# The Criminal Brain

# The Criminal Brain

*Understanding Biological Theories of Crime*

Nicole Rafter

NEW YORK UNIVERSITY PRESS

*New York and London*

NEW YORK UNIVERSITY PRESS
New York and London
www.nyupress.org

Library of Congress Cataloging-in-Publication Data
Rafter, Nicole Hahn, 1939–
The criminal brain : understanding biological theories of crime /
Nicole Rafter.
p. cm.
Includes bibliographical references and index.
ISBN-13: 978–0–8147–7613–1 (cl : alk. paper)
ISBN-10: 0–8147–7613–2 (cl : alk. paper)
ISBN-13: 978–0–8147–7614–8 (pb : alk. paper)
ISBN-10: 0–8147–7614–0 (pb : alk. paper)
1. Criminal behavior—Genetic aspects. 2. Criminal anthropology.
3. Criminal anthropology—History. I. Title.
HV6047.R334    2008
364.2'4—dc22        2008018675

New York University Press books are printed on acid-free paper,
and their binding materials are chosen for strength and durability.
We strive to use environmentally responsible suppliers and materials
to the greatest extent possible in publishing our books.

Manufactured in the United States of America
c   10 9 8 7 6 5 4 3 2 1
p   10 9 8 7 6 5 4 3 2 1

*In memory of Susette Marie Talarico, 1946–2007*

# Contents

# List of Illustrations

# Preface

All early theories of crime were biological. Indeed, until the early 20<sup>th</sup> century, biological theories and criminology were virtually synonymous. But then biological theories were pushed aside by sociological explanations of criminal behavior. Although a few die-hard eugenicists kept biological theories alive, by the end of World War II, when people realized what the Nazis had done in the name of biology, these explanations were firmly rejected and consigned to the dustbin of history—to stay there, many hoped, forever.

Biological theorizing was not dead, however, but only dormant. Even in the 1960s, when sociological deviance theories were at the height of their influence, biological criminology was staging a comeback. Developing slowly at first and emerging mainly in genetics, neuroscience, and psychology, it gathered momentum as the century came to a close.

Many criminologists were insufficiently aware of this new and growing body of research on criminal biology. I was no exception, and to the extent that I was aware of it, like other sociologically oriented criminologists I dismissively lumped the new work with Nazi science, biological determinism, and gulag-like mental hospitals. Yet as I read more deeply, I discovered that much of the new work was scientifically persuasive and that it differed radically from its predecessors. Gone were the determinist, antienvironmentalist explanations of earlier periods. Gone, in fact, was the nature-nurture split itself, with its simplistic assumption that the causes of human behavior can be neatly sorted into two categories, one biological and the other environmental. While many of us weren't looking, scientists had adopted a new mode of explanation, the biosocial model that promises to dominate criminology and other behavioral sciences for decades to come. The 21<sup>st</sup> century, so often touted as "the century of biology" in general, is likely to become the biosocial century in criminology.

The biosocial model recognizes an interaction of biological and social forces. Acknowledging that we are all biological beings, it pictures social forces acting on biology much as a landscape acts on the river running through it, channeling and even redirecting its course. If a poor woman cannot afford nutritious food while she is pregnant—a socioeconomic cause—her baby may be born with biological deficits that place it at greater risk for later criminal behavior than the baby of a well-nourished mother. If young children are traumatized by abuse or even by witnessing abuse, not only do they not forget about it—the traditional view—but the trauma can alter the development of their brains in ways that encourage later criminal behavior. In the new view, the biological and social causes of crime twine together inseparably, constantly interacting. The river and landscape shape one another.

This is the approach of much of the new biocriminology. We may be critical of it, but it is crucial that we at least understand it. To foster that understanding is one of the purposes of this book. Given the dangerous potential of biological theories of crime—their apparent implication that we might be able to change offenders' biology, or that we should prevent them from reproducing—laypeople and specialists alike need to learn how to evaluate research and policy in this area.

Biocriminological ideas often have the ring of truth. In a society like ours, saturated with biological assumptions and inclined to explain phenomena biologically—not just crime but sexual preference, intelligence, and the love of peanut butter—we are primed to accept them. Yet we know from experience that today's scientific truths may become tomorrow's castoffs. How, then, can we decide when to act on the seemingly hard-scientific findings of biocriminology? How can we prepare for a future in which demagogues may propose crime-control programs based on biology?

My approach to such questions is to put them in historical context, analyzing how past biological theories of crime related to the social situations in which they emerged, and trying to draw lessons from those examples for the future. The story told here is in many respects the story of the emergence and growth of scientific criminology itself. I investigate the production of criminology over time, looking at how research on crime was defined and redefined as a science, how it reacted to the hard-science discoveries of different eras, and how it was colored by broader political currents. By tracing the birth and growth of enduring ideas in criminology, as well as by recognizing historical patterns in the interplay of politics and science, we can better appraise the new biocriminology. One of my goals is to give readers points of entry into the new theories and to suggest ways of interpreting and evaluating their still unfamiliar ideas.

Over the many years I have been writing this book, I have accumulated many debts. I am grateful to St. John's College, Wolfson College, and the Centre for Socio-Legal Research, all of Oxford University, for opportunities and resources to do the research. The Peabody Museum Archives of Harvard University and the Dartington Hall Trust Archive in Totnes, England, gave me access to key documents. As always, my chief support has been Robert Hahn. Mary Gibson, with whom I translated and edited the criminological works of Cesare Lombroso, helped me work out the meanings of these foundational texts of scientific criminology. Frances Heidensohn, another source of support from the very beginning of this project, was particularly helpful—despite her misgivings—with my research on Hans Eysenck. Simon Cole of the University of California, Irvine, shared his sophistication in the history of science and proved to be a fine editor. Others who read and commented on individual chapters were Neil Davie of the University of Lyon; Mary Gibson of John Jay College; Stephen Tibbetts of California State University, San Bernardino; and Per Ystehede of the University of Oslo.

While I cannot begin to thank individually all the people who have contributed in one way or another to this project, I do want to note with special gratitude the assistance of Garland Allen, Andrew Arpey, Peter Becker, Piers Beirne, Donna Bishop, Jenny Brown, Lynn Chancer, Amy Farrell, Sarah Gleason, Alex Hahn, Sarah Hahn, Elizabeth Horan, Clay Mosher, Steven Noll, Simon Singer, Doug Starr, Victor Swenson, Mariana Valverde, Nicholas Wachsmann, Geoff Ward, Richard Wetzell, Judy Yarnall, and Lucia Zedner. Ilene Kalish, my editor at New York University Press, entered my title contest and put up with pesky questions while providing expert guidance and support. Susan Ecklund, my copyeditor, and Despina Papazoglou Gimbel, NYU Press's managing editor, also did a superb job of polishing the manuscript and moving it through the publication process. Students in my biological theories of crime course at Northeastern University shaped many of my ideas, and one of them, Danielle Rousseau, helped me assemble the illustrations for this book. The book is dedicated to Susette Talarico, a dear friend at the University of Georgia whose decades-long struggle with breast cancer and generosity of soul inspired those so fortunate as to know her.

An earlier version of chapter 2 appeared as "The Unrepentant Horse-slasher: Moral Insanity and the Origins of Criminological Thought," in *Criminology* 42 (2004): 977–1006, and an earlier version of chapter 3 as "The Murderous Dutch Fiddler: Criminology, History, and the Problem of Phrenology," in *Theoretical Criminology* 9 (2005): 65–96; all rights reserved, copyright SAGE Publications Ltd., 2005,_http://online.sagepub.com/. Parts of chapter 7 appeared earlier as "Earnest A. Hooton and the Biological Tradition in American Criminology," in *Criminology* 42 (2004): 735–771, and as "Somatotyping, Antimodernism, and the Production of Criminological Knowledge," in *Criminology* 45 (2007): 101–129. A version of chapter 8 will appear as "Criminology's Darkest Hour: Biocriminology in Nazi Germany," in the *Australian and New Zealand Journal of Criminology* 41 (2) (2008): 288–307.

# 1

## Introduction

*Crime, History, Science*

The Van Nest murder case of 1846, while unique in its tragic details, illustrates many of the issues typically raised by biological explanations of crime. The killings occurred in an isolated farmhouse on the shore of one of New York's Finger Lakes, on a March evening just as the seven members of the Van Nest family and their hired man retired to bed. Someone slipped into the house and butchered the farmer, his pregnant wife, his elderly mother-in-law, and his two-year-old son, whose small body was eviscerated by the knife, leaving several feet of intestines dangling from the wound. Within days the authorities arrested William Freeman, a man in his early twenties of African and Native American descent. Freeman confessed to the massacre, although he was never able to clearly explain why he had singled out the Van Nests. At times he suggested that he had been revenging himself for an earlier wrongful imprisonment (a case in which none of the Van Nests had been involved) and at others that he "had no reason at all."[1]

While still in his teens, William Freeman had been sentenced to five years in prison for horse theft—a crime for which he was evidently framed by the actual thief, a far more sophisticated man. In any case, Freeman maintained his innocence, and as he served his time in New York State's formidable Auburn Prison, he became increasingly bitter about the conviction, especially as he was cruelly flogged for rule infractions. But he showed no signs of mental peculiarity until after an altercation with one of the prison's keepers. When ordered to strip for a flogging, Freeman instead attacked the keeper, who struck back, hitting the prisoner so hard on the head with a wooden plank that the board split. From then on, Freeman suffered from deafness and an inability to think clearly. He deteriorated mentally to the point of becoming (one eyewitness reported) "a being of very low, degraded intellect, hardly

Freeman stabbing Van Nest child. Unknown artist, commissioned about 1846 by traveling showman George J. Mastin. Note the child's dead father in the doorway. The Mastin murals reflected public horror at the massacre of the Van Nest family; at the same time, they inflamed sentiment against the black assassin of the white family. Fenimore Art Museum, Cooperstown, New York.

above a brute."[2] On release, Freeman sought the arrest of the people who had had him locked up; when he got nowhere with that approach, he started planning another sort of revenge. His determination to right his wrongs may have come to include the Van Nests because when he sought work at their homestead shortly before the massacre, the farmer had declined to hire him.

Freeman's arrest triggered a ferocious debate that became typical of cases in which an appalling crime is attributed to biological abnormality. In the majority were the local citizens who initially tried to lynch Freeman and then demanded that he be legally hanged. These included members of a first jury, which determined that Freeman was "sufficiently sane in mind and memory, to distinguish between right and wrong,"[3] and of a second jury, which found him guilty of the crime. "Many of the voices that screamed for retribution," writes Andrew Arpey in his book on the Freeman case, "did not hesitate to cite the killer's race as a source of his depravity." The other side included a local clergyman, who, observing that the community treated its black population as outcasts, asked, "Is not society in some degree, accountable for this sad catastrophe?" Freeman's brother-in-law agreed, claiming that white men's mistreatment turned his people into "brute beasts."[4] A former New York State governor, William H. Seward, and his law partners volunteered to defend Freeman, arguing before the two juries that the prisoner was insane ("unable to deduce the simplest conclusion from the plainest premises")[5] and thus not responsible. Seward managed to get a stay of execution and, eventually, an order for a new trial, for which he enlisted the assistance of a number of physicians and psychiatrists, including Dr. Amariah Brigham, superintendent of the local lunatic asylum and one of the country's leading authorities on insanity. But Freeman, having declined mentally to the point of idiocy, died before the new trial began. In his autopsy report, Brigham wrote that he had seldom seen such extensive brain disease.[6]

In Freeman's case, biological abnormality was offered not as an account for criminal behavior in general but as an explanation for Freeman's particular offenses. Shortly after the Van Nest murders, a local newspaper editor, speculating on the rumor that a relative of Freeman's had been executed for murder six years earlier, reasoned that there "must be some bad blood running in the veins of the Freeman tribe,"[7] a conclusion that seemed to him especially compelling in view of the killer's Indian (and therefore presumably violence-prone) ancestry. Unlike later biological theorists, the editor did not try to claim that crime in general is caused by a biological factor such as "bad blood." In its broad contours, however, the case resembled many others that preceded and followed it in the history of biological theories of crime: a crime or sometimes series of crimes that seemed monstrous and inexplicable; a mentally disordered defendant; medical and legal specialists who were confident that mental abnormality had caused the criminal behavior; and a philosophical tension between free will and determinism. Moreover, the Freeman case became a focal point for issues of criminal responsibility and punishment that were coming to a head in the broader community, and in this respect, too, it was typical of notorious cases in which a novel biological defense is attempted for the first time.

Among those issues, most influential was an intensifying debate over proposals to eliminate capital punishment. Abolitionists held that Christians should practice forgiveness while retentionists fought back with biblical exhortations for retribution. Opinions were further inflamed by a growing debate over the insanity defense: Should insanity be defined in terms of severe mental illness or the more stringent requirement that the defendant had at the time of the offense been totally incapable of distinguishing right from wrong? (If the latter standard were used, Seward grumbled, the insanity defense could *never* be used, for it would require a "complete obliteration" of memory, attention, and reason of which "the human mind is not capable.")[8] Should courts allow a defense based on the new diagnostic category of *moral insanity*, according to which a person can be ethically insane while normal in other mental functions? And how should insanity be determined? The latter was a particularly hot issue for those who suspected that Freeman was feigning madness.

Related was a debate over court leniency and its effects. In the view of some members of the Auburn community, an acquittal by reason of insanity in a case immediately preceding the Van Nest murders probably encouraged Freeman to think he could get away with murder. Another such acquittal would foster more violence. Here the opposition countered that it was legal harshness that had sent the innocent young man to prison for horse theft in the first place and that had led, ultimately, to the Van Nest killings. Further exacerbating feelings about the Freeman case was a growing debate over the causes of human action. Is criminal behavior determined by social and biological factors beyond the individual's control, as the popular science of phrenology was then teaching, or do humans freely choose their courses of action? The Freeman trial, then, played out in the context of heated arguments over major social issues such as capital punishment, the insanity defense, the appropriate degree of severity in criminal punishments, and the causes of criminal behavior.[9] Politically, legally, and racially, the case raised contentious issues, pitting medicine against law, religion against science.

There have been periods in which biological theories aroused strong resistance, as Brigham's and Seward's explanations did in mid-19th-century New York, but at other times biological theories have enjoyed easy acceptance. Just twenty-five years after William Freeman's trials, for example, Americans were far more receptive to biological explanations of crime, and in the early 20th century, the feeblemindedness or weak

Hanging Freeman. Unknown artist, commissioned about 1846 by traveling show-man George J. Mastin. Freeman in fact died in prison before his second trial be-gan. This painting reflects the outcome that Mastin anticipated from the trial–or, like many members of the local community, hoped for. Fenimore Art Museum, Cooperstown, New York.

intelligence explanation of crime became almost instantly popular, a kind of fad. But today, efforts to explain criminality in terms of what sociologist Nikolas Rose terms the "biology of culpability" once again arouse strong reactions.[10]

Currently, liberals tend to view biological theories as efforts to shift responsibility away from social factors that cause crime and onto criminal individuals. Conservatives embrace biological theories more enthusiastically but grow uneasy when one speaks (as I do throughout this book) of their history, a perspective suggesting that scientific truths are contingent upon social factors. Sociologists look askance at the identification of biological "risk" factors and other indications that social influences do not fully explain crime. On the other hand, biocriminologists—meaning those who produce biological theories of crime[11]—tend to dismiss sociological and historical analyses as a distraction from the important work of scientific research. The political fault lines have shifted since the mid–19th century, when the liberal faction, including Seward and Brigham, proposed the biological explanation; but the polarization itself recurs, and today's issues remain much the same as they were when William Freeman sat, bewildered, in the prisoner's dock.

These issues resurfaced in the case of Andrea Kennedy Yates, the Houston, Texas, woman who in 2001 systematically drowned her five children in a bathtub. Yates had been a bright, athletic student, and she had worked as a nurse until 1993, when she married Rusty Yates, became pregnant six times in seven years (one pregnancy ended in a miscarriage), and adopted Rusty's evangelical religion. Rusty insisted that she homeschool the children and take full care of them herself (part of the time the family lived in a former bus), circumstances that placed heavy burdens on Andrea and isolated her from social support. One of her few close friends was a religious extremist who taught that "the role of women is derived from the sin of Eve."[12] Andrea deteriorated mentally after each pregnancy, attempting suicide, hallucinating, mutilating herself, denying the children food. When her father (for whom she had also been caring) died in 2001, she became catatonic. A doctor prescribed antipsychotic drugs but warned the couple that they should have no more children, given that childbirth triggered Andrea's most severe mental problems. They ignored his advice, however, and after Andrea gave birth to their last child, she went into postpartum psychosis (a condition far more severe than postpartum depression). She confessed immediately after drowning the children, explaining that she was not a good mother, that the children were not developing correctly, and that she was possessed by Satan.[13]

In her first trial, Andrea Yates was found guilty of capital murder and sentenced to life in prison. The jury rejected the defense argument that postpartum psychosis made it impossible for her to tell right from wrong, reasoning that she would not have phoned the police immediately after the killings, or attributed them to Satan, had she not recognized the evil of her action. Rusty divorced her and remarried. But the case reopened in 2005 when it was discovered that a prosecution witness had given false testimony. On retrial, a jury found Yates not guilty by reason of insanity, deciding that due to postpartum psychosis she had in fact *not* known right from wrong when she killed the children. As a result, she is now incarcerated in a mental hospital rather than a prison.

Andrea Yates in court. Andrea Yates walks into the courtroom during the closing arguments in her retrial for capital murder. Yates, charged in the 2001 drownings of her five children in the bathtub, pleaded not guilty by reason of insanity—postpartum psychosis—in her first trial but was convicted. In 2006, however, the earlier decision was overturned and she was declared insane at the time of the crime. Associated Press.

Many of the same factors that had galvanized the public in the Freeman case did so again during Andrea Yates's trials: the atrocious and inexplicable nature of the crimes, the multiple victims and the fact that they included an infant, the mentally disordered defendant, and the relative novelty of the defense. Vituperative Internet postings testified to the way this case, too, tapped into the hot-button issues of the day. Columnist Mona Charen felt that Rusty should also have been put on trial: "The word negligent doesn't even begin to describe his malfeasance. How is it possible that a man who knows his wife's sanity has been compromised by childbirth can nonetheless impregnate her five more times . . . ? How could he leave her alone when he knew she was, at the very least, suicidal?"[14] Others were outraged by what they saw as the court's leniency: "So, she'll be out of that mental institution in a few years," wrote one blogger. "The term 'Justice System' is an oxymoron." And another: "This bitch could very well have been sane. Throw away the key . . . why take chances?"[15] Once again, factors in the social context help explain such inflamed anger—in this case, evangelicalism; debates over women's proper roles; the still-rankling memory of John Hinkley's successful insanity defense after he tried to kill President Ronald Reagan; and the unfamiliarity of the postpartum psychosis defense.

While there is currently a good deal of resistance to biological explanations of crime, that opposition is likely to crumble over the next several decades. Such hostility is often strongest when new biological theories are first proposed, shaking up tried-and-true ways of thinking about crime. But when a new theory resonates with other culturally dominant factors, as current genetic, evolutionary, and neurological explanations do, opponents often come around. If my prediction is correct, we are on the threshold of a major shift that could lead to various genetic and other biological "solutions" to criminal behavior.[16] Whether or not the shift leads to a brave-new-world scenario in which, say, babies' genes are inspected for criminogenic risk factors, depends on how we decide to shape our future. And that, in turn, depends on how well informed we are about the past and present biological theories of crime.

## Why Bother with Biocriminology?

Biological theories raise profound and inescapable issues about the nature of justice. If William Freeman had been hung, would an innocent man have been executed? Had he been sent to Brigham's Utica State Lunatic Asylum, would justice have been achieved, or would the Van Nest victims have gone unavenged? Which of the two Andrea Yates juries got it right—the one that found her guilty, or the one that acquitted her? If some crimes are indeed biological in origin, then it is impossible to achieve justice or to improve crime prevention without grasping the nature of such causes. And yet few ideas are more dangerous than that of innate criminality, which has long been associated with eugenics, the science that promises to eradicate social problems by cleansing the gene pool. In the past, eugenic solutions have led to sterilizations, life imprisonment to prevent reproduction, and (in the Nazi instance) wholesale executions of mere suspects in minor crimes.

No one today advocates executing people with allegedly criminogenic genes, but less draconian forms of eugenics continue to find advocates. Former U.S. education secretary William Bennett has remarked, "If you wanted to reduce crime, you could . . . abort every black baby in this country and your crime rate would go down."[17] In the 1990s, a grassroots group called Children Requiring a Caring Kommunity (CRACK) started offering drug-addicted and alcoholic women $200 to go on long-term birth control or be sterilized.[18] Due to technological advances, genetic theories of crime now raise the specter that fetuses might be inspected for genetic risk factors, with abortion required for those that don't pass muster. We already have genetically modified crops; maybe gene policing and genetically modified criminals are not far behind. Indeed, the possibility of genetically modified humans has already been raised by movies such as *Gattaca* (1997). But criminologists are not debating or even recognizing the ethical implications of eugenic measures looming on the horizon or already in place, perhaps because those measures seem less dramatic today than in the Nazi era, enabling us to contemplate without alarm the quiet genetic death of individuals such as those CRACK mothers. Then, too, it is easier to contemplate (or ignore) eugenics measures against criminals than against more "innocent" groups.

Today's biocriminologies call for critical attention quite apart from the eugenics issues they raise. Recent work in biochemistry, genetics, and neuroscience is revitalizing biocriminology and understandings of the workings of offenders' brains. The decoding of the genome, the intensifying study of gene-environment interactions, improvements in the understanding of human brain development and functioning—these and other aspects of biological research are affecting criminological theory. For instance, recent investigations indicate that gene-linked traits such as impulsivity may increase people's likelihood of engaging in criminal behavior. Although no behavioral geneticist expects to discover anything so simple as a crime gene, it is nonetheless true that twin studies and other evidence point to the influence of heredity on offending.[19] In addition, interest is growing in the contested but provocative field of evolutionary psychology, according to which at least some criminal behavior may have an evolutionary basis—may, in other words, be genetically programmed into offenders' brains. And yet the ways in which biological sciences are applied to criminality are sometimes suspect, as in the William Bennett example and also in the case of criminologists who, with little background in the hard sciences, rush to appropriate the new findings. We need to be able to evaluate biological claims about criminal behavior, just as the juries that condemned William Freeman and Andrea Yates needed to be able to intelligently weigh defendants' biological arguments.

Furthermore, the history of biological theories can help us understand the nature of criminology itself—its scope, development, and means of generating knowledge. The scientific study of crime actually began with biological theories, in the late 18$^{th}$ century. They were the first type of scientific explanation for criminal behavior, and they dominated for a full century before sociological explanations began to flower. The history of biological theories of crime is in many ways the history of criminology itself. And yet most criminology textbooks and even histories of criminology show little awareness of the evolution of biological theories. Even more disconcerting, contemporary biocriminologists themselves seem unaware of their own intellectual background and traditions.[20] *The Criminal Brain* offers a genealogy of biocriminological knowledge that goes back to the first efforts to analyze crime scientifically.

## *The Making of Criminological Knowledge*

Until the 1960s, histories of science conceived of science as a progressive march of knowledge in which, if everyone stayed in line, collected facts, and followed the procedural rules, research would yield ever more complex and valuable truths. This teleological approach was built on the principles of positivism, a philosophical position that emerged in the 18$^{th}$ century in reaction to then-dominant theological and metaphysical ways of knowing and that viewed facts as neutral, objective truths. "Science in the positivist view," writes historian Robert N. Proctor, "is a rational and cumulative enterprise; science grows through accretion of the new and replacement of the old."[21]

The assumptions of scientific positivism held firm until 1962, when Thomas Kuhn published *The Structure of Scientific Revolutions*, arguing that even the hard sciences define their problems and procedures in terms of a dominant paradigm or core set of assumptions about the nature of science. Kuhn's argument threw positivist assumptions into doubt. Together with the work of the French philosopher Michel Foucault,[22] it opened up the possibility of both social histories and sociological studies of scientific knowledge, the approaches I use here. These approaches ask basic questions about the making of scientific knowledge: How is this kind of information generated, validated, disseminated, reconfirmed, and eventually superseded? How (in this particular case) is criminology—the scientific study of crime and criminals—produced? How is it shaped by social factors? How does it decide what counts as a fact, and how does it evaluate the credibility of claims about the nature of crime and criminals?

*The Criminal Brain* is not the first history of biological theories of crime, but it is the most complete and up-to-date. In 1938 Arthur Fink published *Causes of Crime: Biological Theories in the United States, 1800–1915*, a book rich in detail but, as its subtitle indicates, limited in coverage. Moreover, today its approaches to both history and science are severely dated.[23] Fifty years later, Henry Werlinder published *Psychopathy: A History of the Concepts*, a Swedish doctoral dissertation that covers more ground and links mid-20th-century ideas about psychopaths to earlier ideas about born criminals, degenerates, and the morally insane.[24] But Werlinder's book, too, is dated today, and, because it was published in Sweden, it is difficult to access. Stephen Jay Gould's *Mismeasure of Man* (1981) took on craniometrists, criminal anthropologists, and intelligence testers, exposing their scientific pratfalls; but Gould, an evolutionary biologist and paleontologist, was a specialist in neither criminology nor historiography. Since then, some excellent general and specific histories of criminology have appeared.[25] Only a few of these deal with biological theories, however, and none attempts comprehensive coverage.

One barrier to social histories of criminological knowledge is the fact that the term *criminology* did not enter common usage until the late 19th century, and criminology as an academic discipline did not take shape until even later.[26] How are we to talk about criminology before "criminology"— that is, before the study of crime became a specialized field of study with that name? It seems clear that we do not want to include 17th- and 18th-century pronouncements on crime by preachers and pamphleteers— material that in no sense constituted research on crime and which, in any case, as Paul Rock points out, could not "evolve or reproduce itself as a specific discourse."[27] (Rock calls such material "proto-criminology.") But it seems equally clear that we would want to include the work of early 19th-century phrenologists and others who *did* attempt to apply scientific methods to the study of crime, even though they did not think of their work as "criminology." (Historians of psychology, facing a similar problem, have solved it by covering early scientific psychological research even when it was not formally labeled "psychology"[28]—a solution parallel to the one I adopt here.) In this book, I use "criminology" to refer to all efforts to study crime scientifically, irrespective of whether the authors thought of their work as "criminology." Changes in the meaning of "criminology" as the field evolved, together with shifts in the meanings of "science" itself, also form part of my story.

The mere raising of questions about the production of scientific knowledge can make people uncomfortable, for it seems to call into question the activity that sits near the apex of our cultural values: science itself. If the content of biological theories of crime can be affected by the social climate in which they are produced, by competition between scientists, or by government funding policies, does that mean that there are no ultimate scientific truths?[29] Sociologists and philosophers of science respond variously to this question, with some taking the positivist position, according to which facts are neutral, objective, accessible truths, and others taking the constructionist position, according to which facts are historically contingent, shaped by the social circumstances in which they are produced. My own position is constructionist, meaning that we must look to social context to understand how scientific facts are made.

Constructionists and positivists argue over the degree to which scientific knowledge is relative—shaped by social context—but the details of this debate are unimportant here. The social history and sociology of criminological knowledge do not force us to confront the really tough constructionist issues raised, for example, by scientific studies of gravity or astrophysics. Just a moment's reflection shows that it is impossible to reduce criminological explanations to, say, hardwiring of the brain, since the very definition of criminality is so clearly a social phenomenon, determined by cultural definitions of right and wrong, police department arrest policies, the composition of juries, the social backgrounds of criminologists, and the politics of science itself.[30] My interest lies in identifying the social forces behind the sciences of the criminal brain. While scientists must aim at objectivity in their procedures, setting themselves the goal of impersonal investigation, they cannot pretend to have discovered pure, undistorted, eternal truths about the world—especially when the object of study is the social phenomenon of crime. To some extent, criminological facts are always constructed.

## *The Goals and Nature of This Book*

I have written this book neither to promote nor to bash biological theories of crime, but to recover their past and discover their fundamental nature. In my view, figuring out how to evaluate new biological theories is the most pressing issue in contemporary criminology. The hard sciences are already revolutionizing the ways in which we investigate the causes of crime and think about preventive measures, and in the years ahead neurological and genetic research will transform criminological thinking. Now—before the train departs—is the time to decide on the direction in which we want biocriminological research to travel. The stakes are high, including not only the organization of social control but also the social organization of science itself—the relative power of sociology versus genetics neuroscience, and the positions we take in ongoing (but, as I suggest, badly framed) debates over whether criminality is a product of nurture or nature, environmental factors, or the biochemistry of criminal brains. I hope to help sociologically inclined readers learn about biological theories of crime, many of which are much more compatible with sociological perspectives than most people think. I also hope to see widespread debate over the goals we want biocriminology to serve in the future.

*The Criminal Brain* is organized around the history of efforts to answer criminological questions scientifically. Instead of attempting to impose today's criteria for "scientific" on the past, I investigate how earlier researchers established and implemented criteria for scientificalness. New biological theories of crime are usually precipitated by developments in the broader culture—by changes in science or new notions of causation that begin to make earlier scientific ideas seem dated. For example, the work of the evolutionist Charles Darwin—especially his *Origin of Species* (1859)—made earlier phrenological explanations, based on the theory of a compartmentalized brain, look obsolete. Not long after Darwin's book on the evolution of plants and animals appeared, criminologists started explaining criminal behavior in evolutionist terms. Another source of change lies in professional jockeying: multiple discourses converge around criminology (anthropological, biochemical, evolutionist, genetic, managerial, medical, neurophysiological, racist, psychological, psychiatric, religious), all vying for jurisdiction. Social control is a valuable area in which to claim expertise, for it gives those who make their claims successfully the authority to identify deviants and manage them; thus over time a number of professions have cast a colonizing eye in the direction of biocriminology.

An additional source of change in biocriminology lies in shifting understandings of the nature of dangerousness and defilement.[31] Fear of crime flows from wellsprings much deeper than worries about stolen silverware or sudden assault; ideas about crime are also colored by broad-ranging and inchoate fears of moral and physical contamination. In the late 18ᵗʰ century, for instance—the so-called Age of Reason, with its emphasis on logic and rationality—biological theories became a means of explaining irrational and immoderate behavior. During Hitler's Third Reich—a regime obsessed with fears of the degradation of Aryan racial purity—biological explanations of crime became a means of identifying those who should be eliminated by sterilization, death through labor, or the guillotine. Thus the story told here is one of shifting social anxieties. I am particularly interested in relationships between the biological sciences and the contexts in which they develop. I am also interested in the implications of biological theories for criminal punishment. Just as biological theories do not develop in a vacuum, so too do they have repercussions beyond themselves, affecting public policy and human lives.

Part I, on biological theories in the 19ᵗʰ century, begins by showing how, around 1800, biological explanations originated almost simultaneously in three countries: the United States, France, and England. These explanations, cast in the form of speculation about the condition of *moral insanity* (today's *psychopathy*), marked the start of not only biocriminology but criminology itself, for they constituted the first efforts to account for crime scientifically, in terms of brain defects. The next chapter covers phrenology, the science that envisioned rehabilitating criminals by changing the shapes of their brains and skulls. Phrenology was succeeded by criminal anthropology (chapter 4), a theory rooted in Darwinism and based on the riveting figure of the born criminal, scarred by the stigmata of criminality and driven to plunder and kill by his primitive brain. The final chapter in part I, on late 19ᵗʰ-century evolutionary theories, attempts to go beyond the usual exclusive focus on Italian developments by investigating the impact of Darwin and other evolutionists on not only Cesare Lombroso but also Henry Maudsley (England), Richard Dugdale (United States), and Richard von Krafft-Ebing (Austria). It concludes with a discussion of the work of the English statistician Francis Galton, the founder of eugenics and a man whose work on crime formed a bridge between evolutionary theories and later genetic explanations of crime.

Part II, on biological theories in the 20ᵗʰ century, opens with a chapter on the weak intelligence explanation of crime that dominated criminology from about 1900 to 1920. Allying itself with the eugenics movement, criminology in this era aimed at identifying and eliminating the "feebleminded," whose bad genes seemed to carry criminality through the generations. Eugenic criminology was more than an effort at crime control; it was also an antimodernist science, a nostalgic effort to cope with the challenges of modern life by using science to return to the social structure and values of a simpler, purer, crime-free past. The next chapter, on constitutional or bodytype theories, concentrates on the midcentury work of Ernest A. Hooton and William Sheldon. Their work contrasted strongly in its eugenicism and antimodernism with the bodytype research of their thoroughly modernist contemporaries, Sheldon and Eleanor Glueck. Criminology's darkest hour arrived with the ascent to power of the Nazis in Germany, the criminological consequences of which are related in chapter 8. Part II concludes with a chapter on contemporary biocriminology; it surveys ongoing research in the areas of acquired biological abnormalities, learning deficits, evolutionary theory, neuroscience, and genetics. Never before has there been anything like this explosion of interest, this diversity of perspective and approach, or this intensity of research into possible biological influences on criminal behavior.

Part III is concerned with the future of biocriminology. Chapter 10 begins by tracing trends over time in the evolution of biological theories of crime—developmental trajectories in their scope, focus, personnel, sophistication, and ways of conceptualizing the human mind. It goes on to compare biological theories of the past and present, concluding that today's biological theories have broken radically with past traditions of reductionism and determinism. While the new biocriminologies have enormous negative potential, especially for encouraging new programs of eugenic criminology, they also have a great positive potential for encouraging environmental improvements aimed at crime reduction.

For many years, scholars on the Left have viewed genetic and other biological explanations of crime as a way of pinning blame for social problems on bad individuals and hence avoiding social solutions—better schools, antiracism measures, antipoverty legislation—that might change the social structure. At the same time, scholars on the Right have used biological theories of crime to shift the attention away from what to them seem like ineffective social programs and, instead, explain the behavior of lawbreaking individuals. The traditional Left and Right positions flourished in a period in which "genetic" was almost synonymous with biological determinism. But today, new understandings of the workings of genes make a "third way" possible (and the older positions obsolete). Genes alone seldom determine personality traits or conditions. While a few diseases have been traced to single genes, most genes work in interaction with other genes and with the environment in which they express themselves.

This new understanding of the complexity, flexibility, and indeterminacy of most genetic development opens the way to generating new position on the very old (and tired) nature-nurture debate. We no longer have to pit nature against nurture; now we can picture the two as working together to achieve gene expression and to produce the individual. We can now also argue that genetics itself suggests that ameliorating social environments— improving schools, taking steps to alleviate racism, acting against poverty— can be effective anticrime measures. Thus in the final chapter of this book I envision a new or third way in which we can harness genetic explanations to programs of social improvement that would lead to crime reduction. I try not to find a compromise between the former positions of the Left and Right but rather to move beyond those old disputes in a way that is consonant both with the view of genetic development as indeterminate and with the aim of environmental measures to reduce crime. I want to enlist modern genetics in progressive social change.

# PART I

# Biological Theories
# in the 19th Century

# 2

# Moral Insanity and the
# Origins of Criminology

Criminology—the effort to account for crime scientifically—emerged, like other social sciences, out of the 18th-century political, philosophical, and scientific upheavals known as the Enlightenment. In the distant background lay the medieval world, with its authoritarianism, political hierarchies, and preference for theological and metaphysical explanations. In the middle background lay the Renaissance, with its rediscovery of ancient scientific texts and its dramatic advances in engineering and the physical sciences. In the immediate background lay the so-called Age of Reason, with its emphasis on logic, rationality, and systematization. The pace of change accelerated during the late 18th century with democratic revolutions in North America and France, growing pressure for humanitarian reforms, and a pell-mell rush to "do" science of all sorts. Among the results were the efforts made by Cesare Beccaria in Italy and Jeremy Bentham in England to replace autocratic systems of criminal punishment with more rational laws and institutions.[1] Enlightenment impulses led, in the early 19th century, to efforts to establish social sciences through nonspeculative or "positive" methods—by establishing facts from which natural laws could then be derived inductively. This was the cultural context—the flow of 18th-century rationalism and enthusiasm for science into 19th-century positivism—in which the first efforts to study crime scientifically took place.[2]

How, specifically, did scientific criminology get started? Who first realized that criminal behavior might be studied as a science, and what did they mean by "science"? How did they picture the mind of the arch-criminal and see it as different from the minds of run-of-the-mill criminals and law-abiding citizens? In what follows, I trace the origins of criminological science to the work of three men: the American psychiatrist Benjamin Rush, the French psychiatrist Philippe

Physiognomical studies by Giovanbattista della Porta. Della Porta, a scientist of the Italian Renaissance, studied human physiognomy or facial expressions. His book influenced the Swiss physiognomist Johann Kaspar Lavater and through him, 19th-century phrenologists and criminal anthropologists. Della Porta was trying to read character—the workings of the human brain—from physiognomy. From *De humana physiognomonia,* orig. 1586.

Pinel, and the English insane asylum physician James Cowles Prichard. Although they used different terminologies, all three developed the concept of *moral insanity,* and all three identified a specific type of criminal—remorseless, incapable of resisting impulses to harm others, and morally savage, but in other respects normal. In their view, moral insanity was innate, and it could be affected by biological factors such as diet and alcohol consumption; but it did not necessarily involve a physical abnormality of the brain or any other part of the body. Next I follow the concept's development, first examining its fate in the United States, where psychiatrists tended to reject the idea but where their counterparts in institutions for the mentally retarded took it up, relabeling it *moral imbecility* and redefining it in hereditarian terms. In England, the concept of moral insanity fared better, although at the end of the century psychiatrists began fusing it with another concept, that of degeneration. In their work, too, moral insanity was redefined as a somatic and hereditary affliction, and morally insane criminals became degenerates, subhumans who had not fully evolved.

## Benjamin Rush and Moral Derangement

Benjamin Rush (1745–1813) is most often remembered as an American patriot and signer of the Declaration of Independence, but politics was only one of many fronts on which he worked for social betterment. A devout Presbyterian and believer in human perfectibility, Rush opposed slavery and the death penalty and advocated, among other reforms, animal rights, equal education for women, and affordable medicine for the poor. The most influential American physician of his day,[3] he taught medicine at the University of Pennsylvania and became famous (in some circles, infamous) for the depleting treatments—restricted diets, massive bloodlettings, purgatives, and emetics—he prescribed to weaken not just patients but their diseases. But his reputation as the founder of American psychiatry rests on his efforts, novel at the time, to treat and possibly alleviate mental illness. Breaking (at least in part) with the older theological understanding of madness as a sign of sinfulness, the Philadelphia physician redefined insanity as a disease.

Rush produced two major commentaries on the causes of criminal behavior, the first an oration titled "The Influence of Physical Causes upon the Moral Faculty" (1786). This was one of the earliest scientific attempts to conceptualize crime and insanity as anything other than sin. In it Rush sometimes speaks broadly of all kinds of immoral activity, while at others he speaks more narrowly of the type of serious repeat criminal behavior that later psychiatrists would call moral insanity. Without preliminaries, Rush dives into his subject: "By the moral faculty I mean a capacity in the human mind of distinguishing and choosing good and evil, or, in other words, virtue and vice." We are born with this capacity; it is "the law written in our hearts."⁴ While the moral faculty may seem to be the same as conscience, Rush insists that the two differ: the moral faculty causes us to act, while conscience evaluates our actions. Rush's goal in this oration is to show "the effects of physical causes upon the moral faculty."⁵ Because his speech is concerned with physical influences that lead to immoral behavior, it can be considered the modern era's first attempt to formulate a biological theory of crime.

Rush distinguishes between total moral depravity, in which the moral faculty and conscience both cease to function, and partial weakness of the moral faculty, in which the offender remains conscious of wrongdoing.⁶ To exemplify partial weakness of the moral faculty, Rush offers "an instance of a woman, who was exemplary in her obedience to every command of the moral law, except one. She could not refrain from stealing," even though she had no real need. "As proof that her judgment was not affected by this defect in her moral faculty, she would both confess and lament her crime, when detected in it."⁷

To exemplify total absence of the moral faculty, Rush draws on the case of a man named Servin who had been described nearly a century earlier by the Duke of Sully. Servin was handsome, brilliant, and extraordinarily knowledgeable—in philosophy, mathematics, drawing, theology ("an excellent preacher"), and languages (he was fluent in Greek, Hebrew, French, and other tongues). Servin excelled, moreover, as a comedian, poet, musician, and athlete. "But now," Rush writes, "for the reverse of the medal": "He was treacherous, cruel, cowardly, deceitful, a liar, a cheat, and a glutton, a sharper in play, immersed in every species of vice, a blasphemer, an atheist. . . . [H]e died in the flower of his age, in a common brothel, perfectly corrupted by his debaucheries, and expired with the glass in his hand, cursing and denying God."⁸

One can be born with a defective moral faculty, Rush continues, or the damage can occur later. When the deficit develops after childhood, it can be caused by a fever, poor diet (eating meat, overeating), immoderate consumption of fermented liquors, extreme hunger, and too much sleep. Climate, too, can undermine the moral faculty, as when the "constant fogs and rains" of a British November "favour the perpetration of the worst species of murder."⁹ Rush's treatment proposals flow directly from this analysis: a vegetarian diet, moderation in alcohol consumption, cold baths, work, and solitude will restore the weakened moral faculty. "Nebuchadnezzar," Rush reports, "was cured of his pride, by means of

2.2 Physiognomical studies by Johann Kaspar Lavater. Lavater tried to turn physiognomy into a science "of the correspondence between the external and internal man." Early criminologists were influenced by his assumption that outer appearance correlates with mental state. They too were looking for a way to understand the mental processes behind facial structures and expressions. From *Essays on Physiognomy*, orig. 1789.

solitude and a vegetable diet."[10] In time, if physicians work to develop "the moral science, it is highly probable, that most of those baneful vices, which deform the human breast, and convulse the nations of the earth, might be banished from the world."[11]

Between the oration of 1786 and *Medical Inquiries and Observations upon Diseases of the Mind* (1812), the book in which he returns to illness of the moral faculty, Rush took charge of mentally ill patients at the Pennsylvania Hospital, thereby greatly increasing his familiarity with mental disease. In this second work he lays out his model of mental functioning more systematically, explaining that the mind has nine faculties or capacities, including understanding, memory, will, the moral faculty, the conscience, and the sense of God. These faculties are "internal senses," and like the external senses, they are innate.[12] When the faculties become diseased or deranged, they may do so singly or in tandem, "and there are cases in which all the faculties are sometimes deranged in succession, and rotation, and now and then they are all affected at the same time."[13] This billiard-ball model, in which one faculty and then another can be knocked out of commission, or all at once, helps explain the distinction between partial and total ethical malfunctioning, which Rush terms *partial* and *total moral derangement*. If moral derangement is partial, involving failure of only the moral faculty, it can coexist with a sound conscience and sense of God, as when people who are starving to death commit cannibalism. When the moral derangement is total, however, the conscience and sense of deity as well as the moral faculty stop operating, and the result is people who commit crimes repeatedly and without remorse.[14] Rush confesses himself unsure as to whether morally deranged people should be held responsible for their criminal acts, but he is certain that, as sick people, they deserve compassion.

The chief significance of Rush's psychiatric work lies in the way he took insanity, including moral derangement—conditions still widely viewed as signs of sin or demonic possession—and redefined them as mental diseases. "Rush's [1786] essay," writes historian Henry Werlinder, "can be seen as a contribution to the battle between physicians on the one side and theologians and philosophers on the other as to priorities in research and treatment of 'madness.'"[15] Rush's work was additionally significant because it attempted to remove criminality from the clergy's hands and incorporate it into the psychiatrist's domain. Rush perceived, before anyone else, that criminality could be thought of as a natural, material phenomenon, susceptible to scientific explanation—in this case, the explanations of psychiatry. As he pondered the causes of crime, he conceived of criminality in terms of physical disease.

### *Philippe Pinel and* Manie sans Délire

In his famous painting of Philippe Pinel (1745–1826), artist Tony Robert-Fleury shows the physician entering a Parisian insane asylum in 1793 and heroically unlocking the chains that shackled inmates to the walls, thus ushering in an era of more humane, medical treatment of madness.[16] The image draws its power partly from its implied comparison with the liberation of the French people during the recent overthrow of the ancien régime. Its romantic gesture signifies a revolution in attitudes toward insanity that was spreading not only in France but throughout Europe and the United States, introducing reforms aimed at curing the mad through "moral" (meaning, in this case, psychological) treatment.[17] Pinel himself associated the French Revolution with the start of a new era in medical science: "The principles of free inquiry, which the revolution has incorporated with our national politics, have opened a wide field to the energies of medical philosophy."[18]

Pinel, as medical director of the Asylum de Bicêtre in Paris and later of a women's asylum, the Salpêtrière, was one of the first European physicians to insist on treating insanity as a disease. Like Rush, Pinel was intrigued by cases in which criminals broke the law repeatedly and, apparently, uncontrollably, even while remaining in all other respects sane. But in contrast to Rush's approach, which had appealed for authority as much to the Bible as to direct observation, Pinel's procedures were closer to what early 19th-century thinkers defined as science.

Pinel opens his *Treatise on Insanity* by praising the "modern" practices of "minute . . . observation" and "analytical investigation." When he first entered the Bicêtre, Pinel recalls, he found "chaos and confusion." He therefore decided to observe "every fact, without any other object than that of collecting materials for future use; and to endeavour, as far as possible, to divest myself of the influence, both of my own prepossessions and the authority of others." This determination to investigate insanity independently and objectively led Pinel to reject the traditional belief that insanity is "an effect of an organic lesion of the brain," a supposition that he found to be, "in a great number of instances, contrary to anatomical fact."[19] Pinel's conclusion that the mind may become ill without a corresponding illness in the brain was bolder than it may sound today, for it implied that the mind, which many associated with the soul, was subject to disease and even death—an implication that seemed to deny the immortality of the soul.[20] However, Pinel turned his back on the theological and metaphysical concerns of the past to insist, on the basis of postmortem examinations and comparisons of the crania of normal, insane, and idiotic subjects, that the mind leads a life of its own, independent of the body—a conceptual breakthrough of considerable consequence for subsequent psychiatric treatments and theories.

Pinel identifies five types of mental derangement: melancholy, dementia, idiocy, mania with delirium, and mania without delirium. Previous authorities, Pinel observes, taught that mania or madness is always accompanied by delirium (hallucinations, delusions), but at the Bicêtre he found "many maniacs" who "at no period gave evidence of any lesion of the understanding."[21] Pinel labels such cases *manie sans délire*, or insanity without delusions. His *Treatise on Insanity* goes on to present, without further analysis, three cases of *manie sans délire*. One, a long and diffuse example, involves a Bicêtre inmate who tried to kill people who had been kind to him. The second involves another Bicêtre inmate, a workman who from time to time experienced "paroxysms of maniacal fury, unaccompanied by any lesion of the intellect"; growing hot all over, he would be "seized by an irresistible propensity to sanguinary deeds," but at the same time he "would answer questions coherently and felt deeply dismayed by his behavior."[22] Filled with remorse, this patient repeatedly attempted suicide.

Neither of these examples bears close resemblance to the condition that Rush had termed moral derangement, but Pinel's third example does:

> An only son of a weak and indulgent mother gave himself up habitually to the gratification of every caprice and passion. . . . The impetuosity of his disposition increased with his years. The money with which he was lavishly supplied removed every obstacle to the indulgence of his wild desires. Every instance of opposition or resistance roused him to acts of fury. He assaulted his adversary with the audacity of a savage . . . . If a dog, a horse, or any other animal offended him, he instantly put it to death. . . . This wayward youth, however, when unmoved by passion, possessed a perfectly sound judgment . . . he distinguished himself by acts of beneficence and compassion. . . . But an act of notoriety put an end to his career of violence. Enraged with a woman who had used offensive language to him, he threw her into a well. Prosecution was commenced against him; and . . . he was condemned to perpetual confinement in Bicêtre.[23]

Pinel developed his analysis of *manie sans délire* independently, before he had an opportunity to read work by Rush.[24] (Rush, in turn, developed his initial analysis of moral derangement before any of Pinel's books had been published.) Even though the two psychiatrists reached similar conclusions within a period of just fifteen years, as scientists they seem to have been working in different eras. Rush started with 18th-century concerns and religious premises; while some of his examples originated in firsthand experience, others came from the Old Testament and Shakespeare. Pinel, on the other hand, based his work on the positivist principles—factual observation, objectivity, induction, skepticism—that would dominate 19th-century science. His concept of *manie sans délire* proved to be far more influential than Rush's moral derangement, partly because Pinel's student Esquirol became famous in his own right and carried his teacher's work forward, and partly because American psychiatry, clinging to the old-fashioned religious principles and somatic assumptions evident in Rush's work, advanced more slowly. The version that seemed more scientific eventually won the day.

## James Cowles Prichard and Moral Insanity

The English physician James Cowles Prichard (1786–1848) conducted scientific research on several fronts, producing, before the age of thirty, *Researches into the Physical History of Man* (1813), an influential study in anthropology and ethology. Subsequently he wrote a book on mental diseases, and later still, having served as senior physician of a hospital in Bristol, England, he published *A Treatise on Insanity* (1835), the text that turned "moral insanity" into a standard, if disputed, psychiatric term. Prichard made no reference to Rush's work, with which he probably was unfamiliar. He did recognize Pinel as a forerunner but felt that Pinel's *manie sans délire* paid too little attention to cases of insanity consisting of "a morbid perversion of the affections and moral feelings exclusively." By extending Pinel's concept to include purely "moral" or psychological disorders, and by redefining it as *moral insanity*, Prichard hoped to make his own mark on the study of mental disease.[25] He succeeded: Prichard's writings on moral insanity became the basis for his future fame as well as for much of subsequent 19th-century theorizing about innate criminality.

In his *Treatise*, Prichard defines moral insanity as

> a form of mental derangement in which the intellectual faculties appear to have sustained little or no injury, while the disorder is manifested principally or alone, in the state of the feelings, temper, or habits. In cases of this description the moral and active principles of the mind are strangely perverted and depraved; the power of self-government is lost or greatly impaired; and the individual is found to be incapable, not of talking or reasoning upon any subject proposed to him, for this he will often do with great shrewdness and volubility, but of conducting himself with decency and propriety in the business of life.[26]

The morally insane, Prichard emphasizes, are logical in their thought processes and indeed can "display great ingenuity" in justifying their misconduct.[27] Their other traits include extreme irascibility and constant, malicious plotting against others who have done nothing to provoke such antagonism. Moral insanity may express itself in a propensity to theft or fire setting, or in sexual obsessions such as erotomania, satyriasis, and nymphomania.

The causes of moral insanity remained a mystery to Prichard, although he noted that the problem could appear in members of families with "an hereditary tendency to madness," as well as in individuals who had previously suffered an attack of madness, epilepsy, or fever. But although he found the causes "obscure,"[28] Prichard stressed that morally insane behavior could not be attributed to ordinary motives such as revenge or to intellectual derangement. He also rejected explanations of similar behaviors being offered at the time by practitioners of the popular science of phrenology. Phrenologists, Prichard felt, had failed to prove their doctrine with "positive" (factual) evidence and were occasionally guilty of illogical reasoning. More promising for future understanding of moral insanity, in Prichard's view, was a new form of experimental surgery in which physicians removed parts of animals' brains and then observed the results. (One researcher "found that a duck, after he removed its cerebellum, could only swim backwards.")[29] None of these considerations brings Prichard closer to pinpointing the causes of moral insanity, but they do enable readers to pinpoint his criteria for good science: factual evidence, logical reasoning, painstaking experimentation.

To exemplify moral insanity, Prichard reports the case of a servant who begged to be dismissed from her post because she experienced "the most irresistible desire" to "tear in pieces" a child entrusted to her care.[30] He also describes an elderly soldier who killed a little girl on the edge of a woods, then raped her and sucked her blood. Eventually the soldier confessed, very calmly, even with "an air of gaiety and satisfaction."[31] Some of Prichard's other examples might today be deemed cases of irresistible impulse, bipolar disease, or Alzheimer's disease.

Prichard lamented juries' tendency to consign morally insane defendants to the gallows; jurors simply failed to grasp that someone who answers questions rationally can also be insane. Reviewing numerous cases in which the law had punished such unfortunate victims of disease, Prichard argued that morally insane criminals should, instead, be confined in asylums. (Here again we find psychiatry vying for professional control over criminality, but now, in a sign of success in the secular takeover of criminality, the opponent is no longer the clergy but the legal profession.)

With Prichard, the concept of moral insanity acquired new authority and scientific status. Simply as a term, *moral insanity* made more immediate sense than its predecessor terms did to physicians familiar with faculty psychology and its notion of a moral faculty or faculties. Daniel Hack Tuke, a prominent English psychiatrist of the next generation, praised Prichard for focusing English psychiatrists on this form of mental disease.[32] At the same time, American psychiatrists, having themselves failed to produce innovative work in this area, looked to England for inspiration and adopted Prichard's concept of moral insanity as a focal point for their own debates.[33] Prichard's influence, for instance, permeated the trial (described in the previous chapter) of William Freeman for the murder of the Van Nest family, with the defense attorneys attempting, unsuccessfully, to argue that Freeman suffered from moral insanity.[34]

## Moral Insanity Becomes Hereditary

Theorizing about moral insanity or uncontrollable criminality was an international phenomenon from the start. It had three national points of origin, with Rush, Pinel, and Prichard—despite their only partial awareness of one another's work—addressing the issue independently. After Prichard published his *Treatise*, "moral insanity" entered the vocabulary of psychiatrists not only in the United States, France, and Britain but also in Italy, Germany, and Canada. The term became part of the international language of mental disease, with psychiatrists keeping track of usages in other countries through travel, exchanges of letters, subscriptions to foreign journals, and the "developments abroad" sections of their own professional journals. It became the term that medical men and legal authorities throughout the Western world used to explain criminal behavior that was shocking, undeterrable, and remorseless.

Moral insanity owed its ability to thrive as a concept to several factors, most important the recognition it gave to the role of emotions in mental disease. Today, mental illness is nearly synonymous with emotional disturbances, but in the 17th and 18th centuries, when it was viewed as a disease of the brain, it was nearly synonymous with intellectual disturbances, usually defined as a disease of the brain and hence the mind. Moral insanity made its debut as a diagnostic category just as psychiatrists were broadening their understanding of the causes of human behavior to include the will, attitudes, feelings, and such utilitarian considerations as the pursuit of pleasure and avoidance of pain.[35] "The realm of [mental] unsoundness changed its character," historian Hannah Augstein writes of early 19th-century ideas of insanity; "increasingly, cases of insanity became known where patients did not seem to dwell in some delusive state."[36] The concept of moral insanity reflected and contributed to this shift in the boundaries of insanity to include emotional disturbance. Late in the century, in fact, a commentator titled a paper "Moral or Emotional Insanity."[37]

This shift was encouraged by the Romantic movement's fascination with the drama of emotional states,[38] and by the popularity of phrenology, a science that paid as much attention to the affective as to the intellectual faculties and that, at least in the eyes of its supporters, had an air of scientific sophistication.[39] Another factor that made moral insanity appealing as an idea was the 19th century's intense interest in the legal implications of insanity. Even when moral insanity itself was not raised as a defense, the sensational trials of the 19th century—that of William Freeman for the massacre of the Van Nests; that of Daniel M'Naghten for killing someone whom he mistook for the prime minister of England and believed to be conspiring with the pope against him; that of the U.S. presidential assassin Charles Guiteau—riveted international attention on issues of the diagnosis of insanity, freedom of will, and responsibility.[40] Such debates illuminated the conceptual usefulness of moral insanity.

Progressive American psychiatrists accepted the idea of moral insanity and used it diagnostically.[41] One of them, Isaac Ray, even became a champion of the theory, writing about it extensively and defending it against his more conservative colleagues. Ray's *Treatise on the Medical Jurisprudence of Insanity* traces the idea of *moral mania* (as he termed moral insanity) back to Pinel's *manie sans délire*[42] and adopts Prichard's definition, describing moral mania as "a morbid perversion of the natural feelings, affections, inclinations, temper, habits, and moral dispositions, without any notable lesion of the intellect."[43] Ray conducted no new research for his *Treatise*, which, as a legal rather than a scientific text, quite legitimately drew its examples from writings by others.[44] But he did assemble a treasure trove of examples of homicidal mania, habitual theft, erotic mania, and repetitive fire setting that he had gleaned from history and law books. The examples are aimed at revealing the essence of moral mania: criminal behavior committed by people who have no motive, cannot control themselves, and lack remorse.[45] Echoing earlier theorists, Ray argues that people who are driven to crime by moral mania are not responsible for their behavior. He believes that their acts are "the result of physical disease, instead of moral depravity."[46] Given that they suffer from a kind of brain disease, such people should not be punished but rather given medical care. That Ray paid so much attention to moral insanity in what became the standard 19th-century work on the jurisprudence of mental disease (the *Treatise* went through five editions and was admired on both sides of the Atlantic) helped cushion the concept against the disapproval of his American confrères.

Eventually, however, moral insanity became a lightning rod for tensions that divided American psychiatry. Ray's stature could not save the concept from attacks by colleagues who refused to recognize even the possibility of emotional madness without accompanying disability. The psychiatrists' professional group, the Association of Medical Superintendents of American Institutions for the Insane, was a closed and parochial organization in the later part of the 19th century;[47] it was, moreover, dominated by Dr. John P. Gray, superintendent of New York's Utica Lunatic Asylum, a man of conservative, moralistic views who never doubted the immortality of the human mind.[48] Gray insisted that insanity is "simply a bodily disease in which the mind is disturbed more or less profoundly, because the brain is involved in the sickness. . . . The mind is not, in itself, ever diseased. It is incapable of disease or of its final consequence, death."[49] Gray thus slammed shut the door on even the possibility of moral insanity, a disease of the mind itself.[50]

Although the ferocity of Gray's opinions may have discouraged his more timid colleagues from endorsing the theory of moral insanity, as some scholars have argued,[51] it is also true that, by 1860, factors in the broader social context had started undermining support for the concept. Phrenology fell into disrepute. The M'Naghten Rule of 1843, formulated in England but adopted in the United States as well, stressed cognitive, not affective, factors in determinations of legal insanity; to avoid conviction, criminal defendants claiming insanity had to show that they had not known the nature and quality of their act, or, if they had known it, had not understood that it was wrong. Lawyers and conservative psychiatrists argued that if moral insanity were accepted as a defense in criminal trials, people would lose all sense of responsibility. In addition, many physicians in addition to Gray sensed a heresy lurking in the apparent dualism of moral insanity theory: if the mind could sicken, then it might die, and the soul might die with it—quite contrary to the religious doctrine of the immortality of the soul. Rush's hope for human perfectibility had long since fallen by the wayside, done in by an increasing pessimism about America's ability to solve its social problems. But the greatest threat to the concept of moral insanity was the growing popularity of the new theory of degeneration, which explained human ills such as insanity, criminality, and poverty in somatic and hereditarian terms.[52] By the end of the century, few American psychiatrists or social-policy makers could conceive of a mental affliction that did not also involve physical *and* intellectual decay.

While American psychiatrists eventually rejected the concept of moral insanity, rejection did not lead to the idea's extinction.[53] Rather, the idea jumped jurisdiction to be adopted by superintendents of institutions for the mentally retarded, who transformed moral insanity into "moral imbecility," an affliction that more clearly "belonged" in their domain. Led by Isaac Kerlin, the most powerful superintendent in his jurisdiction, the Association of Medical Officers of American Institutions for Idiots and Feeble-Minded Persons produced a series of papers that redefined "moral insanity" as "moral imbecility" by merging the older concept with degeneration theory and thus defining it as a somatic condition. These superintendents then used "moral imbecility" to argue for enlarging their own professional scope and authority.[54] In sum, they took advantage of the opening provided by the psychiatrists' rejection of moral insanity to renovate the concept and make it their own.

For a while, circumstances in England looked more favorable for the survival of the concept of moral insanity in its original form as a mental disease that did not affect intellectual capacity. The British association of psychiatrists, the Medico-Psychological Association, was a less contentious group than its American counterpart, partly because it was not a closed and defensive organization, partly because it was not polarized by strong personalities such as those of Isaac Ray and John Gray. Although some of its members fretted that moral insanity might become a "stepping-stone" for criminals hoping to evade justice,[55] English psychiatrists worked to collect more precise examples of the condition, discuss treatment possibilities, and clarify the distinction between partial and full moral insanity. In a particularly thoughtful essay titled "Lecture on Moral Insanity," John Kitching, a physician who had gained firsthand experience with the affliction as medical superintendent of England's York Retreat, a private mental hospital, described moral insanity as a violent but localized storm: whereas the major forms of insanity sweep through the mind "as a storm of wind may sweep an entire ocean, and produce wild confusion and turbulence from shore to shore," at other times the sea "may be subject to a gale which shall blow over the region, within circumscribed limits, and leave the rest in entire or comparative calm."[56] Kitching's metaphor helped clarify the difference between total and partial or moral insanity.

The most spectacular case of moral insanity in the English psychiatric literature of the late 19th century was presented by Daniel Hack Tuke at the 1885 annual meeting of the Medico-Psychological Association, where he reported on the case of W.B., a horse slasher of whom he had learned during a recent trip to Canada. (Tuke derived his report from W.B.'s records at the Kingston, Ontario, asylum. Because his report is lengthy, I summarize it here, quoting only briefly from Tuke's original. His version, as first printed in the *Journal of Mental Science* in 1885, includes photographs of W.B.)[57]

> Born in 1843, W.B. had begun as a boy to torment other children and torture domestic animals. He whipped a younger brother, almost killing him, and then "was apprehended for cutting the throat of a valuable horse belonging to a neighbour." He confessed to this act and to maiming and killing other animals as well. Jailed for twelve months, he returned and tried to strangle a younger brother. An attempt to smother an infant sibling and several thefts led to a seven-year penitentiary sentence. "His next escapade was the result of an accident. B. and his father were at a neighbour's one evening, and while paring apples, the old man accidentally cut his hand . . . severely. W. B. . . . became restless, nervous, pale," and went to a nearby farmyard, where "he cut the throat of a horse, killing it." While hiding in the woods, he raped a little girl. At that point, W.B. received a life sentence. He was pardoned, however, and went on to castrate a horse, gash its neck and abdomen, and amputate part of its tongue. Sent to an insane asylum, he escaped, attempted rape, and committed a number of minor offenses. Back in the asylum he tried to castrate a fellow inmate and punctured the stomach of another with a fork. He was fond of his stepmother but confessed that he planned to rape her. W.B. could be "a quiet and useful man," Tuke concludes, "but he could never be trusted. He had a fair education and enjoyed reading newspapers."[58]

In W.B., Tuke and his colleagues found a perfect example of moral insanity—a man normal in all respects aside from the fact that for years on end he committed revolting acts of violence without experiencing an iota of remorse. The concept of moral insanity (or, as Tuke sometimes calls it here, "moral imbecility") helped to explain such otherwise inexplicable behavior.

For the decade following 1870, the *Journal of Mental Science* rarely mentioned moral insanity, and when the discussion did resume, the concept had been transformed by the degenerationist idea that humans can devolve and move backward, down the evolutionary ladder. It did not undergo as complete a name change as in the United States, where *moral imbecility* became the preferred term, nor did it so dramatically leap into another jurisdiction; it simply absorbed the lessons of evolution and the new somaticism to emerge as a more general theory of innate criminality, one that could account for a wider range of offenses.[59] The *Journal of Mental Science* broke its silence on the issue in July 1881, with the article "Moral Insanity" by Dr. George H. Savage, resident physician at Bethlem Royal Hospital, that so radically redefined the concept as to leave little of its original meaning intact. Moral insanity here is no longer distinct from intellectual insanity but is, rather, tightly linked to it. Moreover, Savage now explains its innateness in hereditarian terms: the morally insane either inherit the condition from unsound parents or were conceived while their parents were feverish or syphilitic.[60] In addition, moral insanity now explains not only crimes but also minor deviancies—eccentricity, childhood naughtiness, lying, bullying, incessant masturbation. Like Rush, Pinel, and Prichard, Savage associates moral insanity with criminality ("it is almost impossible to draw a definite line between the criminal and the person who is more truly morally insane"),[61] together with uncontrollable, undeterrable lawbreaking, but that core is almost all that survives of the original concept.

Although the concept of moral insanity had not been discussed in the *Journal of Mental Science* for a decade, Savage clearly had been rethinking its definition in light of the teachings of the evolutionists Herbert Spencer and Charles Darwin and of the degenerationist psychiatrist Henry Maudsley.[62] His call to his colleagues for more discussion of moral insanity triggered a flood of responses in the same vein.[63] Other psychiatrists, too, had been rethinking the matter, and they, too, were ready to reinterpret Prichard's theory in degenerationist terms.

Moral insanity slipped readily into degenerationist discourses on moral savagery and social reversion. In a talk of 1884, Tuke explained that in some forms of moral insanity, "the higher levels of evolution with which the altruistic sentiments are associated have become the seat of . . . morbid changes." In other cases, "in which the character has always been morally sub-normal, the highest level of evolution reached is a low one . . . and the altruistic sentiments are feebly developed."[64] Here Tuke draws on the idea of evolution to distinguish between acquired and congenital moral insanity. Later, citing Herbert Spencer, he notes that what seems abnormal in civilized society may be normal under barbarism. Some people revert "at birth . . . to the condition of a prior ancestry," while others begin normally only to have "disease . . . destroy the activity of those sentiments which have been more recently evolved."[65] Another physician agreed with Tuke wholeheartedly: "Without doubt the moral sense is the latest acquirement of civilization, and one of the first to be lost."[66] Tuke himself interpreted the horse-slashing W.B. as a "reversion to an old savage type, . . . born by accident in the wrong century."[67] By the 1880s, then, leading British psychiatrists were combining the older concept of moral insanity with ideas of Spencer and Darwin to produce a degenerationist version of the theory. They did not mention the work of the Italian psychiatrist Cesare Lombroso, but the idea of moral insanity had led them to conceive of an offender very like the born criminal Lombroso had identified in his recent work *Criminal Man*.[68]

## The Roots of Scientific Criminology

Thus roots of criminological thought lie in the field that we today call psychiatry, specifically in discourses on the affliction that came to be called moral insanity. And thus a history of criminological thought must begin with the biological theorizing of the late 18th and early 19th centuries and must include developments on both sides of the Atlantic, specifically in the United States, France, and England. The broader origins of these criminological efforts lay in the Enlightenment drive to study phenomena scientifically. Also influential in the genesis of what became criminology was the Enlightenment impulse toward reform, an urge symbolized by the dramatic image of Pinel liberating the insane and realized in programs of so-called moral treatment within institutions for the mentally ill.[69] All three of the physicians who initiated the discourses on moral insanity—Rush, Pinel, and Prichard—were primarily interested in the causes and treatment of mental disease. All three, in the course of analyzing the diseases of the mind, came across an anomalous type of case—insanity without the usual delusions, hallucinations, depressions, and rages. Approaching the problem from various angles, they elaborated versions of the theory of moral insanity to account for the anomalies. In their work, moral insanity can be affected by physical factors, but it does not show up in biological abnormalities. None of them professed to account for all types of criminal behavior. Rather, they looked at a particular type of criminal behavior—recidivistic, often violent, apparently uncontrollable, committed by offenders who appeared incapable of remorse—and explained it in terms of mental abnormality. Writing at the end of the so-called Age of Reason, they conceived of dangerousness as irrationality—immoderate, illogical, and inexplicable behavior. To them, these extreme departures from standard ways of reasoning and behaving seemed a departure from human nature itself. Later moral insanity theories biologized the concept, turning moral insanity into a somatic and hereditary condition.

In an illuminating passage in *Knowledge and Social Imagery*, the sociologist of science David Bloor argues that social philosophers of the Enlightenment differed importantly from those of the late 19th century in the way they thought about the individual's relation to the state and society. Enlightenment social thought was "individualistic and atomistic," conceiving "of wholes and collectivities as . . . sets of individual units" whose nature was "unchanged by being brought together. Thus [for Enlightenment thinkers] societies are collections of individuals whose essential nature . . . is not bound up by society." Instead, human rights and the essential rationality of human nature are universals, invariant across time and place, regardless of social situation. It follows (although Bloor does not specifically make this point) that human rights and human nature cannot be undermined by a sick society; indeed, the idea of a "sick" society was foreign to Enlightenment thought. Bloor's generalizations apply well to the teachings of Rush, Pinel, and even, to some extent, those of Prichard, even though he wrote a bit later. They also apply well to those who opposed William Freeman's moral insanity defense, for those opponents, too, believed that human nature is universal and immutable. In contrast, Bloor continues, in late 19th-century thought, the "notion of pre-social naturalness is replaced by the idea of our essentially social nature. It is society which is natural," a belief that carries with it "organic images of family unity." In late 19th-century social thought, the individual unit exists "in a state of intimate unity with the whole."[70] From this it follows that a sick society can poison the individual, and conversely, that a sick or degenerate individual can infect the body social. Bloor's distinctions help explain why crime became a more threatening phenomenon over the course of the 19th century. Ideas about the relation of the individual to the state colored ideas about the significance of crime.

It is hardly surprising that, around the year 1800, someone, somewhere, would start using the methods of science to study criminality, not only out of perplexity about the nature of extreme forms of lawbreaking but also to rescue explanations of crime from theologians and clerics. Positivism was starting to provide new tools for understanding social phenomena; eventually someone would start to apply them to crime. Given the social organization of late 18th- and early 19th-century Western society—a world with no social sciences, in which medical superintendents of insane asylums were the only professional group that might conceivably have the expertise to explain extraordinary forms of criminal behavior—psychiatrically inclined physicians were naturally the first to move into this field. As the physician and phrenologist J. G. Spurzheim explained, "It is the particular duty of the physician to consider the diseased state of man."[71] Nor was it surprising that medical men extended their expertise from illnesses of the body to those of the mind and brain, especially in an era when many believed that body and mind were intimately connected and when, as Spurzheim further remarked, it was becoming clear that emotions such as grief, jealousy, and hopeless love could harm physical health.[72] However, the retrospective predictability of the development around 1800 of a psychiatric explanation for undeterrable criminal behavior does not mean that the concept of moral insanity, as formulated by Rush, Pinel, and Prichard, was historically inevitable. The manner in which the concept emerged, its meanings, its reception, and its subsequent influence depended on a host of factors, including social expectations of science and the specific intellectual, religious, and professional concerns of the originators.

The 19th-century debates over moral insanity constituted a dramatic challenge to the religious understandings of insanity and criminality that had prevailed for centuries. As late as 1838, Isaac Ray, the American specialist in the medical jurisprudence of insanity, felt that he had to defend himself against criticism by charging that "to attribute it [insanity] to the visitation of God . . . is a questionable proof of true piety."[73] Similarly, in an 1841 report, directors of an American insane asylum felt they had to explicitly oppose the belief that insanity is "'a visitation of [God's] wrath and vengeance, or a reproach.'"[74] The idea of moral insanity helped physicians, lawyers, policy makers, and the general public pass over the abyss separating theological from scientific reasoning. Eventually it helped American and English psychiatrists accept the idea of biologically based psychological disease as a cause of crime.

A concept as radical as that of moral insanity naturally had to struggle for acceptance. Courts resisted incorporating it into jurisprudence because cases of moral insanity (as psychiatrists readily admitted) were difficult to diagnose. A prosecutor in the Freeman case, for instance, argued that if the jury accepted the defense of moral insanity, society could "bid adieu to all hopes of punishing the atrocious crime of murder," at least until that remote and unlikely day when advances in medical science enabled physicians to "enter the murderer's heart or analyze his mind and discover the influences by which it is operated."[75] But the ultimate reasons for resistance were neither legal nor scientific but philosophical and religious. Participants on both sides of the Atlantic were debating the nature of the human mind and soul. The concept of moral insanity forced them to deal with difficult issues of free will and determinism, and it demanded that they rethink the sources and nature of evil behavior. Those who accepted the moral insanity explanation of criminal behavior did so because it seemed scientific—the same reason that people accept genetic and neurological explanations today.

The early and late versions of the moral insanity concept differed considerably. Rush's version was barely distinguishable from his religious beliefs, while later theorists, as they themselves emphasized, shared a "repugnance to invoke the supernatural in accounting for the phenomena of human life."[76] Early theorists considered moral insanity a rare phenomenon; their degenerationist descendants discovered it everywhere. Whereas Rush and other early proponents identified heredity as a predisposing cause in *some* cases of moral insanity, later theorists could barely conceive of moral insanity apart from bad heredity. Whereas moral insanity was initially explained in terms of faculty psychology, by the end of the century the terms had shifted to those of what we would now call evolutionary psychology. The early theorists utilized a variety of scientific methods to investigate moral insanity: case study, the empirical collection of facts, induction, postmortems and crania comparisons (Pinel), even experimental animal vivisection (Prichard). The later theorists, too, were wedded to scientific investigation, but they used additional methods, including genealogical research, measurements of cranial capacity, and the testing of mental and physical abilities.

These differences notwithstanding, moral insanity—although but a prototypical and rudimentary instance of biocriminology—had traits that became characteristic of such theories. It tended to be reductionist, boiling the causes of crime down to an abnormality of the brain. To explain bizarre criminal behavior, it looked first (though not exclusively) to factors inside the offender, not outside in social conditions. Moral insanity theory began with the assumption that biology is a key cause of human behavior, including criminal behavior. It scientized criminality, thus beginning to shift lawbreaking out of first the metaphysical and then the legal realm and into the medical jurisdiction, where it was interpreted as a form of disease. The notion of moral insanity, moreover, implied a basic difference between offenders and law-abiding citizens, between them and us; its emphasis, in other words, fell on human differences, not commonalities. Although it was a "soft" deterministic theory, one that conceived of biology as susceptible to environmental modification, it nonetheless raised fundamental issues about free will. And it implied that the key to better crime control would lie in making the criminal justice system (or parts of it) more scientific in approach. These characteristics did not appear in every version of moral insanity theory, nor were they well developed. But with the benefit of hindsight, we can see that over time they became typical of biological explanations of crime.

To return to the beginning: understanding the origins of the scientific study of crime calls for examining not only the original texts but also the context in which they appeared. Moral insanity theory emerged in the period between the flowering of 18th-century rationalism and the onset of 19th-century hereditarianism. It began at a time when criminals were assumed to be normal human beings with free will and the capacity for utilitarian cost-benefits analyses. The penitentiary system, introduced in the early 19th century, presupposed such rationality while at the same time aiming to reinforce it.[77] By the 1870s, however, criminals seemed irrational and undeterrable, governed by a malignant heredity over which they had no control. Moral insanity theory, picturing the arch-criminal as intellectually sane but morally mad, hovered between these two poles, criminalizing offenders' minds, but only partially, and sometimes holding out hope that diseased moral faculties might be restored to normality.

# 3

# Phrenology
## The Abnormal Brain

Phrenology—the early 19$^{th}$-century system of reading character from the contours of the skull—produced one of the most radical reorientations in ideas about crime and punishment ever proposed in the Western world. In the area of jurisprudence, its practitioners worked to reestablish criminal law on a new philosophical basis; to overhaul ideas about criminal responsibility; and—in a retributivist age—to develop a rehabilitative rationale for sentencing. In the area of penology, phrenologists opposed capital punishment and developed a plan for rehabilitating offenders that influenced criminal justice for the next 150 years. But it was in the area of criminology that phrenologists proved themselves most innovative, for they developed the first comprehensive explanation of criminal behavior, one that overlapped with the theory of moral insanity but was far more inclusive and systematic.

On the basis of their understanding of the brain as an aggregation of independent organs or "faculties," phrenologists could explain every form of criminal behavior from petty theft through wife beating to homicide. They had guidelines for distinguishing between sane and insane criminals; they introduced the idea that people vary in their propensity to commit crime; and they could account for differences in crime rates by age, nationality, race, and sex. Phrenologists could even explain the behavior of criminals whom we today would call serial killers and psychopaths, as in this case from one of phrenology's basic texts:

At the beginning of the last century several murders were committed in Holland, on the frontiers of the province of Cleves. For a long time the murderer remained unknown; but at last an old fiddler, who was accustomed to play on the violin at country weddings, was suspected in consequence of some expressions of his children. Led before the justice, he

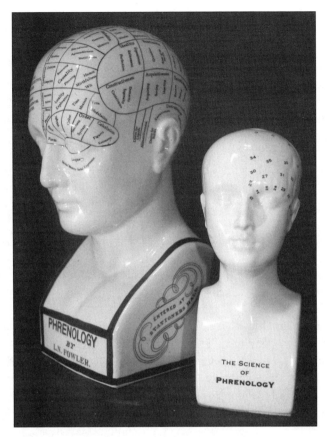

Phrenological heads. Phrenologists tried to diagnose criminality and other abnormal mental states by studying the contours of the skull. Then, to restore the brain to normality, they tried to reduce the size of overdeveloped mental "faculties" and to increase that of underdeveloped faculties. Photograph by Danielle Rousseau.

confessed thirty-four murders, and he asserted that he had committed them without any cause of enmity, and without any intention of robbing, but only because he was extremely delighted with bloodshed.[1]

At a time when most people would have explained the Dutch fiddler's behavior in terms of evildoing, phrenologists attributed it to an innate brain defect. Their criminological ambition and scope—their desire to develop a science of criminal behavior—excited liberal thinkers on both sides of the Atlantic.

Phrenologists' writings on criminal jurisprudence, penology, and criminology were part of a much broader, all-encompassing biosocial explanatory system that aimed at scientifically accounting for not only criminal behavior but *all* human behavior (and a great deal of animal behavior as well). Their system rested on five fundamental assumptions:

1. The brain is the organ of the mind.
2. The brain is an aggregation of about thirty separate organs or faculties, such as Combativeness, Covetiveness, and Destructiveness, that function independently.[2]
3. The more active an organ, the larger its size.
4. The relative size of the organs can be estimated by inspecting the contours of the skull.
5. The relative size of the organs can be increased or decreased through exercise and self-discipline.[3]

These fundamental ideas, all but the last of them formulated about 1800 by the Viennese physician Franz Joseph Gall, became the basis of an international movement to develop a science of phrenology and spread its gospel. The movement occurred in two stages: a scientific phase, from about 1800 to 1830, when the phrenological system was developed, mainly by physicians and psychiatrists; and an overlapping popularizing stage, from about 1820 to 1850, during which phrenology became a fad, complete with social clubs, marketers, and hucksters. But the timing and duration of these phases differed by place, and although phrenology itself underwent little development after the 1840s, its ideas segued into the theory of degeneration that underpinned concepts of deviance in the late 19th century. Indeed, some phrenological societies remained active into the 20th century.

Like other very early students of social behavior, phrenologists adopted methods previously developed in the natural sciences, assuming that the social world could be studied using the same procedures. They collected data, formulated hypotheses, and made positivist assumptions about the possibility of direct, objective apprehension of social phenomena. During its scientific phase, phrenology intersected with a range of other scientific endeavors, including anatomy, anthropology, physiology, psychology, and psychiatry, and it used a range of scientific procedures, including empirical observation through animal vivisection and autopsies, induction, and deduction. (Some phrenologists also claimed to use the experimental method, but their failure to experiment rigorously proved to be a scientific Achilles' heel.) Phrenology constituted an ambitious and complex effort to break with older metaphysical and theological explanations of behavior and replace them with an empirical science.

What did phrenologists say about the causes of crime? In what ways was their work an antecedent of today's biocriminologies? How did they move beyond the rudimentary positivism of early moral insanity theorists to develop criminology as a science? In what follows, I first establish the social context in which phrenologists worked and summarize the substance of their thinking about the causes of crime, about reform in the area of criminal jurisprudence, and about penology or the treatment of prisoners. The final section discusses their doctrine's significance as a form of biocriminology.

## Phrenology: Context and Doctrine

Phrenology, like moral insanity theory, emerged out of the Enlightenment drive to replace metaphysical and theological explanations with scientific accounts of natural and social phenomena. "One fact is to me more positive and decisive than a thousand metaphysical opinions," declared Johann Gaspar Spurzheim, one of phrenology's founders, in a phrase much admired by his followers.[4] The new emphasis on observation and human reasoning as sources of knowledge was reinforced by democratic revolutions in North American and France—vivid demonstrations of the possibility of breaking free of older systems. With democracy came the ideal of universal education and the bold notion that any educated person might at least dabble in the study of natural phenomena. Phrenology grew out of this enthusiasm for scientific explanation and these democratic impulses. Insanity and criminality, previously interpreted as willful violations of God's laws, now seemed as though they might be comprehensible in scientific terms. At the same time, the fall of authoritarian regimes, their gradual replacement by bourgeois industrial societies, and the growing distaste for older, retributivist punishments that harmed or destroyed the body created a demand for new methods of social ordering and discipline.[5] This, very roughly, was the situation about 1800, when phrenology made its first appearance.

Two more specific developments lay in phrenology's immediate background: the theory of moral insanity and the science of physiognomy.

In very early remarks on what became known as moral insanity, the psychiatrist Benjamin Rush had conceived of the mind as a congeries of independent "faculties," thus presaging the phrenological conception of the brain as a series of autonomous organs.[6] Thereafter, moral insanity theory and phrenology developed on parallel tracks, sometimes converging in the work of medical men such as Amariah Brigham, who endorsed both doctrines. Physiognomy was described by its greatest popularizer, the Swiss theologian Johann Kaspar Lavater (1741–1801), as "the science or knowledge of the correspondence between the external and internal man, the visible superficies and the invisible contents."[7]

Lavater was hardly the first physiognomist—he was preceded, for instance, by the 16th-century Italian scholar Giambattista della Porta (see figure 2.1), whose book on physiognomy stimulated much of the later work on the science of faces, including criminal anthropology. However, Lavater was the first modern practitioner to attempt to establish physiognomy on a scientific basis. He was certain that he could read people's character from their faces, a conviction he elaborated in his *Essays on Physiognomy*, a work first issued in German (1775–1778) and published in English on both sides of the Atlantic by 1795. His *Essays*, with their drawings of facial expressions (see figure 2.2) and claims to constitute a scientific psychology, enjoyed remarkable success, appearing in more than 150 editions by 1850.[8] Particularly popular were illustrated pocketbook versions that readers could use to gauge the character of new acquaintances and passersby. (Lavater taught, for example, that long foreheads indicate comprehension; short ones, volatility; and "perfect perpendicularity . . . , want of understanding.")[9] Physiognomy, like its successor science of phrenology, illustrates the early 19th-century hunger for a science of human behavior. Both fields began with the assumption that outer appearances must reflect inner states. But the differences between the two are also instructive. Although Lavater hoped that physiognomy would become a full-fledged science, he did not attempt rigorous study, as phrenologists did. His assertions are based more on appeals to common sense ("everyone knows," "no one can deny")[10] than on systematic data collection, and he did not attempt to *explain* the correlations he observed.[11]

Phrenology itself began in late 18th-century Vienna, with research in craniology by its founder, Franz Joseph Gall. Gall's collaborator and most influential follower, the German physician Johann Gaspar Spurzheim, described how Gall arrived at his doctrine:

Dr. Gall, from his earliest youth, was attentive to the difference which existed between his brothers and sisters, and his school-fellows. He was particularly vexed, that while several of his school-fellows learned by heart even things which they did not understand, with great facility, he had the utmost difficulty in engraving in his memory a small number of words. On the other hand, however, he found that he excelled them in the powers of reflection and reasoning. He afterwards observed that in those individuals who had so great a verbal memory, the eyes were very prominent; and this observation was the commencement of all his future inquiries into psychology.[12]

It took years of study, however, for Gall to find the right track. For instance, he wasted time trying to correlate people's talents with "the whole form of their heads."[13] But Gall persisted, inviting people of all social classes and vocations into his house, talking with them to determine their character, and studying areas of their heads until he was able to correlate character traits with specific areas of the skull. Having no children, Gall was able to spend his money and spare time on research. He made casts of people's heads, collected skulls, and stopped people on the street if he noticed on their heads "any distinct protuberance."[14] In time, he wrote up his findings in a six-volume work, *On the Functions of the Brain and Each of Its Parts*, first published in French in 1825.[15] This work was eventually translated into English,[16] but its late date of publication (1835) and unwieldy size meant that it was not much read in Britain or the United States. (In fact, Gall opposed a shorter edition on the grounds that readers should have all the facts at their disposal.)[17] The relative inaccessibility of Gall's work in Britain and America created a void filled by more timely and less cumbersome books on phrenology.

Spurzheim compressed, systematized, and extended Gall's system in a single, English-language text, *The Physionomical System of Drs. Gall and Spurzheim*, that along with his other books became the basis for the phrenological movement in Britain and the United States. Spurzheim identified six organs in addition to Gall's original twenty-seven and, ingeniously, developed an easy-to-follow and easily reproduced head chart indicating the organs' locations. (Gall seems to have done much of his instruction from actual skulls on which he penned the outlines of the organs, a method that would have involved hauling skulls to demonstrations.)[18] Even though Gall believed that climate, food, and drink can modify the faculties, and in fact used such changes to explain racial and ethnic differences in body build and character, he had only long-term modifications in mind.[19] Spurzheim, in contrast, taught that individuals' faculties can be modified in the course of a lifetime. "Bring men into favorable situations calculated to call forth their feelings, and these will be strengthened," Spurzheim wrote. "In order to cultivate benevolence, one should not frequent only the society of rich and opulent persons, and learn by heart descriptions of charity; he must experience misery himself."[20] Thus Spurzheim gave the essentially deterministic doctrine an optimistic twist, adding the possibilities of self-help and treatment. In his view, the "inferior faculties"—those most responsible for crime—"stand in need of constant regulation."[21]

Spurzheim settled in England, where he gave compelling anatomical demonstrations to illustrate Gall's system. His proselytizing efforts eventually carried him to the United States, where he was lionized by East Coast intellectuals and invited to lecture on anatomy at Harvard medical school. These exertions exhausted him, however, and he unexpectedly died in Boston in November 1832. Thousands attended the funeral,[22] a sign that the doctrine was already becoming a cause.

While the social identities of phrenology's supporters differed over time and by country (sometimes by city), the first-stage advocates seem generally to have been middle-class reformers. Among the most enthusiastic were George Combe and his brother Andrew Combe, residents of the Scottish city of Edinburgh, where, for reasons that historians have explored extensively, phrenology took its strongest and deepest hold.[23] The substantial literature on the subject identifies phrenology's advocates as liberals, some with a radical and utopian bent, most of them antimetaphysical and, in France, also anticlerical.[24] They tended to be not members of social elites but up-and-coming young Turks. The early 19th century was in any case a period of aspiration and widespread optimism. ("The most important way of preventing crime," wrote Spurzheim, "is that of improving mankind.")[25] In this context, phrenology provided a philosophical basis for reformers who hoped to rationalize governance and institute new means of maintaining order in the democratic state.

Phrenology's appeal lay partly in its implicit social and political hierarchies. The doctrine naturalized the idea of social hierarchy through its division of labor between the head and lower parts of the body; it also taught the importance of harmony, balance, and cooperation among the parts, and of obedience to natural law. Gall's system not only put the topmost part of the human form in charge but also hierarchically ranked the faculties.[26] It located the lower propensities (Amativeness, Combativeness, Destructiveness), which man was said to share with animals, on the lower section of the skull. Even more ignominiously, it relegated some of them to the back of the head. (Thus Amativeness—sexuality—was to be found to the rear and at the base of the skull.) Gall's intellectual faculties lay more toward the front and center of the skull, while at the top, crowning the whole, lay the moral faculties of Benevolence, Veneration, Firmness, Hope, and Conscientiousness. Here was a model of order not only for the individual but also for society, one in which goodness, rationality, and intelligence would control impulsivity, animalistic tendencies, and criminality. Toward the 1850s, as the century's early optimism faded into middle-class apprehension about the dangerous classes, the hereditarian ideas implicit in phrenology become more prominent, and phrenology began to look more like a system of inherited ability.[27] Sir Francis Galton's research on the inheritance of ability and the possibility of breeding better humans were but a step away.[28]

Spurzheim's *Physiognomical System of Drs. Gall and Spurzheim* remains an impressive book: clear, well organized, comprehensive, and closely argued. The first section, on the structure of the brain and nervous system, serves a credentialing function: based on dissections and other direct observations of the brain, it shows itself to be the work of careful anatomists. Spurzheim enumerates past obstacles to scientific study of the brain and nervous system, including "the mania of forming systems upon a few solitary facts" and metaphysical assumptions. "The schoolmen . . . say, the soul is simple, and therefore its material residence [the brain] must be simple also, and all the nerves must end in one point; in other words, the nerves can have only one origin, because each individual has but one soul."[29] Deriding such metaphysical reasoning as "frivolous speculation," Spurzheim calls instead for close observation of "natural facts." We should "forsake hypothetical reasoning in order to follow the simple methods of experience. . . . [We must adopt] a rational mode of judging from experiment and observation."[30] Later in the book, having explained the phrenological system in detail, Spurzheim proudly claims, "We never venture beyond experience [direct observation]. We neither deny nor affirm any thing which cannot be verified by experiment."[31] John Abernethy, a London surgeon who rejected phrenology but knew and admired Spurzheim, reported, "Dr. Spurzheim . . . [said] to me that it matters not how many coincidences we may observe [between character and cranial protuberances]; one contradictory fact must disprove them all."[32] Moreover, Spurzheim made a point of displaying his evidence for all to see. To some laymen and physicians thirsting for scientific understanding of human behavior, phrenology seemed to unlock the secrets of the human soul.

To understand why it was phrenology and not some other science that became the basis for the first fully developed theory of crime, we need to look at the way the personal interests and research skills of phrenology's founders intersected with the scientific context in which they worked and the cultural contexts in which their doctrine took root. The scientific context was one of widespread interest in applying scientific methods to the study of social phenomena, and researchers had no reason to doubt that natural science methods would work just as well for the investigation of social and psychological events. Earlier, the utilitarians Jeremy Bentham and Cesare Beccaria had offered a rational choice framework for explaining criminal behavior, but utilitarianism was hardly a full-blown psychological or social theory, and in any case, punishment simply did not seem to deter criminals. The work of A. M. Guerry, Adolphe Quetelet, and Siméon-Denis Poisson on crime statistics—another sign of the hunger for social science—lay in the future (albeit the very near future), and none of these men was primarily interested in the causes of crime.[33] However, Lavater had recently elaborated his physiognomical system for reading the face for signs of trouble; and moral insanity theorists, drawing on faculty psychology, were already developing their faulty-mind theory of criminality. Thus the very first efforts to study deviance scientifically had already set this type of work on an explanatory trajectory heading toward the brain.

This was the general scientific situation in which Gall and Spurzheim undertook their search for an explanation of human behavior. Their anatomical skills and empirical approach satisfied scientific requirements, but their doctrine's radical materialism—its reduction of free will and human nobility to bundles in the brain—meant that at first phrenology had few followers. Indeed, it might have sunk without a trace had Spurzheim not serendipitously found a receptive social and cultural context in Edinburgh and the United States; had he not softened the doctrine's determinism to make Gall's phrenology palatable to reformers; and had the doctrine not attracted the superb publicist George Combe. Moreover, as the next sections show, phrenology provided middle-class reformers with exactly the science they needed to wage their jurisprudential and penological crusades. Specialists in mental disease and related fields similarly discovered a scientific friend in phrenology. Through this fortuitous, stochastic process, then, phrenology found receptive constituencies—and thrived until changing circumstances, including criticisms of its scientific claims, made a successor science appear more persuasive.

## Explanations of Crime

Spurzheim's chapter "The Organ of the Propensity to Destroy, or of Destructiveness," in his *Physiognomical System*, illustrates both his methods and phrenology's applicability to the study of crime. He begins by observing that animals vary in their propensity to kill, even within species and breeds. "Gall had a little dog which had this propensity in so high a degree, that he would sometimes watch several hours for a mouse, and as soon as it was killed he left it; notwithstanding repeated punishment he had also an irresistible propensity to kill birds." In man, too, Spurzheim continues, the destructive propensity manifests itself with different degrees of intensity. Some people are merely indifferent to animals' pain; others enjoy seeing animals killed; and still others experience "the most irresistible desire to kill." Spurzheim gives many examples, including that of the Dutch fiddler, and explores their implications. The examples seem to demonstrate that "the propensity to kill is a matter independent of education and training," a function of mental organization alone. Spurzheim also reports on the related research of Philippe Pinel, the French psychiatrist who at about the same time was observing in madmen a similarly "fierce impulsion to destroy," and he gives many of Pinel's examples.[34]

To Spurzheim, the conclusion seemed inescapable: there must be an organ of the brain that determines the propensity to kill, and it must function independently of other propensities, which continue to work normally even in extreme cases like that of the Dutch fiddler. Gall had earlier identified an organ of Murder, having found a well-developed protuberance at the same spot in the skulls of two killers.[35] However, Spurzheim objects to naming an organ "according to its abuse" and therefore changes the name of Murder to Destructiveness, attributing to it the propensity not only to kill but also to take self-protective and constructive measures: "to pinch, scratch, bite, cut, break, pierce, devastate . . . . We are convinced, by a great number of observations, that the seat of this organ is on the side of the head immediately above the ears. . . . It is commonly larger in men than in women; yet there are exceptions from this rule."[36] In short, on the basis of numerous examples,

Spurzheim has identified the primary cause of homicide: overdevelopment of the organ of Destructiveness, which is the seat of both negative and useful forms of destruction.

The other faculties most relevant to criminology in Spurzheim's organology are Amativeness, Combativeness, Covetiveness, and Secretiveness. (Anticipating television's antipornography filters, he discreetly presents his discussion of Amativeness in Latin.) In these instances, too, Spurzheim insists that no organ is in and of itself evil; rather, the disproportionate enlargement of a faculty is the factor that leads to imbalance in a person's mental system and hence to criminal behavior. Covetiveness, for example, can be useful; we desire money and thus work for it. But when the organ of Covetiveness becomes overdeveloped, it leads to a propensity to steal:

> Another individual of good breeding was from infancy given up to this inclination; betook himself to the military service in hopes of being re-strained by the severity of its discipline; and, as he contrived to steal, was in danger of being hanged: struggling still against this propensity, he stud-ied theology and became a Capucin; his propensity followed him into the convent, and he took trifles, such as candlesticks, snuffers, scissars [sic], drinking-cups and glasses; but not concealing the stolen objects, he ac-knowledged that he had taken them home [so] that the proprietors might have the trouble of carrying them to their houses again.[37]

The organ of Covetiveness is located a bit above the ear, toward the forehead. It, too, is usually more developed in males than females.

A deterministic doctrine, phrenology attributed criminal behavior not to free will but to abnormal brain organization.[38] The fault might lie in poor heredity, poor environment, or a disease that had damaged the faculties—but not in individual choice. Yet phrenologists did not preach a gloomy, predestinarian message. Most people, they believed, are born with their faculties in harmonious balance; normality is the standard, and normal people, having been born responsible, do not commit crimes. "The functions of a well formed and healthy brain," wrote the English phrenologist Marmaduke Sampson, "must always be consistent with virtue. From this you will see at once that all acts of an opposite nature must be attributed to a corresponding unsoundness in [an] organ."[39] Moreover, because post-Gall phrenologists conceived of the brain as plastic, malleable, and capable of change, they were able to combine their determinism with an optimistic,

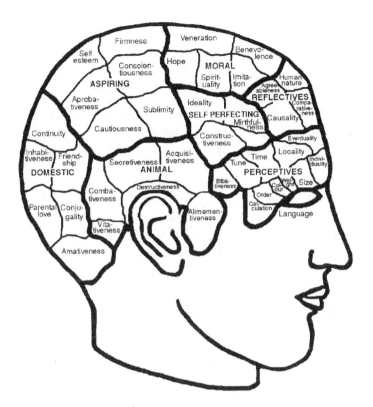

The science of phrenology. Charts like this one helped phrenologists identify the mental faculties beneath different areas of the skull. Courtesy of The Old Melbourne Jail and the Australian National Trust.

rehabilitative approach to crime and other social problems without a sense of contradiction. Conceiving of character traits as heritable but not fixed, they could simultaneously argue that criminals are not responsible for their crimes *and* that, with treatment, they can be cured of criminality. Sampson, who tended to take extreme positions, viewed *all* criminals as "patients" who should be sent to moral hospitals.[40]

In practice, most phrenologists dodged the full implications of their doctrine for free will by developing a typology of mankind according to degree of criminal responsibility. For example, the Edinburgh lawyer George Combe, the third most influential proponent of phrenology after Gall and Spurzheim, delivered a lecture titled "Human Responsibility" in

Boston in the late 1830s in which he explained, "Men may be divided into three great classes. The first comprehends those in whom the moral and intellectual organs are large, and the organs of the propensities [lower impulses] proportionately moderate in size." These men have free will and should be punished if they commit crimes. Members of the second class, whose organs are all large and about equal in size, have stronger criminal impulses but are still responsible. In members of the third class, the organs of the propensities are large and the moral and intellectual faculties small. These are the "habitual criminals," the "incorrigibles"; "they are moral patients and should not be punished, but restrained, and employed in useful labour during life, with as much liberty as they can enjoy without abusing it."[41] In effect, Combe recommended totally indefinite sentencing for criminals in the third group, predicating release on their reformation.[42] His typology reflected ideas about social worth as well as about degrees of criminal responsibility: those in the first class were, by implication, most fit to govern, and those in the third class most in need of governance.

Other phrenologists, too, created typologies based on the idea of biological variations in degree of criminal responsibility. Like Combe, James Simpson, an English lawyer, ranked humans into three classes according to their criminal propensities:

> *First*, those whose criminal appetites or propensities are so powerful as to overbalance the restraining force of their moral and intellectual faculties . . . . The *second class* of mankind are very numerous, those whose *animalism* is nearly as strong as in the first class, but whose moral and intellectual powers of restraint are . . . much greater . . . . External circumstances in such persons turn the scales . . . . The *third* class are the good ground. . . . It is *physically* possible for such men to rob, or steal, or torture, or murder, but it is *morally* impossible.[43]

Simpson's divisions, more clearly than Combe's, illustrate phrenological thinking about the relative impact of nature (biology) and environment ("external circumstances") in crime causation. Biology determines the behavior of both law-abiding men and lawbreakers. Environmental factors have their strongest impact on members of the "very numerous" second class—those most improvable by education in the free world and treatment in prisons. While phrenologists' classifications of criminals by degrees of responsibility and free will differed in their particulars, together they formed the nucleus of the idea that later flowered in Cesare Lombroso's hierarchical typology of criminal man.[44]

Although the major phrenological texts on issues of crime and justice were produced by professional men like Simpson and George Combe, anyone could add to the store of phrenological knowledge about crime. From Sydney to Stockholm, York to Heidelberg, and Rochester, New York, to Lexington, Kentucky, amateur phrenologists studied the heads of living and dead criminals, mailing their findings in to phrenological journals and reporting them at meetings of phrenological societies. The 1834–1836 volume of the *Phrenological Journal and Miscellany*, for example, included a reader's article on a tame ram with unusually well-developed Destructiveness who violently butted adults and terrorized children. The same issue carried speculations on the relation of Benevolence and Destructiveness in a certain pirate (he had become a buccaneer to revenge himself on Spaniards for some cruelty) and character analyses of the head casts of recently executed murderers. Relatedly, when in 1848 an explosion sent a metal rod flying through the head of a Vermont railroad worker named Phineas Gage, the local physician wrote up the case in such as way as to support phrenology, and on the basis of hearsay the *American Phrenological Journal* reported that

> after the man recovered, and while he was recovering, he was gross, pro-fane, coarse, and vulgar. . . . Before the injury he was quiet and respect-ful. . . . [T]he iron rod passed through the regions of BENEVOLENCE and VENERATION, which left these organs without influence in his character, hence his profanity, and want of respect and kindness; giving the animal propensities absolute control in his character.[45]

Thus phrenology enabled ordinary people to contribute to scientific knowledge, including knowledge about the causes of crime.

## Phrenology and the Criminal Law

Phrenology took root in a period of remarkable upheaval in criminal jurisprudence, one in which revulsion against harsh punishments, especially of minor first offenders, property offenders, and the mentally ill, surged through western Europe and North America. A transnational campaign against capital punishment took hold, and as the first penitentiaries were built, citizens noisily debated the purposes of these new penal institutions.

This rethinking of fundamentals of criminal jurisprudence occurred against a background of industrialization and urbanization that pushed legislators to find new methods of assuring the survival and cooperation of the working class, including public health improvements, universal education, and measures to reform criminals.[46]

Engaging widely and deeply in this movement for criminal law reform, phrenologists rejected the principles of retribution and deterrence on which this body of law had traditionally rested. "Convicts are almost never reformed under the present system," Simpson pointed out, voicing one common objection.[47] George Combe found another argument in the statistics on crime being published by the Belgian Adolphe Quetelet: the stability over time in Quetelet's rates of crime and conviction seemed to prove that "crimes arose from causes in themselves permanent, and which punishment does not remove."[48] Since punishment has no discernible impact on crime rates, Combe reasoned, then reformation should become the goal of criminal law. Marmaduke Sampson, in turn, insisted that punishment is "irrational" and deterrence impossible, since all criminals are sick and not responsible for their acts. Punishment actually increases crime by damaging offenders' constitutions and leading to transmission of their enfeeblement to the next generation.[49]

Thus phrenologists advocated a jurisprudential overhaul to reorient criminal law toward reformation and (in the case of those who proved incorrigible) social defense. "There were ages when criminal legislators thought it their only duty to punish or revenge," wrote Spurzheim, and in which "the animal powers dictated the penal laws. . . . Now-a-days, it is admitted that the penal code ought to have for its objects the prevention of [offenses] . . . , the correction of those who have failed in their duty, and securing the community against incorrigible members."[50] Phrenologists lobbied against debilitating punishments that might brutalize the faculties: the whip, the treadmill, and unrelieved solitary confinement. Some also lobbied for an end to transportation, a measure devoid of reformative value. Insisting that "in dealing with criminals we are dealing with *mind*," George Combe and other phrenologists recommended individuation of punishment to recognize differences in capacity and predisposition toward crime.[51] To C. J. A. Mittermaier, a law professor at the University of Heidelberg, one of the great advantages of phrenology was the way it encouraged lawmakers to find means to cultivate criminals' Benevolence and impede "the undue development of those organs which are liable, through abuse, to produce evil, such as Destructiveness." Another advantage, in Mittermaier's view, lay in phrenology's guidance to judges trying to determine criminal responsibility; the doctrine made it clear that "accountability . . . is influenced by the condition of the organs which we find in the offender."[52] *Do no harm* and *fit the punishment to the criminal*— these were the twin pillars on which phrenologists based their programs for reformation.

The long-term thrust of these views was toward redefinition of the concept of dangerousness. Whereas 18th-century jurisprudence defined dangerousness in terms of offense seriousness, late 19th-century jurisprudence defined it in terms of the individual criminal's biological predisposition and capacity for crime.[53] Toward the century's end, the process of redefinition built up pressure for fully indefinite sentencing and eugenic approaches to crime control. Phrenology helped set this process of redefining dangerousness in motion. Conceptually, it lay roughly at the midpoint between the two poles.

Phrenologically inclined psychiatrists joined the battle to exempt the mentally ill from criminal punishment. Mentally ill offenders who committed homicide were routinely hanged in the first half of the 19th century, there being no other recourse under laws that recognized only raving lunacy as an excuse for crime. Phrenology provided a way out of this dilemma with its view of the brain as a group of independent organs, any one of which could become diseased. Amariah Brigham, the physician who so ardently tried to save William Freeman from the gallows, used phrenological theory to show that Freeman was morally insane, although still capable of some intellection.[54] Isaac Ray, another American psychiatrist and one who had been profoundly influenced by phrenology in his youth, argued for recognition of partial moral mania, a condition in which "the derangement is confined to one or a few of the affective faculties, the rest of the moral and intellectual constitution preserving its ordinary integrity." "With no extraordinary temptations to sin," Ray continued, "but on the contrary, with every inducement to refrain from it, and apparently in the full possession of his reason," the morally insane offender "commits a crime whose motives are equally inexplicable to himself and to others."[55] Such offenders should be excused from the full brunt of criminal punishment. John Kitching, an English psychiatrist more tentatively committed to phrenology than Brigham or Ray, also argued that partial insanity should serve as an excuse for crime before law: "The rope-end or cat will not cure moral insanity."[56] Such arguments, although some of them were rejected in court, contributed to the campaign for greater leniency for mentally ill offenders and to establishment of hospitals for the criminally insane.

Curtailment of capital punishment in general was another legal reform that owed its success in part to phrenologists. Public sentiment against the death penalty was growing in any case, but phrenologists brought to the cause a united and vociferous insistence on abolition. Public executions brutalize onlookers, they argued, exciting destructive propensities and deadening moral sensibilities.[57] Moreover, they continued, it is folly to punish people who are not responsible (as, in the phrenological view, many criminals were not by definition). Life imprisonment of murderers would satisfy the same end of social defense.[58] Marmaduke Sampson, over-the-top as usual, not only argued that the death penalty stimulates crime; he offered to take members of a gallows mob and treat them for one month to "the wholesome influence of moral advice, coupled with *prison discipline* and *medical treatment*," after which "it is probable that most of them would abstain from attending the execution at all."[59] While Sampson was unusual among phrenologists in his optimism about the faculties' pliability, he was typical in his opposition to capital punishment.

Phrenologists' deterministic and materialistic analyses of criminal behavior, and their apparently sacrilegious recommendations for criminal law reform, scandalized traditionalists in the legal establishment. J. J. S. Wharton, an author of treatises on law, addressed a forty-four-page letter to Prime Minister Sir Robert Peel exhorting him to ignore Marmaduke Sampson's proposals to abolish the death penalty and establish moral hospitals. In metaphorical agitation, Wharton blasted Sampson's theory as "moral-crushing, religion-destroying . . . blighting the flourishing plant of moral accountability, withering the pure precepts of our christianity, and howling forth in its annihilating blasts the impunity of crime!"[60] Phrenologists' iconoclasm on jurisprudential matters gave many people pause. However, it proved attractive to those searching for a new philosophical basis for discipline and social control—so much so that, by the end of the century, the reforms phrenologists had advocated were by and large in place, though shorn of their organological language.

## Phrenology and Punishment

Phrenology, as historian Roger Cooter has observed, provided a "rational scientific umbrella" for "a vast range of ideas and beliefs which in themselves had little need of Gall's doctrine."[61] Nowhere was this truer than in the case of penology, an area in which phrenologists advocated a range of reforms that long outlived phrenology itself. To phrenologists, it seemed obvious that incarceration was the best possible punishment: prisons isolated criminals from the rest of the population, so they could not damage the moral faculties of innocents, while at the same time isolating criminals from enfeebling influences in the broader society. Phrenology's heyday coincided with the period in which American states began to build penitentiary-type prisons. Should these new institutions follow the Pennsylvania model of unbroken solitary confinement, or should they adopt the practice of the prison at Auburn, New York, of solitary cells at night and group labor during the day? In deciding this and other penological issues, Gall's followers were guided mainly by George Combe and the American jurist Edward Livingston, the phrenologists who wrote most extensively and authoritatively on prison policy. Both men began with the idea that prisons should be designed to rehabilitate, and both endorsed measures to encourage convict self-improvement.

These ideas animated penology on both sides of the Atlantic for the next 150 years. They had been formulated originally by Gall, for whom the goal of criminal law should be "*to prevent crime, to reform malefactors and to protect society against the incorrigible*,"[62] and they became key to the international prison reform movement that ushered in the rehabilitative goal and started formally in Cincinnati, Ohio, in 1870.[63] Phrenology was but one current flowing into this reform movement, but it was a strong one. The movement's leaders had grown up steeped in the phrenological notions that pervaded early 19th-century American culture.[64] When they formulated their Declaration of Principles in 1870, these leaders incorporated the penological ideas of phrenology but avoided the doctrine's terminology. Some speakers avoided it just barely, as shown by examples from the keynote address of Zebulon Brockway, "The Ideal of a True Prison System for a State":

- "The science of man forms the foundation of all systems for his government";
- "legalized degradation [whipping] . . . of any . . . criminal inflicts injury upon the whole social organism";
- "What is the molecular condition or quality of those who gravitate to vicious and criminal society and practices? How is the mind affected by a degraded physical organism? How [is] . . . the moral

sense obscured by such a mind? . . . What cures and tones up? How can a system be planned . . . to cure criminals, to stamp out crime, and to heal the social disease thus developed, without first obtaining a diagnosis of it?"[65]

Phrenological ideas lived on in works such as Brockway's speech, helping to create the "scientific umbrella" of which Cooter speaks.

A well-ordered prison, in the phrenologists' view, was fundamental to the restoration of balance among criminals' faculties. Convicts should have fresh air and decent food. Corporal punishment, which only stimulates the lower faculties, must be prohibited, as must extended periods in solitary confinement. The prisoner's daily routine, George Combe explained in a letter to his German friend Mittermaier, must train him in "habits of sobriety, order, and industry, and at the same time, he must be furnished with intellectual, moral, and religious instruction."[66] Combe was serious about educating prisoners, estimating that there should be a teacher for every eight to ten convicts.[67] Mittermaier himself hoped that prison administrators would "study the individuality of the criminals, and direct their treatment in reference to it," diagnosing and treating offenders much as physicians diagnosed and treated patients.[68] Such recommendations, seconded by other phrenologists, laid the groundwork for later schemes that aimed at classifying prisoners scientifically.

At the time, however, phrenology's theories of rehabilitation had but spotty impact on prison practice. Mid-19th-century penitentiary superintendents sometimes gestured toward individualization of treatment by bringing in a phrenologist to study convicts' heads, especially when an eminent outside phrenologist dropped by for a visit. At the Melbourne jail in Australia, an official made death masks of executed criminals, including the bushranger Ned Kelly, in the hope of contributing to penological science. A thoroughgoing attempt to achieve prisoner reformation occurred at the women's section of New York's Sing Sing prison, where in the mid-1840s Eliza Farnham, an important phrenologist in her own right,[69] introduced flowers, music, and lecturers.[70] This program, whatever its effects on the prisoners' moral and intellectual faculties, enraged John Luckey, the chaplain in the nearby men's division of Sing Sing, who had Farnham fired. And so died what was apparently the only systematic phrenological attempt to turn a prison into a moral hospital.

The phrenological recommendation that appealed most to prison administrators was the tiered system of rewards for good behavior. Edward

Phrenological illustration of a male criminal. In her notes on this illustration, the phrenologist and penologist Eliza W. Farnham wrote: "G.P., a negro imprisoned for petit larceny. He is exceedingly wanting in reflection and judgment; but is possessed of strong passions, quick perceptions, and much eccentricity of mind. . . . The drawing indicates great want of reflective power, good perception, and not a little conceit." The observations refer to G. P.'s "faculties." From Farnham's appendix to Marmaduke B. Sampson's *Rationale of Crime*, 1846.

Livingston proposed this system in his penal code, a plan for Louisiana that, though never implemented, excited enthusiasm among phrenologists in the United States and Europe.[71] Livingston outlined a graded system through which convicts would work their way up, enticed and reinforced by improved conditions along the way. They would start their sentences in the lower tier, characterized by solitary confinement, coarse food, and denial of opportunities to work. The inducements of promotion to the higher tier—books, better food, opportunities for labor—would encourage them to exercise their higher faculties.

Phrenologists with little direct involvement in prisons were impressed by the way Livingston's system might encourage convicts to *choose* the path of improvement.[72] Prison administrators, on the other hand, were probably more attracted by the system's potential for increasing control of convicts. At any rate, a graded system that could reward good behavior was soundly endorsed by the 1870 prison congress.[73] Even earlier, it was implemented in famous experiments in prisoner reform by Alexander Maconochie at the Norfolk Island, Australia, penal colony and by Sir Walter Crofton in Ireland.[74] Maconochie's work, in particular, may have been inspired by phrenological principles.[75]

During his 1838–1840 phrenological tour of the United States, George Combe visited prisons to collect evidence that might enable him to decide which system, the Pennsylvania or Auburn, was best.[76] Both approaches to convict discipline seemed to have virtues and drawbacks. Under the

Pennsylvania system of perpetual solitary confinement, convicts grew weak, and their brain organs became flaccid. (The exception: the cerebellum, or organ of Amativeness, which tended toward enlargement due to the Pennsylvania system's many opportunities for masturbation.) Under the Auburn system, on the other hand, prisoners were less susceptible to "deep moral and religious impressions."[77] Thus Combe suggested combining the two approaches. Convicts should begin their sentences in solitary, with no opportunity for labor or other distractions while their lower organs softened and became vulnerable to moral influences. The next step should be "a very effective course of moral, intellectual, and religious instruction." During it, the convict would "be advanced to greater and greater degrees of liberty, of self-regulation, and of social enjoyment, in proportion as he shewed himself to be capable of acting virtuously and wisely."[78] Next would come day release on "moral probation"—a presagement of the late 19th-century innovation of parole.

As they worked out the details of their penological program, phrenologists recognized a residual group of convicts who would need to be held for life, or close to it, on totally indefinite sentences. Some conceived of this group as convicts guilty of atrocious crimes.[79] Others thought the category would consist of habitual offenders—those convicts who, by definition, would have grossly overdeveloped lower faculties and very small intellectual and moral organs. Yet others designated it for the "incurables" and "incorrigibles" who could or would not respond to the prison's rewards system.[80] (George Combe expected these to include idiots and the insane.) It was an incoherent group, conceptually, but it came to play a large role in later discussions of dangerousness and of prisoner classification, especially after eugenicists appeared to have found a scientific way to identify incorrigibles.

"No sound system of criminal legislation and prison discipline," wrote George Combe, "can be reached while the influence of the organism on the dispositions and capacities of men continues to be ignored."[81] This idea lay at the heart of phrenology's program for penological reform. The specific influence of that program on subsequent theory and practice can be difficult to gauge, partly because some reformers were reluctant to identify themselves with phrenology,[82] and partly because others had absorbed phrenological principles but dropped the nomenclature. But it is undeniable that phrenologists' proposals to rationalize and medicalize prison management, put forth close to the inception of the prison system, and their vision of scientific rehabilitation continued to drive Western penology right through till the onset of the antirehabilitation movement in the 1970s.

By the 1830s, phrenology had begun to lose its plausibility among intellectuals and professionals. Some close students of the doctrine, like the English surgeon John Abernethy, had asked tough questions from the beginning. (How, Abernethy had snidely demanded, are the organs coordinated? "By committees of the several organs, and a board of control?" Abernethy also worried about negative labeling: "Suppose a man to have large knobs on his head which are said to indicate him to be a knave and a thief, can he expect assistance and confidence from any one?")[83] The social philosopher Auguste Comte, the psychiatrist Isaac Ray, and others who had begun as converts to phrenology gradually lost faith.[84] Still others, of course, had never seen anything in the doctrine in the first place, other than blasphemy and misplaced sympathy with criminals. While phrenology remained popular through midcentury and phrenologists continued to gather empirical proofs of their doctrine, to the scientifically inclined it became increasingly clear that almost any evidence could be regarded as confirmation of such a multifaceted theory.[85] Nor did phrenologists conduct experiments to see if their doctrine could be refuted, even though the ideas of experimental design and theory testing were taking hold in science more generally. The aspect of phrenology that may have harmed it most, scientifically, was its redundancy: even advocates eventually realized that one could reach the same conclusions about the nature of human behavior without recourse to organology.[86] In any case, by 1850, social problems were starting to appear less tractable than they had seemed in the sunny light of the century's early decades. Alarmed, social theorists and policy makers were no longer able to start from phrenology's premise that most people are biologically normal and naturally good. Many of those who had endorsed phrenology now abandoned it in favor of the newer doctrine of degeneration, with its more hereditarian cast and implications for more coercive measures of social control.[87]

## Phrenology as Biocriminology

In today's terms, phrenology was both a biological and a social science, combining the two in ways that made it a precursor of several recent sciences that also explain behavior in biosocial terms. One is sociobiology, the attempt of the 1970s and 1980s to establish biological bases for all social

Phrenological illustration of a female criminal. Again referring to the phrenological faculties, in her comments on this illustration Farnham writes, " L.W. is a female who has been long notorious in New-York for her depravity and abandonment of character. . . . In her head benevolence is well developed, but the whole moral region beside is exceedingly small. The drawing indicates extreme narrowness and smallness of the whole coronal region." From Farnham's appendix to Marmaduke B. Sampson's *Rationale of Crime,* 1846.

behavior.[88] A second is evolutionary psychology, the controversial effort to explain certain social behaviors primarily in terms of natural selection. (A branch of evolutionary psychology, evolutionary criminology, which today attempts to trace criminal behaviors to evolutionary processes, is discussed in chapter 9.) A third is modern genetics, which as we shall see (again in chapter 9), adopts a biosocial model in which gene expression depends on environment.[89] Moreover, some cognitive scientists, echoing phrenologists' faculty psychology, now speculate that the human brain is composed in part of mental modules or innate structures with specialized functions, although no one today argues for rigid localization or compartmentalization of mental faculties.[90]

Phrenology is now remembered primarily for the popular culture of its second stage: the manufacture of inkwells and caneheads shaped like phrenological skulls, with the brain's organs marked out for study; the calling in of phrenological experts to examine the heads of job applicants; the quackery of itinerant practitioners of "bumpology." It has been dismissed as a medical cult, a discredited science, dead science, pathological science, and pseudoscience. But if we examine phrenology in its own social context and see what its advocates were trying to do in the area of criminology, it becomes clear that phrenologists produced an early science of crime—in fact, the first comprehensive scientific explanation of criminality. Criminology was far from phrenology's central interest, any more than were criminal jurisprudence or penology; but in its effort to explain all human behavior, phrenology happened to develop a remarkably systematic and broad-ranging set of ideas about crime, criminals, and punishment.

Phrenologists carried efforts to scientize criminology and criminal justice much farther than moral insanity theorists. Whereas the notion of moral insanity applied to only a minute segment of the criminal population—those with severe mental disease (today's "psychopaths")— phrenology confidently offered scientific explanations for the behavior of the entire gamut of offenders, from calculating pickpockets through the murderous Dutch fiddler. The distinctions between moral insanity theorists and phrenologists were not clear-cut, of course, since a single commentator like Amariah Brigham might argue for moral insanity on phrenological grounds. However, insofar as the two theories were distinct, it is fair to say that phrenology developed a much more ambitious agenda for bringing science to bear on criminal behavior.

As a science, the phrenological theory of crime was characterized by reductionism, determinism, and a naturalization of social phenomena. It was reductionist in that it boiled down something complex (the causes of crime) into something simple (irregular protuberances and declivities of the brain). While it did not ignore environmental influences on criminal behavior, it traced even those back to the condition of the brain's various faculties. It was a determinist criminology insofar as it claimed that the brain's faculties dictate one's behavior. However, phrenologists took a "soft" determinist stand on the causes of crime, arguing that brain abnormalities *can* lead to criminality but not that they are bound to do so. Indeed, phrenologists attributed a degree of free will to all but the most hardened criminals, and even in those cases, they believed that a well-designed penal regimen might bring about improvement. As for the third characteristic, phrenologists naturalized criminality in that they made it seem part of the world of nature, a biological given. Whatever the offense, it was caused by the brain's configuration. They also naturalized social hierarchies and a whole value system, showing that nature itself gave pride of place to the faculties of veneration, benevolence, conscientiousness, and so on—those that should guide moral behavior.

As we shall see, subsequent biological theories, too, were often characterized by reductionism, determinism, and a naturalizing tendency, although in different ways and with different degrees of emphasis. Also typical of later biological theories were the simplicity and straightforwardness of phrenology's explanation of crime. Until relatively recently, biological theories generally put forth uncomplicated, easily graspable explanations, and they have proposed simple solutions. They tended to tell tidy and satisfying stories about the nature of crime and criminals.

One of phrenology's most instructive lessons is political. Today, biocriminology is often associated with conservative and at times retrograde positions on political and social issues—the reason that liberals tend to reject it out of hand. But phrenology was promoted by liberals, reformers at the forefront of progressive change in criminology and criminal justice. In the early and mid-19<sup>th</sup>-century, the *opponents* of phrenology were the conservatives, people who clung to the soon-to-be-outmoded notions of crime as sin and insanity as total derangement. The history of phrenology encourages us to break the traditional association of biocriminology with standpattist or even reactionary political views. Although biocriminology has often been conservative, politically and socially, phrenology shows that it is not necessarily so.[91]

# 4

# Criminal Anthropology

## *The Atavistic Brain*

Cesare Lombroso, the Italian physician, psychiatrist, and self-styled anthropologist, was undoubtedly the most significant, if also the most puzzling and contradictory, figure in the entire history of criminology. As the founder of the field of criminal anthropology, Lombroso was the first to fully realize the implications of the idea that crimes and criminals might be subjected to scientific study. He claimed that there is a criminal type: the born criminal, whose propensity to offend is innate, constitutional and incurable. Born criminals, he asserted, are atavisms or throwbacks to a more primitive form of life, dangerous and incorrigible by virtue of their very being—what we today would call their genes. Lombroso's work constituted the first true criminology, a theory comprehensive in scope (unlike moral insanity) and independent of another doctrine (unlike the phrenological explanation of crime).

Lombroso was born in 1836 in Verona, in northern Italy, to a Jewish family whose religious beliefs he put aside in favor of what he called "the sole authority of our times: Science."[1] He studied medicine in Italy and Austria, and very early in his career began working in lunatic asylums, where he made a close study of insanity. A stint as a military physician in southern Italy, where the army was trying to impose northern notions of law and order on fiercely independent peasant populations, confirmed for him the northern Italian stereotype of southerners as savage and criminalistic.[2] After his army service, Lombroso conducted studies of pellagra, a disease ravaging Italy's peasantry, causing mental as well as physical deterioration, and pursued his interest in insanity and psychiatry. The period in which he matured intellectually coincided with the unification of Italy (1860–1870) and its foundation as a modern state. Lombroso hoped to help the new nation, much of it mired in archaic governmental traditions, establish itself on a scientific basis by adopting

Cesare Lombroso. Lombroso, an Italian physician, psychiatrist, and student of anthropology, authored *Criminal Man*, the first work to specifically offer a scientific explanation of crime.

positivist approaches toward crime and punishment.[3] While Lombroso has been depicted as an arch-conservative, in fact he was a liberal (he even converted to socialism in later life). In the words of Alexandre Lacassagne, a founder of French criminal anthropology, "Lombroso was a man of the avant-garde, perhaps a utopian."[4]

In 1876, the pivotal year of his life, Lombroso was named professor of legal medicine at the University of Turin. This was also the year in which he published the first edition of *Criminal Man*, the book that eventually made him world famous. The core idea of *Criminal Man*, that of the atavistic born criminal, had first come to him (he explained melodramatically) a decade earlier, when, on a "cold grey November morning, I was deputed to make the *post-mortem*" of Villella, a brigand from Calabria, in southern Italy. His realization that Villella's skull resembled the crania of "inferior animals, especially rodents,"

> was not merely an idea, but a revelation. At the sight of that skull, I seemed to see all of a sudden, lighted up as a vast plain under a flaming sky, the problem of the nature of the criminal—an atavistic being who reproduces in his person the ferocious instincts of primitive humanity and the inferior animals. Thus were explained anatomically the enormous jaws, high cheek-bones, prominent superciliary arches . . . found in criminals, savages, and apes, . . . [their] love of orgies, and the irresistible craving for evil for its own sake, the desire not only to extinguish life in the victim, but to mutilate the corpse, tear its flesh, and drink its blood.[5]

This was a lot to infer from the skull of one old man, but Lombroso's histrionic vision gave criminal anthropology its foundational myth—a myth of the origins of not only crime but also criminology.[6]

Lombroso was not as unique as he liked to think when he conceived of criminals as less evolved than law-abiding people, for British commentators had been making a similar point for at least a decade. In *The Criminal Prisons of London*, the investigative reporters Henry Mayhew and John Binny had observed that habitual criminals "are a distinct body of people . . . , the human parasites of every . . . community."[7] The Scottish prison physician J. Bruce Thomson had described a criminal type related to degenerates, Australian bushmen, moral idiots, and Gypsies.[8] And Henry Maudsley, a fashionable London psychiatrist, had written that there is "a distinct class of beings, who herd together in our large cities . . . propagating a criminal population of degenerate beings."[9] In fact, Lombroso may have gotten some of his inspiration from these British forerunners, for he cites Thomson's work in the first edition of *Criminal Man*, Maudsley's in the second. But in truth, evolutionist ideas were being discussed throughout Europe and the United States, and both the British forerunners and Lombroso drew on a common pool of intellectual influences, including anthropology, degeneration theory, phrenology, physiognomy, and scientific racism. It is not surprising that several people almost simultaneously came up with the idea of the criminal as a poor evolver, animalistic and savage. But Lombroso pursued this idea more consistently and drew out its implications more elaborately than any of the others.

For the rest of his life, Lombroso devoted himself to elaborating, confirming, and publicizing the lessons of Villella's skull. *Criminal Man* went through five editions, the last published in 1896–1897;[10] Lombroso also wrote a companion volume, *Criminal Woman*, and other spin-offs. His research attracted students to the University of Turin, where they formed the nucleus of his Positivist school of criminology. In 1880, Lombroso founded a journal, *Archivio di psichiatria, antropologia criminale e scienze penali (The Archive of Psychiatry, Criminal Anthropology, and Penal Sciences)*, to serve as an outlet for his own work and that of his followers.

Any discussion of criminal anthropology must begin with Lombroso's work because for a while, the two were synonymous. What did Lombroso say about the causes of crime, and where specifically did his ideas come from? How did he propose to deal with criminals? How was his work received and developed by others? In what follows, I begin with a review of Lombroso's doctrine, arguing that it was heavily informed by his earlier racist (but at the time quite standard) anthropological research. Then I discuss his work as a science and explore what he said about its implications for criminal justice. I conclude by arguing that Lombroso was the only criminologist who actually shifted the paradigm or framework for thinking about crime and criminals. Before Lombroso, despite the inroads made by moral insanity theorists and phrenologists, for most educated people the standard framework was still that of religion—crime as sin. Lombroso persuaded people throughout the Western world that crime was a natural phenomenon that could be studied by science.

## The Criminal: Body, Skull, and Brain

On his desktop Lombroso kept two objects: an immense phrenological bust and Villella's skull. The bust reminded him of criminal anthropology's predecessor in the science of deciphering the human brain while the skull incorporated almost all the wisdom of criminal anthropology, if one knew how to decipher its messages. The criminal, Lombroso taught, could be recognized by the anomalies that blemished his body and mind. In Villella's case the crucial anomaly was his median occipital fossetta, the unusual indentation at the base of his skull that Lombroso deemed atavistic. Using craniometry—anthropological techniques for measuring the bones and capacity of crania—Lombroso discovered that the skulls of most criminals were unusually small or malformed; some had a median occipital fossetta, like Villella's, and others had "monkeylike anomalies." "I cannot avoid pointing out," he wrote, how closely the cranial abnormalities of criminals "correspond to characteristics observed in normal skulls of the colored and inferior races."[11] Further reminding Lombroso of savages were other aspects of criminals' skulls—their prognathism (the forward thrust of the lower face), their large jaws, and their receding foreheads. In short, criminals looked like Africans, Australian aborigines, or apes.

In good positivist fashion, Lombroso set about collecting data to prove his fundamental intuition of the criminal's atavistic nature. Earlier in the century, anthropologists and phrenologists had learned how to gauge the size of the brains of dead people by filling their skulls with pellets and then weighing the results. Following suit, Lombroso used his steadily growing collection of criminals' skulls to make inferences about the size and nature of the criminal brain, which he concluded resembled that of "the rodent or lemur, or the brain of a human fetus of three or four months."[12] Additional evidence for his atavism theory came from anthropometry, the measurement of body parts and functions. The criminal proved to be less sensitive to pain than the normal or law-abiding man. In physiognomy or facial expression, criminals were not necessarily hideous, and some were even handsome, but "there is nearly always something strange about their appearance."

> It can even be said that each type of crime is committed by men with particular physiognomic characteristics, such as lack of a beard or an abundance of hair. . . . Thieves are notable for their expressive faces and manual dexterity, small wandering eyes that are often oblique in form, thick and close eyebrows, distorted or squashed noses, thin beards and hair, and sloping foreheads. Like rapists, they often have jug ears. Rapists, however, nearly always have sparkling eyes, delicate features, and swollen lips and eyelids. Most of them are frail; some are hunchbacked.[13]

Thus in body as in skull and brain, the criminal was an abnormal, backward being. More confirmation came from Lombroso's discovery that, like savages, criminals tattooed themselves.

Further investigation revealed the born criminal to be scarred mentally as well as physically. Not only were most criminals backward intellectually compared with honest men; "even in criminals of genius, there is an aspect in which the intellect is defective: they do not have the mental energy for continuous and diligent labor."[14] Criminal man, moreover, suffers from moral blindness: he is vain, vindictive, bloodthirsty, remorseless,

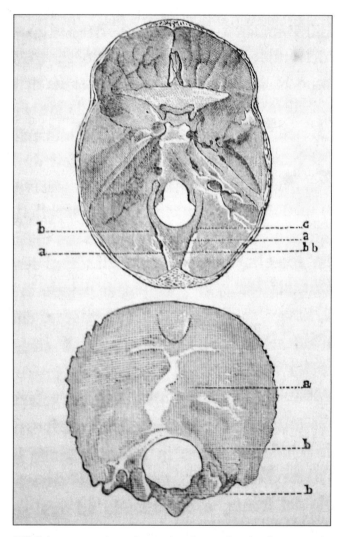

Villella's cranium. According to Lombroso, the idea for criminal anthropology came to him as "a revelation" as he studied abnormalities in the skull of the brigand Villella. This drawing comes from a book on race, evolution, and anthropological anomalies that Lombroso published years before *Criminal Man*. Lombroso, a northern Italian, deemed Villella racially inferior (and hence criminalistic) partly because he came from southern Italy. From *L'uomo bianco e l'uomo di colore*, 1871.

and undeterrable. Although he experiences violent passions ("In their emotional intensity, criminals closely resemble . . . savages"),[15] he is unable to maintain loving relationships. He is illogical, deeply religious in a showy sort of way, imprudent, and incapable of foresight.

Eventually Lombroso developed a typology of criminals, conceding that in addition to the born criminal there are "less obvious but much more frequent forms of the criminal" who are "closer to normal man."[16] Less marred by anomalies, these other types included the criminal of passion (motivated by love, political fervor, or honor), the occasional criminal, the insane criminal, and the mattoid (mentally unstable and full of grandiose political or religious ideas). However, the born criminal remained central to Lombroso's thinking, and he was able to "confidently estimate the actual proportion of born criminals to be close to 40 percent of all offenders."[17]

Lombroso was a century ahead of his time in paying attention to criminal woman as well as criminal man. As early as the first edition of his magnum opus, he tried to determine the characteristics that made female offenders different from their male counterparts, concluding that "the few violent women far exceed men in their ferocity and cruelty." During the French Revolution, Parisian women "forced a man to eat his own roasted penis; and . . . threaded human bodies on a pike. Thus Shakespeare depicts Lady Macbeth as more cruel and cold than her male accomplice."[18] Working with Guglielmo Ferrero, the young lawyer who later married his daughter Gina, Lombroso in 1893 issued a separate volume titled *La donna delinquente* (*Criminal Woman*), the first book ever written on this subject and one that influenced thinking about female criminality well into the 20th century.[19] Here he compares the criminal woman not only to criminal man but also to the "normal" woman and the prostitute.

Lombroso begins *Criminal Woman* by showing that normal women are biologically, intellectually, and emotionally inferior to normal men. "Woman . . . feels less, just as she thinks less."[20] But some women are better than others; there are two basic types, one good (law-abiding, feminine), the other bad (criminalistic, masculine, primitive). That there are fewer female than male born criminals is simply another sign of women's atavism—here too they fall behind men. (The illogic of this argument, given his earlier argument that it is atavism that turns men into criminals, made Lombroso acutely uncomfortable; but he was so committed to his belief in female inferiority that he could not work his way out of the logical cul-de-sac.) Even worse than the female criminal—more morally degenerate—is the prostitute: "The women's crime that corresponds most closely to men's crime . . . is that of prostitution."[21] Thus among women, the prostitute is the true born criminal.

The roots of Lombroso's criminology lay in *L'uomo bianco e l'uomo di colore* (*The White Man and the Man of Color*), an untranslated work that is little known but indispensable to grasping his intellectual development.[22] From this study he derived his identity as an anthropologist and some of the fundamental ideas for criminal anthropology.[23] Based almost entirely on works written by others, *L'uomo bianco e l'uomo di colore* was published in 1871, just before Lombroso turned his attention to crime, and it positions itself dead center in the intellectual tradition that became known as scientific racism. Scientific racism, constructed out of anthropology, natural history, phrenology, and physiognomy, used techniques such as craniometry and anthropometry to create typologies and hierarchies of human races. Scientific racism was widely accepted in the 19th century by educated white Europeans and Americans, who used it to justify their ventures in colonialism and imperialism. Even though Lombroso never left Europe, in a sense he became a colonialist within his own country, extending state control over a population deemed inferior, subjugating criminals to anthropological and legal scrutiny.[24]

Like other scientific racists, Lombroso owed his first debt to Carolus Linnaeus, the botanist and zoologist who first categorized human races, and his second to Charles Darwin, whose *Origin of Species* (1859) suggested to Lombroso that "the zoologically superior species are formed through the perfection of the inferior."[25] His third debt was to Ernst Haeckel, the German naturalist whose immensely influential theory of recapitulation argued that the human fetus, as it develops, passes through earlier evolutionary stages, from fish through reptile and on to mammal.[26] Armed with these ideas, in *L'uomo bianco e l'uomo di colore* Lombroso asked "whether we white men . . . owe our primacy to our bodies or to accident."[27]

The conclusion was foregone: while pretending to make inductions based on facts, *L'uomo bianco e l'uomo di colore* dedicates itself to proving white superiority and attributing it to superior physical organization. Assuming (as he was soon to do again in *Criminal Man*) that "we are the children of our organs," Lombroso showed that people of color are inferior to whites anatomically, morally, and intellectually—a line of argument soon to be replicated in his next work, but with people of color replaced by criminals. (In *Criminal Man* he even assumes that criminals tend to have dark skins.) The original race was black, Lombroso contended, but it evolved into the yellow and then the white race, most "perfect" of all. One proof, Lombroso

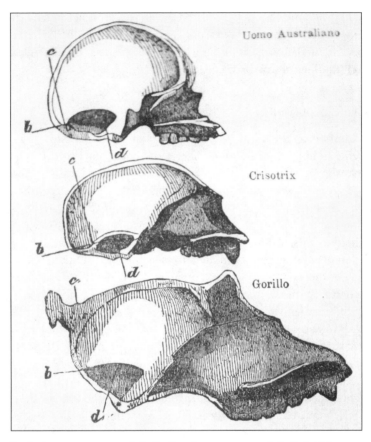

Evolutionary sequence of skulls. Lombroso compared skulls in this early book, *L'uomo bianco e l'uomo di colore* (*The White Man and the Man of Color*), much as he later compared the skulls of criminals and noncriminals. Here he studies differences in the skulls of an Australian man, a squirrel monkey, and a gorilla.

continued in a passage showing that he already had the thesis of *Criminal Man* in mind, is that in their moral and physical insensibility, the yellow races and redskins of America are similar to European criminals. Another proof lay in the skull of Villella (a dark-skinned southern Italian), the contours of which reminded Lombroso of the crania of lower creatures.[28] In this book on the anthropology of race, Lombroso also speaks of atavism and heredity—central concepts in his later work—and even uses some of the same kinds of evidence (folktales, drawings of Bushman women with large bottoms) that he used in his later work on criminals. The writing of *L'uomo bianco e l'uomo di colore* prepared him, in terms of subject matter, theory, method, and even his approach to displaying visual evidence, for the criminological work to come.

## *The Causes of Crime*

For Lombroso, the ultimate cause of crime was atavism: "The most horrendous and inhuman crimes have a biological, atavistic origin in those animalistic instincts that, although smoothed over by education, the family, and fear of punishment, resurface instantly under given circumstances."[29] He used the third edition of *Criminal Man* to prove this proposition by tracing the origins of crime to primitive organisms (insect-eating plants, murderous ants, cannibalistic tadpoles) that obviously lacked free will but nonetheless seemed criminalistic in nature. In addition, drawing on Haeckel's theory that individual organisms recapitulate the evolution of their entire species, Lombroso argued at length for the inherent criminality of children, a tendency to cruelty that seemed to confirm that people are born with the savage instincts of their ancestors. (To demonstrate this, he went into nursery schools to study rates of masturbation, truancy, and fidgetiness.) But "these abnormalities tend to disappear with proper education," at least when the children are not born delinquents.[30]

While atavism remained the fundamental cause of crime for Lombroso, he also recognized a multiplicity of secondary or immediate factors: weather (crime rates rise with the temperature); "race" (a tribe of professional thieves in India specializes in stealing, the men of a certain Italian town in swindling); civilization (the more civilized a nation, the more pickpockets, blackmailers, and alcoholics it will have); heredity (crime runs in families); and sexuality (malformed genitals lead to sex crime). But even though Lombroso distinguished between ultimate and secondary or immediate causes, in truth his thinking about the causes of crime was massively incoherent. He did little to explain how the ultimate and immediate causes interrelated, and as time went on, he proposed other ultimate causes— mental disease and moral insanity, epilepsy, and degeneration—without clearly articulating their relationship to atavism.

As a psychiatrist who attended patients in institutions for the criminally insane as well as regular prisons, Lombroso almost automatically associated mental illness with crime. "Few would doubt that crime is often caused by cerebral afflictions," he wrote in the first edition of *Criminal Man*, "and,

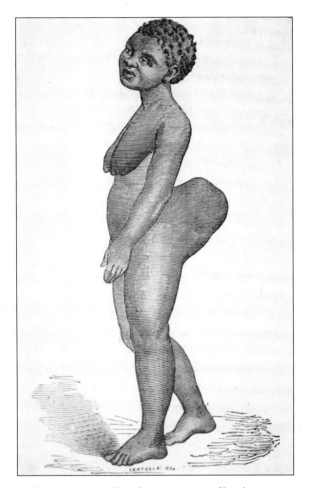

Bushman woman. Like other Europeans of his day, Lombroso was transfixed by the idea that "savage" women had
anomalies of the buttocks and sexual organs. This idea fed
into his criminological theory of the criminal as a savage
being, a throwback with telltale physical abnormalities.
From *L'uomo bianco e l'uomo di colore*, 1871.

above all, madness."[31] Indeed, his entire background prepared him to reach
this conclusion. By the third edition, he was arguing that criminality was
nearly identical to moral insanity, even while continuing to insist that
atavism was the "predominant factor" in the etiology of crime.[32] In the
fourth edition, he added epilepsy to atavism and moral insanity as ultimate

causes of crime. "The identification of epilepsy with born criminality and moral insanity will seem absurd to those who define epilepsy in terms of convulsions," he admitted. But he could also diagnose "hidden epilepsy": "What I call the epileptic type includes not only obvious epiphenomena but also secondary characteristics, bringing together all the traits of the morally insane and the born criminal in a pronounced way."[33] Because those "secondary characteristics" of epilepsy (unpredictability, ferocity, insensitivity, and calmness after committing a crime) were in fact the same traits with which he had previously defined moral insanity and inborn criminality, the whole exercise of isolating the causes of crime became circular. Lombroso's tendency to augment and garble the causes of crime became even more pronounced in the fifth edition, where he occasionally suggested that degeneration, an innate tendency to decay, was an ultimate factor in the etiology of crime.[34]

But no matter how obscure and confused his dicta on causes, Lombroso's basic position was clear. "Crime is a natural phenomenon," and because it is fundamentally biological in its origins, legal debates over criminal responsibility are pointless. "Most criminals really do lack free will."[35] To understand and prevent crime, we need to understand the criminal, and the place to begin is with the born criminal, whose biological deviations and mental abnormalities prove that he (or she) is a throwback to a primitive form of life.

## Criminal Anthropology as a Science

Lombroso and his followers defined themselves over and against the so-called Classical school of criminology, which was not really a "school" at all in sense of a distinct group of theorists or practitioners but rather an international orientation toward crime and punishment. Predating Lombroso's work by about a century, the classical approach grew out of Enlightenment thought and was associated in particular with Jeremy Bentham, the English philosopher of utilitarianism, and Cesare Beccaria, the Italian whose little book *On Crimes and Punishments* laid out the principles of the classical perspective.[36] That approach, concerned with crime, not criminals, began with the assumption that humans are rational creatures with free will and that, therefore, the purpose of punishment should be deterrence. The classicists also assumed that the chief cause of crime is self-interest, but otherwise they took little notice of the causes of crime. In brief, they did not produce what we today think of as criminology.[37]

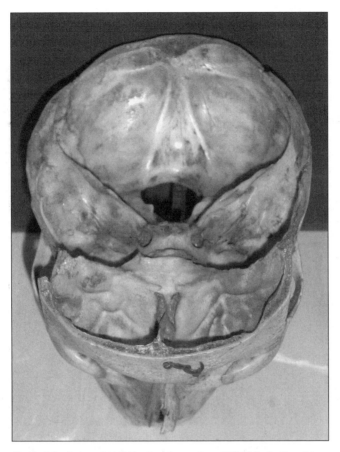

Skull of the brigand Villella. Lombroso kept Villella's skull on his desktop, a memento of the origins of criminal anthropology and a symbol of his science of criminals' abnormalities. Courtesy of the Museo Lombroso (Turin). Photograph by Mary Gibson.

By defining themselves as members of an opposing Positivist school, Lombroso and his followers meant that they used scientific methods to discover the causes of crime. Positivism, the scientific approach to the study of social phenomena that began early in the 19th century, was still in the process of maturation when Lombroso entered the scene; and although moral insanity theorists and phrenologists had tried to apply its principles to crime, they had not gotten very far. Lombroso embraced positivism vigorously and did a great deal to develop it as the basis of what later generations would call criminology. He and other members of his Positivist school (also called the Italian school or school of criminal anthropology) called for scientists to collect facts and then build on them through induction. The Positivist school *did* become a "school" in its own right: Lombroso's followers elaborated and applied his theory in Italy, and criminal anthropology spread quickly abroad, where others embraced the idea of a science of crime even while critiquing the "science" in Lombroso's work.

Lombroso folded a range of methods into the science of criminology. "As a psychiatrist rather than a natural scientist," he wrote retrospectively; "I simply replaced the abstract approach of the past," meaning the legalistic perspective of the Classical school, "with clinical and anthropological methods in the individual study of the madman and the criminal." The "clinical methods" that he spoke of here included those of medicine, psychiatry, and psychology. ("My book," he observed of *Criminal Man*, "is nothing if not a tract on the criminal mind.") The clinical methods also included forensics. (Lombroso claimed to be the first person in Italy to conduct a forensic examination in a criminal case.) The "anthropological methods" of which he spoke included anthropometry, craniology, and ethnology. Lombroso also drew on an American study on the heredity of crime that utilized a genealogical methodology—Richard Dugdale's *"The Jukes"*[38]—and he pioneered in the use of methods that today would be called sociological. He tried to use control groups, for example, by comparing prisoners with the insane and with "normal" or law-abiding people, and he amassed reams of statistics on all aspects of crime and criminality.

His enthusiasm for positivism notwithstanding, Lombroso failed as a scientist in almost every respect. His work was often sloppy and self-contradictory. For instance, on a single page of *Criminal Man* he writes first that "nearly all criminals have jug ears" and then, a little later, that "jug ears are found on 28 percent of criminals."[39] Historian Robert Nye describes the methodological beating that Lombrosian science took from French critics at the Second International Congress of Criminal Anthropology, where the French anthropologist Léonce Manouvrier

> compared Lombroso's theories to the disgraced system of Franz Joseph Gall, accused Lombroso's criminal type of being a sort of "ideal harlequin," and subjected the Italian efforts at statistical analysis to a rigorous examination. Tellingly, he pointed out Lombroso's failure to collect measurements within discrete series according to race, sex, and class, and dismissed the

value of statistics on criminal anomalies which were never compared with equally broad samples of "honest" men. Manouvrier . . . concluded ironically by accusing Lombroso of having done anthropology the disservice of "criminalizing" anatomical characteristics. "One will only be able to console himself at being a born criminal by remembering that he is an honest man even so."[40]

Another French anthropologist, Paul Topinard, refused to recognize criminal anthropology as part of his field, while the French sociologist Gabriel Tarde pointed out that criminal anthropology could not explain the differences between male and female crime rates, since criminals of both sexes were said to share the same cranial anomalies. Worst of all was a crack by Lombroso's former disciple, Moritz Benedikt, who "added to Topinard's remarks . . . by saying, amidst general hilarity, 'It is easy to make hypotheses: why not say the *fossette* [median occipital fossetta] indicates a predisposition to hemorrhoids for example?'"[41] Italians, too, were aghast at Lombroso's "science."[42]

Lombroso's science had fallen victim to his personality. Perhaps the best way to understand Lombroso's research methods is through a description by his daughter Paola of his typical day:

> . . . composing on the typewriter, correcting proofs, running from Bocca [his publisher] to the typesetter, from the typesetter to the library and from the library to the laboratory in a frenzy of movement . . . ; and in the evening, not tired and wanting to go to the theater, to a peregrination of two or three of the city's theaters, taking in the first act at one, paying a flying visit to another, and finishing the evening in a third.[43]

In his research as in his typical day, Lombroso rushed madly about, seldom checking his data, haphazardly adding up columns of figures, frenetically churning out articles and books but not always (perhaps even seldom) taking time to review materials for consistency and logic. Another biographical detail helps explain his willingness to include folklore, pictures of freaks, popular maxims, Shakespeare's characters, and improbable anecdotes as evidence for his theories. Historian Delfina Dolza writes of Lombroso's "almost total inexperience with the practical aspects of existence, his childlike innocence," and a gullibility so extreme that his children felt a need to protect him.[44] This naïveté, while it does not excuse his failings as a scientist, at least makes it a bit easier to understand

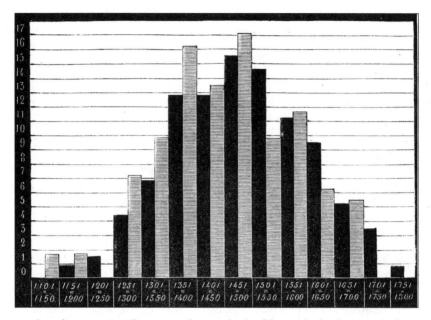

Lombroso's science. Lombroso seized on methods of the newly developing social sciences to illustrate his findings. This graph illustrates the cranial capacity of 121 male criminals (hatched bar) compared with "normal" men (black bars); the figures along the bottom indicate the cranial capacities (probably in cubic centimeters). As this graph shows, Lombroso attempted to use control groups but not random selection. From the third edition of *L'uomo delinquente* (*Criminal Man*), 1884.

Lombroso's readiness to incorporate evidence that others, including his contemporaries, sometimes found ludicrous.

But his embrace of odd bits of evidence, especially visual evidence such as mug shots, crime maps, tattoos, wax death masks, and pickled criminal brains, probably helped persuade nonscientists of the validity of criminal anthropology. Visual displays filled an increasing number of pages in his books as time went on until in the final, four-volume edition of *Criminal Man*, an entire separate volume, *The Atlas*, was devoted solely to images. The displays also appeared in the Lombroso museum in Turin, the first of what became a series of criminological museums in major European cities. (On Lombroso's death, the Turin museum received two new artifacts: his desk, ornamented as in life with his phrenological bust and Villella's skull, and a jar in which his brain was preserved, for further study.) Although today we can only guess at the meanings that Lombroso thought would emanate from the objects he displayed, the artifacts continue to testify to his artless trust that they would prove the validity of criminal anthropology.[45]

Neither Lombroso's texts nor his displays can be dismissed simply as bad science or pseudoscience. Notwithstanding their naïveté and scientific clumsiness, they demonstrate his devotion to empiricism. In the best scientific tradition, he determinedly presented his data so others could examine them. He refused to curb what he recognized as his

> overexuberant use of facts and figures, which may cause the less attentive to lose the thread of my argument. Cutting back on the data would have meant falling short of the positivist method, an approach which, in such a contentious field, has the advantage of showing the evidence for my conclusions. My data also provide others with material for correcting and improving my theories.[46]

In contrast to the classicists, the positivists attempted to study crime according to scientific principles. And for a while, Lombroso's followers held the day. During the last quarter of the 19th century, they were generally recognized as *the* experts on criminal behavior. Despite international disputes over methodologies and findings, criminal anthropology was the leading and very nearly exclusive form of criminology worldwide.

## Criminal Anthropology and Criminal Justice

Lombroso tried to apply scientific principles to criminal justice as well as criminology, beginning with policing. "Hitherto policing was conducted much as wars used to be waged: randomly and on the basis of hunches," he wrote. "Successful investigations depended on the astuteness and dedication of a few individuals. What we need now is to apply the scientific method to the identification of criminals." Arguing that scientific policing must "develop innovative defenses against the new weapons offered to criminals by urbanization and the development of modern life,"[47] Lombroso advocated surveillance, silent alarms, private security companies, and undercover policing. In addition, he was a great fan of the Bertillon method of identifying criminals, a prefingerprinting procedure that involved taking prisoner photographs and then filing them according to a system that enabled police to identify recidivists even if they assumed aliases.[48]

Lombroso dreamed of revamping the criminal justice system so that it would incorporate his criminology and react to offenders according to their

Criminal women. Unlike other early criminologists, Lombroso understood the importance of gender to the study of criminal behavior, and he included observations on women from the first edition of *Criminal Man* onward. Eventually he developed this data into a separate volume on *Criminal Woman* (1893). This table of criminal faces comes from the third edition of *L'uomo delinquente* (*Criminal Man*), 1884.

degree of innate dangerousness. To determine defendants' or prisoners' degree of riskiness, psychiatrists and forensics experts should be called in to examine them, much as physicians diagnose the sick. Lombroso spent a great deal of time arguing for probation, juvenile reformatories, and other intermediate punishments that would keep offenders who were not particularly dangerous out of ordinary prisons. But for the atavistic born criminal, whose backward brain could never be reformed, the only solution was lifelong incarceration in special institutions for the incorrigible. In one of his rare eugenical passages, Lombroso argued that prisons for incorrigibles "would gradually reduce that not inconsiderable proportion of criminality that stems from heredity factors . . . . There would be a return to the process of natural selection that has produced not only our race but the very justice that gradually came to prevail with the elimination of the most violent."[49] Late in life, Lombroso began to advocate "that extreme form of natural selection, death" for criminals who "repeat bloodthirsty crimes for the third or fourth time."[50]

The seeds of these ideas about scientific punishment had been planted by phrenologists, with their tripartite typologies of offenders and calls for sentences to fit the types, including indefinite sentences for incorrigibles. Moreover, the seeds were already being forced into bloom by experiments with indeterminate sentencing in Australia, Ireland, and the United States. Lombroso's genius in the realm of punishment was to gather together a number of innovative ideas, christen them the "social defense" position, and develop for this stance a political rationale. Society has the right to defend itself against criminals, he taught, even if the latter are not morally responsible. "Crime is necessary," he declared, meaning that it is a natural phenomenon, like germs, "but so is defense against it. . . . When we justify punishment in terms of social defense, it becomes more logical and effective."[51]

Social defense constituted an important philosophy of punishment, proposed by Lombroso as a replacement for the Classicists' philosophy of deterrence. It protected him against charges of wanting to coddle criminals when he proposed measures for rehabilitating the reformable, and it gave him the justification he needed for dealing harshly with recidivists. A philosophy similar to the theory of incapacitation, but broader, the social defense justification for punishment was Lombroso's primary, if seldom recognized, contribution to criminal justice theory.

To his discussions of criminal justice reforms, Lombroso brought decades of experience as a doctor in institutions for normal and lunatic criminals. He had testified as an expert witness at trials, conducted forensic examinations, and exchanged ideas with Italy's leading prison superintendents and specialists in criminal jurisprudence. Thus it is unfair to charge him with naïveté about run-of-the-mill offenders, as historian David Garland does in the course of contrasting what he sees as the abstractions of Italian criminal anthropology with the more practical, sensible criminology generated by British psychiatrists of the same era.[52] Whatever the differences between late 19th-century Italian and British criminology, they cannot be traced to an unfamiliarity on Lombroso's part with criminal justice, for few if any criminologists have produced theory while at the same time working so closely with offenders and criminal justice officials.[53]

## Lombroso as a Paradigm Shifter

Lombroso's overwhelming significance to the development of criminology derives from four intellectual feats: (1) his synthesis of the study of crime with other sciences and fields of inquiry; (2) his use of the medical model to frame nearly all aspects of his new perspective on criminal behavior; (3) his production of blueprints that gave liberal states new ways of dealing with deviants; and, above all, (4) his transformation of criminology from an offshoot of phrenology into a full-fledged science.[54]

Lombroso synthesized the study of crime with a wide range of other fields and endeavors, some old (biology, law, medicine, pedagogy, psychiatry), some new (anthropology, ethnology, evolutionism, genealogical research, psychology, sociology), and some so newly hatched that they as yet had no name (forensics, penology, sexology). He defined his territory very broadly, attributing crime to causes ranging from weather and race through alcohol abuse and heredity and on to age, sex, and oversized genitals. This meant that criminology could draw concepts, data, and methods from a number of contemporary fields of inquiry. It enabled Lombroso to link criminality, conceptually and causally, to other forms of deviance: cretinism, degeneration, epilepsy, genius, insanity, monstrosity, prostitution, and primitive savagery. His new science could borrow credibility and a degree of familiarity from better established fields of study. Paradoxically, by fusing criminal anthropology with other fields, Lombroso enabled it eventually to become an area of inquiry in its own right, a distinct type of knowledge. Its progress toward independence can be traced through changes in Lombroso's titles at the University of Turin: first professor of legal medicine and public hygiene (1876), then professor of psychiatry and clinical psychiatry (1896), and finally professor of criminal anthropology (1906).[55] He—and his field—had arrived.

Lombroso's second major intellectual feat, and a second reason for his enduring significance, was his consolidation, extension, and popularization of the medical model. Although the understanding of criminality as a sickness—mental, physical, or both—had germinated in the late 18th century, most people continued to think of lawbreaking in terms of sin and free will, with struggles between these two views playing out in famous trials such as that of William Freeman in the United States and that of Callisto Grandi in Italy.[56] Joining this debate at a moment when public opinion was ripe for change, Lombroso not only legitimated the medical model but also turned it into a metaphor capable of encompassing many— maybe all—forms of deviance, including large jaws, odd handwriting, emotional instability, tactile insensitivity, homosexuality, lack of remorse, and premature wrinkles. All deviations from what he and his followers defined as *normale* became signs of disease, warning signs of potential criminality that called for interpretation and treatment by medical men. To be sure, Lombroso left plenty of room for nonmedical experts to contribute to criminological research, including botanists (for carnivorous plants), sexologists, and zoologists, but he adopted the medical model as his basic explanatory framework. It is ubiquitous in his writings, the overarching dome under which he gathered other forms of explanation. Partly as a result of Lombroso's work, the understanding of criminality as a medical problem became dominant and almost automatic, an assumption more than a proposition.

Lombroso's production of criminological and penological blueprints offered liberal states new ways of dealing with deviants—something for which they keenly felt a need in the late 19th century, and a third source of his significance. The nation of most concern to him was, of course, his own. Unified geographically by 1870, Italy was nonetheless characterized politically by radical disunity, a country more in name than in fact, with subjects who identified with their hometowns rather than the new national government. A story about those who rallied around the hero Garibaldi, leader of the revolution that led to Italian unification, illustrates the dimensions of the problem: many of the revolutionaries, although they were fighting for Italia, had never heard the word before, and some thought that "La Talia" might be the name of an official's wife.[57] After centuries of fragmentation into fiefdoms ruled by the Catholic Church and European powers, the new nation had to build a central legal system from scratch and figure out how to deal with problematic populations like criminals and the insane. "The *Risorgimento* [unification] had 'made Italy,' but it had not 'made Italians,'" writes historian Daniel Pick. "This was the implicit problematic of Lombroso's researches. Criminality was taken as the very sign of the weakness of the nation. . . . His work sought to settle the definition of the political subject, by fixing more clearly and inexorably those who were beyond the pale of polity and society."[58]

While the situation differed considerably in other countries, the late 19th century was a period when many modernizing nations felt a need to revamp their systems of social control. (The U.S. states, for instance, were just beginning to institute statewide police systems.) Industrialization, urbanization, immigration, and war had created a whole new set of problems in governance, including the formation of an urban subproletariat. Lombroso's work, with its scientific separation of the orderly from the disorderly, and its clear, rational, and constructive-sounding recommendations for dealing with the disorderly, had tremendous appeal. As Pick explains, "The designation of the criminal is bound up, in complex ways, with the opposing but reciprocal process of defining the good citizen."[59]

Fourth, Lombroso made it possible to think of crime as a problem that might be studied scientifically. He had his predecessors, the physiognomists, phrenologists, and prison physicians who had created kinds of protocriminology. But it was Lombroso who, conceiving of crime as a natural phenomenon that could be subjected to empirical analysis, invented criminology, the science of crime and criminals. Lombroso's bid to remove the definition of crime from the hands of clerics and lawyers was a momentous move, not only because he was the first to make it for crimes generally but also because he was successful. He is the only criminologist who can begin to qualify as a paradigm shifter in Thomas Kuhn's strict sense of term, as someone who shattered traditional ideas about what science could and could not do and who began a scientific revolution (albeit in this case a minor revolution, confined to a single field of inquiry).[60] Lombroso shifted the focus from the crime to the criminal, where it remains to a large extent today. He altered the definition of crime so that it came to mean not only lawbreaking but also anything abnormal or harmful. He all but redefined dangerousness, from act to state. ("For the first time," observes historian David Horn, "one could be a criminal (that is, a danger to society) without having committed a crime.")[61] He

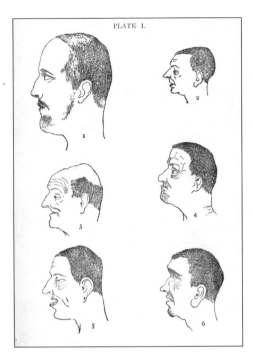

Heads of criminals. These drawings appear in Havelock Ellis's famous book *The Criminal,* which disseminated criminal anthropology to the English-speaking world. In his commentary, Ellis describes the first man, who got a life sentence for murder, as having "a most determined villainous expression, but a massive forehead." The implication is that with such a big brain, the man cannot be all bad.

invented a semiology of the body, a system of decoding meanings in the body's signs, and he developed a multiplicity of new ways of representing the deviance of the criminal body—through photographs, bar graphs, charts, death masks, and even a museum of criminal anthropology.

Endorsing a radical materialism, Lombroso's *Criminal Man* turned criminology's focus away from the mind (a construct compatible with the idea of an immortal soul) to the brain (an organ whose physicality ruled out metaphysical speculation of any sort). In the Italy of his day, perhaps only a nonpracticing Jew like Lombroso—an outsider to Catholicism who had turned his back on all forms of nonempirical belief—could have achieved the psychological distance necessary to thus sever criminology from morality and religion.[62] (This is not to say that Lombroso managed to conduct his science without thick colorations of his own moral opinions, but he did endorse objectivity as an ideal.) Even where it was most vociferously contested, criminal anthropology set the terms for debates over the study of crime, dictating the methods and types of evidence to be used and framing the way the new field of inquiry would develop.

Here again I part company with David Garland, who has argued that "the very idea of a science devoted to 'the criminal' seems to have been something of an historical accident, originally prompted by a claim that was quickly discredited: namely, that 'the criminal type' was an identifiable anthropological entity. Were it not for the contingency of that intellectual event there might never have been any distinctive criminological science, or any independent discipline."[63] The issue is not just that the idea of the criminal type, far from being quickly discredited, as Garland claims, remained viable for decades in France, Portugal, Spain, South America, Italy, Germany, and the United States, and arguably in Britain (which is Garland's focus) as well.[64] Even more problematic is Garland's claim about the accidental quality of the founding of the science of criminology. Given the Enlightenment scientific project of creating new empirical knowledges based on systematic thinking, and given the considerable curiosity from the end of the 18th century about the causes of crime, the development of a science of the criminal seems almost inevitable. That development seems doubly so given the need of modernizing democracies to find new methods for disciplining the disorderly and reminding "good" citizens of their opposite: the demonic, subhuman born criminal. Nothing made the work of Lombroso himself inevitable, of course, nor was there anything predictable about the way in which he braided together strands of degeneration theory, evolutionism, scientific racism, moral insanity theory, the remnants of phrenology, and fledgling ideas about heredity to produce the discourse of criminal anthropology. But it seems probable that someone, somewhere, would have ended up founding a science of the criminal. Indeed, in the years before the first appearance of *Criminal Man*, J. Bruce Thomson and Henry Maudsley very nearly did. Lombroso shifted the paradigm, introducing a scientific approach to the study of crime; but the old moralistic and metaphysical paradigm was already teetering on the edge of obsolescence.

Criminal anthropology foreshadowed much of what is happening in biocriminology today. Its typology, separating born criminals from other offenders, anticipated today's familiar distinction between the life-course persistent and the adolescence-limited offender.[65] Its core theory of the criminal as atavism echoes in today's evolutionary criminology. And (as chapter 9 shows) Lombroso's work uncannily anticipated current genetic and neurological explanations of crime.

# 5

## Evolutionary Theories
### *The Degenerate Brain*

Evolutionism—meaning all natural explanations of organic development, Darwinian or otherwise—fundamentally influenced 19th-century ideas about deviance in general and crime in particular. We would have to look to today's genetics revolution to find a science comparable in its repercussions on thinking about social problems and human nature itself. But very little is known about how evolutionism shaped criminology in its formative stages. We do have some understanding of how evolutionary theory affected Cesare Lombroso's theory of criminal anthropology, with its evolutionarily backward born criminal, but the impact of evolutionism on other criminologists remains, for the most part, unexplored.[1]

Like a river dispersing in a delta, its tributaries seeking out the most promising tracks, late 19th-century criminology flowed in a number of directions. Although it was dominated by criminal anthropology, there was no single dogma of criminal anthropology, and criminology in fact developed along various lines as thinkers in different countries and different fields tried to come to grips with evolution's implications for crime. This chapter explores some of those variations. It also traces the emergence of eugenics, the would-be science of speeding up human evolution through programs of differential breeding. The eugenics movement addressed the entire gamut of social problems, but curtailing the reproduction of criminals was among its major concerns.

Criminology germinated in a context of deepening gloom about governance. This mood differed markedly from that of the first half of the 19th century, which had been a period of optimism on both sides of the Atlantic. To legislators and policy makers in the earlier period, social problems had seemed solvable, humans rational, and the world, notwithstanding its ever faster pace of change, still a familiar and manageable place in which to live. But about 1850 the mood had begun to shift, albeit at a different pace and to a different extent depending on country and region. Urbanization, industrialization, the widening divisions among social classes; political restiveness among workers; a sense of crisis in social control among middle-class reformers—these and related factors combined to create a more pessimistic mood, one receptive to the sorts of dour hereditarian conclusions that appeared in late 19th-century criminology. "There cannot be the very slightest doubt," wrote the British psychiatrist S. A. K. Strahan in 1892, "that much of the disease, both physical and mental, which afflicts this and every other civilised people on the face of the earth is to a large extent the result of hereditary transmission of a degenerate constitution or predisposition to disease, brought about by the deteriorating influences of civilised life."[2]

In the United States and Europe, people grew apprehensive about the future. Village communities with their settled hierarchies were eroding, and traditional approaches to social problems were proving inadequate to meet the century's economic and social upheavals.[3] "Crime," in the words of historian Martin Wiener, became "a central metaphor of disorder and loss of control in all spheres of life."[4] That sense of disorder was intensified by Darwin's work on evolution and other scientific developments that overturned what had seemed to be eternal truths about creation, humans' place in the universe, and their relationship to God. Earlier, one had been able to count on the truths dispensed from the Sunday pulpit, but evolutionism forced one to question the Bible itself. This mood of dejected confusion formed the social and political context in which late 19th-century criminologists worked, borrowing evolutionary ideas here, adopting hereditarian premises there, and weaving both into scientific explanations of criminal behavior.

In addition to Lombrosian criminal anthropology, what other types of criminological explanation thrived in the late 19th century? Did the others, too, incorporate the idea of evolution by coming up with a theory of the atavistic criminal? Were their authors any less shaky and evasive than Lombroso when it came to accounting for the alleged heredity of crime? And were any of them forerunners of today's biocriminologists? In what follows, I start by teasing apart two major explanatory themes in 19th-century evolutionist thought: the idea of evolution in the sense of species development, on the one hand, and the idea of evolution as inheritance or heredity, on the other. In practice, the two themes often intertwined, but because criminologists tended to stress one or the other, it is useful to begin by distinguishing between them. Next I investigate the impact of these themes on the work of four authorities on the nature of crime—Henry

Maudsley, Richard Dugdale, Cesare Lombroso, and Richard von Krafft-Ebing. Following these examples, I discuss the work of the statistician Francis Galton, who founded the eugenics movement and whose work on heredity formed a bridge between late 19th-century and early 20th-century criminological ideas. In conclusion, I draw connections between the early evolutionist theories discussed in this chapter and today's biological theories of crime.

## Evolution as Species Development

Charles Darwin's *Origin of Species*, the work most closely associated today with evolutionary theory, did not appear until 1859, but well before that, pre-Darwinian explanations of evolution had forced educated people to grapple with the implications of nontheological, naturalist accounts of the origins and development of life. The study of geological formations whose great age seemed to contradict the Bible's account of creation;[5] the unearthing of fossils that called into question the biblical doctrine of immutability of the species; the return of Darwin and other sea voyagers with the remains of strange creatures that again evidently contradicted creationist assumptions about the origins of life—such developments challenged theological and philosophical truisms, even while they stimulated interest in the scientific study of natural and social phenomena. How might one fit criminals into this emerging picture of vast reaches of time and of change that occurred through struggle and adaptation? The concurrent growth of "scientific" racism, with its apparently incontrovertible hierarchies of race and human worth, raised an additional question about the nature of crime: might not even Western criminals be somehow closer to dark-skinned savages than to highly evolved, civilized whites? What light did new ideas about natural evolution, social evolution, and even individual evolution throw on the origins of crime and criminals?

### Natural Evolution

By the 1860s, the idea that plants and animals evolve was fairly well accepted; where debates arose was over the nature of the engine that drove the evolutionary process. Early in the century, in his two-volume study *Philosophie zoologique* (1809), the French zoologist Jean-Baptiste Lamarck had put forth an influential theory according to which organisms evolve out of "needs" to adapt to new types of environments. Lamarck's use of

Petrus Camper's facial angles. In this study from about 1794, the Dutch scientist Petrus Camper traces the evolution of the skull from an orangutan through a Mongolian and European to the ideal: a statue of Apollo. The idea of evolution preceded Darwin, as this example shows, and scientific racism thrived before the 19th-century began. Both ideas fed into criminal anthropology.

the word *besoins*,[6] which can be translated as either "needs" or "wants," led Darwin and others to belittle this aspect of his explanation on the grounds that it is silly to attribute "wants" or desires to lower forms of life, yet Lamarck's defenders insisted that he meant nothing more than a "need" to adapt to new circumstances.[7] A second key point in Lamarck's theory, and the one that turned out to have greater criminological significance, was that of use-inheritance, according to which "frequent and sustained use of any organ gradually strengthens this organ, develops and enlarges it . . . ; while the constant lack of use of this organ imperceptibly weakens it . . . and ends by making it disappear."[8] In this view, acquired traits are preserved by heredity and passed on to descendants. Nearly every 19th-century evolutionist incorporated Lamarck's use-inheritance theory into his own explanation, and in fact neo-Lamarckians (not Darwinians) dominated discussions of evolution late in the century in the United States as well as France. Lamarck's use-inheritance became the basis of the century's central criminological concept, that of degeneration.

Darwin drew on Lamarck's theory of use-inheritance, especially in two of his later books, *The Descent of Man* (1871) and *The Expression of the Emotions in Man and Animals* (1872), but in *The Origin of Species* his key explanation of "descent with modification" or evolution lay in natural selection, the idea that organisms vary and that those best suited to win in the struggle for existence survive while others become extinct. Darwin's was a sterner view of evolution than Lamarck's; it pictured not a "soft" adaptationist process of satisfying "wants" or "needs" but rather a heartless, wasteful, perhaps even pointless process. The Darwinian picture was more difficult—almost impossible—to reconcile with belief in a compassionate deity. The evolutionary process has no goal in *The Origin of Species*, nor is it necessarily progressive. It has no teleology—no design, purpose, or final cause.

What did Darwin's view imply for criminology? First, it implied that the world is a tough place, one in which the struggle between criminals and law enforcement might be an aspect of the struggle for existence. Moreover, it contradicted basic religious beliefs about justice and the power of good to conquer evil. It suggested that if criminals are more powerful than the law-abiding, then they will win—an implication that countered religious accounts in which a deity ensures that justice and righteousness will prevail. Criminals—it seemed to follow from Darwin's position, though he himself engaged in none of these speculations—cannot adapt to the civilized world, as they might if Lamarck's position were correct; rather, they can harm it irreparably.

A second set of conclusions that readers drew from Darwin's book was that criminals are lower forms of life, less evolved and less adapted to existence in the civilized world. Logically, readers might have drawn the opposite conclusion and speculated that criminals are more "fit" for the struggle for existence than honest men and women, or at least equally so; evidently more than logic was at work here, though, for theorists claimed that criminals were biologically inferior to normal, law-abiding men (by which, of course, they meant themselves). Although Darwin himself said no such thing in *The Origin of Species*, others, including Lombroso, were quick to reach this conclusion. Developmentally, they taught, criminals occupy a lower rung on the evolutionary scale, and their brains are more brutish than those of honest people.

Darwin's most powerful contribution to criminology was a misunderstanding that he tried valiantly to avoid: the widespread misinterpretation of his position as a "monkey theory" of descent. Darwin in fact argued that monkeys and men descended from a common ancestor,[9] and in *The Origin of Species* he had taken pains not to attribute purposefulness to the evolutionary process or to say that one form of life evolved into something better. However, many readers of *The Origin of Species*, including nearly all influential 19th-century criminologists, rushed past those points to conclude that the law-abiding are among the most perfect products of evolutionary progress and that criminals must therefore be closer to less evolved forms of life—apes and dark-skinned savages.

Whereas 18th-century legal theorists such as Bentham and Beccaria had assumed that criminals are like other people, making their decisions according to the same utilitarian calculus, criminals now became hairy and crude, closer to beasts than to law-abiding men and women. This portrait turned up not only in social science literature but also in popular works such as Robert Louis Stevenson's *Dr. Jekyll and Mr. Hyde* (1886), in which a cultivated physician is overwhelmed by his brutish alter ego. Lawbreaking began to seem less significant as an act than as a sign of an innate biological condition, that of criminality.

### Social Evolution

Nineteenth-century thinking about crime was deeply affected by the idea of not only natural evolution but also social or moral evolution, and here too Darwin was a major influence. In *The Descent of Man*, Darwin wrote of the evolution of the moral sense from its undeveloped state in primitive societies to its full development in modern, civilized nations.

> The greatest intemperance with savages is no reproach. Their utter licentiousness, not to mention unnatural crimes, is something astounding. As soon, however, as marriage, whether polygamous or monogamous, becomes common, jealousy will lead to the inculcation of female virtue; and this being honoured will tend to spread to the unmarried females. . . . Chastity eminently requires self-command.[10]

Thus "the moral sense is fundamentally identical with the social instincts."[11] Moral capacities such as self-command and conscience, encouraged by marriage, eventually become a permanent aspect of human nature, partly through use-inheritance but mainly through natural selection.[12] Thanks to social evolution, moral standards have risen since man's early history, and they are likely to continue to rise.

Almost as influential on criminological theory were the ideas about social evolution enunciated by the English philosopher Herbert Spencer, the most popular and prolific science writer of his day, whose vast stream of books on evolution shaped opinion worldwide. Conceiving of "society as organism," Spencer taught that society evolves just as the individual organism does, passing through the same stages from infancy to maturity and in the same order.[13] (Spencer meant the metaphor of society as an organism almost literally, arguing, for example, that merchants, by helping goods circulate through society, play a role comparable to the body's vascular system.)[14] This comparison had profound implications for the interpretation of harms caused by crime: if criminality is a biological condition, and if society is an organism, then crime damages not only the immediate victim but also the body social. This argument in turn reinforced the medical understanding of criminality, according to which the criminal is sick, capable of infecting the social body. In time the medical model fed into eugenics programs that proposed to strengthen the social body by eliminating criminals and others of the unfit.

Spencer's organicism led him to articulate the policy that became known as *social Darwinism*, the view that governments should not interfere with evolution by helping the unfit. "State-meddlings" would foolishly support inferior organisms in their struggle to survive, whereas evolution would cause them to expire. Moreover, state welfare drains resources from the fit: "That the average vigour of any race would be diminished did the diseased and feeble habitually survive and propagate; and that the destruction of such . . . leaves behind those who are able to fulfil the conditions of life; are almost self-evident truths."[15] Thus Spencer's idea of social evolution implied a set of crime control policies: do nothing to help the criminal classes so they will die out and leave the nation's stock improved by their demise.

Individual Evolution

If evolution occurs in nature and in society, perhaps it also occurs on the individual level—or so reasoned evolutionists drawn to the concepts of atavism, monstrosity, and reversion. (In fact, evolution does not occur on the individual level.) Criminologists were immediately attracted to atavism, monstrosity, and reversion as ways to explain the apparent backwardness of criminals.

Atavism or throwback theory, as we saw in the last chapter, held that some people are representatives of an earlier stage in human evolution. This throwback concept, although it turned up in many evolutionist writings, was fostered by the work of the German morphologist Ernst Haeckel. Haeckel's law that ontogeny recapitulates phylogeny maintained that the development of the individual embryo recapitulates the evolution of its species, passing through the same or similar developmental stages. As evidence Haeckel offered images of various animal embryos in the process of development, evolving through the stages of fish and amphibian.[16] His recapitulation law was eventually repudiated, but, in the words of the evolutionist Stephen Jay Gould, it "ranks among the most influential ideas of late nineteenth-century science,"[17] and it deeply affected criminology. With Haeckel's images of evolving embryos before their eyes, people aspiring to explain crime could easily conceive of criminals as atavisms, creatures who had been born before fully maturing as members of the human species. One could even picture criminals as hunched creatures, with forward-thrust, misshapen heads like those of Haeckel's human embryos in their penultimate stages. Haeckel's theory also reinforced suspicions that criminals were like savages, human types who had not yet fully evolved, and it encouraged Lombroso's extensive commentaries on the innate criminality of children, a group that, in his view, had not finished evolving.

Closely related to the notion of atavism was that of monstrosity. Here the idea was that evolution sometimes produces grotesque body parts, such as extra digits and misplaced brains,[18] or grotesque conditions, such as albinism, dwarfism, and gigantism.[19] For Darwin, "monstrosity" was a morally neutral term: "By a monstrosity I . . . [mean] some considerable deviation of structure in one part, either injurious to or not useful to the species, and not generally propagated."[20] But criminal anthropologists took monstrosities and other anomalies as signs of backward evolution on the individual level. Interest in monstrosity fed into the notion of a criminal scarred by physical and psychological deformities—Lombroso's born criminal. It led to portrayals such as that in which the American social reformer Henry Boies enthusiastically described criminals as "the imperfect, knotty, knurly, worm-eaten, half-rotten fruit of the race."[21]

The possibility of individual evolutionary change was further encouraged by the notion of reversion, a slow version of atavism and monstrosity. Whereas atavism premises saltation or a jump backward, and monstrosity is a onetime anomaly, reversion was said to involve an almost imperceptible process of devolution or return to an earlier evolutionary state. The idea of reversion was closely related to the theory of degeneration discussed in the next section, but it merits mention here because it was so strongly reinforced by the idea of moral reversion put forth by Darwin and Spencer. In *The Descent of Man*, Darwin wrote that "with mankind some of the worse dispositions, which occasionally without any assignable cause make their appearance in families, may perhaps be reversions to a savage state."[22] And Spencer, in often-quoted passages, argued that the most recent achievements of civilization are the first to be lost when trouble sets in. Spencer pictured this kind of reversion in terms of a relapse by cultivated white men into savagery: "In the Australian bush and in the backwoods of America, the Anglo-Saxon race, in which civilization has developed the higher feelings to a considerable degree, rapidly lapses into comparative barbarism: adopting the moral code, and sometimes the habits, of savages."[23] Similarly, psychiatrists explained the condition of moral insanity as a reversion to a primitive state.[24] Thus individual evolutionary change could occur through reversion as well as atavism and monstrosity. In all three cases, it signified a decline toward a more primitive, amoral condition.[25]

Criminologists who conceived of evolution primarily in terms of species development thus tended to be concerned with visible, physical indicators of change, although some spun off to speculate on social and moral change as well. Their theories, with their interest in morphological differences, encouraged speculation about criminals as a separate species, or as throwbacks in the present species, or as creatures whose anthropological oddities signified their dangerousness. Lombroso's writings on criminal anthropology were the ones that became most famous, but many other commentators produced similar discourses. For example, before he had ever heard Lombroso's name, the English psychiatrist Henry Maudsley explained that the criminal class constitutes "a degenerate or morbid variety of mankind, marked by peculiar low physical and mental characteristics. . . . They are scrofulous, not seldom deformed, with badly-formed angular heads; are stupid, sullen, sluggish, deficient in vital energy, and sometimes afflicted with epilepsy."[26] In the United States, a physician at New York's Bloomingdale Asylum, fresh from his first encounter with Lombroso's work, wrote, "With the struggle for existence, and (let us hope) with the 'survival of the fittest' we are all familiar; but there is also another struggle going on in our midst, with far different results, the chief of which is the *Survival of the Unfittest*, and it is the question of the criminal as a distinct type of the human species."[27] A few years later another American physician spoke of "the evil instincts natural to uncivilised man," warning that "the instinctive criminal is an abnormal and degenerate type of humanity."[28] All such declarations represented efforts to extract from the notion of species evolution lessons about the genesis of criminality and the nature of criminals.

## *Evolution as Inheritance*

In addition to the idea of species evolution, a second major evolutionist theme influenced early criminological thought: the concept of inheritance. It is impossible to entirely separate the two, but it is useful to consider them apart, if only momentarily, to see what 19th-century criminologists meant when they spoke of inheritance as a cause of lawbreaking.

When evolutionists tried to explain how change occurs over time, they often invoked the notion of inheritance or heredity. "Like begets like" was a familiar concept: farmers harvesting their crops, fanciers breeding their pigeons, and parents gazing fondly on their children realized that there must be some mechanism through which traits pass from one generation to the next. "Heredity is that mysterious influence which foreordains that the offspring shall be in the likeness of its parents," wrote S. A. K. Strahan in his popular book on heredity.[29] But no one knew how that "mysterious influence" worked until genes were identified in the early 20th century. Nineteenth-century theorists had to limp along with makeshift terms such as *elements, gemmules, germ plasm,* and *unit characters,* even while admitting, with Darwin, that "the laws governing inheritance are quite unknown."[30]

For 19th-century social theorists, far and away the most influential conceptualization of inheritance was the notion of degeneration. Those who wrote about degeneration posited an innate condition—degeneration or degeneracy—that causes other afflictions, including criminality, epilepsy, insanity, and pauperism. Degenerationists viewed the stuff of heredity (whatever it might be) as plastic, malleable, and capable of infinite gradations of change; thus they believed that degeneration might manifest itself in any number of physical and social diseases, showing up as criminality in a grandfather, alcoholism or epilepsy in his daughter, and insanity (or insanity *with* criminality, alcoholism, and epilepsy) in her child. They also conceived of a constant interplay or circular feedback loop between the condition of degeneration and its manifestations, so that criminality might be both a result and a cause of degeneration.

Although degeneration theory meshed poorly with Darwin's teachings about natural selection, it fit perfectly with (and indeed ultimately rested upon) the Lamarckian notion of use-inheritance, meaning the inheritance of acquired characteristics. According to degenerationists, those who drink heavily, fornicate frequently, become slothful, or fail to discipline their minds are in danger of devolving or going backward on the evolutionary scale; they also risk passing their degeneracy on to their descendants. "The man or woman whose family has a clean bill of health," as Strahan put it, "can by wicked and vicious habits build up insanity, or epilepsy, or phthisis, or gout, etc., to be handed down to posterity."[31] If, however, they obey the laws of virtuous living, they may be able to avoid this fate.

The degenerationists' Bible—their counterpart to what *The Origin of Species* was for Darwinians—was the *Traité des dégénérescences physique, intellectuelles et morales* (*Treatise on Physical, Intellectual, and Moral Degeneration*; 1857) of Bénédict Auguste Morel, the chief physician of a French insane asylum. Morel defines degeneration in terms of maladaptation or morbid deviation.[32] Whoever carries the germs of degeneration becomes ever less capable of performing ordinary tasks and thinking clearly. Degeneration curbs the afflicted individual's potential and progressively weakens his or her descendants. Morel takes pains to explain that he is not talking about a regression toward the mean but rather a morbid deviation away from normality that leads to criminality, madness, sterility, and early death.[33] Degeneration, a condition of moral, intellectual, and physical atrophy, "can be congenital or acquired, complete or partial, susceptible to improvement or entirely incurable."[34] In nearly all cases it will be passed on to the next generation, and the next after that, undermining health until the line becomes extinct. Degenerative conditions, Morel continues, are caused by violations of the moral law, abuse of one's body, and failures to cultivate one's mind. Sometimes the causes lie in the environment, as when a marshy region produces people who are stunted, pallid, and slow of gait. Degeneration is also induced by alcohol and opium abuse, by living in overcrowded urban areas, and by poverty and disease.

The aspect of Morel's theory that affected criminology most powerfully— indeed, shaping the thought of major theorists well into the 20th century— was his insistence on interchangeability in the results of degeneration. Just as the causes of degeneration might be physical, moral, or intellectual, so might the results be physical deformities, criminality, insanity—or all at once. Interchangeable, the signs of degeneration were merely temporary manifestations of the inner condition, the rot silently coursing through the degenerate's veins. This notion of interchangeability facilitated the work of criminologists who tried to trace the flow of an ancestor's bad heredity through the generations, for any disability in later family members served to prove an inherited predisposition to degenerate. The easy interchangeability of degenerative traits also swelled the ranks of those who could be considered criminally inclined: feeblemindedness, epilepsy, hysteria, and almost any other sign of a "defect" became a warning of lawbreaking potential.

Criminality or even potential criminality could now be found anywhere, secretly lurking in the germ plasm, waiting to erupt.

Drawing on statistics analyzed by Adolphe Quetelet and others, Morel warned that degeneration was on the rise. "The ever growing number of suicides, of misdemeanors, of crimes against property, if not against persons, the monstrous precocity of youthful crimes, the pollution of the race . . . are irrefutable facts," evidence of degeneracy's relentless increase.[35] Even though his fundamental position was that degenerate lines eventually become sterile, Morel was so alarmed by the apparent rise in the tide of degenerates that he fell into contradiction, warning that degeneration can lead to an explosion in the number of inferior beings, a calamity comparable to the barbarian invasions of ancient civilizations.[36] Later degenerationists, rejecting the possibility of a sterility-and-death outcome in favor of the view that degenerates are outmultiplying the healthy, forecast equally grave dangers from hereditary crime.

Few ideas in the history of criminology have had greater impact than that of degeneration.[37] Although today it has been nearly forgotten, in the 19th century degeneration was *the* way of talking about the inheritance of criminality:

> In the case of the criminal incapable of true reform, we may feel morally sure that he has come of a degenerate line, and that if he have offspring some measure of his innate viciousness will be transmitted. (W. Duncan McKim)[38]

> The offspring of degenerate, degraded, defective, or diseased parents are of the necessity of nature below the normal standard, physically, mentally, or morally, at birth—even if not malformed or tainted with a diseased diathesis, neurotic, tuberculous, scrofulous, intemperate, or other. Some may be rescued from their inherited tendency by intelligent and favorable care and cultivation; but without extraordinary attention nature will reproduce in them—it cannot do otherwise—an aggravation of parental defects. (Henry Boies)[39]

And degeneration was *the* way of conceptualizing the relationship of criminality to other social problems:

> In the majority of cases, criminality appears in only one, two, or three members of a family, the brothers and sisters showing the taint in various

ways. One will be scrofulous, or a deaf-mute, another insane, idiotic, epileptic, a suicide, a prostitute, etc., as the case may be. (S. A. K. Strahan)[40]

Vice, crime, and insanity may be regarded as merely different phases of degeneracy which so resemble one another that we are often at a loss when we would distinguish between them. (W. Duncan McKim)[41]

An idea with immense explanatory power, degeneration carried ominous undertones of genetic decay.

Those implications grew more distressing as the century moved toward its conclusion. So long as degeneration theory remained rooted in the "soft," Lamarckian understanding of heredity as malleable, it offered hope for improvement. (If someone can degenerate, then she or he can also regenerate; reform is possible.) However, later theorists became "harder" in their determinism, adopting the view that the mechanism of heredity— whatever it might be—is particulate: unchangeable and impervious to environmental reforms. The latter view interlaced with the increasingly pessimistic mood of the late 19th century and with the growing alarm over social pollution by degenerates. It shifted the blame for social problems from social conditions to "degenerates" themselves.

## Four Evolutionist Approaches to Crime

Now we can return to the original question: how did evolutionism affect the reasoning of people who wrote about crime? I have already indicated some of their general responses, but to grasp the richness of variation in the reactions—the multiformity of late 19th-century criminology—it is useful to look at specific examples. Thus in what follows I examine the work of four men—Henry Maudsley (England), Richard Dugdale (United States), Cesare Lombroso (Italy), and Richard von Krafft-Ebing (Germany). The first three were among the most influential authorities on criminality of their era, while Krafft-Ebing was the century's outstanding specialist in sex crime. I selected these four examples partly for geographical diversity: Italian work has dominated histories of early criminology, but we also need to know about theories generated elsewhere. I also chose the examples for the diversity in their approaches to crime: their varied perspectives, I hoped, would reveal differences in the impact of evolutionism. I focus on a single work by each author: in Maudsley's case, *Responsibility in Mental Disease* (1874),

his most specifically criminological book; in Dugdale's case, *"The Jukes":
A Study in Crime, Pauperism, Disease and Heredity* (1877), his only book;
in Lombroso's case, *Criminal Man* (originally 1876), his most famous
book; and in Krafft-Ebing's case, *Psychopathia Sexualis* (originally 1886),
his pioneering work on sexual pathologies.

Thus I cover four influential criminological texts produced during the
twenty-five-year period in which evolutionism had its first impact on
theories of crime.[42] Varied in background and approach, the four texts
show that 19th-century authorities on crime absorbed evolutionist ideas
unevenly, eclectically, even idiosyncratically, depending on their time,
location, background, and personal proclivities.

### Henry Maudsley and *Responsibility in Mental Disease*

Henry Maudsley (1835–1918), the most distinguished psychiatrist in late
19th-century England, held a chair in medical jurisprudence at University
College, London, and edited the *Journal of Mental Science*, the main
periodical of British psychiatry, from 1860 to 1878. He also helped to
shift the profession of psychiatry out of the lunatic asylum, where it
had originated, and into the community. Developing a lucrative private
practice, he accumulated sufficient wealth to found London's famed
Maudsley Hospital, which he hoped would provide early treatment for
the mentally ill, thus enabling them to avoid institutionalization. His
*Responsibility in Mental Disease* became one of the most cited vehicles
in the English-speaking world for the idea that the criminal is "born,
not made."[43] (It was translated into several foreign languages as well.)
Maudsley's pessimism about the reformability of criminals fit well
both with his own personality—by all reports, he was a joyless man,
opinionated and unsparing[44]—and with the period's general gloominess
about environmental solutions to social problems.

Maudsley viewed criminality as a form of insanity, and insanity as a
disorder of the brain, a sign of a malfunctioning nervous system. Neither
the insane nor criminals can escape their condition, which is inherent
and hereditary: "There is a destiny made for man by his ancestors." Thus
criminals are not responsible for their misdeeds ("The wicked are not
wicked by deliberate choice . . . but by an inclination of their natures").
Because criminals are "manufactured" by evolution, it is impossible to
reform them through punishment. Criminality, Maudsley concluded in
a much-quoted passage, is an "intractable malady. . . . The dog returns

to its vomit and the sow to its wallowing in the mire . . . . How can that which has been forming through generations be *re*-formed within the term of a single life? Can the Ethiopian change his skin or the leopard his spots?"[45] Like Africans and animals, criminals are biologically doomed to inferiority.

Evolution in the sense of species development was one of the two basic concepts undergirding Maudsley's interpretation of criminality. His understanding of evolution was based on Darwin, but on a very superficial reading of Darwin. Maudsley claimed (as Darwin did not) that evolutionary processes are the chief and indeed only determinant of criminal nature. In his utterly determinist view, evolution damns criminals to their fate from generations back; its effects are as inescapable as they are horrifying. Criminals are in fact almost a separate species, "a distinct . . . class of beings," "marked by defective physical and mental organization."[46] Maudsley here comes close to Lombroso's criminal anthropology, although he does not call criminals atavisms, as Lombroso would soon do, nor does he attempt to develop a science of criminality.

In formulating his opinions on the evolution of the criminal, Maudsley drew on teachings about social and moral evolution that could be found in both Darwin and Spencer. Spencer, for example, had recently written that societies evolve, becoming ever more civilized, but that they are in danger of losing their most recent achievements when a situation becomes unstable. Similarly, Maudsley considered morality a product of evolution. The moral sense, he explained, is an acquired characteristic that first appeared in the "primitive family and tribe" as a result of its need for self-protection. Thereafter, the moral sense became hereditary, part of the brain's organization. But because morality and conscience were acquired late in the evolutionary process, they are the "first to suffer when disease invades the mental organization."[47]

A more immediate influence on Maudsley's ideas about the imperfect evolution of the criminal was the work of the Scottish prison physician J. Bruce Thomson, who late in life published two extraordinary and widely influential articles. These reports, which were among the earliest statistical studies of crime, were based on Thomson's encounters with thousands of convicts, and both were published in Maudsley's *Journal of Mental Science*. The first—and the one that Maudsley cites in his *Responsibility in Mental Disease*—argues that "there is a criminal class distinct from other civilized and criminal men . . . marked by peculiar physical and mental characteristics"; their disease is hereditary and incurable.[48] The second article, following hard on the heels of the first, argues "that great criminals are wholly without the moral sense, [and] that violent and habitual criminals are, as a class, moral imbeciles."[49] Thomson expounds on the physical deformities of such criminals, their "low type of physique indicating a deteriorated character which gives a family likeness to them all"; and he designates them a "marked hereditary breed."[50] Thomson's statistical data and his description of hereditary criminals as anthropological freaks became bricks and mortar to Maudsley and others building their own theories.

Evolutionist ideas of inheritance were the other basic concept that undergirded Maudsley's understanding of criminality, and here the chief influence was Morel's degeneration theory. Maudsley had read Morel early in his career, when he was a novice asylum physician and desperate for guidance on mental disorders.[51] He swallowed degeneration theory whole and never modified it, even while merging it with ideas about evolution as species development. Morel's influence shows up, for instance, in Maudsley's explanations of the inheritance of criminal behavior. The chain of events leading to criminality, Maudsley writes, begins with some sort of moral failing. The results do not necessarily appear in the next generation; rather, the tendency to degenerate "may be entirely latent in it, not coming to the surface in any form until the third or fourth generation. But it will run on in the stream of family descent" until it "reaches a pathological evolution which entails the decay and extinction of the family."[52] From degenerationism, Maudsley also took the notion of the easy interchangeability of defects among degenerates. People with a hereditary disposition to insanity might become criminals, dipsomaniacs, or epileptics.

Maudsley gave equal weight to the developmental and the hereditarian strands within evolutionism. That is, he emphasized the idea of the criminal as an evolutionary failure *and* the idea of the criminal as a degenerate. This equal emphasis was unusual, at least among the four authorities examined here. To reach his conclusions about criminality, Maudsley had cobbled together scientific ideas drawn first from Morel, whose degeneration theory formed the substructure, and then from Darwin, Spencer, and Thomson, whose more anthropological evolutionism he fused with Morel's teachings in a seamless web.

Maudsley always thought of himself as a specialist in mental disorders, not criminal behavior, but when he wrote about criminality he did so with vast conviction—magisterially, vividly, almost exultantly—laying down the law of biological determinism like an Old Testament prophet, creating a powerful evolutionary criminology and becoming one of the most effective exponents in Victorian England of the idea of innate criminality. Driven by his unrelenting biological determinism, Maudsley ended up making eugenic recommendations for the control of crime, albeit vague ones. "When we observe what care and thought men give to the selective breeding of horses, cows, and dogs, it is astonishing how little thought they take about the breeding of their own species," he remarked, recommending prevention of propagation as one method of checking the increase in insanity and criminality.[53]

### Richard Dugdale and *"The Jukes"*

Maudsley could thunder on about criminals as a product of evolution, but he could not prove it. Just as he published *Responsibility in Mental Disease*, however, a volunteer researcher for a New York State charity was designing a study that, when completed, seemed to prove at least half of Maudsley's claim: that criminality is inherited. Using an ingenious research design,[54] Richard L. Dugdale's *"The Jukes": A Study in Crime, Pauperism, Disease, and Heredity* electrified theorists and policy makers on both sides of the Atlantic. (Lombroso, for example, cited it within the year.) For many, *"The Jukes"* was the study that scientifically proved that criminality (not to mention pauperism, promiscuity, and profligacy) is transmitted from generation to generation. Actually, Dugdale himself hesitated to draw hereditarian conclusions from his data, noting that he did not have enough information to prove conclusively that heredity is more powerful than environment.[55] No one paid attention to his caveats, however, as social reformers rushed to implement the implications of *"The Jukes"* by instating eugenic measures.[56]

Dugdale (1841–1883) was an anomaly among late 19th-century authorities on crime; whereas the majority of the others had a medical background and specialized in psychiatry, he was a young businessman and lacked professional training.[57] Although he knew a little about statistics before he started, he basically made up his social science methodology as he went along. Dugdale himself described his entrance into the work: "In July, 1874, the New York Prison Association having deputed me to visit thirteen of the county jails of the State and report thereupon, I made a tour of inspection . . . . No specially striking cases of criminal careers, traceable through several generations, presented themselves till _____ county was reached. Here, however, were found six persons, under four family names, who turned out to be blood relations in some degree."[58] Relying on the records of local institutions and on the memories of physicians, employers, and older residents of the area, Dugdale discovered that "these six persons belonged to a long lineage, reaching back to the early colonists, and had intermarried so slightly with the emigrant population of the old world that they may be called a strictly American family. They had lived in the same locality for generations, and were so despised by the reputable community that their family name *had come to be used generically as a term of reproach*."[59]

Pursuing his genealogical research, Dugdale constructed immense family trees of the original six jail inmates and their relatives, going back for seven generations and placing, at the head of all the branches, a man born about 1750 whom he called Max. The family in its entirety, including all its blood relations and their partners, he dubbed "The Jukes," always using quotation marks to remind readers that the "family" included relatives by marriage who in fact had different surnames.[60] To his genealogical charts Dugdale added notes summarizing the information he had picked up on each individual; of a fifth-generation member, for example, we read: "Laborer; at 30, g. lar., c. jail, 90 d; assault and bat., c. jail, 90 d; 49, rape x of his niece, S. Sing, 5 y.; no property." If we read the foldout charts from left to right, moving through the generations and studying Dugdale's notes on individuals ("harlot," "o. relief," "vagrant," "syphilis," "tried suicide twice," "mulatto child," and so on), we can follow what seems to be the inheritance of degeneration.

For the first time, or so it appeared, someone had documented the flow of bad heredity through the generations. One could watch as the number of Max's progeny swelled in the fourth and fifth generations and then thinned out, an apparent confirmation of Morel's prediction of sterility and death for degenerate lines. Moreover (eager positivists noted), one could quantify the results in terms of numbers of inebriates, paupers, criminals, and so forth, and do cross-tabulations of, for example, conviction offenses by age at first offense. One could also count the costs in terms of "o. relief" or public welfare: "Over a million and a quarter dollars of loss in 75 years [Dugdale wrote], caused by a single family 1,200 strong, without reckoning the cash paid for whiskey, or taking into account the entailment of pauperism and crime of the survivors in succeeding generations, and the incurable disease, idiocy and insanity growing out of this debauchery."[61] Even though Dugdale himself concluded that his data indicated the need for environmental improvements such as better education for the poor, readers understandably drew hard-hereditarian conclusions from his charts and figures.

## TABLE II.

| Second generation. | Third generation. | Fourth generation. | Fifth generation. | REMARKS. |
|---|---|---|---|---|
| Ada, harlot before marriage. { | A. × B, no crime*. | { A. B. × X, crime<br>{ A. B. × D. X, reputable | A. B. X, crime<br>A. B. D. X, reputable | Preponderance of males } Bastard line.<br>Semi-successful ....... } |
| | A. × C, no crime | A. C. × B. C., no crime | A. C. B. C., no crime | Legitimate. Preponderance of girls. |
| | A. × D, no crime | A. D. × X, no crime | No crime | Legitimate. Distinct:vely pauper line. |
| | A. × X, no crime | A. X. × E. X, pauper | A. X. E. X, pauper | |
| Bell, harlot before marriage. { | B. × X, no crime | { B. X. × X, reputable | Honest | Successful branch } Bastard line. |
| | B. × C, no crime | { B. X. × X, crime | B. X. X, crime | Criminal branch } |
| | | B. C. × X, no crime | | Legitimate. |
| Clara, of good repute ....... { | C. × X, not traced | ........ | ........ | Legitimate. Not traced. |
| | See A. × C and B. × C. | | | Legitimate. |
| Delia, harlot before marriage { | D. × X, no crime | { D. X. × X, crime | D. X. X, crime | Legitimate. |
| | | { D. X. × B. C, no crime | D. X. B. C, no crime | Bastard line. |
| Effie, reputation unknown. | E. = X*.<br>E. × X, no crime | E. X. × X, crime | Not traced | Bastard line and barren.<br>Legitimate. |

B

**\* Explanation.** **× Married.** **= Cohabiting with.**

Chart of the "Juke" family. Richard Dugdale's charts of the prolific "Juke" family seemed to scientifically prove that criminal tendencies and other negative traits are inherited.

What is most interesting about Dugdale's work, in terms of my question about the impact of evolutionism on criminology, is that he entirely ignores the idea of evolution as species development, instead devoting his essay almost exclusively to evolution as inheritance—degeneration theory.[62] In contrast to Maudsley, who placed equal stress on species development and heredity, Dugdale seems ignorant of debates over *The Origin of Species* (which had been published about fifteen years earlier) and other work on evolution as organic development. He cites neither Darwin nor Spencer. To judge from his footnotes, Dugdale's main influences were the corresponding secretary of the Prison Association, Dr. Elisha Harris; Maudsley; and one of J. B. Thomson's famous hereditarian tracts on prisoners. Even Morel's name—which one might expect to be used frequently in this Morelian study—turns up only once, and that in a quotation from Elisha Harris. Dugdale, it seems, was not only a younger and less mature writer than Maudsley; he was neither well read nor particularly interested in the great evolutionist debates swirling around him.

But Dugdale's obliviousness to evolution in the sense of species development made not a jot of difference to his impact on others, which was immediate and profound. Dugdale's emphasis (or seeming emphasis, since he disowned it) on the hereditary nature of criminality jump-started the eugenics movement and foreshadowed today's work on genes and crime. And his methodology, although it was very nearly unique, did not remain so for long as imitators rushed to create genealogical trees for other bad families.[63]

### Cesare Lombroso and *Criminal Man*

Like Maudsley, Lombroso was a psychiatrist, but he also thought of himself as an anthropologist, and that additional orientation made all the difference in their explanations of crime. Whereas Maudsley was interested in both aspects of evolutionism—the physical development of species and inheritance—Lombroso downplayed inheritance relative to species development and other "anthropological" aspects of evolution. Inheritance failed to fire his enthusiasm as the notion of atavism did. Thus in answer to the question, How did evolutionism affect Lombroso's work? the answer is that it fixated him on his famous notion of the backward-evolving, anthropological criminal.

To be sure, one should not entirely dismiss the significance of inheritance in Lombroso's arguments for the existence of criminal man. He devotes a section to inheritance in the second edition of *Criminal Man*, reporting in detail on *"The Jukes,"* describing similar bad families, and claiming that "criminality itself is hereditary."[64] Earlier in this same edition he writes of the hereditary influence of "race" on criminality, giving as one example Sicilians' tolerance of violence, a trait they inherited from Arab ancestors: "In Sicily today, following the tradition of the original Arab settlers, both uprisings and brigandage are intertwined with politics. Brigandage provokes neither horror nor revulsion in people of this area as it would in groups with a greater proportion of Aryan blood." Similarly, Gypsies inherit thievishness and vengefulness, passing these traits on to their children, and Jews transmit low crime rates.[65] Lombroso's belief that hereditary factors contribute to criminality occasionally led him to speculate on what we would now call the eugenic effects of life sentences.[66] He thought of anomalies—the "stigmata" of crime—as degenerative (that is, heritable) traits, and eventually he added degeneration to atavism as a cause of crime. Yet he showed little interest in how heredity works,[67] nor did he investigate its effects with the obsessiveness with which he measured criminals' crania and catalogued their tattoos. Moreover, the addition of degeneration to his deck of explanations for crime had little effect on the anthropological, evolutionist core of Lombroso's teachings. Inheritance was merely the icing on the cake of his central, developmental arguments for the existence of criminal man.

It is tempting to think that Lombroso may have modeled his work on that of Darwin, who had published his major books on evolution (1859, 1871) in the decades leading up to the first edition of *Criminal Man* (1876). Indeed, Lombroso's lifelong effort to identify the born criminal can be seen as a sustained response to a question with which Darwin opens *The Descent of Man*: "Is man subject to . . . malconformations, the result of arrested development, . . . and does he display in any of his anomalies reversion to some former and ancient type of structure?"[68]—a question to which Lombroso's answer, in terms of lawbreakers, was a resounding "Yes!" Like Darwin before him, Lombroso starts from naturalistic premises, assuming that human social phenomena have a biological explanation and that evolution can account for even the psychology of human behavior. Again like Darwin, he assumes a continuity of behavior among animals and humans. His descriptions of murderous ants and thievish bees, much ridiculed by critics, merely extend Darwin's anthropomorphic claim that "the lower animals are excited by the same emotions as ourselves."[69] Lombroso may have hoped to become the Darwin of the criminal.[70]

It is, however, more probable that Lombroso derived the evolutionist basis for his criminal anthropology not from Darwin but from Italian sources. Even before Darwin's ideas reached the peninsula, Italy's scientists took great interest in both evolution and anthropology. *L'uomo bianco e l'uomo di colore* (*The White Man and the Man of Color*; 1871), Lombroso's early work on the origins of races, already held the core idea of *Criminal Man*—that of atavism or regression to an earlier stage of evolution[71]—and in that book (as Lombroso scholar Renzo Villa observes), "Lombroso cites neither . . . Haeckel nor Darwin, except in brief notes." Nor, Villa continues, did he have any need to rely on foreign sources, for in Italy "these were the years of hottest debate on biological evolution and the origins of man,"[72] polemics that drew on native sources. In any case, in Italy during the years in which Lombroso was formulating his thesis about criminal man, there was no such thing as pure Darwinism but rather a synthesis of evolutionary thought that mixed together ideas of Lamarck, the French biologist Geoffrey Saint-Hilaire, Haeckel, phrenology, and Paolo Marzolo (one of Lombroso's earliest mentors), among others.[73] So rather than modeling his work on that of Darwin, Lombroso probably developed it on a parallel track, using some of the same sources and eventually discovering and citing Darwin in support of his own evolutionary project.

Due to his profound investment in his theory of atavism and his self-identification as an anthropologist, Lombroso put his misshapen born criminal at the center of the criminological enterprise. Indeed, what made Lombroso unique—and far more famous criminologically than Maudsley and Dugdale—was his dramatic delineation of this figure. The born criminal was firmer in its outlines than other theorists' protean degenerate, who kept changing identities, becoming insane, epileptic, inebriate, and pauperized. Lombroso's atavistic born criminal, in contrast, had a distinctive profile and was difficult to forget—a menacing survivor from the primitive evolutionary past.

### Richard von Krafft-Ebing and *Psychopathia Sexualis*

Richard von Krafft-Ebing (1840–1902), a dominant figure in 19th-century psychiatry and a founder of the study of human sexuality, played an important role in the modernization of psychiatry; like Maudsley, he helped relocate psychiatric work from the asylum into the community. However, Krafft-Ebing was less arrogant than Maudsley, establishing ties with other European intellectuals, including Lombroso, whose work Krafft-Ebing cited frequently and mined for examples. (Reciprocating, Lombroso wrote the introduction to an Italian edition of Krafft-Ebing's famous *Psychopathia Sexualis*.) Krafft-Ebing taught at the universities of Strasbourg, Graz, and Vienna; in the latter city he seems to have been on good terms with another early student of sexuality, Sigmund Freud.[74] Darwin's *Descent of Man*, with its extensive discussions of plant and animal sexuality and its assumption that sex is both natural and necessary to evolution, probably emboldened Krafft-Ebing, Freud, and others to initiate the study of human sexuality.[75] A liberal, Krafft-Ebing denounced anti-Semitism and nationalism, supported pacifism, and in time became an opponent of sodomy laws.

In *Psychopathia Sexualis*, which went through twelve editions after its initial appearance in 1886, Krafft-Ebing describes sexuality as the driving force behind social progress. "Sexual feeling," he explains, "is really the root of all ethics, and no doubt of aestheticism and religion. The sublimest virtues . . . may spring from sexual life." Drawing on evolutionary theory and citing Lombroso, he sketches the trajectory of social evolution from the open and shameless sexuality of savages through the gradual development of civilization to modern, monogamous family life. Trouble sets in because sexuality "may easily degenerate into the lowest passion and basest vice."[76]

Immersed in Morel's ideas, Krafft-Ebing applied the Frenchman's concept of degeneration to sexual deviance, sometimes elaborating to explain how degeneration works. For instance, Krafft-Ebing believed that worrisome life circumstances increase tensions in the nervous system, stimulating sexuality and leading "the individual as well as the masses to excess . . . . In . . . periods of civic and moral decline the most monstrous excesses of sexual life may be observed."[77] Extending this argument to homosexuality—at the time a serious crime—Krafft-Ebing wrote of it as a "functional sign of degeneration," one that is usually accompanied by a hereditary psychopathic taint, psychological anomalies, and either decline in intellectual powers or eccentricity.[78]

Like other degenerationists, Krafft-Ebing associated abnormality with backward evolution into savagery. In his discussion of sadism, for example, he remarks that "from the history of civilisation and anthropology we know that there have been times, as there are savages to-day that practise it, where brutal force, robbery, or even blows that rendered a woman powerless, were made to obtain love's desire. It is possible that tendencies to such outbursts of sadism are atavistic."[79] Rape and other sex crimes indicate a loss of inhibitory control over primitive urges; they are signs that civilized man is devolving or literally "going ape."[80]

Krafft-Ebing used degeneration theory to address one of the fundamental questions in forensic psychiatry: how to determine criminal responsibility. Like other psychiatrists of his day, he looked to the body itself for answers to questions about the human mind, searching for signs of degeneration in physical anomalies such as cleft palates and club feet, in unusual cranial measurements, and in family trees that might reveal hereditary degenerative tendencies. We can differentiate between those sex criminals who are diseased and those who are merely vicious, he wrote, by looking for the signs of degeneration. Anomalies can help us tell which sex offenders are genuinely ill. Those who suffer from the disease of perversion (as opposed to the mere vice of perversity), in Krafft-Ebing's view, should not be held responsible for their offenses, although they should be removed from society.[81]

While degenerationist explanations of sexual deviancy predominate in Krafft-Ebing's work, in the 1890s he began to supplement them with evolutionist arguments that drew more heavily on developmental (or what he called "anthropological") models.[82] (Thus he reversed the progression of Lombroso's thinking, which had begun with developmental evolution and later added the hereditarian theory of degenerationism.) German evolutionist thought had long emphasized morphology and embryology, as in the case of Haeckel. Drawing on this tradition, Krafft-Ebing discussed homosexuality as a form of arrested development or return to an earlier evolutionary state in which the organism is bisexual. According to the "law of mono-sexual formation," lower evolutionary forms are bisexual but over time evolve into something more perfect, the heterosexual ("mono-sexual," meaning attracted only to the opposite sex). However, one may regress to earlier, bisexual stages, with males picking up female traits and females acquiring the "thought, sentiment, action, even external appearance . . . of the man."[83]

Although evolutionist explanations constitute significant subthemes in *Psychopathia Sexualis*, Krafft-Ebing is mainly interested in identifying and classifying sexual pathologies, and at times his degenerationism has a pro forma feel, as though he were rehearsing a dogma that had ceased to engage him. Moreover, in the 1890s he began pulling away from the insistent biologism of 19th-century psychiatry and toward more psychological and psychoanalytic explanations of sexual deviancies, a tendency that can be seen in the conclusion to his discussion of sadism. Here he repeats the standard Darwinian and Spencerian lines about the evolution of the virtues, explaining that compassion—the emotion that holds primitive impulses toward cruelty in check—evolved most recently and thus is first to go when reversion sets in. But he concludes this passage with a notable aside about sadistic responses to threats, writing that the instinct to fight and destroy, "so important in prehistoric conditions," lives on "in the ideas engendered by civilisation, like that of 'the criminal,'" in which "it finds new objects."[84] Thus seemingly civilized people become punitively sadistic, wanting to torture and kill criminals and other enemies. Here Krafft-Ebing transforms an evolutionist explanation into an almost psychoanalytic account.

In Krafft-Ebing's late work, criminological thought has absorbed evolutionism and is beginning to move on to new types of theory. Whereas Maudsley and Dugdale were confirmed degenerationists, and Lombroso never swerved from his basic anthropological evolutionism, Krafft-Ebing is starting, at the century's end, to find the old evolutionist modes of explanation inadequate. He is feeling his way toward new approaches to defining and accounting for deviant behaviors.

## Galton and the Transition to Genetic Criminology

While Krafft-Ebing's late work hinted at the beginning of a major conceptual shift, that of Francis Galton helped accomplish the actual transition from the evolutionist explanations of 19th-century criminology to the genetic (and quasi-genetic) explanations that followed. Galton, who was born into a prosperous scientific family (Charles Darwin was a cousin), was left independently wealthy at the age of twenty-two by the death of his father and thus could pursue his manifold scientific interests at will. Close friends with some of the leading scientific writers of his day, including Darwin and Spencer, Galton very early in his own scientific career began to study the inheritance of mental abilities or intelligence—a phenomenon perhaps suggested by his own distinguished pedigree. He invented ways to apply statistics to evolutionary biology and came close to disproving the inheritance of acquired characteristics. Galton also coined the term *eugenics*, a word that soon attached itself to the nascent movement to improve human beings through selective breeding. The eugenics movement became a magnet for people involved in the social control of problem populations, giving them an apparently scientific foundation for their work and a program for social reform.

Especially important to the future of criminology was Galton's theoretical work on heredity, which seemed to prove that traits like intelligence could be inherited and thus to confirm that "nature" or heredity is more important than "nurture" or environment to the development of human behavior. In fact, Galton was the first to frame the evolutionist issue of inheritance in terms of nature versus nurture, a dichotomy he introduced in the title of his book *English Men of Science: Their Nature and Nurture* (1875).[85] This conceptualization shifted the debate among criminologists from one about the relative importance of species evolution versus inheritance in the causation of crime to one about the relative importance of heredity versus environment, an opposition—Galton's work seemed to show—in which heredity was the hands-down winner. Galton's nurture-versus-nature dichotomy dominated criminological debates for the next century.

*Inquiries into Human Faculty and Its Development* (1883), the work in which Galton coins the term *eugenics* (good stock), is also the most criminological of his books, including as it does material on composite photography of criminals and on Dugdale's book *"The Jukes,"* as well as a wide range of other topics such as statistics and differences in human intelligence. Galton's understanding of criminality is similar to that of Maudsley, Dugdale, Lombroso, and Krafft-Ebing insofar as he repeats the now-standard description of criminals as degenerates. Yet degeneration per se is of less interest to Galton than what it seems to demonstrate about the need to control human reproduction: "In every race of domesticated animals, and especially in the rapidly-changing race of man, there are elements, some ancestral and others the result of degeneration, that are of little or no value, or positively harmful.... [Thus] the natural characteristics of every human race [group or strain] admit of large improvement in many directions easy to specify."[86] Similarly, while Galton repeats the now tried-and-true principles of criminal anthropology, writing that the criminal class is by heredity closer to primitive societies than modern civilizations,[87] his most pressing concern is to point out that we could breed "superior strains or races" by "so favoring them that their progeny shall outnumber and gradually replace that of the old one."[88]

Galton played a pivotal role in the inauguration of modern genetics. As biographer Ruth Schwartz Cowan explains, "Many of the founders of modern genetics were inspired by his work, particularly ... *Natural Inheritance*, which appeared in 1889, just at the beginning of the twenty-year period in which modern genetics was born. What they found in his book was simply this: an operational definition for a word which had long been poorly defined—the word was 'heredity.'"[89] Most evolutionists, Cowan continues, still used the vague term *inheritance*, conceiving of it as some kind of force whereby

Composite photograph of prisoners. Francis Galton thought that by making composite photographs of criminals–superimposing a number of photographs on top of one another–he might arrive at a portrait of the average criminal. Galton eventually abandoned this method because it washed the "villainy" out of the features, but others pursued it. This composite from Ellis's book *The Criminal* (1890) combines images of thirty-eight prisoners at New York's Elmira Reformatory.

like begets like. The term *heredity*, according to Cowan, rarely turned up in English science writing before Galton started using it systematically to signify an intergenerational relationship, one that could be measured in individuals and populations. Moreover, Galton conceived of heredity as particulate, carried by discrete factors and not by amorphous "germ plasm"; in this respect, too, he paved the way for modern genetics. Thus, Cowan concludes, "the new science of genetics was based upon a definition of heredity that Galton had invented and first put to use."[90]

In *Inquiries into Human Faculty*, even more than in the perfunctory quality of some of Krafft-Ebing's late comments on degeneration, we see signs of criminology's end-of-the-century recovery from evolutionism. Galton has digested the idea of evolution and is ready to go beyond it, to use it "to further the ends of evolution more rapidly."[91] Even though criminality was not one of Galton's central concerns, his work presaged a major shift in criminology: from its 19th-century preoccupation with species evolution and degeneration to its early 20th-century interest in the particulate heredity of supposedly criminogenic traits, especially that of weak intelligence. Naturally, Galton did not bring about this change single-handedly. August Weismann's late 19th-century disproof of use-inheritance; the 1900 rediscovery of Gregor Mendel's work; and the subsequent introduction of basic genetic concepts (gene, genotype, phenotype)—these developments also served as midwives to early 20th-century eugenic criminology, as did the 1911 development by the eugenicists Henry H. Goddard and Charles B. Davenport of a family-tree methodology for documenting the transmission of supposedly single-gene traits (criminality, feeblemindedness, alcoholism) across generations.[92] But Galton's ideas formed a link between older and newer criminological concepts, making it possible to leave behind 19th-century ways of analyzing criminality.

Galton was a transitional figure in the history of criminology in four ways. First, his rejection of the vague concept of "inheritance" in favor of the more precise, particulate, and fixed "heredity" marked the beginning of the end for degenerationist views of crime as a manifestation of inner decay, easily interchangeable with other pathologies. That is, his work prompted criminologists to move away from "soft" hereditarianism and toward newer, "harder" ways of conceptualizing the relationship of criminality to heredity. Second, by more tightly coupling the ideas of developmental evolution and heredity, Galton largely eliminated the late 19th-century latitude to explain crime primarily in terms of backward species development (as Lombroso did) *or* degeneration (as did Dugdale). In today's language, he made it difficult to think of evolution in nongenetic terms. Third, Galton helped transform eugenic criminology from the vague, social Darwinist recommendations for eliminating criminals put forth by Maudsley and others into a vital part of a social movement replete with a name (*eugenics*), a science, and a program. Fourth and finally, his work marked the start of a criminological era in which the agenda for biocriminologists became a search for genetic factors that predispose offenders to crime. The search was impeded for a while by the flowering of sociological explanations in the early and mid–20th century and by revelations of the misuse of genetics by Nazi scientists. However, genetic criminology has since recovered its footing and is today advancing (as chapter 9 shows) at a rapid pace.

## The Evolutionist Heritage

Evolutionism created a crisis to which criminologists reacted by adopting the language and concepts of natural science. The crisis lay in evolutionism's implication of a nature without design. The very idea that species might be mutable flew in the face of the Old Testament story of God making every type of creature, complete and unchangeable, at the dawn of creation. And with the idea of species mutability came the possibility that morality, law, and all the fundamental arrangements of family and state might also be mutable, subject not to divine law but to the contingent, brutal laws of evolution. But if the world had not been designed by God, what was the source of morality? If nature, as Tennyson claimed, was "red in tooth and claw," might not human nature (or at least criminal nature) be innately brutish and violent? If so, did a criminal law based on assumptions of criminal responsibility become irrelevant? To address these questions, writers on criminological issues borrowed from Darwin, Haeckel, Lamarck, Morel, Spencer, and others, applying concepts such as atavism, degeneration, reversion, social evolution, and struggle for existence to the phenomenon of lawbreaking. About 1870, criminological thinking entered an evolutionist stage.

Late 19th-century authorities on crime drew on evolutionist ideas in a wide range of ways, creatively and piecemeal. Some, such as Maudsley, wove hereditarian and developmental-evolutionary ideas together so tightly as to bind them inseparably. Lombroso emphasized developmental evolution over heredity, while Dugdale, ignoring developmental concepts like atavism and natural selection, focused on inheritance. Krafft-Ebing drew on both concepts but tacked them on to his case studies in a way that suggests they were already losing their explanatory force. When Galton turned his attention to crime, he sidelined the idea of the criminal as an evolutionary laggard to concentrate on his central theme of hereditary worthiness.

To some extent the evolutionists were influenced by national scientific traditions—or the absence thereof. Maudsley's criminological thought stood squarely at the crossroads where English evolutionism intersected with research by British prison physicians such as J. Bruce Thomson. Dugdale, although he was a phenomenon unto himself, working at the outset of American sociology and evidently with no sense of belonging to a scientific tradition, nonetheless drew, like the other three, on the fundamental concepts of degeneration theory, the international lingua franca for analyzing social problems. Lombroso's criminal anthropology emerged from pre-Darwinian Italian work on evolution and anthropology, although he later drew further inspiration from the English evolutionists— Darwin, Maudsley, Spencer, Thomson. And Krafft-Ebing incorporated the morphological and embryological interests of German evolutionism.

Today as in the 19th century, developmental-evolutionist and genetic explanations of crime split off into separate discourses. Genetic criminologists, represented most prominently by Terrie Moffitt and her colleagues,[93] avoid speculating about evolution, concentrating instead on individual genetic differences that seem susceptible to biological explanation. Their work recalls that of Dugdale in its stress on nature-nurture interactions, although they conceptualize those interactions in terms of not soft but hard heredity. Today's evolutionary criminologists, on the other hand, tend to avoid speculating about genes—or at least about the functions of specific genes. Attributing criminal behavior to innate traits or instincts that at one time served an adaptive or reproductive function,[94] their work recalls that of Maudsley, Lombroso, and Krafft-Ebing. A third important strain in current theorizing, that of criminological neuroanatomists, argues that there are significant physical differences between the brains of at least some criminals and noncriminals.[95] It is tempting to term this third discourse neo-Lombrosian (especially when, paralleling the Italian's displays of criminal crania and pickled brains, it offers as evidence MRI images of criminals' prefrontal cortexes), but it has nothing to do with the idea of atavism and is compatible with environmental as well as genetic explanations. (Chapter 9 discusses current trends in biocriminology in more detail.)

There are, of course, marked differences between past and current biological theories of crime. Those of the present eschew both scientific racism and biological determinism. Unlike degenerationists, whose soft biosocial model was based on the idea of use-inheritance, today's genetic criminologists begin with a hard biosocial model according to which environmental factors may affect the *expression* of genes. And yet key assumptions from 19th-century biocriminology reappear in current work. Most basic is the assumption that lawbreakers differ from law-abiders at some biological level—that criminal behavior signifies, in at least serious cases, an underlying condition of criminality. This is not a hypothesis that grew out of research but rather a fundamental premise that provides a research starting point. Neither genetic nor evolutionary nor neuroanatomical criminologists arrived at their notion of a "biology of culpability"[96] through induction. Rather, like their 19th-century predecessors, they began by surmising that criminality is rooted in biology, and *then* they set out, from their various perspectives, to prove this. While few of them demonstrate awareness of their intellectual ancestry, they nonetheless draw on biological traditions as old as scientific criminology itself.

# PART II

# Biological Theories
# in the 20<sup>th</sup> Century

# 6

## Stupidity Theories

### The Backward Brain

In May 1927, Justice Oliver Wendell Holmes Jr., of the U.S. Supreme Court handed down a decision in the case of *Buck v. Bell, Superintendent* based on the feeblemindedness theory of crime.[1] The case involved Carrie Buck, a young woman who had been committed, involuntarily, to the Virginia State Colony for Epileptics and Feeble Minded. Virginia had passed an act authorizing involuntary sterilization of such residents on the grounds that the so-called feebleminded were a social menace and that their affliction was hereditary.

Justice Holmes described Carrie as "a feeble minded white woman . . . the daughter of a feeble minded mother in the same institution, and the mother of an illegitimate feeble minded child." Like many social leaders of his day, Holmes hoped to make government more efficient. He was concerned "that the Commonwealth is supporting in various institutions many defective persons who if now discharged would become a menace but if incapable of procreating might be discharged with safety and become self-supporting with benefit to themselves and to society." In his view, "heredity plays an important part in the transmission of insanity, imbecility, &c." If Carrie were not sterilized, she was likely to become the "parent of socially inadequate offspring" who would "sap the strength of the State" and "swamp" it with "incompetence." In words that would become famous, Holmes concluded, "It is better for all the world, if instead of waiting to execute degenerate offspring for crime, . . . society can prevent those who are manifestly unfit from continuing their kind. . . . Three generations of imbeciles are enough."[2]

And so Carrie Buck was sterilized in the name of crime control. Irving Whitehead, the lawyer who served as her advocate, had argued that sterilization would violate Carrie's "constitutional right of bodily integrity." Moreover, he had warned, if a government were able "to rid itself of those citizens deemed undesirable according to its standards," a "reign of doctors

Carrie Buck and her mother, Emma. Carrie Buck's case led the U.S. Supreme Court to authorize sterilization on the grounds that she was an imbecile, the daughter of an imbecilic mother, and thus someone doomed to bear imbecilic and criminalistic children. But Carrie Buck was not "feebleminded" after all; the court allowed itself to be misled by a false science of criminality. This photograph shows Carrie and Emma Buck at the Virginia Colony for Epileptics and Feebleminded on the day before the *Buck v. Bell* trial in Virginia. Arthur Estabrook Papers. M.E. Grenander Department of Special Collections and Archives, University of Albany Libraries.

will be inaugurated and in the name of science new classes will be added, even races may be brought within the scope of such regulation, and the worst forms of tyranny practiced." Whitehead's prediction was realized most completely in Nazi Germany, but the Nazis' sterilization law was based on American eugenics legislation.

Whitehead actually intended to lose Carrie's case—and he did.[3] Perhaps he would have been less successful in this aim had he not masked with constitutional arguments his close friendship and political alliances with those who sought to use Carrie as a test case, a prelude to many further sterilizations. Yet Whitehead's words did underscore the key issue. The Supreme Court was asked to void the constitutional right of a helpless young woman to "bodily integrity" because science predicted that her children would be criminals with feeble brains.

This chapter deals with the feeblemindedness theory of criminality—or *theory of deviance* might be a better term, given that Carrie had not committed a crime. The feeblemindedness theory rocketed into public consciousness around 1900, fueled by the newly invigorated eugenics movement—the campaign to encourage the "fit" to have more children and prevent the "unfit" from "breeding." The idea of the criminalistic imbecile became the basis of a crusade, a social movement to prevent crime by sexually immobilizing people deemed subnormal intellectually. I call the theory *eugenic criminology* and its advocates *eugenic criminologists*.

In some ways this chapter is an exercise in getting hold of slippery terms, for eugenic criminologists used language carelessly and self-indulgently—as indeed Justice Holmes did in his *Buck v. Bell* decision. When they claimed that "the feebleminded" were criminalistic, they often meant that only some very "high grade" people with mental retardation ("morons"; "defective delinquents") were criminally inclined—people in whom only experts could detect the mental defect. And when they claimed that most criminals are feebleminded, they often meant that *some* people convicted of crime had tested below average on intelligence tests. But their failures to define their terms meant that they could entertain the prospect of locking up and perhaps sterilizing large segments of the population ("the unfit"). Thus this chapter has to focus on ways in which linguistic imprecision became a means for eugenic criminologists to fantasize about what they thought would be a better world—a world with no more imbeciles.

For a brief period, the feeblemindedness explanation of crime became the most broadly—and enthusiastically—endorsed explanation of lawbreaking in U.S. history. Judges, university presidents, lawmakers, journalists, novelists (think of Lennie Small, the accidental killer in John Steinbeck's *Of Mice and Men*), ex-president Teddy Roosevelt ("we have no business to permit the perpetuation of citizens of the wrong type"),[4] Winston Churchill, psychiatrists, prison superintendents, and the heads of institutions such as the Virginia State Colony assumed the theory's validity and helped propagate it. It was the first "American" theory of crime—the first influential explanation of criminal behavior formulated primarily in the United States, although similar discourses were generated abroad, with lots of international give-and-take. And it was the first genetic theory of crime.

With the rediscovery of Mendel's laws of inheritance in 1900 and acceptance of the understanding of heredity as a phenomenon unaffected by environment, eugenics came into its own, becoming the basis of a reform movement that stretched from coast to coast and across the Atlantic into the heart of Europe.[5] It attracted the energies of many Americans, from housewives volunteering to make heredity charts in Faribault, Minnesota, to families competing in a Fitter Families Contest at the Texas State Fair.[6] While eugenicists had varying motivations, most of them hoped to restore America to an earlier, less complicated condition uncontaminated by immigrants, socialists, morons, and criminals, and generally they were driven by something very like a search for purity or lost innocence.[7] Control of criminals and the feebleminded was just one aspect of the eugenics agenda, which encompassed such causes as birth control and immigration restriction; but it was perhaps the most magnetizing aspect, attracting eugenic fieldworkers, institutional superintendents, prison reformers, psychiatrists, psychologists, wealthy philanthropists, and at least one Supreme Court justice to its cause. The eugenics movement as a whole began to lose steam around 1920, deflated by disproofs of its teachings about heredity and sobered by the grim realities of World War I. But some eugenicists remained missionaries for decades longer, and even today people are quick to associate criminality with mental retardation and bad heredity.[8] Long after eugenic criminology had been discredited, it continued to influence both the operation of criminal justice systems and scientific thinking about the causes of crime.

What made eugenic criminologists decide that the feebleminded were a menace and that crime could be reduced by preventing people like Carrie Buck from having children? Why did officials who worked closely with the mentally retarded and knew them to be no more criminalistic than anyone else, jump on this crime-control bandwagon? In what ways did the new science of genetics seem to confirm the theory of the feebleminded criminal? In what follows, I describe the unfolding of eugenic criminology in the early years of the 20th century. Then I argue that this movement in social control was in large part a movement in class control, one in which middle-class, "old" American eugenicists set out to defend themselves against groups they considered morally and biologically inferior. Continuing this argument, the next section maintains that eugenic criminology was essentially an antimodernist science, an effort to restore the world to a simpler, premodern past in which traditional social class relationships and traditional value systems would remain intact. The chapter's penultimate section follows the slow fade of eugenic criminology while demonstrating that, Lazarus-like, the theory continues to return from the dead. In conclusion I return to Carrie Buck, showing that none of the charges made against her by Justice Holmes was true.

## Eugenic Criminology

The belief that low intelligence is somehow linked to criminality lay dormant in evolutionist theory, waiting to emerge from its chrysalis. As early as 1870, J. Bruce Thomson had explained that criminals are abnormal in intellect as well as in their physical characteristics and moral sensibility, a claim he supported with studies suggesting that 12 percent of Scotland's adult prisoners suffered from some sort of "mental weakness." Worse, "so far as could be determined *the majority were congenitally weak-minded*"— their defects inherited.[9] Similarly, Lombroso: "If it were possible to measure the average intellectual capacity of criminals with the same accuracy with which we measure their cranial capacity, I am sure the results would be identical. The average would be lower than normal."[10]

The Hungarian criminal anthropologist Moriz Benedikt, in *Anatomical Studies upon Brains of Criminals* (1881), found that "the brains of criminals exhibit a deviation from the normal type," a frontal lobe abnormality indicating "deficiency—deficient gyrus development."[11] And according to *The Criminal* (1890), the influential work on criminal anthropology by the English eugenicist Havelock Ellis, the criminal's intelligence is characterized by two traits: stupidity and cunning. While these traits may seem incompatible, they "are in reality closely related, and they approximate him to savages and to the lower animals. Like the savage, the criminal is lacking in curiosity, the foundation of science, and one of the very highest acquisitions of the highly-developed man." True, criminals are often astute. "But what is this astuteness? It is an instinctive, innate faculty, which does not depend on real intelligence, and which is . . . found . . . in children, in the lowest savages, in women, and also in imbeciles."[12]

Thus were the associations woven, thread by thread, in one evolutionist study after another, among criminals, imbeciles, and other underdeveloped groups such as women, children, and savages. "Real intelligence," as Ellis called it, became a caste mark, the sign of "the highly-developed man." As the interwoven associations began to form full cloth, "intelligent" became a code word for the good, law-abiding, middle-class citizen. The term helped wedge a cultural and social divide between the worthy and unworthy, the healthy and the degenerate, the man of science and the man without curiosity—a restructuring of social values around the polarities of the intelligent and the imbecilic. The two groups now differed not in degree but in essence: in their germ plasm, their "heredity."[13]

### On the Cusp: Goring's *The English Convict*

In the early 20th century, one of the most impressive demonstrations of the mental backwardness of criminals was made by Charles Goring's *The English Convict* (1913). It is rare to find a book that says the opposite of what the author claims to have said, but Goring's book is one of those rarities. An English prison physician, Goring aimed at refuting the "superstition" of Lombrosianism. Indeed, he declared unequivocally that "there is no such thing as an anthropological criminal type." But his very next sentence stated "that, on the average, the criminal of English prisons is markedly differentiated by defective physique—as measured by stature and body weight; by defective mental capacity—as measured by general intelligence; and by an increased possession of wilful anti-social proclivities."[14] *The English Convict*, as Lombroso's daughter happily noted, actually constitutes "one of the most important and best arguments in favor of criminal anthropology."[15]

Goring became the first major British criminologist of the 20th century and an international leader in the criminalization of mental backwardness. America's premier criminological journal ran not one but several reviews of his book on the grounds that "no other recent research has attracted as much attention among criminologists, both in America and in Europe, as Dr. Goring's *The English Convict*."[16] This book is of interest here not only because it was a significant work of biocriminology but also because it shows how biological theory evolved after 1900, moving steadily toward acceptance of the idea that low intelligence somehow causes crime. Gradually criminologists shed the outward, anthropological trappings of evolutionist theory, looking inward from the skull to discover the backward brain. This brain was not *evolutionarily* backward in the sense of atavism but *intellectually* backward in the sense of mental defectiveness. Goring's criminal formed a link between the born criminal of evolutionist theory and the genetically doomed, feebleminded criminal who immediately followed.

Goring perpetuated the British tradition, inaugurated by J. B. Thomson and his cohort, whereby criminology was generated by prison physicians. However, to the study of his sample of 4,000 convicts Goring brought the statistical methods of Quetelet (mean values and the normal distribution), Galton (correlation and regression), and Karl Pearson (standard deviation, correlation, and regression coefficients).[17] By the time Goring undertook the analysis of his data at the Galton Eugenics Laboratory in London, such work had taken on the title of *biometrics*, meaning the statistical study of biological phenomena. Armed with biometrics, Goring was well prepared to take a significant step forward in criminological theory—and he did, insofar as he resisted the idea of a distinct criminal type and insisted on continuity of criminals with normal men.

However, that step did not make him nearly so anti-Lombrosian as he fancied,[18] and when it came to the study of criminal intelligence, his work suffered from a crucial methodological drawback: he had collected his data on prisoners' intelligence just before the advent of Binet's method of gauging ability by means of tests that could arrive at a "mental age." Instead, Goring had relied on "general impressions of mentality" by one or more prison officials, on the basis of which he then classified convicts into five categories: intelligent, fairly intelligent, unintelligent, weak-minded, and imbecile. Goring gives no criteria for forming these "general impressions of mentality"—a striking omission in a book fixated on the minutiae of careful measurement. This vagueness about the measurement of intelligence constitutes a key difference between Goring's work and the Mendelizing feeblemindedness studies that soon followed.

Goring's findings are easily summarized: Criminals (by which he meant men in prison) are shorter, intellectually weaker, and more antisocial than other men. Criminality can be eradicated only through eugenic measures. "Our figures [show] the comparatively insignificant relation of . . . environmental conditions with crime, and the high . . . association of feeble-mindedness with conviction for crime, and its well marked relation with alcoholism, epilepsy, sexual profligacy, ungovernable temper, obstinacy of purpose, and wilful anti-social activity—*every one of these, as well as feeble-mindedness, being heritable qualities.*"[19] Mentally defective criminals are particularly likely to commit arson, although they also have high rates for maiming animals and raping children. "The criminal" is "unquestionably a product of the most prolific stocks in the general community," although that fertility is curbed somewhat by imprisonment.[20] Here we see in action the building of the stereotype of the rapidly reproducing, ultradangerous feebleminded criminal.

*The English Convict*, widely reviewed and highly respected due in part to its heft (it runs to 440 oversized pages) and its statistical tables (another 84 pages), became a pivot point in the development of eugenic criminology, a strong demonstration that the criminal is a hereditary mental defective. It shows criminology on the cusp of the great changes brought on immediately after its publication by intelligence testing and the adoption of the Mendelian formula for inheritance. The next phase in biocriminology, that of the genetically doomed criminal imbecile, is all there in potentiality; what Goring lacks is the idea of "hard" or particulate heredity and a scientific method of measuring criminals' intelligence.

### Proving the Inheritance of Feeblemindedness

All the basics of eugenics were assembled in the late 19th century, including the image of the feebleminded as criminalistic and, after 1883, the term *eugenics* itself. What jolted eugenics into new life about 1900, turning it into a vigorous social movement, were two developments in genetics. First was the rediscovery of Gregor Mendel's work on heredity, showing that parental traits do not blend in offspring but rather are inherited in predictable ratios of dominants to recessives. Mendel's experiments with garden peas suggested that Francis Galton had been right when he postulated that traits are inherited as particles or unchangeable unit characteristics (what we today call genes). The second stimulant was August Weismann's disproof of the notion that acquired characteristics can be inherited. Weismann's work, like Mendel's, indicated that the germ plasm is impervious to changes in the environment.

These two scientific developments galvanized eugenicists. They seemed to make clear the impossibility of improving society by improving social conditions; from now on, reformers would have to prevent those with negative traits from reproducing.

Needed next was a demonstration that feeblemindedness and other negative traits are transmitted as unit characters, like height in Mendel's experiments with garden peas. This problem was solved by Henry H. Goddard, the psychologist at the Vineland, New Jersey, Training School for Feeble-minded Boys and Girls, who early in the 20th century emerged as a national leader of the campaign to criminalize the feebleminded.[21] The Vineland institution, too, emerged as a leader in this project: not only did it include on its staff Henry Goddard, the first professional psychologist to specialize in mental retardation;[22] it was also able to attract funding for eugenics research. Samuel Fels, a wealthy soap manufacturer and another eugenicist, helped support Goddard's investigations.

To demonstrate that feeblemindedness is inherited according to Mendel's formula, Goddard produced a pedigree study of a family he nicknamed the Kallikaks (from the Greek, meaning "the good-bads"). In the background lay Dugdale's *"The Jukes"* and the studies of other degenerate clans it had inspired such as "The Tribe of Ishmael" (1888), "The Smoky Pilgrims" (1897), and the Zeros (1907).[23] Goddard trained an assistant, Elizabeth S. Kite, in the techniques of "eugenic field research"—meaning methods of tracking down members of degenerate families—and sent her off into New Jersey's Pine Barrens to find relatives of a Vineland inmate ("Deborah Kallikak"). Using eyeball methods to estimate the intelligence of the people she met, together with suppositions about the intelligence of their long-dead relatives, Kite cobbled together a preliminary report, which Goddard then polished up into one of the most famous of all eugenics tracts: *The Kallikak Family: A Study in the Heredity of Feeblemindedness.*

*The Kallikak Family* traces two branches of a single family, both sired by Martin Kallikak Sr., at the time of the Revolutionary War. The bad branch, flowing from Martin's illicit liaison with "a nameless feeble-minded girl," included more than 180 illegitimate, alcoholic, epileptic, and (especially) feebleminded and criminalistic descendants, ending with Deborah, who, institutionalized as she was at Vineland, would fortunately end that line. The other branch, stemming from Martin's marriage to "a respectable girl of good family," included 496 descendants, "men and women prominent in every phase of social life."[24]

Thus nature had thoughtfully provided in the Kallikaks a controlled experiment showing that heredity determines character and that "no amount of education or good environment can change a feeble-minded individual into a normal one."[25] Goddard's contribution lay not only in reporting this remarkable natural testimony on the heredity of feeblemindedness but also in illustrating it with an ingenious iconography that enabled readers to visualize the march of bad heredity through the generations.[26] Indicating males with boxes and females with circles, and marking the center of each box or circle with an "N" for "normal" intelligence or an "F" for feeblemindedness, Goddard's famous chart of Martin Kallikak's progeny visually confirmed the supposition that feeblemindedness is a recessive unit character, inherited according to Mendel's law.

Also needed was an efficient method of identifying the feebleminded, and in this case, too, Goddard came to the rescue. At the time he became director of research at the Vineland institution, in 1906, there was no efficient method of identifying the feebleminded and classifying them by "grade" or teachability. So serious was the problem that the superintendent of Vineland shipped Goddard off to Europe to see if he could find useful methods there. Goddard learned of the paper-and-pencil tests being developed by the French psychologist Alfred Binet and his collaborator,

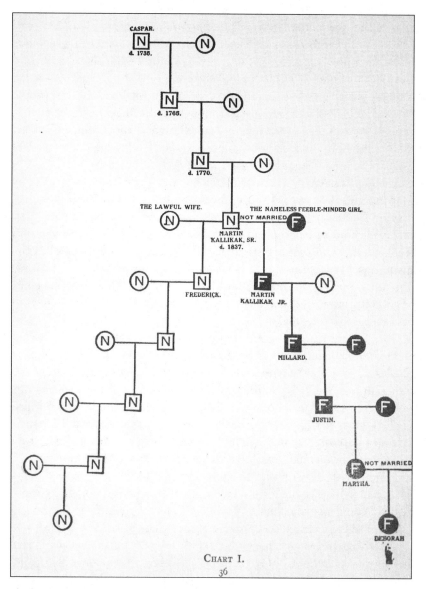

CHART I.

36

The heredity of feeblemindedness. This heredity chart from Henry H. Goddard's book *The Kallikak Family* (1912) seemed to prove scientifically that feeblemindedness ("F") and normal intelligence ("N") are inherited as unit characteristics. Goddard's research methods, which enabled him to determine the intelligence of people who had died nearly 200 years earlier, pointed to eugenic solutions to social problems.

Dr. Théodore Simon, a method that keyed questions to levels of mental development and enabled testers to scale results by "mental age." Returning to the States, Goddard translated, revised, and published Binet's questions. "Between 1910 and 1914," Kite reported in an explanatory brochure, "20,000 booklets and 80,000 record blanks were printed and distributed from the Vineland Laboratory alone," to which she helpfully added, "Copy of the scale, with Goddard's explanation of its use and application can be secured from the Committee on Provision for the Feeble-Minded [a leading eugenics organization], Empire Bldg., Phila. Price, 15 cents."[27]

The lid was off the pot, but the pot was full of worms: untrained testers, unstandardized tests, and questions that were too tough at the upper levels or that called for subjective answers. (A question for mental age XII, for instance, called for definitions of charity, justice, and goodness.)[28] The psychologist Lewis Terman, yet another eugenicist, issued a revision of the Binet tests that introduced the concept of intelligence quotient or IQ, but it was years before intelligence testing achieved anything close to objectivity (some would argue that we are not there yet). The early years of IQ testing, then, were something of a free-for-all, and as result, many perfectly normal children and adults were misdiagnosed as feebleminded.

### Proving the Imbecility of Criminals

Binet testing enabled Goddard to clear up some of the terminological confusion that had reigned for decades in the area of mental retardation and to specify exactly which members of the genus *feebleminded* were bound to become criminals. He proposed defining the levels of mental retardation by mental age: *idiots* would be those who tested under one or two years, *imbeciles* those who tested at mental ages three to seven, and *morons* (a term Goddard invented from Greek for "childish" or "foolish") those who tested between eight and twelve and seemed so normal that only trained professionals like himself could identify them. Goddard's aim in introducing the new term was partly to sensitize the public to morons' unfitness and increase the likelihood of their institutionalization: "One of the most helpful things that we can do would be to . . . help the general public to understand that 'morons' are a special group and require special treatment,—in institutions when possible, in special classes in public schools, when institutions are out of reach."[29] The superintendents of institutions for the mentally retarded accepted the new terminology, and a campaign to identify previously undetected morons got under way.

Goddard's contribution to criminology was to equate the moron with the moral imbecile. Among both prison officials and specialists in mental retardation, the suspicion had been growing for decades that the feebleminded were inherently criminalistic. Goddard confirmed this suspicion by Binet-testing Vineland's moral imbeciles, a group of twenty-three of the institutions' most disobedient children, some with "marked sexual disturbance." All twenty-three tested between the mental ages of nine and twelve, thus cementing, in Goddard's mind, the identity of the moral imbecile and the moron.[30] Drawing on Haeckel's recapitulation theory, Goddard hypothesized that the "primitive" instincts

> that lead the child to become what we loosely call a moral imbecile, ripen about the age of nine years; now if a child is arrested in his development at just about that time then he is a liar, a thief, a sex pervert, or whatever else he may be, because those instincts are strong in him. . . . Had he been arrested in his development a year or two sooner, he would not have been a moral imbecile because the instincts that lead to it had not developed.

Or, if development stopped later, "he would have developed sufficient reasoning power to enable him to overcome and control those instincts." Morons, because their moral evolution stopped "at just that critical period of nine," would inevitably be liars, thieves, and other criminal types.[31]

This conclusion was all the easier to make due to the long-standing tradition of using moral and social criteria to diagnose feeblemindedness, on the one hand, and intellectual criteria to diagnose criminality, on the other. For instance, it was not at all unusual in the late 19th and early 20th centuries to decide that women who had engaged in premarital sex were feebleminded, criminalistic, or both. (Such reasoning lay behind New York State's founding of a eugenic custodial institution for "feebleminded" women.)[32] Thus the superintendents of institutions for the feebleminded did not object when Goddard used social and moral criteria to equate the moron with the moral imbecile. (Soon thereafter, in fact, he started called the moron a "criminal imbecile.")[33] Indeed, they welcomed his clarification, for by now most of them were administering large institutions on extensive acreage, and they needed rationales for retaining morons, mischievous though they might be, to do the farming and other heavy work for which otherwise the officials would have had to hire labor. (Of course, since those diagnosed as morons by Goddard's Binet tests were in many cases probably normal in intelligence, or close to it, they in particular were likely to act out when institutionalized—again confirming the equation of morons with offenders.)

The feebleminded had been criminalized, but to show that the equation of the feebleminded and the criminal worked in both directions, a final step was necessary: to "moronize" the criminal. This step was easily accomplished by Binet-testing institutionalized delinquents. Large proportions of these populations, as Goddard reported in *Feeble-mindedness: Its Causes and Consequences,* flunked the tests; in fact, the better the tester, the larger the proportion of morons in the test results.[34] Generalizing from juvenile delinquents to adult criminals, Goddard estimated that 25 to 50 percent of all convicts, if tested, would prove to be mentally defective. "The so-called criminal type is merely a type of feeble-mindedness," he concluded. Then, openly bidding to replace the criminal anthropologist as the chief authority on crime, Goddard claimed, "It is hereditary feeble-mindedness not hereditary criminality that accounts for the conditions."[35] The criminal had become feebleminded or (to use yet another favorite phrase of this period so rich in terminology for mentally retarded people) a "defective delinquent."

## Social Class and Social Control

The effort to control the feebleminded criminal constituted a movement in not only crime control but also social class control. It was a social reform movement in a period of social reform movements, one often termed the Progressive Era. Progressives were concerned with a wide array of social issues, from political corruption and alcohol consumption to land conservation and enabling women to vote. They included social control professionals who embraced the gospel of eugenics. Eugenic criminology involved three classes: the "unfit"; the moneyed elite whose members financed the movement; and the Progressive social control professionals who did the legwork on eugenic legislation and criminal justice reform. The social class interests that coursed just below the surface of the feeblemindedness theory of crime help explain its content and its appeal to eugenic criminologists.

Ostensibly, the eugenics movement aimed at the reproductive immobilization of the feebleminded, but because feeblemindedness was now regarded as fundamental, *the* cause underlying other social problems, when eugenicists spoke of *the feebleminded,* they referred to other unfit types as well. These included unreformable convicts, paupers, anarchists, immigrants from southern and eastern Europe, the insane, and strikebreakers. In the view of Martin Barr, a specialist in mental retardation, the high-grade feebleminded included the "queer, nervous, misanthropical, moody; the weak dude; the silly coquette"; the lustful; gossips; "the dipsomaniac; the kleptomaniac; the pyromaniac"; murderers, harlots, agents provocateurs; epileptics; hypochondriacs; and egotists—and this is far from the end of his list. According to Barr, all were "born" moral imbeciles who should be committed to institutions for the feebleminded to protect "the pure stock from contamination."[36] In this usage, the *feebleminded* was synonymous with the *unfit* and roughly equivalent to the subproletariat: unreliable, inefficient, or uncompliant workers, the unemployable, and others who sapped state coffers in their need for welfare.[37] In the pulsating language of eugenics, the *feebleminded* could indicate people with mental retardation or an entire social class that needed to be brought under control. The term's vagueness merely increased its political usefulness.

The second class, members of the moneyed elite, helped finance eugenic criminology. Andrew Carnegie, Samuel S. Fels, Daniel Guggenheim, Mary Harriman, John D. Rockefeller Jr., William Rockefeller, Mortimer L. Schiff, and F. W. Vanderbilt were among the plutocrats who contributed, either directly or through foundations they had funded.[38] Some underwrote the research for or publication of studies of Juke-like bad families; some contributed to training police officers to recognize morons on the streets of New York City; and John D. Rockefeller Jr., who was probably the most deeply involved, financed the founding of a eugenic prison on land he had owned in Bedford, New York. They contributed because they, too, wanted to participate in the period's reforms—because they, too, were allured by the Progressive ideals of increasing efficiency and purifying society. Moreover, participating in civic reforms gave them a way to demonstrate that—notwithstanding their often heartless business maneuvers—they were responsible citizens. The fight against the feebleminded criminal, moreover, offered ways to strengthen their self-interests, as when Adolph Lewisohn, a well-to-do industrialist with an interest in a disciplined workforce, chaired a committee to centralize and improve the efficiency of New York's prison industries.[39] In its vague way, the movement to control the feebleminded promised to weed out slackers and to institute reproductive controls on the unemployable and those who depended on state welfare. While these wealthy contributors probably achieved far less than they had hoped, their reforms did contribute to the restructuring of social values that occurred during the Progressive Era, a shift to greater emphasis on efficiency, workplace discipline, and promotion through merit.

Third, the movement to control crime by controlling reproduction of the feebleminded attracted middle-class reformers. This was true of most Progressive causes, but eugenic criminology drew in a special subtype of middle-class reformer: social control professionals, the segment of the labor market that began to emerge in the late 19th century.[40] The workplace identities (and incomes) of social control professionals such as psychiatrists, mental testers, social workers, and prison administrators rested on their claims to expertise; thus, not surprisingly, they hoped to see society reorganized as a meritocracy, one administered by those who were worthy, intelligent, and well trained—Progressive men and women like themselves.[41] Hence their hearty endorsement of the medical model, which located the source of social problems not in social or economic factors but in inherited "fitness." Socially problematic groups, as sociologist L. J. Ray points out, were "the antithesis of the professional middle class" in that they were considered "both inherently degenerate, and highly fertile."[42] By imposing eugenic constraints on the feebleminded, social control professionals furthered their own interests while at the same time excising the "festering sores" of the body social.[43]

Nowhere were the social class interests involved in eugenic criminology better illustrated than in a Princeton University lecture series given in 1919 by Henry Goddard and published as *Human Efficiency and Levels of Intelligence*. In this model of Progressive reasoning, Goddard begins by claiming, on the basis of U.S. Army test results, that 45 percent of the U.S. population is intellectually subnormal. To improve national efficiency, he recommends giving everyone a mental test and then assigning workers to jobs graded according to the level of intelligence required. "An ideally efficient society then would be made up of the right proportion of individuals to do all the different types of work that are to be done and each man doing the work for which he is just capable."[44] Next Goddard defines "delinquency" (by which he means adult as well as juvenile criminality) in terms of "social and moral" inefficiency: "Delinquency is an offense because it impairs the efficiency of the group."[45] Most crimes are committed by the feebleminded, but these delinquents are not responsible for their offenses because they are mentally subnormal. Ninety percent of feebleminded delinquents should be placed in institutions for the feebleminded. This will require a threefold expansion of that institutional system—"a big expense; but what compensation!"[46] Crime would be reduced by 25 to 50 percent,

---

### Test 8

Notice the sample sentence: People *hear* with the  *eyes*  *ears*  *nose*  *mouth*
The correct word is *ears,* because it makes the truest sentence.

In each of the sentences below you have four choices for the last word. Only one of them
is correct. In each sentence draw a line under the one of these four words which makes
the truest sentence. If you can not be sure, guess. The two samples are already marked
as they should be.

---

SAMPLES { People *hear* with the   *eyes*   *ears*   *nose*   *mouth*
{ *France* is in   *Europe*   *Asia*   *Africa*   *Australia*

|  |  |
|---|---|
| 1. The *apple* grows on a   *shrub*   *vine*   *bush*   *tree* | 1 |
| 2. *Five hundred* is played with   *rackets*   *pins*   *cards*   *dice* | 2 |
| 3. The *Percheron* is a kind of   *goat*   *horse*   *cow*   *sheep* | 3 |
| 4. The most prominent industry of *Gloucester* is   *fishing*   *packing* *brewing*   *automobiles* | 4 |
| 5. *Sapphires* are usually   *blue*   *red*   *green*   *yellow* | 5 |
| 6. The *Rhode Island Red* is a kind of   *horse*   *granite*   *cattle*   *fowl* | 6 |
| 7. *Christie Mathewson* is famous as a   *writer*   *artist*   *baseball player* *comedian* | 7 |
| 8. *Revolvers are made by*   Swift & Co.   Smith & Wesson   W. L. Douglas B. T. Babbitt | 8 |
| 9. *Carrie Nation* is known as a   *singer*   *temperance agitator*   *suffragist*   *nurse* | 9 |
| 10. *"There's a reason"* is an "ad" for a   *drink*   *revolver*   *flour*   *cleanser* | 10 |
| 11. *Artichoke* is a kind of   *hay*   *corn*   *vegetable*   *fodder* | 11 |
| 12. *Chard* is a   *fish*   *lizard*   *vegetable*   *snake* | 12 |
| 13. *Cornell University* is at   *Ithaca*   *Cambridge*   *Annapolis*   *New Haven* | 13 |
| 14. *Buenos Aires* is a city of   *Spain*   *Brazil*   *Portugal*   *Argentina* | 14 |
| 15. *Ivory* is obtained from   *elephants*   *mines*   *oysters*   *reefs* | 15 |
| 16. *Alfred Noyes* is famous as a   *painter*   *poet*   *musician*   *sculptor* | 16 |
| 17. The *armadillo* is a kind of   *ornamental shrub*   *animal*   *musical instrument* *dagger* | 17 |
| 18. The *tendon of Achilles* is in the   *heel*   *head*   *shoulder*   *abdomen* | 18 |
| 19. *Crisco* is a   *patent medicine*   *disinfectant*   *tooth-paste*   *food product* | 19 |

World War I Alpha test. The Alpha Test, of which this is a partial example, was
used to test the intelligence of literate army recruits. Leading to the diagnosis of
many normal men as feebleminded, it fueled eugenic criminology.

and because the regular criminal justice system would be bypassed, court
and prison costs would be reduced as well. To assure that the best shall
rule, governments should not permit the feebleminded to vote; nor should
they educate the feebleminded to read and write. Rather, the feebleminded
should be trained to be cooks, factory workers, and so on, depending on
local needs. Eventually, they can be released from institutions to live and
work in nearby communities.

Goddard is clear that his topic is "the social control of the unintelligent
and inefficient."[47] He envisions a society in which science in the form of
mental testing would steer decision making—with mental testers at the
helm. By denying the feebleminded both education and the vote, he would
turn them into a permanent underclass. While Goddard did not speak

for everyone involved in the work of social control, his Princeton lectures illustrate how social control of the feebleminded could segue, in the minds of Progressive professionals, into social control of the entire underclass.

Yet the interests of middle-class professionals in controlling the feebleminded criminal were symbolic as well as instrumental, reflecting (as born-criminal theories over time have tended to do) fundamental fears of defilement. In the late 18ᵗʰ and early 19ᵗʰ centuries, at the close of the so-called Age of Reason, born-criminal theorists explained criminality in terms of the condition that seemed to them to most defile humanity and reduce people to the levels of beasts: total irrationality of the moral faculty or "moral insanity." In the late 19ᵗʰ century, the great era of evolutionism, born-criminal theory again reflected fundamental social fears, in this case anxiety about failing to progress or even devolving, a fear reflected in anthropological and degenerationist explanations of criminality. In the early 20ᵗʰ century, with the advent of genetics, defilement lay in having bad germ plasm.

More specifically, eugenic criminologists' anxiety lay in the thought of *undetectable* pollution. The Progressive Era was an idealistic and even utopian period, shot through with yearning for improvement and moral purity. For early 20ᵗʰ-century eugenicists, writes historian Harry Bruinius, "America, more than any other nation, held the promise of being a land of innocence, free from the defects of the past."[48] The feeblemindedness scare reflected fear of defilement through deception, misunderstanding, or ignorance. People wanted to keep their innocence intact, but feeblemindedness theory suggested that they and their society could be tricked, deceived by an unknowable, underlying contamination— undetected bad germ plasm. Hence the moron: the unrecognizable pollutant, dangerous and corrupting, cloaked in deceptive normality, the secret menace in their midst.

Thus some aspects of eugenic criminology, particularly its loathing for the mentally retarded, may be explained by the metaphorical and symbolic dimensions of "the menace of the feebleminded." The reformers had much more at stake than social control of the small proportion of the population that was genuinely retarded—and that, in any case, was not unusually criminalistic. They vilified the feebleminded because this group represented a threat to their social class and traditional way of life; because they defined themselves in opposition to it; because they believed in meritocracy. Worst of all, they felt defiled by a group that seemed both fecund and dirty in its very essence, befouled in its germ plasm.

Fig. 53.—Group Examination Beta, Form 0, Test 6, Picture Completion.

World War I Beta test. The Beta test, of which this is a partial example, was used to test the intelligence of illiterate army recruits. It, too, provided evidence for eugenic criminology and the social class prejudices that undergirded it.

## *The Science of Nostalgia*

Yet another way to understand eugenic criminology is to look at it as science, and here a comparison with Lombroso's science is instructive. Lombroso never doubted that science would automatically lead to truth and improve the world. He assumed that science was part of progress and that progress, in and of itself, was both good and inevitable. Eugenic criminologists, in contrast, were unsure that science, left to itself, would make the world better; nor did they share Lombroso's faith in the beneficence of progress. Rather, their science was shaped by a set of impulses that might be called *antimodernist*.

Eugenic criminology was part of a much larger effort to come to terms with ways the world had changed since the late 19th century—the growth of cities and of social class divisions, the fragmentation of work, secularization, the increasing emphasis on rationalist and positivist approaches to social problems, and what seemed to be life's ever-growing unpredictability. Evolutionary theory, industrialization, and world war had made it impossible to continue believing that (in the words of historian Dorothy Ross) "a beneficial order existed in history."[49] These changes precipitated the *modernist* movement, a current in social thought that was broad and amorphous, and that remains difficult to define.[50] Although it is associated mainly with the arts and architecture, modernism affected the sciences as well.

Some scientists—those aligned with modernism—decided to live with the issues of uncertainty presented by the world's changing circumstances; accepting the realities of their time, they tackled problems straightforwardly, without reference to their personal regrets and nostalgias. But others evinced antimodernist reactions. In both Europe and the United States, as social histories of science have shown,[51] antimodernism manifested itself in efforts to yoke science to the restoration of a more spiritual existence; in interest in the irrational; in rejection of mass culture; in nostalgia for the past; and in a retreat into eugenical racism. Historian Anne Harrington characterizes the antimodernist reaction in science as a quest for wholeness and "reenchantment." Harrington explains that in Germany in the period 1890–1933, some scientists rethought the "epistemological and methodological standards for science. Under the banner of Wholeness, these scientists argued, in varying ways, that a transformed biology and psychology—one that viewed phenomena less atomistically and more 'holistically,' less mechanistically and more 'intuitively'—could lead to the rediscovery of a nurturing relationship with the natural world."[52]

The antimodernist tradition that Harrington identifies in the history of German science is one in which many eugenic criminologists, American and European, participated. They were drawn to and used specific sciences—intelligence testing, eugenics, genetics—to satisfy their nostalgia for a simpler, more innocent world. In background, most eugenic criminologists were middle-class Anglo-Saxons; many had grown up in positions of privilege, at a time when class divisions seemed firmer and more settled. The new world of the 20<sup>th</sup> century was one of promise but also of upheaval. They hoped science would restore the "enchanted," innocent world of their childhood, uncomplicated by problems like immigration, crime, socialism, sexuality, urbanization, and poverty. Eugenic criminology seemed to offer an opportunity to return to a world where their sort were still firmly in control. Like other antimodernists, eugenic criminologists hoped that science could reinforce traditional values, in their case by demonstrating the importance of "intelligence"— good character, moral principles, and Anglo-Saxon background—while fending off the tides of change.

Antimodernist science was less a reaction against science itself than a series of attempts to harness science to antimodernist ideals. In its way, it was utopian. It was simultaneously rational and irrational,[53] and its paradoxical nature helps explain the rapid leaps in eugenic criminology from "the feebleminded," meaning people with mental retardation, to "the feebleminded," meaning all of the unfit. Eugenicists were devoted to science and its ideal of objectivity, but they did not test hypotheses in the modernist scientific mode, nor did they care much about the quality of their information. Instead, they amassed data in a manner that now seems unscientific, and they used those data to reach conclusions that satisfied nostalgic longings.

Eugenic criminologists, then, were not antiscience—quite the contrary: they wanted to use science to improve the world. But they were *antimodernist* scientists, men and women who hoped that science would enable them to hang onto the world they were losing. They were closer to Galton, who wanted to *use* science to make the world better, than to Lombroso, who was confident that science would make the world better without assistance, with science shaping values, not the other way around. The next chapter gives additional examples of antimodernist impulses, for they also lay behind Earnest Hooton's midcentury attempt to resurrect criminal anthropology and William Sheldon's introduction of somatotyping.

## Retractions and Resurrections

By the 1920s, eugenic criminology had lost its appeal as a popular cause. Improvements in mental testing cast doubt on the early findings of Goddard and other psychometricians, making it more difficult to label criminals feebleminded. The Mendelian model of inheritance, basic to the eugenics' movement's inflated claims, became its Achilles' heel as geneticists realized that feeblemindedness, criminality, and the other signs of degeneration could rarely if ever be inherited as single units. Psychiatrists, concerned about psychologists' claims that they could identify criminally irresponsible defendants through mental testing, moved to regain their power to determine criminal responsibility by redefining dangerousness in terms of "the psychopath," a figure who clearly fell into their jurisdiction.[54] Eventually, even psychologists converted to the view that psychopathy or mental illness was a fundamental cause of criminality.[55] Another tide turner was the psychiatrist William Healy's widely admired book *The Individual Delinquent*, a work that argued against simplistic, monocausal theories of crime in favor of a psychiatric, multifactorial approach.[56] On the other side of the Atlantic, Cyril Burt's *Young Delinquent*, the British counterpart to Healy's book, also rejected hereditarian theories in favor of a multicausal environmentalism.[57] As the wind went out of the sails of the eugenics movement,[58] standard-bearers in the criminalization of the mentally retarded conceded that they had been wrong. Walter E. Fernald, head of the Massachusetts institution—he who had announced in 1908 that "every imbecile . . . is a potential criminal"—admitted a decade later that "not all the feeble-minded are criminalists and socialists and immoral and anti-social . . . . We have really slandered the feeble-minded."[59]

The equation of criminality with feeblemindedness was further weakened by the rise of sociological theories of crime. Starting about 1900, sociologists added their voices to the biological discourses that until then had dominated criminology. Not only did sociologists seek the causes of crime in social factors; they also demanded better use of statistics in criminological theory. In 1931 Edwin Sutherland, fast becoming one of America's leading sociologists, published a devastating review of approximately 350 studies of intelligence and crime, concluding dryly that "feeble-mindedness has not been demonstrated to be a generally important cause of delinquency."[60]

But so effective had the campaign against the feebleminded been, and so powerfully had it appealed to deep-seated anxieties, that decades passed before the recantations and refutations reversed the tide. The progression can be traced in criminological texts. *Crime, Abnormal Minds, and the Law*, a textbook published in 1923, has chapters on other deviant types as well, but it opens with a chapter titled "The Defective Criminal" and observes that in this case, "permanent segregation . . . may be the kindest and most efficient form of treatment."[61] A decade later, Sheldon Glueck and Eleanor Glueck published *Five Hundred Delinquent Women*, a study of inmates at the Massachusetts reformatory for women, the majority of whom had been sentenced for prostitution and other sex offenses. While the Gluecks scrupulously noted that "little of a conclusive nature is yet known about the heredity of mental disease or its relation to criminality," they show the eugenicist's moral contempt for "this swarm of defective, diseased, antisocial misfits," recommending for them totally indefinite sentences.[62] Another decade later, in the 1940s, the popular textbook *New Horizons in Criminology* rejected the idea that mental retardation is mainly inherited and that the feebleminded are inherently criminal or vicious.[63] But this refutation and others like it did not entirely kill off eugenic criminology.

For instance, a return to feeblemindedness theory, albeit to a pale and attenuated form of the doctrine, occurs in *The Bell Curve* (1994), the controversial book by psychologist Richard Herrnstein and political scientist Charles Murray. Herrnstein and Murray argue that "cognitive ability is substantially heritable" (between 40 and 80 percent);[64] that social class is now determined largely by intelligence; and that the top of the social class hierarchy is occupied by a cognitive elite. Occupations, Herrnstein and Murray continue, sort us out by intelligence, so that the people with the highest IQs get the best jobs and earn the most money; this process, which keeps our society efficient and productive, is fair and good. Conversely, low IQ is one of the main determinants of poverty and crime.

In many ways, *The Bell Curve* merely updates points Henry Goddard had made seventy-five years earlier in *Human Efficiency and Levels of Intelligence*, but in this case, instead of three social classes, only two are relevant, those at the tail ends of the bell curve: the cognitive elite and the underclass, the bright and the dumb, us and them. (Indirectly addressing this change, Herrnstein and Murray maintain that middle-class professionals have *become* the elite.[65] The authors also recognize that the great mass of American society lies between the two extremes, but this group is irrelevant to their central argument.) Like the label "feebleminded," Herrnstein and Murray's "low cognitive ability" is a broadly inclusive term, covering recent immigrants, criminals, the unemployed, the chronically ill, the divorced and the illegitimate, and those who rely on welfare. While they do not claim that low intelligence is the sole cause of crime, Herrnstein and Murray do view it as *one* of the leading causes, and while they do not make specifically eugenic recommendations, they edge close to doing so. Like Goddard, they want to see a matching of low-IQ people with low-IQ jobs; they, too, worry that the underclass is undermining democracy; and they, too, endorse government by a meritocracy in which their own kind will be in charge.

What are we to make of these similarities? Herrnstein and Murray echo Goddard because they, too, engage in antimodernist science, using science in an attempt to restore a premodernist world. Following the lead of Edmund Burke, the Irish political philosopher revered by American conservatives, Herrnstein and Murray regard the French Revolution as a "perversion of the egalitarian ideal" because it tried to make people equal, whereas they are not.[66] Describing their viewpoint as "decidedly traditional,"[67] they idealize hierarchical, paternalistic social arrangements. Like earlier feeblemindedness theorists, they practice a science of nostalgia. Their work demonstrates once again how closely some Americans associate "intelligence" with "merit" of all kinds, including the merit of obeying the law. It illustrates how easy it is to envisage a society in which science (in the form of mental testing) might guide social control and create a near-permanent underclass.

Both *Human Efficiency* and *The Bell Curve* teach us to beware of stupidity theories of crime, at least those pitched on a biological foundation. The mental-measurement sciences, as chapter 8 on Nazi criminology further demonstrates, have proven themselves all too liable to misuse as instruments for social control.

Another return to quasi-eugenical ideas about crime control can be found in a 2001 paper contending that legalized abortion contributed significantly to recent reductions in crime rates. Economists John J. Donahue and Steven D. Levitt mention neither eugenics nor mental retardation, but they do argue that crime rates began falling eighteen years after the U.S. Supreme Court decision in *Roe v. Wade* legalized abortion, eliminating significant numbers of people from the population as they would have reached their high-crime years. Legalized abortion, Donahue and Levitt maintain, accounts for about 50 percent of the recent drop in crime. They also maintain that crime rates began declining even earlier in states that allowed abortion before *Roe*.[68]

This paper precipitated an avalanche of debate, with some critics going to far as to argue the reverse—that violent crime actually increases with rises in abortion rates.[69] It now seems likely that the legalization of abortion had no more than a small effect (if any) on crime rates, but the controversy is important in showing how the ideas of birth prevention and crime control continue to coalesce, magnetizing one another. In the future, as genome reading becomes more common, we are likely to see a new wave of quasi-eugenic explanations of crime rates and new proposals for gene-based programs of crime control.

## The Lesson of Eugenic Criminology

The life story of Oliver Wendell Holmes Jr. is a case history in worthiness: Holmes was a Harvard University graduate (B.A. and law degree); a Civil War hero; an internationally influential legal theorist; chief justice of the Massachusetts Supreme Judicial Court; and for thirty years an associate justice of the U.S. Supreme Court. His face has appeared on a postage stamp, and his life has been memorialized in a play, a television special, and several biographies. But when it came to Carrie Buck, Justice Holmes was wrong on every point.

In "Three Generations, No Imbeciles," his iconoclastic article on Carrie Buck's case, Paul Lombardo of the University of Virginia shows that neither Carrie nor her mother nor her daughter was an "imbecile." In fact, Carrie and her daughter were intellectually normal; her mother may have been so as well, although there is too little evidence to be sure. Lombardo further reports that Carrie was not "immoral"—the basis of the moral degeneracy charge against her, and of Holmes's amazing prediction that if left unsterilized, she would bear "degenerate offspring" who would eventually be executed for their crimes. In fact, Carrie had borne an illegitimate child because she had been raped.[70]

One piece of evidence introduced against Carrie at her original sterilization hearing was a deposition from Harry Laughlin, the assistant director of the Eugenics Record Office at Cold Spring Harbor, New York. Laughlin was naturally the person to turn to for evidence on the innate criminality of the feebleminded, for it was he who had written the Model Eugenical Sterilization Law on which Virginia's law—the one being tested by Carrie's case—had been based.[71] A few years later, the Nazis used Laughlin's model act as the basis for their own eugenic sterilization legislation. In gratitude, they awarded him an honorary degree at Heidelberg University for his contributions to racial hygiene.[72]

The mistakes of history have nothing to do with good or bad intentions. Holmes, Laughlin, the eugenic criminologists who labored in the trenches to detect defective delinquents—even Hitler—threw themselves into the work of political and social reform. With the possible exception of Hitler, who may have been more cynical in the matter, they trusted science to guide their reforms. Eugenics not only provided persuasive evidence—in the form of bad-family pedigrees and intelligence test results; it also said what they wanted to hear about moral degeneracy.

How are we to avoid such mistakes in the future? This is far from an abstract question, for we will soon again be facing the temptation to prevent crime through genetic engineering. One lesson of eugenic criminology is to be critical of science, especially when it claims it can identify potential criminals through biology. We need to scrutinize such science and remind ourselves that neither science nor crime occurs in a social vacuum. We need to be especially mistrustful when scientific criminology tells us what we may want to hear about others whom we mistrust or fear. As we head further into the era of the genome, we must resist the temptation to consider genetic engineering as a solution to crime—even if we act with the best of intentions. The result is almost bound to be the "reign of doctors" of which Irving Whitehead warned in Carrie's case, with "new classes . . . , even races," being subject to biological regulation and ultimately to "the worst forms of tyranny."[73]

# 7

## Constitutional Theory
### *Bodytypes and Criminality*

Does body shape have anything to do with criminal behavior? In the mid–20th century, there emerged a criminological school with precisely that message. Proponents thought of themselves as "constitutional" theorists, meaning that they sought the causes of crime in the way the body is constituted or formed. The theory had European roots, but by the 1930s it had moved to the United States, specifically to Harvard University, where it was developed by the anthropologist Earnest A. Hooton, the physician-psychologist William Sheldon, and the criminologists Sheldon and Eleanor Glueck. But there was another site of development as well—Nazi Germany—and this connection helped drive constitutional theory off the criminological research agenda. Criminology textbooks mentioned it over the years, but otherwise little further was heard of constitutional theory until late in the 20th century, when a minor revival took place.

The original proponents' choice of the label "constitutional" for bodytype theory was unfortunate, for the term was so vague that it could refer to any number of other theories as well. Physiognomy, the late 18th-century folk science of reading character from people's faces, could be considered constitutional, and it was certainly a forerunner of the constitutional theorizing under discussion here. The same was true of phrenology, which attempted to diagnose criminality from the contours of the skull. Criminal anthropology, too, was a constitutional theory, as well as another antecedent, as were degenerationist theories. Indeed, all biological theories of crime, including those that invoke genetics, can be considered constitutional, for all trace crime to the nature of the criminal body and, at least by implication, to the makeup of the criminal brain.

Related to this terminological weakness are questions about what fields are (or should be) involved in the study of the relations between bodytypes and crime. Is constitutional theory a psychological explanation of crime?

(Sheldon called his work "constitutional psychology.")[1] Anthropological? (Hooton spoke of Sheldon's "constitutional anthropology.")[2] Is it in some sense a psychiatric theory, as its background in German psychiatry suggests? Is it fundamentally genetic? And given some of its proponents' willful disassociation from mainstream criminology, at what point does it enter the criminological domain?

This chapter traces the history of constitutional theory and evaluates its content. It also continues following the trajectories of eugenic criminology and antimodernist tendencies in biocriminology. In the last chapter I argued that eugenic criminology, as it developed into the 1920s, was essentially an antimodernist science, one that marshaled scientific (or quasi-scientific) tools in efforts to recapture a premodernist world, one less subject to conditions of uncertainty, less fluid in its social class structure, and less affected by urbanism, immigration, prostitution, and the other problems of then-modern life. By the mid–20th century—the focus of this chapter—eugenic criminology had fallen from favor. It breathed its last gasp, at least in the form of thinking about criminals as hereditary degenerates, in the work of Hooton and Sheldon. These two men were also the theorists who brought to a culmination antimodernist tendencies in 20th-century criminology. This chapter pays a good deal of attention to their biographies in an effort to understand the origins of their eugenic and antimodernist messages about the causes of crime.

Hooton and Sheldon were both deeply pessimistic about the fate of mankind. They worried about the unhealthiness of modern bodies, a deterioration they generally attributed to the consumption of impure foods, lack of exercise and self-discipline, and loss of the traditional, rural values of hard work and independence. Moreover, they associated this psychophysical deterioration with criminality. Hooton and Sheldon hoped that their scientific work would help reinstate what they saw as early American traditions of self-reliance and simple, healthy living; this renewal would somehow lead to (or follow from) a genetically purer society, one that by definition would be little bothered by crime. Their antimodernist ideas had counterparts in Nazi Germany, with its focus on maintaining the purity of the national "stock," its glorification of the heroic body of the Nordic superman, and its program of reducing crime by cleansing the nation's germ plasm. But the differences were more important than the similarities: while Hooton and Sheldon supported sterilization, they were horrified by Nazi eugenics, and both participated in the struggle against Germany during World War II.

In what follows, I review the history of bodytype research and then turn to the life and work of Earnest Hooton, who first tried to revive criminal anthropology and, when that failed, turned to constitutional studies. The next section covers the life and work of William Sheldon, whose constitutional research produced a famous finding about delinquents' bodytypes. Sheldon himself, however, barely slowed down to acknowledge this finding as he rushed ahead in pursuit of a crackpot scheme to save the world. A third section, on the constitutional research of Sheldon and Eleanor Glueck, argues that their work—although outwardly similar to that of their colleagues Hooton and Sheldon—was actually quite different in sensibility and goals: modernist to their antimodernism. The final section, on the minor resurrection of interest in bodytype theorizing in the late 20th century, argues that it had less to do with a renewed interest in constitutionalism per se than with the return to biocriminology more generally.

## The Origins of Bodytype Research

From ancient times, scientists have looked for associations between body and mind, physical states and behavior. The Greek physician Hippocrates (ca. 450–380 BCE) identified links between body and behavior in the humors (blood, yellow bile, black bile, and phlegm), substances whose proportion and balance determined health and disease. Shakespeare played with morphological beliefs when he gave Julius Caesar the line "Let me have men about me that are fat." Physiognomists and phrenologists tried to read the mind from the body by focusing on the head, while 19th-century degenerationists focused their investigations more broadly, on the devolution of the entire body. Their interest in the entire constitutional state was perpetuated by 19th-century racial anthropologists like Lombroso who assumed that different racial and ethnic groups would have different personalities and inclinations. In Italy in the late 19th and early 20th centuries, a school of medical anthropologists (Di Giovanni, Naccarati, Viola) began developing the notion of bodytypes.[3] However, the key figure in this movement to examine the entire body for signs of inner states was the German psychiatrist Ernst Kretschmer.

Kretschmer was interested not so much in crime as in mental disease. In *Physique and Character: An Investigation of the Nature of Constitution and of the Theory of Temperament* (1925), he identified two primary bodytypes, the pyknic, or fat (which correlated with manic depression), and the asthenic, or skinny (which correlated with schizophrenia, as did

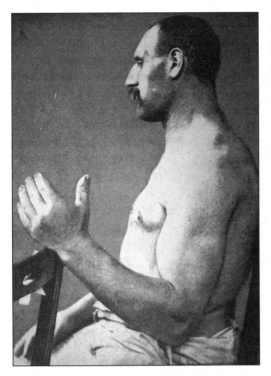

Bodytyping by Kretschmer. The German psychiatrist Ernst Kretschmer, a pioneer in efforts to correlate bodytypes with mental illnesses, identified an athletic type that correlated with schizophrenia among the patients in his hospital. Kretschmer's *Physique and Character* (1925) influenced later Nazi ideas about physical worthiness and fed into American research on bodytypes and criminality.

a third, athletic physique). Illustrating his bodytypes with photographs of his mental patients, Kretschmer emphasized that the forms vary along continua and merge in various combinations (such as a mixture of asthenic with athletic). When the Nazis came to power, he refused to support them, but other German psychiatrists went on to forge an "Aryan criminology"[4] from older Continental traditions that biologized lawbreaking and insisted on its hereditary nature.

At the same time, as part of a much broader search for explanations of human differences, American psychologists undertook constitutional research, seeking possible correlations of physique with intelligence levels, mental diseases, and behavioral traits. A study by two Columbia University psychologists exemplifies the stage that morphological research had reached just before Hooton and Sheldon appeared on the scene. These psychologists, H. E. Garrett and W. N. Kellogg, took all their body measurements from nude photographs of Columbia College freshmen. The images, shot in the university's gym for posture studies, gave three views of each subject (front, rear, and side). Like other American morphological researchers of this period, Garrett and Kellogg concluded that constitutional research was not a particularly promising avenue of inquiry.[5]

### Earnest Hooton: From Criminal Anthropology to Bodytyping

In 1939, the well-known anthropologist and Harvard professor Earnest Hooton published two books, *The American Criminal* and *Crime and the Man*, based on statistical analysis of one of the largest surveys of criminals ever compiled.[6] These books were widely reviewed, and Hooton became a spokesperson on criminological matters, quoted in leading newspapers and invited to deliver prestigious lectures. He was a controversial figure, with some reviewers fiercely attacking his methods and conclusions. But other contemporaries regarded Hooton as a major criminologist, and textbooks regularly summarized his work.

Hooton was born in 1887 in Clemansville, Wisconsin, the son of a Methodist minister and a schoolteacher from Canada. He attended Lawrence College in Appleton, Wisconsin, studying classics and working part-time at the Waupun State Penitentiary, an experience to which he later traced his interest in criminals.[7] But when he entered University College, Oxford, as a Rhodes scholar, his interest swerved from the classics toward anthropology. "Some of my teachers were interested in the scientific study of Roman religion or of Roman archeology," Hooton explained later, "and from these men I received the inspiration to learn more about the peoples of antiquity. Ultimately that led me into anthropology."[8]

Hooton joined the Harvard University faculty in 1913 on a one-year appointment and remained until his death forty-one years later, a period during which he became one of the most powerful anthropologists in America. His research and publications went through three overlapping phases. During the first, which began in 1915 and ended in 1930, he conducted scientific research on skulls to produce two well-regarded monographs.[9] In his middle phase, which began in 1926 and ran until about 1940, Hooton undertook large-scale surveys of living populations—including the criminals study—and began publishing popular science books on race, evolution, and eugenics.[10] During the third phase, from 1940 to 1954, he pursued the possibility of correlating various human bodytypes with different personality traits and abilities while at the same time undertaking practical research (for example, he used anthropometric methods to help the U.S. Army determine the optimal size for cockpits and gun turrets) and continuing to produce general-audience books.[11]

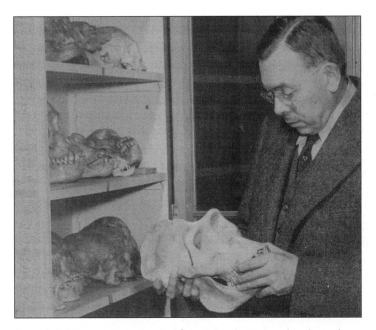

Earnest A. Hooton. In the mid-20th century, the Harvard anthropologist Earnest A. Hooton tried to resuscitate criminal anthropology and link it to a eugenics program that, he believed, would rid the world of criminals. Courtesy of the Hooton Archive, Peabody Museum, Harvard University.

As this overview suggests, Hooton's intellectual trajectory carried him away from purely scientific work addressed to other scholars and toward practical matters of concern to government or business. The change was driven in part by Hooton's disappointment with the poor reception of his criminals study; in part by a growing desire to make his research useful; and in part by developments in the field of anthropology, which matured in directions that sometimes disappointed Hooton or outran his expertise. At a time when his colleagues took increasing interest in cultural and social anthropology, Hooton continued to view biology as the primary influence on the development of individuals and groups, insisting that "environment is the universal alibi of human failure."[12] To younger anthropologists, Hooton seemed mired in the "scientific" racism of the past.[13]

Hooton died suddenly of a heart attack in 1954, at the age of sixty-six. Although he had won nearly every honor available to an American anthropologist, he died a frustrated and anxious man. He had come of age before World War I and died almost a decade after the end of World War II, a period characterized by wrenching change and brutal events. While Hooton participated actively in civic life,[14] he also reacted to the crises of his times by becoming ever more nostalgic for his Wisconsin boyhood, a world he associated with physical and mental vigor, self-reliance, freedom from automobiles and other dependency-inducing machines, and women who nursed their babies instead of feeding them noxious formulas.[15] In this simpler past, people read books and thought for themselves; in what was for Hooton the modern present, people mindlessly followed dictators and, at home with their families, passively watched television. (A cartoon by Hooton shows a family degenerating in front of a television set; even the dogs are becoming morons.)[16] The welfare programs of the New Deal brought out Hooton's social Darwinist spleen, for they seemed to coddle an already weak segment of the population that might better be allowed to die off.[17] Deeply disturbed by the apparent downward rush of civilization, Hooton predicted social, political, and genetic doom.

### The Criminals Study

Hooton's criminals study originated in a course he had introduced in 1916, "Criminal Anthropology and Race Mixture"—perhaps the first course in criminology per se in America.[18] According to his lecture notes, Hooton's background reading for this course included Havelock Ellis's *The Criminal* (1890), Charles Goring's *The English Convict* (1913), William Healy's *The Individual Delinquent* (1915), Hans Kurella's *Cesare Lombroso: A Modern Man of Science* (1910), and several works by Lombroso himself.[19] From this reading Hooton concluded that the anthropology of criminals deserved further investigation. His efforts in this direction bore fruit in 1926, when one of his former criminal anthropology students, Sheldon Glueck, now teaching in Harvard's Department of Social Ethics, introduced Hooton to Dr. Winfred Overholser, a state official who could help him gain access to jail and prison inmates.

A central goal of Hooton's criminals study became to validate Lombroso's idea that criminality somehow marks offenders' bodies. Although he criticized Lombroso's methods and logic, Hooton remained convinced that the Italian had been a great scientific innovator. Second to Lombroso in influence on the criminals study was Charles Goring, whose mammoth work *The English Convict* had attempted to refute Lombroso.

Hooton admired Goring's statistical abilities, and although he objected to the Englishman's "violent prejudice against Lombroso,"[20] he modeled his own study on Goring's work.

With Overholser's help, Hooton gained access to prisoners in Massachusetts and beyond. His samples, including control groups, eventually totaled about 17,000 subjects. The prisoner groups consisted of nonrandom samples collected from ten states; the controls, too, were nonrandom samples, of groups such as militiamen, hospital outpatients, and firemen. Hooton hired two graduate students to travel to state prisons and take about twenty physical measurements of each inmate. In addition, the students were to make "morphological observations" on thirty-three factors such as hair quantity, forehead slope, and earlobe notches, and to cull data from the prison records on about ten "sociological" factors such as marital status and number of prior convictions. After he was well into the data collection phase, Hooton discovered that the students' information was not always reliable and that many of the prison records were incomplete. Moreover, he came to realize that some of the morphological factors (such as the amounts of head and facial hair) could be affected by environmental factors (such as the availability of prison barbers). However, he proceeded to code data on about 125 variables.

Hooton originally planned to report his results in a three-volume work called *The American Criminal*. The first volume was to discuss "white" state prisoners born in the United States of native-born parents; the second was to cover native-born white prisoners of foreign parentage and foreign-born white prisoners; and the third volume was expected to cover Negro, Negroid, and Mexican state prisoners. As it turned out, due to high production costs and poor sales, the first volume was the only one to be published.[21] Hooton also published *Crime and the Man*, intended as a popular-audience digest of the project as a whole. However, *Crime and the Man* proved to be an even more complex book, partly because it encompassed much more data and partly because, to analyze these data, Hooton devised a tortuous new method that produced in effect a completely new set of findings. Thus the second book, far from being a mere digest of the first, actually constituted a different work entirely.

While Hooton's criminals project was ostensibly an exercise in criminal anthropology, it heralded the constitutional theory to come. The project boiled down to a massive search for something—anything—abnormal in the physiques of criminals. And because Hooton insisted, for reasons that only a very old-fashioned anthropologist like himself could understand, on

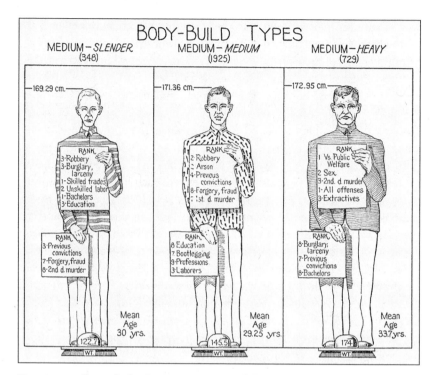

Hooton on offenses by bodytype. In *Crime and the Man,* Hooton attempted to correlate body build with offense type, background, and marital state–with almost incomprehensible results. Reprinted by permission of the publisher from *Crime and the Man* (p. 95) by Earnest Albert Hooton, Cambridge, MA: Harvard University Press, copyright 1939 by the President and Fellows of Harvard College. Copyright renewed by Mary C. Hooton.

first breaking down his results by race and birthplace and *then* hunting for differences, he ended up with a large number of physical types. *The American Criminal,* comparing the white, native-born, native-parented criminals to law-abiding citizens of the same ethnic origin, concludes that "criminals are inferior to civilians in nearly all of their bodily measurements."[22] It further reports on physical differences among criminals by offense type. First-degree murderers, for instance, proved to be older, heavier, and taller than other criminals, and although second-degree murderers, too, were older, they had less chest depth and shorter heads. Hooton did not conceive of these multitudinous groupings as *constitutional* types, but he was moving in that direction.

For *Crime and the Man,* with its broader database, Hooton invented a labyrinthine method of analysis that involved constructing nine "racial groupings" and then studying the frequency with which their members committed specific offenses. Much of this analysis has the effect of constructing national and ethnic stereotypes, as in "the typical Italian criminal is a murderer, someone who assaults another, or someone who is prone to rape."[23] To drive home the meaning of these race-ethnic comparisons, Hooton presented his findings in visual illustrations.

*Crime and the Man* in fact carries two sets of illustrations, the first a series of facial "mosaics" drawn by an assistant to demonstrate differences detected by Hooton among criminals from various states. For example, the top half of one page presents a frontal and side composite view of an Old American Criminal from Kentucky, showing his narrow forehead, short ears, and thick, membranous lips. Below it are frontal and side views of an Old American Criminal from Texas, showing his wavy hair, heavy beard, and long earlobes.[24] These composite portraits add more types to Hooton's already rich criminal typology, and by emphasizing physique, they take yet another step on the path toward constitutional theory.

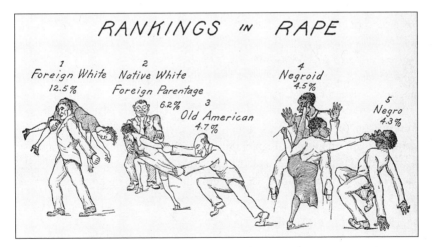

Hooton on rape by race and ethnicity. In this illustration Hooton attempts to correlate rape rates with race and ethnicity. Reprinted by permission of the publisher from *Crime and the Man* (p.302) by Earnest Albert Hooton, Cambridge, MA: Harvard University Press, copyright 1939 by the President and Fellows of Harvard College. Copyright renewed by Mary C. Hooton.

The second series of illustrations, drawn by Hooton himself, consists mainly of graphlike scenes in which cartoon figures representing racial and ethnic types are associated with various offense rankings. One graph, for example, shows British criminals with spectacles and books, Irish criminals with jugs of whiskey, and Teutonic criminals with beer steins, swastikas, and bayoneted rifles—all perched on top of or beside bars of a graph indicating "significant offense differences."[25] With their crude race-ethnic stereotypes, these cartoons suggest significant physical differences among human groups, divisions somehow related to criminality.

Hooton did not try to hide the eugenic goal of his criminals studies. Indeed, one of the major lessons of a review of Hooton's criminological work is that, even on the brink of World War II, neither this leading anthropologist nor his publisher, Harvard University Press, hesitated to promote eugenics. *The American Criminal* openly aims at encouraging eugenic measures against criminals. It begins by explaining that attempts to reform the criminal justice system or the criminal are "futile . . . if the germ plasm which produces that criminal is scum." Criminality, Hooton continues, is a "social cancer" that "demands the knife."[26] Hundreds of pages later, *The American Criminal* ends with more eugenical remarks: white, native-born criminals with native-born parents are "low-grade human organisms" and probably mentally as well as physically backward. Criminals' inferiority is very likely hereditary in origin. Thus, Hooton concludes, criminals can be eliminated only "by the extirpation of the physically, mentally and morally unfit, or by their complete segregation in a socially aseptic environment."[27]

Similarly, *Crime and the Man* concludes that criminals are "inherently inferior organisms" who cannot be reformed. First offenders might be allowed to reproduce so long as they are permanently isolated on a federal reservation to which they could import their wives. Habitual criminals "should be permanently incarcerated and, on no account, should be allowed to breed." Democracy is collapsing due to the "progressive biological deterioration of the people."[28] Something has gone wrong constitutionally.

### Hooton and Constitutional Theory

Academic reviewers panned Hooton's criminals books for their unrepresentative samples, unsophisticated used of statistics, and unrelenting biological determinism. Nonetheless, Hooton shaped the future of criminology and became midwife to constitutional theory through his influence on the Gluecks and Sheldon.

Hooton's eugenic prison. Hooton titled this cartoon "Tailpiece" because it was the last illustration in his book, but the title also refers to the cartoon's content. "Crime can be eradicated, war can be forgotten," Hooton wrote beneath this drawing, if we "control the progress of human evolution by breeding better types and by the ruthless elimination of inferior types." Reprinted by permission of the publisher from *Crime and the Man* (p. 397 ) by Earnest Albert Hooton, Cambridge, MA.: Harvard University Press, copyright 1939 by the President and Fellows of Harvard College. Copyright renewed by Mary C. Hooton.

For years the Gluecks and Hooton lived within walking distance of Harvard Yard; they interacted not only professionally but also socially, having a number of colleague-friends in common and sharing, at least during the 1930s, an interest in eugenics. In *The American Criminal*, Hooton acknowledges Sheldon Glueck's key role in getting the study started, and elsewhere he praises the Gluecks as "our best criminologists."[29] The Gluecks in turn thanked Hooton for statistical advice in *Five Hundred Delinquent Women* and for help with funding and research in *Unraveling Juvenile Delinquency*.[30] Moreover, they dedicated their book *Physique and Delinquency* to "the late Earnest A. Hooton, teacher and friend, who long ago directed our attention to the possible role of body build in human behavior."[31]

Hooton's influence on the Gluecks was indirect, manifesting itself through both general support for biological research and specific professional favors. He introduced them to William Sheldon, whose technique of somatotyping or classifying people by bodytypes deeply affected their later research, and to the physical anthropologist Carl C. Seltzer, a Hooton protégé who collaborated with the Gluecks on *Unraveling Juvenile Delinquency*. Hooton's own bodytype research, conducted after completion of the criminals books, did not focus on criminals, but it made him a valuable colleague as the Gluecks investigated possible relationships between bodytype and juvenile delinquency.

In Sheldon's case, Hooton was less a colleague than a mentor. Sheldon was an unlikely candidate for mentoring in 1938, when he met Hooton— nearly forty years old, with a doctorate in psychology and a medical degree, plus psychiatric training in Europe. But he had already demonstrated the lack of focus that characterized much of his professional life, having worked as a rancher, oil field scout, and instructor at several universities. He had been "obsessed" (he informed Hooton) since his midtwenties by the notion of "constitutional study."[32] Hooton enabled him to move into this line of research, which Sheldon pursued, one way or another, for the rest of his life.

Sheldon, in turn, reinvigorated Hooton's research agenda by introducing him to somatotyping just as the criminals study wound down. Somatotyping, as a method of classifying bodies across nonracial dimensions, helped Hooton escape from the rigidities of his race-ethnic taxonomies and gave him a way to pursue an issue that had emerged, without clear results, during the criminals study: that of the nature and behavioral implications of various bodytypes. Starting in 1947 and continuing for at least three years thereafter, he conducted a somatotype study for the U.S. Army. Although the army would not allow him to discuss this work,[33] at least he was able to report to the primatologist Robert M. Yerkes his general finding that "the knowledge of personality and temperament, etc., can be acquired more easily through [body] classification than by . . . approaches to less tangible aspects of the individual." (Perhaps jocularly, he went on to try to interest Yerkes in "a scheme of classification of body types for chimpanzees.")[34]

Hooton's constitutional work was only one of his many interests, and he came to it late in life, after turning away from criminology in disappointment over the dismal reception of his criminals books. His contribution to criminology (such as it was) lay primarily in the criminal-anthropology tradition. But latent in Hooton's criminals books lay the seeds of constitutional theory, which emerged during his subsequent, brief collaboration with Sheldon and encouraged Sheldon and the Gluecks to pursue their own work on the relationship of bodytypes to criminality.

## William Sheldon and Constitutional Psychology

When Hooton first met Sheldon, at a conference of the Association of Physical Anthropologists, he was so electrified that he offered on the spot to bring Sheldon to Harvard.[35] Declaring Sheldon to be "a genius" and his work "of utmost importance to a number of sciences,"[36] within three months he had obtained a stipended appointment for Sheldon at Harvard's Peabody Museum, where he himself worked. "I am profoundly impressed with [Sheldon's] work in constitutional anthropology," he told a correspondent.[37] Hooton wrote dozens of letters on Sheldon's behalf, introduced him to colleagues, arranged for reviews of his work, lectured enthusiastically on somatotyping, and lauded Sheldon in print. His gifts to Sheldon included the term *somatotyping* (or at least *somatyping*), which he coined to refer to the endeavor that Sheldon had been calling "anthrotyping."[38] Hooton also praised Sheldon to prospective publishers and pushed journalist friends to write stories on Sheldon's research.

Yet within eighteen months Hooton had wearied of Sheldon as a colleague. " I find it very difficult to fit Dr. Sheldon into the social and professional life of this Department and the [Peabody] Museum," Hooton confessed in confidence to Sheldon's grant supervisor at the Whitney Foundation, who had contacted him for an evaluation.

> He has succeeded in alienating many of the men in the Department. . . .
> He also has a tendency to assume alternately a familiar and facetious manner and a domineering, demanding attitude which has ruffled nearly every single person with whom he has come into contact. . . . I still believe in Dr. Sheldon's work and I like him personally very much indeed. . . . However, I have found proteges who are easier to help.[39]

By the time Sheldon left Harvard in 1942, he had worn out this relationship through arrogance and unreliability. This was part of a larger pattern in which Sheldon taxed his supporters to the breaking point.

William Herbert Sheldon was born in 1898 in Warwick, Rhode Island, to an old New England family; his father bred poultry and dogs competitively. Sheldon's early familiarity with the idea of breeding better species, and his pride in his Anglo-Saxon pedigree, fed into his lifelong advocacy of eugenics. After undergraduate work at Brown University, Sheldon enrolled in the University of Chicago for a doctorate in psychology. In Chicago he encountered Sante Naccarati, an Italian anthropologist about ten years older than himself who was studying correlations of bodytypes with temperament.[40] Sheldon's choice of a dissertation topic, "Morphologic Types and Mental Ability," was very likely encouraged by Naccarati's example. Sheldon went on to earn a medical degree and then, with a travel grant from the heiress Dorothy Whitney Elmhirst, set off in 1934 on a lengthy European tour that proved to be the intellectual turning point of his life.

The trip began at Dartington Hall, the estate in Devon, England, where Dorothy Whitney Elmhirst and her husband, Leonard, had recently established a utopian community, modeled on a medieval village but dedicated to fostering progressive education and the arts. During his six weeks at Dartington Hall, Sheldon worked on what became his first book, *Psychology and the Promethean Will*.[41] This work, composed during the unsettled period in which Hitler came to power and the Spanish Civil War began, speaks at length about modern dilemmas and argues the need for a Promethean savior, a hero who will sacrifice himself for the good of humanity by uniting psychology with religion—a program set forth here by Sheldon, who by implication is the Promethean hero.[42] Although the book says nothing about bodytypes, its redemptive vision became the underpinning of the bodytype research that followed.

From Dartington, Sheldon moved on to Germany, where he met twice with Kretschmer, studying firsthand the German's methods for associating bodytypes with categories of mental disease.[43] He also visited Freud, whom he advised to "anchor" his system in "physical anthropology." (Freud declined; the proposal, Sheldon later explained, "was too radical for him.")[44] On the same trip Sheldon met the Swiss psychiatrist Carl Jung, whose hereditarian ideas about spiritual healing shaped Sheldon's emergent philosophy. The 1930s, then, were years in which Sheldon completed his extensive education, chose bodytypes as his primary research interest, and developed the philosophical platform on which he built his somatotyping program.

Over the next fifteen years, Sheldon held research positions at several universities, published a number of books on somatotyping, and attracted a following of disciples, intellectuals, philanthropists, and reformers. One follower was the British-born novelist and social critic Aldous Huxley, who wrote a long essay for *Harper's* magazine greeting somatotyping as a new science that might prevent war, help with the diagnosis and cure of diseases, guide educational policy, and "mak[e] it possible for us to know who we and other people really are."[45] But despite his powerful backers and impressive credentials, Sheldon never held a regular academic appointment, and in some cases, his university affiliations carried little or no salary. When his funding ran out for the last time, Sheldon was saved by Dorothy Iselin Paschal, a friend who shared Sheldon's interests in eugenics and early American coins. She moved him and his research projects into her New York City apartment and later into her home in Cambridge, Massachusetts. Sheldon worked out of an office in the latter (he titled it the Biological Humanics Foundation), collaborating with acolytes and tinkering with his somatotyping techniques until his death at the age of seventy-eight.

Sheldon attracted supporters by promising that his research would have a wide application to social ills. Some supporters financed his investigations and publications. (These included Dorothy Whitney Elmhirst; Eugene McDermott, founder of the company that became Texas Instruments; the Rockefeller Foundation; and the Viking Fund.) Others, such as Huxley and Hooton, promoted it through writings and personal contacts. Many of his supporters began as advocates of his Promethean philosophy without subjecting his research to scientific scrutiny.[46] Harper and Brothers, one of the nation's most reputable publishing houses, kept bringing out his books, thus giving them an imprimatur of respectability, a reputability underscored by positive articles like Huxley's and good reviews in the popular press.[47] Although Sheldon was openly eugenical, his preachments did not offend supporters—indeed, the eugenical thrust of his message no doubt attracted supporters such as Hooton and Paschal. When a patron became disillusioned and withdrew, as the Elmhirsts did in the late 1930s,[48] and Hooton in the early 1940s, Sheldon attracted a new supporter, less through the empirical virtues of his work than through its scientistic promises.

## The Somatotype Series

Sheldon published four books on constitutional psychology, meaning the physical determinants of personality: *The Varieties of Human Physique* (1940), *The Varieties of Temperament* (1942), *Varieties of Delinquent Youth* (1949b), and *Atlas of Men* (1954). The first introduced somatotyping and used it to identify three basic male physiques; the next tied these physiques

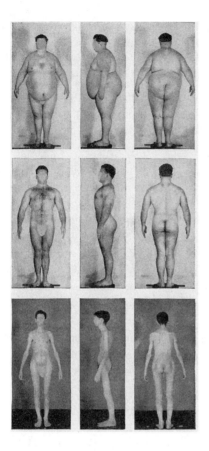

Three extreme types of human physique. The frontispiece to William H. Sheldon's *Varieties of Human Physique* (1940), this illustration presents the bodytypes on which he built a theory of criminal behavior. Another eugenicist, Sheldon hoped to eliminate crime and other social problems by preventing reproduction by people with inferior "protoplasm."

to three basic temperaments; the third applied somatotyping to a sample of male delinquents; and the fourth presented a taxonomy of the eighty-eight male somatotypes that Sheldon had identified so far. For *The Varieties of Human Physique*, Sheldon's database consisted of three-way photographs, borrowed from various university physical education departments, of 4,000 naked college men. To determine these men's bodytypes, Sheldon scored the photographs on morphological components, concluding that there are three basic types: *endomorphs* (soft and round), *mesomorphs* (muscular and compact), and *ectomorphs* (linear, fragile, and intelligent).

This was little more than Kretschmer's taxonomy relabeled and reapplied. Sheldon's innovations were, first, the conceptualization of the "components" (endomorphy, mesomorphy, and ectomorphy) as continuous variables each of which is present to some degree in every individual, and, second, the method of scoring so that every individual could be associated with three numbers—that person's somatotype. (For example, an extreme endomorph—an obese man with almost no muscularity or fragility—would have a 7-1-1 somatotype.) In addition, although he gave no evidence to prove the point, he was more insistent than previous bodytypers on the hereditary nature of one's bodytype. Sheldon concludes *The Varieties of Human Physique* with a eugenic vision in which somatotyping will eventually enable us to breed better people and predict their choices in clothing style, home location, and life partner.[49]

*The Varieties of Temperament* takes the next step of identifying biologically determined attitudes, beliefs, and motivations associated with the basic bodytypes. In this case, too, Sheldon ends up with a threefold typology: *viscerotonia* (the relaxed, sociable, gluttonous temperament), *somatotonia* (dominated by muscular activity and a drive toward action and power), and *cerebrotonia* (restrained, asocial, dominated by the cerebrum). The one-to-one correspondence of the temperaments with the basic bodytypes is not surprising, given that Sheldon did not derive the temperaments empirically but imposed them on his data.[50] Nor is it surprising, given that he himself did the ratings, that there proved to be a +.80 correlation of the three temperamental characteristics with the basic bodytypes of the 200 men whom he studied for this volume. The book ends with assurances that constitutional psychology will eventually be able to wipe out diseases and, by guiding "discriminate breeding, . . . strengthen the mental and spiritual fiber of the race."[51]

In *Varieties of Delinquent Youth*, "a field report on constitutional psychology in action,"[52] Sheldon compares 200 "more or less delinquent" male residents of a home for transient or troubled young men with the 4,000 college men of *The Varieties of Human Physique*. He himself selected the 200 subjects out of 400 youths who had passed through Boston's Hayden Goodwill Inn in the period 1939–1942. To measure their degree of criminality, he devised an "Index of Delinquency, or Index of Disappointingness" based on scores for (1) mental insufficiency; (2) medical insufficiency ("organic shortcomings"); (3) psychiatric insufficiency (including ratings on a DAMP RAT, or homosexual syndrome scale—Dilettante, Arty, Monotophobic, Perverse, Restive, Affected, Theatrical); and (4) persistent though not necessarily criminal misbehavior. Most of *Varieties of Delinquent Youth* is devoted to detailed case histories. For each man Sheldon gives the standard three-view photographs, a somatotype score, a gynandromorphy (*g*) score for the degree of feminine characteristics, a thoroughbredness (*t*) score, a criminal history (nearly all the subjects were truants, runaways, or petty thieves), an intelligence quotient, and an Index of Disappointingness (ID) score. He also identifies a PPPP trait (poor protoplasm poorly put together). This volume ends with eugenic yearnings for a Promethean savior who will overcome the world's Dionysian delinquents—a well-balanced, 4.5-4.5-4.5 hero who will institute a new biological humanics.

The finding that excited later criminologists—that the delinquent boys tended to be mesomorphs, relative to the college students—was the first major substantive message to emerge from Sheldon's somatotyping project. It was based on just sixteen cases—those of the youths charged with or convicted of an actual crime.[53] Sheldon himself was not impressed by the result, partly because he suspected that famous generals, businessmen, and politicians—equally energetic and uninhibited characters—were also mesomorphs. Moreover, he recognized that these adjudicatable delinquents were physically superior to the other youths, excelling in "general strength and general athletic ability."[54]

Sheldon was far more interested in the "essential inadequacy" of the other subjects, most of whom he found to be characterized by "the spoor of insufficiency." In his view, *Delinquency is behavior disappointing beyond reasonable expectation.*"[55] Physically, the worst delinquents are those whose reproduction leads "toward biological catastrophe." Due to "irresponsible reproduction," humanity is no longer evolving but "devolving" into "social chaos, wars . . . , and the confusion necessarily attendant upon the pathology of increasing urbanization." The book ends on an apocalyptic note: the only way to staunch devolution is "a biological humanics."[56] In other words, to prevent biological devolution, Sheldon recommends not specific eugenic remedies such as sterilization but his own vague, visionary program.

*Atlas of Men*, the final book in the series, aims at creating a "biological humanics" or "science of man resting on biological descriptions and procedures." Drawing on 1,175 cases, many of them hospital patients with "more or less constitutional" diseases such as diabetes and thyroid disorders, it sets out to present a "basic structural taxonomy of human beings."[57] Sheldon presents examples of the eighty-eight male somatotypes he has identified to date, beginning with a 1-1-7 case and ending with a 7-4-1.

The most distinctive characteristic of Sheldon's constitutional psychology books—and the one that caused scandals when he started somatotyping women—was their nude photographs. These constituted a powerful visual rhetoric and, together with Hooton's illustrations for his criminals books, made of constitutional theory the most visual form of criminology since Lombroso

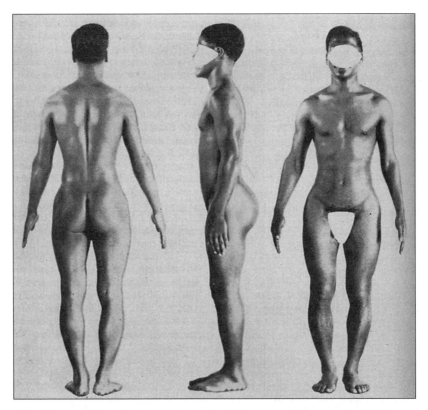

A Sheldon example of "primary criminality." This young delinquent fit Sheldon's definition of mesomorphy, the athletic build that he associated with law-breaking. In his case notes, Sheldon draws on racial and other stereotypes, comparing the youth to a tiger and a "cat on the prowl" and describing him as "gifted in music. He has what is known as hot rhythm." The young man's father "was a powerful full-blooded Negro. Mother a mulatto, considered feebleminded and easily led." From *Varieties of Delinquent Youth* (1949).

began illustrating his notion of criminal man. A 1995 *New York Times Magazine* article, resurrecting Sheldon as "the posture-photo mastermind," suggested that he might have snapped the likes of Hillary Rodham in a "master-race eugenics project."[58] But physical education departments had been clicking nude student photographs at least since the turn of the century, and initially Sheldon had borrowed posture-study photos from physical education departments. In later years he did indeed photograph his own subjects, but by then the making of such images was common practice.

The key question, in any case, is not who took the photographs or for what purpose but what information the images convey about their subjects. Somatotype photography forms part of the history of the idea of objectivity, meaning the development of the belief that science needs to censure the personal and that, therefore, the photographed object has greater validity than a drawing (say) of the same object.[59] Somatotype photographs also form part of a long tradition in social science research in which, in the words of visual anthropologist Marcus Banks, "'we' do visual things to 'them' or conduct research on 'their' visual forms."[60] In Sheldon's images as in 19th-century photographs of exotic aborigines or Lombroso's drawings of tattooed criminals, the subjects are naked while the investigator is not. *They* are controlled and subjected to scrutiny; the investigator remains invisible and free to circulate their images. The pictures embody power relations—and encourage readers to participate in them. They define their subjects, including those 200 delinquents, as people to be looked at, not as people qualified to do the looking—inferior creatures to be scientifically scrutinized and categorized for the social good.

In sum, Sheldon claimed that crime is caused by inherited biological inferiority. Delinquents are less worthy beings than college men; they are mesomorphs whose behavior is governed by their muscular physiques and not their cerebrums, Dionysian types from whom the world needs saving. Sheldon's goal was not to prevent crime or even to predict it but to prove his thesis that delinquents are carriers of "poor protoplasm poorly put together." In fact, he proved the opposite, for his actual delinquents turned out to be healthy, vigorous young men. Nonetheless, in Sheldon's view, his constitutional psychology series demonstrated that biology is destiny, the chief determinant of character and behavior.

### Sheldon as an Antimodernist

Sheldon, the most obviously antimodernist scientist discussed in this book, was absolutely clear about his opposition to modern life and his desire to use science to reinstate the values he associated with the past. Indeed, it was his clarity about this goal—and about his calling as a modern Prometheus who would reverse the world's rush to modernity—that attracted disciples to him.

*Psychology and the Promethean Will*, Sheldon's first book, set forth the antimodernist values that dominated his thinking for the rest of his life. In a scathing attack on the modern world, he objected to its fragmentation, superficiality, and materialism, conveying his objections through a portrait of "the waster": "The waster loves to *do* things, to wield power . . . , to use up things fast . . . . He is hearty, big, expansive . . . . The waster is particularly prominent in America . . . . He is . . . an open enemy of character. Above all else he hates 'principles.'"[61] To embody his own values, Sheldon created the figure of the "man of character" with a "reverent mind," the sensitive idealist who, like Prometheus, heroically brings "new light" to the rest of mankind.[62] Sheldon's antimodernism is further revealed by the book's goal: to coordinate psychology, religion, and medicine so as to minister to "the divided soul" produced by the modern world, and to reintegrate feeling with intellect so that people can once again have a sense of wholeness and peace.

Shared misgivings about modern life were what drew Sheldon and the Elmhirsts together, creating the basis for their friendship in the 1930s and leading to the Whitney Foundation's funding of Sheldon's work.[63] Dartington Hall, 800 acres of pristine farmland surrounding a restored 13th-century abbey, embodied the Elmhirsts' longing for rural community and their own premodernist values, even while its programs advanced progressive education and modernist art and architecture. To Sheldon, it symbolized opposition to "an ever increasing urbanity."[64]

Sheldon associated urbanity—his code word for modernism—with a cultural and intellectual takeover by Jews: "As a race, the jews are arty, and they become more intensely urban with every generation," he wrote in one of his first letters to the Elmhirsts from Germany.[65] Later the same week in a letter to Leonard Elmhirst he expressed similar resentments: "There is one basic principle which underlies all of my thinking . . . . It is a deep and intellectual resistance to the movement of the human mind toward urbanity." One must resist the "pull . . . to become urban" and to give in to "jewish psychology," which wants "to level all minds, and urbanize all human life."[66] There is no sign in the correspondence that the Elmhirsts shared Sheldon's anti-Semitism or his enthusiasm for eugenics, but they, like many of their generation, feared that trends in modern life would eventually obliterate traditional values.

Sheldon's scientific antimodernism comes out not only in the constitutional series but also in his book *Early American Cents, 1793–1814: An Exercise in Descriptive Classification*, a work that did for rare coins what *Varieties of Delinquent Youth*, published the same year, did for delinquents: classifying specimens by size and quality, describing them in minute detail, and displaying them in photographic plates. In fact, it is tempting to see this work as a fifth book in the constitutional psychology series. Sheldon associated his family's collection of antique pennies with social stability and a simpler, more rural America, a time when "a home without a box or bag of the old coppers secreted somewhere about the house, was something of a rarity."[67] Pennies research enabled him to return nostalgically to "the New England village where I was born" and "long winter evenings about the open fire" when the family would roast chestnuts and sort through the old coppers.[68] In the pennies book as in *Varieties of Delinquent Youth*, he indulged an antimodernist scientific impulse—one that harks back to the descriptive taxonomies of the 18th and 19th centuries—to classify partly for the joy of ordering things; both "exercises in descriptive classification" linked him to the better regulated, less chaotic life of his boyhood.

But in the course of his coins research, Sheldon indulged in another impulse as well—theft. After his death the American Numismatic Society discovered that, while studying coins in its collection, Sheldon had substituted lower-grade pieces and made off with 129 valuable early American cents for which he then devised false pedigrees.[69] It is difficult to reconcile this elaborate switch-and-steal scam with Sheldon's admiration for "the man of character," other than by noting that his biography indicates frequent self-excuse, self-deception, and outright prevarication. But clearly, for him the coins had symbolic as well as financial value, reminders as they were of a past he idealized.

Recognition of the antimodernist currents in Sheldon's work throws new light on his search for a causal relationship between body shape and criminality. His goal was twofold: to prove that delinquents are dysgenic *and* to enlist science itself in his salvationist project. Thus his relative disinterest in the mesomorphy-delinquency correlation. His ambitions were much more lofty: to save aristocratic ectomorphic stock from being "killed off" by urban conditions, competition from inferior stocks, and the leveling effects of democracy.[70]

## Crime, Constitution, and the Gluecks

Sheldon's constitutional psychology books received uniformly negative reviews from social scientists. Critics charged that because *Varieties of Delinquent Youth* had not begun with a random sample, it could reach no valid conclusions about the distribution of delinquents' bodytypes.[71] They also charged that Sheldon's "delinquents" were not in fact delinquent, since most had not violated the criminal law. Several critics raised fundamental issues about the utility of "types" derived from a priori reasoning and subjective ratings,[72] while others found that Sheldon had mismeasured his photographs, made computational errors, and failed to use appropriate statistics.[73] Notwithstanding these criticisms (and more),[74] Sheldon's finding of a mesomorphy-delinquency correlation was replicated by follow-up studies, some using more reputable methods.[75] Of these replications, the most careful and complete was that which emerged from Sheldon and Eleanor Glueck's milestone study, *Unraveling Juvenile Delinquency.*

Perhaps the most thorough study of delinquency ever conducted, *Unraveling Juvenile Delinquency* was based on information on 500 delinquent boys and a matched sample of 500 nondelinquent boys who lived in Boston and were studied from a wide range of angles, including family and personal background, intelligence, school adjustment and achievement, companions, church attendance, health, and physique.[76] For that aspect of the study focusing on "bodily constitution," the Gluecks used Hooton and Sheldon as consultants; for the actual photograph measurements of the boys, and their subsequent classification into physical types, they used Hooton's protégé Carl C. Seltzer. At the time, somatotyping was an innovative technique.

The Gluecks came up with three findings about bodily constitution: the delinquents were "somewhat superior in physique"; they matured a little later, physically; and they were characterized by mesomorphy, meaning that they were "a predominantly bone-and-muscle, tightly-knit, and energetic type."[77] Additionally, the Gluecks discovered in their delinquents a masculine or "virile element," meaning that these boys were more angular and well-muscled, and not as rounded, weak, and feminine as the controls.[78] While they suspected that the morphology of the delinquents was affected by heredity, they found it impossible to be sure.[79] In sum:

> The picture that emerges is one that portrays the delinquent as a more masculine and more mesomorphic physical specimen than the non-delinquent. This is evident in the delinquent's greater lateral breadth of torso tapering from the shoulder to the hips, in the heavier development of the arms, and in the possession of a smaller face and head anchored very firmly on the wide shoulders. It is a picture which tends to approximate the typical masculine type.[80]

Unlike Sheldon, the Gluecks did not attempt to reduce criminality to biological factors alone but rather emphasized that physique was only one factor among many affecting delinquent behavior. Indeed, in comparison to the criminological work of Hooton and Sheldon, that of the Gluecks was a model of cautious, antireductionist, well-informed social science.

Six years later the Gluecks dedicated an entire book, *Physique and Delinquency*, to detailed analysis of their data on the physical constitutions of the 1,000 *Unraveling* subjects and its possible implications for criminality. From the start they made it clear that, although this volume focused on physique and delinquency, they did not mean that physique plays an outstanding role in the genesis of crime.

Mesomorphic delinquents, the Gluecks found in *Physique and Delinquency*, were "more highly characterized" than nonmesomorphic delinquents "by traits particularly suitable to the commission of acts of aggression (physical strength, energy, insensitivity, the tendency to express tensions and frustrations in action), together with a relative freedom from such inhibitions to antisocial adventures as feelings of inadequacy, marked submissiveness to authority, emotional instability, and the like."[81] These traits, like the physique types, may be genetic in origin, although again, the Gluecks warn, is impossible to be sure. Moreover, they report, not all mesomorphs have the same constellation of traits, and although boys with this type of constitution generally have a "greater delinquency potential,"[82] there is no single cause of delinquency; nor is there any such thing as a "delinquent personality."[83] The Gluecks conclude on a sociological note, hypothesizing that mesomorphs may have higher rates of delinquency simply because, being more energetic, they are more inclined to act out "under the pressure of unfavorable sociocultural conditions." Less energetic endomorphs, in contrast, have a lower delinquency potential and are "less likely to act out their 'drives.'"[84] Thus in the hands of the Gluecks, the famous mesomorphy-delinquency correlation is reduced to a biosocial factor that may in some cases increase the push toward lawbreaking—hardly a dramatic assertion.

In the late 1990s, criminologists Robert J. Sampson and John H. Laub followed up on the Gluecks' work on physique. (Their reinvestigation was not part of the revival of constitutional theory discussed later in this chapter but rather an aspect of a larger research project using the Gluecks' data.) The Sampson-Laub study shed new light on the validity of constitutional theory while at the same time bringing supplementary data and new types of analyses to bear on the issue of bodytype and crime.

Recalculating the Gluecks' data, Sampson and Laub found that mesomorphs were indeed overrepresented among the official delinquents.[85]

But they also found that mesomorphy in adolescence had no discernible influence on later criminality in the Gluecks' sample of delinquents. Moreover, Sampson and Laub continued, the mesomorphy-delinquency correlation might stem "in part from how juvenile justice officials reacted to large, stout, and muscular boys compared to non-mesomorphs (e.g., weak or plump boys)."[86] Indeed, the correlation might have been influenced by the fact that "mesomorphy correlates with ethnic background—37 percent of Italian boys were rated as extreme mesomorphs compared with only 18 percent of non-Italians. . . . Prejudice against Italians, which was known to exist in Boston at the time of the Gluecks' study . . . may have contaminated the results."[87] Thus this follow-up study, while reconfirming the mesomorphy-delinquency correlation, identified social factors that could explain it.

### The Gluecks as Modernists

Earlier the Gluecks had published *Five Hundred Delinquent Women*, a study that occasionally becomes eugenic in its tone and recommendations.[88] However, even *Five Hundred Delinquent Women* had little antimodernist material (complaints of fragmentation in the contemporary world, nostalgia for the more complete world of the past, contempt for immigrants and criminals, and so on). Nor did eugenic overtones appear in their subsequent work where, in passages on physique, they comment on neither the inferiority of outsider groups nor the deterioration of the nation's germ plasm. In fact, their delinquents had admirable bodies—virile, healthy, and energetic.

While further research may turn up personal material indicating antimodernist tendencies in the Gluecks' thought, in their publications they are modernist. They accept the realities of their time—immigration, poverty, delinquency—and address the problem of delinquency straightforwardly, analyzing it without moralization. They assume that science can help solve social problems, and they are eager to make suggestions for rehabilitating offenders and improving the criminal justice system. All these characteristics are typical of modernist social science.

Why did the Gluecks not share the antimodernist attitudes of Hooton and Sheldon? The fact that they were Jews, and that Sheldon had been born in Warsaw, meant that the Gluecks had less to romanticize about America's past than Sheldon and Hooton; nor could they identify with the Protestant, Anglo-Saxon heritage that eugenic criminologists extolled. Although the Gluecks could hardly have been classified as "unfit" (Sheldon was a professor at Harvard Law School), they were no doubt aware of anti-Semitism in Europe and the United States (perhaps even the anti-Semitism of their colleague William Sheldon). Moreover, Eleanor, despite her doctorate and prestigious publications, never rose higher than research associate due to discrimination against women. Laub and Sampson describe her as "an outcast from mainstream academia at Harvard."[89] Whatever its sources, the Gluecks' modernism sharply distinguished them from their fellow constitutionalists.

## *The Return of the Bodytypers*

Reacting to Nazi eugenics, most mid-20th-century criminologists dismissed biological theories out of hand, and constitutional theory all but disappeared from view. But toward the century's end, scholars in the United States and Great Britain started returning to William Sheldon's discovery of a delinquency-mesomorphy correlation. In the United States, this mini-trend began with *Crime and Human Nature* (1985), the widely discussed book in which Harvard University professors James Q. Wilson and Richard Herrnstein reintroduced the notion of *criminality*, defining it as an individual's propensity to commit crimes or equivalent acts.[90] With this book, the pendulum began to swing back toward the "nature" pole in the nurture-nature debate.

Wilson and Herrnstein discuss somatotyping in the context of a chapter titled "Constitutional Factors in Criminal Behavior," the goal of which is "to establish the fact [*sic*] that individuals differ at birth in the degree to which they are at risk for criminality."[91] They begin with physiognomy ("It is possible that these enduring beliefs are based on more than prejudice"); move on to Lombroso ("Goring may have gone too far in dismissing . . . Lombrosian criminal anthropology"); review Goring ("Goring acknowledges [*sic*] the existence of criminal tendencies"); and then cover Hooton's *American Criminal* ("this most careful [*sic*] of all anthropological studies").[92] Next they devote eight pages to Sheldon's work (including reproductions of five somatotype photographs and two diagrams from *Varieties of Delinquent Youth*), but they mention the Gluecks' far less determinist work only in passing. Their extensive discussion of Sheldon's research implies that his somatotyping approach was valid, just as the material quoted earlier in this paragraph suggests that earlier "constitutional" studies provided scientifically valid proof that some people are innately criminalistic.

"The evidence leaves no doubt," Wilson and Herrnstein conclude, "that constitutional traits correlate with criminal behavior."[93] Actually, the evidence that they cite most extensively—Sheldon's *Varieties of Delinquent Youth*—leaves every reason for doubt. Although subsequent studies did confirm Sheldon's mesomorphy-delinquency correlation, the original finding had been based on selected cases and set forth in the context of a eugenic superman theory. Had Wilson and Herrnstein been acting responsibly as social scientists, they would not have devoted so much space to an uncritical review of the scientistic minutiae of Sheldon's methods. One is tempted to conclude that these authors were willing to use any evidence, even contaminated evidence, to support their "nature" interpretation of criminal behavior.

But there is an additional way to interpret this scientific lapse. Wilson and Herrnstein may have been attracted to Sheldon's work, and not to that of the Gluecks, because they shared his dismay over the direction of the modern world. *Crime and Human Nature* is not explicitly antimodernist, but its calls for reestablishment of the nuclear family, encouragement of personal responsibility, and reaffirmation of "the moral order of society,"[94] suggest a longing for a simpler, uncorrupted past. That Wilson and Herrnstein match Sheldon's biologism step for step, reporting his details on delinquents' broad chests, low waists, relatively long arms, and so on, and that they make the somatotyper's research seem credible, may reflect antimodernist sentiments of their own.

In Great Britain, the revival of constitutional theory began even earlier, in the writings of Hans Eysenck, the iconoclastic psychologist whose work, although it was vigorously critiqued by sociological criminologists, proved to be a harbinger of the renewal of biocriminology that continues into the present. As early as 1964, in *Crime and Personality*, Eysenck reported at length on constitutional theory, which reinforced an explanation of criminal behavior that he himself had developed. (He equated Sheldon's "cerebrotonic," or brainy and law-abiding, type with the law-abiding type that he himself called the introvert.)[95] Later, in *The Causes and Cures of Criminality*, Eysenck returned to constitutional theory, this time adding material on criminal stigmata. While rejecting Lombroso's picture of born criminals marked with telltale stigmata, Eysenck asserted that "minor physical anomalies . . . are more frequently found in criminals than in noncriminal groups."[96]

Notably, Eysenck's work bore no trace of antimodernism. Similarly, another contributor to the revival of constitutional theory, the psychologist

Adrian Raine, writes straightforward science, presenting facts and evaluating research findings without laments on the condition of the modern world. In *The Psychopathology of Crime*, where he summarizes the findings of constitutional research, Raine stresses that "ultimately, the link between body build and crime/delinquency may be mediated largely through *social* mechanisms. For example, body build may be linked to delinquency because having a larger, more muscular body build allows bullying to be an effective strategy." Raine also insists "that no factor linked to crime should be viewed in the anachronistic terms of genetics versus environment."[97]

In sum, in the last decades of the 20th century, Wilson and Herrnstein, Eysenck, and Raine revived constitutional theory in the sense of discussing it seriously. But their commentaries were signs not of a rekindling of enthusiasm for constitutionalism itself but of the return to biocriminology more generally. Collectively, their work shows a petering out of the antimodernist tendencies that had characterized scientific biocriminology since the start of the century. Those antimodernist tendencies, closely linked with eugenic criminology, left traces in the work of Wilson and Herrnstein, but otherwise they had worn off.

Quite apart from the particulars of constitutional theory, biocriminology is unlikely to return to the antimodernist themes of the past. One hundred fifty years have passed since Darwin's *Origin of Species* and changes in 19th-century society set off the crisis of modernism. People have learned to live with uncertainty, with the lack of religious verities, and with the fragmentation and anonymity of urban life that triggered antimodernism. Social science has adopted standards for objectivity that leave little room for moralization of the phenomena being studied,[98] and people now have different expectations of science itself. While they may hope that social science will show us how to deal better with crime, they no longer expect it to save the world—or the privileges of their social class.

## The Future of Constitutional Theory

Let us return, then, to the original question: does body shape have anything to do with criminal behavior? The answer: very little. Perhaps a better question would be, What does constitutional theory tell us about those who produced it and the times they lived in?

Inherent in constitutional theory are several problems that would seem to make it an etiological dead end. One is the fact that bodytypes are not static; many of us change shape over time, and although bodytype research has focused on teenagers, no constitutionalist has explained why one's teenage somatotype should be definitive. Another problem is that street crime is by and large committed by young men; thus we should not be astonished to learn that those most likely to commit it are young, high-testosterone youths. Related is the so-what problem: what can we learn about the causes of crime by discovering that it is associated with mesomorphy? The Gluecks struggled heroically to address this issue, and they probably got the answer right: energetic, athletic young men are better equipped, physically, to commit crime than less energetic skinnies or pudgies. But to some ears, this sounds a lot like "boys will be boys."

Constitutional theory played an important, if misunderstood, role in 20th-century criminology, and in retrospect we can see that it presaged today's research into genetics and crime. The new wave of genetic theories is unlikely to be antimodernist in its impulses, however; those motives for biocriminology have withered and died, and we live in a postmodernist world. But in reductionist hands, genetic explanations could easily develop some of the same eugenic implications as earlier constitutional theory. If we trace criminality to an inborn trait of some kind in the bodies of criminals, then it is likely that someone will again propose that we stop criminals from reproducing.

# 8

# Criminology's Darkest Hour

## Biocriminology in Nazi Germany

During the twelve years of Hitler's Third Reich (1933–1945), the Nazis used biological theories of crime to justify the killing of tens of thousands of people—millions, in fact, if we consider that the Nazis justified the extermination of not only lawbreakers but also Jews and Gypsies by attributing to them inherent criminality. The Germans developed a science of "criminal-biology" that they believed could identify hereditary criminals and demonstrate that they needed to be incarcerated indefinitely to prevent their reproduction. With the onset of World War II, in 1939, the Nazis intensified their applications of criminal-biology, drawing on it to select allegedly mentally handicapped offenders, including the criminally insane, for "euthanasia" or "mercy killing." Later still, after Führer Adolf Hitler decided to exterminate all those with "lives not worth living,"[1] the Nazis murdered criminals and others whom they deemed to be hereditary "asocials" in gas chambers or sent them to concentration camps for "extermination through labor."

This aspect of the Nazi regime—criminology's darkest hour—remains all but unknown to criminologists. Indeed, until recently, it was relatively unknown even to historians of the Third Reich. Although these historians had closely analyzed the development of eugenics, genetics, medicine, and other sciences that the Nazis used to destroy indisputably innocent victims, they had paid less attention to the science of criminal-biology, perhaps because its victims, having been accused or convicted of crimes, were considered in some sense suspect or even deserving of their fate.[2] In recent years, however, new research by historians such as Richard Wetzell (*Inventing the Criminal: A History of German Criminology, 1880–1945*) and Nikolaus Wachsmann (*Hitler's Prisons*) has brought the picture of Nazi criminology and criminal justice into focus.[3] This picture reveals a previously unfamiliar dimension to the predations of the National Socialist state—and the murderous potential of biological theories of crime.

In recent years, understandings of Nazi science have undergone rapid evolution as historians abandoned the older view that a few fanatic leaders had forced passive but otherwise virtuous scientists to nazify their methods and findings. This older view was based on a shaky and perhaps untenable distinction between "bad" and "good" sciences; moreover, it was promulgated after World War II by Nazi collaborators who wanted to exculpate themselves.[4] Even more important to the reinterpretation is the growing realization that the older picture distorts the active and enthusiastic collaboration of German scientists with the Nazi regime. The new wave of studies of Nazi science makes it impossible to continue drawing bright lines between good and bad scientists.[5] And the more that historians discover about the workings of Nazi science, the more crucial it becomes to understand why scientists collaborated—to grasp the nature of their relationship with the state that funded their work and their desire to harness science to the goal of race purification. The new interpretation of Nazi science holds that the enlistment of science in a vast and disastrous enterprise such as occurred in Hitler's Germany *could* happen again. If we truly want to prevent such a recurrence, then we must acknowledge that all science is to some degree politicized because it develops in a social context. If "value-free science" is an impossibility,[6] then our task becomes the difficult one of figuring out how to guard against a development that was but an extreme and murderous extension of something— science—that many of us practice daily.

This chapter focuses on criminology and its effects on criminal justice during the Third Reich. It is based solely on English-language sources and is intended as a contribution to the history of not Nazi science but criminology. Everything reported here is known to historians and is based on their research, especially the work of Wachsmann and Wetzell, pioneers in the study of Nazi criminology and criminal justice.[7] However, this line of historical research is unfamiliar to most criminologists.[8] Criminology was still an immature field when the Nazis became interested in it. In countries such as England, France, and the United States, it was turning in sociological directions; elsewhere it developed along biological lines. In Nazi Germany it fed into a political program of mass extermination. German criminal-biology was not directly responsible for that program, but it did provide one justification for it.

While this chapter focuses on criminology and its effects on criminal justice during the Third Reich, it also looks, more briefly, at criminology in

Benito Mussolini's Fascist Italy (1922–1943), another state with a powerful biocriminological tradition, the nature and impact of which historians are now starting to document.[9] The two states are linked by their mutual participation in the larger phenomenon of *fascism*—the belief-system that undergirded the governments of not only Nazi Germany and Fascist Italy but also other mid-20th-century nations from Brazil to Japan. Fascism as a political movement was distinguished by its hostility to various other movements—capitalism, feminism, liberalism, socialism, and traditional conservatism; and it was nationalist ("ultranationalist," to use Kevin Passmore's term)[10] in spirit and policies. Although fascism differed from country to country, it often had strong mystical and ritualistic elements that coalesced with an ethos that was masculinist, militaristic, bellicose, and totalitarian. ("It is a crime not to be strong," Mussolini declared.)[11] A defining characteristic of fascism was its tendency to place the needs of the state before those of the individual, diminishing or obliterating individual rights for the sake of furthering an ideology and preserving a dictatorship. A comparison of the German and Italian cases, even a brief comparison such as that undertaken here, enables us to identify some of the ways in which social context fostered the politicization of biocriminology and to isolate factors that made the German experience far more lethal.

My key questions are these: How did biological ideas shape explanations of crime in Hitler's Germany? How did Nazi science define "criminals"? What events—ideological, legislative, administrative, military, scientific— fed into the development of Nazi biocriminology, and what actions did the Nazis take against crime and criminals? I begin by discussing the immediate background to Nazi biocriminology in the previous government of the Weimar Republic and then examine the development of criminal-biology during the Third Reich and its applications by Nazi police, courts, and prisons. In conclusion, I briefly discuss biocriminology under the Italian Fascists, identifying some of the restraints that kept 20th-century Italian criminal anthropology from becoming as potent a destructive force as German criminal-biology.

## *The Background: Criminal-Biology in the Weimar Republic*

The roots of Nazi biocriminology reach far back into German history, but they lay most immediately in the social unrest of the previous era, that of the Weimar Republic (1919–1933), the government that replaced the German monarchy at the end of World War I and remained in power until Hitler took over. The Weimar Republic was a liberal democracy but unstable, kept precarious by its difficulties in recovering from the war and by extremism on both the Left and the Right. It adopted progressive criminal justice policies, limiting police powers, granting defendants legal protections, and running its prisons as rehabilitative institutions.[12] But this liberalism infuriated conservatives, who, arguing that the government was soft on crime, demanded more law and order. The sense of moral breakdown in the Weimar Republic—a foreboding that affected many groups, not only conservatives—was intensified by urbanization and industrialization;[13] it came to a head after the economic crash of 1929, with the Great Depression and its worldwide repercussions. Large numbers of vagrants, hungry and unemployed, now filled the streets of German cities, overwhelming welfare agencies and becoming symbols of the country's inability to cope with its problems.[14] People began to long for a more authoritarian government that would restore order and, as the up-and-coming politician Adolf Hitler promised, "morally purify the body politic."[15]

As the impression of governmental ineffectiveness grew, crime became a prominent theme. The preoccupation with lawbreaking is manifest in the period's most famous film, Fritz Lang's *M* (1931; the initial stands for *Murderer*). *M* includes scenes of mob violence, a familiar event during the Weimar years. It also depicts a gang of professional thieves, or *Ringvereine*, who are at least as well organized and adept at social control as the police. Furthermore, *M* tells a story of *lustmord*, or sex killing, a phenomenon that erupted in Weimar Germany, mesmerizing its avant-garde artists and unnerving the populace.[16] One of the most spectacular *lustmord* cases was that of Peter Kürten, the "Dusseldorf Vampire," whose real-life sex murders of children are echoed in *M* by the killings committed by the central character, a mentally ill pervert. (To play this part, Lang cast Peter Lorre, a sinister-looking Hungarian Jew and an obvious outsider.) The introduction of fingerprinting and other aspects of scientific policing (some of these, too, show up in *M*) made it easier to detect recidivists, increasing the impression that the number of incorrigible criminals was on the rise. Weimar Germany became a hothouse for the cultivation of a criminology that drew clear lines between us and them, the law-abiding and the criminal.

The strongest influence on German criminology in this period was that of a man who had died years earlier: the Italian criminal anthropologist Cesare Lombroso. Lombroso's key writings, translated into German by the end of the 19th century, shaped the contours of the emerging science of criminal-biology, even though German criminologists did not swallow

The murderer "M." "M," a child rapist and killer played by Peter Lorre, looks in the mirror with self-loathing in Fritz Lang's film *M* (1931). The film reflects social problems in Germany in the period leading to Hitler's regime, including sex crime and mob violence; it also reflects the growing belief that crime is often committed by non-Germanic "outsiders" and likely to be biological in nature. Photo used by permission of Photofest.

Italian criminal anthropology whole. Indeed, like their counterparts in the United States, England, and France, German criminologists such as Gustav Aschaffenburg heavily criticized Lombroso, even while incorporating some of his central ideas.[17] Like Lombroso, they concentrated on the study of not crimes but criminals, and like him they found an explanation for crime in biological abnormality. "No serious person really doubts," wrote German criminologist Johannes Lange, "that we must first look for the causes of crime in the criminal, i.e. in biological material."[18] With modifications, German theorists accepted Lombroso's idea of the born criminal, the biologically and mentally abnormal incorrigible who remains socially dangerous for life.

Leading criminologists also accepted Lombroso's social defense prescription for crime control, arguing that the punishment should fit the criminal, not the crime, and that incorrigibles should be removed from society for life—not to punish, not to rehabilitate, but to keep them from contaminating others.[19] Although Lombroso himself died before eugenics theory became popular, his social-defense philosophy and hereditarian views meshed smoothly with the eugenics ideas that became popular in Weimar Germany. His medicalized notion that society should rid itself of born criminals, using the death penalty when necessary, and his naïve assumption that whatever scientists reported must be true were among the most influential aspects of his legacy. They dovetailed with what historian Mariacarla Gadebusch Bondio describes as a factor contributing to Germans' acceptance of Lombrosian ideas: "blind confidence in scientific explanations of deviance, and the belief in the need to sacrifice individuals for the benefit of society."[20]

Even before the Weimar period began, theorists such as Emil Kraepelin, Aschaffenburg, and Hans Kurella had already defined criminology as a medico-psychiatric speciality and established psychiatrists as authorities on social health and the regulation of deviance.[21] Thus it is not surprising to find that most criminologists of the Weimar era were physicians or psychiatrists (by definition, the latter had medical training)—people predisposed to interpret human behavior in physical terms. To explain why criminology became a medical speciality in Germany at this time, historian Richard Wetzell points to two factors of particular importance. First, the doctrines of Lombroso (himself a psychiatrist) appealed powerfully to psychiatrists through their biological explanations and equation of innate criminality with the psychiatric phenomenon of moral insanity. Second, German psychiatry, like its counterparts in other countries, was seeking a way to expand its professional domain by moving beyond the walls of insane asylums and "colonizing" new deviant groups such as criminals. German psychiatrists concerned with the biological health of the nation as a whole were eager to "place the interests of society above the welfare of the individual patient"[22]—especially when those "patients" were undeserving criminals.

Ernst Kretschmer, a psychiatrist prominent in the Weimar period, contributed indirectly to the development of criminal-biology with research on the relationship between body shape and personality. Kretschmer's *Physique and Character* reports the results of research on patients in his insane asylum.[23] After dividing the patients into two main groups, manic-depressives and schizophrenics, Kretschmer used anthropological tools—calipers and tape measures, photographs and drawings—in the hope of discovering physical differences between them. Kretschmer also constructed family trees to study inheritance of bodytype through the generations. Then, investigating whether the main bodytypes were associated with particular types of personalities, Kretschmer concluded that manic-depressives tend to be quiet and softhearted, schizoids dull and brutal. He himself rejected the possibility of a physical type like Lombroso's born criminal, replete with telltale "ear-flaps,"[24] and he played no personal role in the development of German criminology. (In fact, he resigned his position as president of the German Society of Psychotherapy in protest when the Nazis took over.) However, Kretschmer's research encouraged criminologists to reach Lombrosian conclusions about the influence of biology and heredity on character.

Johannes Lange, another medical man who influenced the development of German criminology during the Weimar period, focused more directly on genetic factors in human behavior. The author of a famous twin study, *Crime as Destiny*, Lange attempted to prove that criminality is an inherited condition by studying sibling pairs. His finding that there was a higher concordance for criminal behavior (measured by imprisonment) among identical twins (77 percent) than fraternal twins (12 percent) seemed to prove that "as far as the causes of crime are concerned, innate tendencies play a preponderant part,"[25] although Lange readily admitted that environment contributes as well.

To locate sets of twins in which at least one of the pair had been imprisoned, Lange had turned for help to the Bavarian Ministry of Justice, an institution with a program of biological research that, like Kretschmer's bodytype investigations, furthered the biologization of criminality in the Weimar years. In 1924, the justice ministry in the south German state of Bavaria established the Criminal-Biological Service to collect data—anthropometric, medical, moral, and psychiatric—on prisoners, their families, and their associates.[26] The goal was to identify "incorrigibles" so that they could be sent to preventive detention. Based on the assumption that morality is rooted in biology, the Bavarian criminal-biological research seemed to prove that assumption, a proof that in turn reinforced hereditarian notions and the acceptance of eugenic solutions. Eventually including files on more than 100,000 people, the program identified a motley group of "incorrigibles," including ordinary criminals, communists, homosexuals, psychopaths, recidivists, and sex offenders, groups that, taken together, constituted an apparently dysgenic nucleus of antisocial people.[27]

The Weimar years, then, saw the development of a new science, criminal-biology, that could easily be used in the next period to further the eugenic goals of the Nazi state. Related to other sciences and scientific subspecialities—old-fashioned criminal anthropology; the new amalgam of genetics, eugenics, and anthropology; psychiatry; bodytyping; genealogical investigations; and twin studies—criminal-biology was distinguished above all by its scientism or unquestioning acceptance of (indeed, enthusiasm for) what scientists identified as true knowledge. Weimar criminology was not a monolith, as Wetzell cautions, for it developed on a number of fronts and through research programs that sometimes produced contradictory results.[28] But the general thrust was toward confirming criminality as a biological condition, identifying a core group of incurables ("habituals," "incorrigibles," "psychopaths"), and demonstrating the heritability of criminality. Weimar criminology differed from the criminal-biology of the Third Reich in degree, not kind: it was less racist, and its eugenics themes were relatively muted. But, as Wachsmann explains, "By the time the Nazis came to power in January 1933, not only was there widespread agreement that certain 'habitual' offenders had to be eliminated from society, but prison officials and criminologists had already taken the first steps in identifying who these offenders were."[29]

## Criminal-Biology in The Third Reich

Criminal-biology was one of several sciences—including anthropology, biology, eugenics, genetics, medicine, psychology, and psychiatry—that, during the Third Reich, actively contributed to the Nazis' goal of cleansing Germany of genetic inferiors, and it cannot be separated from the broader scientific effort of which it formed a part. At the outset of the Third Reich, Dr. Max Planck, president of the Kaiser Wilhelm Society for the Advancement of the Sciences, expressed his and his colleagues' enthusiasm for working closely with the new government, assuring Hitler that "German science is ready to make every possible effort to collaborate in the reconstruction of the new national state, which, in turn, has declared itself to be our protector and our patron."[30] The symbiotic relationship of science with the regime was reaffirmed a decade later when Dr. Eugen Fischer, a leader in Nazi eugenics research, exulted, "It is a rare and special good fortune for a theoretical science to flourish at a time when the prevailing ideology welcomes it, and its findings can immediately serve the policy of the state."[31] From one perspective, Nazi eugenics was part of the antimodernist reaction described in previous chapters, an attempt to mobilize science in addressing the problems and uncertainties of modern life. In any case, the life sciences thrived under the Nazis, criminal-biology among them.

The two scientific programs with which Nazi criminal-biology allied itself most closely were eugenics and racial hygiene. These two terms are often used as synonyms, and indeed eugenics and racial hygiene converged as Hitler unfolded his plans for extermination. Moreover, even in Hitler's Germany, scientists did not sharply distinguish between the two projects. However, if we today are to understand the aims of criminal-biological research, it is important to note the differences between them. The *eugenics* project aimed at improving the quality of the "race" (meaning, most broadly, the "human race") by encouraging superior people to reproduce ("positive eugenics") and discouraging "inferiors" from reproducing ("negative eugenics") through forced exile, marriage prohibitions, incarceration, or extermination. At its most general, eugenics proposed to prevent the reproduction of *everyone* with hereditary defects—not members of a single racial or ethnic group but all the "defectives" within every group—for the good of the whole. Into the 1930s, Jews were among those who, in Germany and elsewhere, supported the eugenics movement, which, criminologically, aimed at identifying hereditary criminals of all races and ethnicities and preventing them from reproducing. All the leading criminologists in the Third Reich supported the eugenic goals of the Nazi regime, albeit with varying degrees of enthusiasm.

*Racial hygiene*, on the other hand—insofar as it can be distinguished from Nazi eugenics—was concerned with identifying ethnic or racial *groups* of people, such as Jews and Gypsies, and restoring Germany to Aryan (roughly, "Nordic" or Germanic) purity. In terms of criminology, racial hygiene intersected with eugenics when specific race-ethnic groups were identified as genetically criminalistic. The complexities of the interaction become clear when we consider that Gustav Aschaffenburg, a leader in the development of criminal-biology, did not realize as late as 1935 that his science could become anti-Semitic—even though he himself had already been ousted from his university post because he was a Jew.[32] Aschaffenburg simply did not grasp that for the Nazis, criminal-biology and anti-Semitism were "complementary parts of a eugenic-racial policy."[33] A few years later, this connection became obvious. It is unclear to what extent those who developed criminal-biology supported racial hygiene as well as eugenics. However, after the Nazis' purge of Jews and political opponents from the criminological ranks (described later), most if not all of the remaining criminal-biologists endorsed both goals, thus merging the aims of the two scientific projects.

Race purification had long been at the top of Hitler's agenda. In the first volume of *Mein Kampf*, written in the 1920s, he had declared that every cultural achievement is "almost exclusively the product of Aryan creative power." The Aryan is "the Prometheus of mankind," the bold creator of the humanities and the arts, whereas the Jew is a parasite, an inveterate liar, and the cause, through interbreeding or "miscegenation," of physical and racial deterioration in Aryan stock.[34] Germany needs laws, Hitler continued, to prevent the breeding of inferior races ("the inferior always outbreed the superior") and to forbid the mating of Jews with "the superior race."[35] The old German empire, "by neglecting the problem of preserving the racial foundations of our national life," made "mongrels" of its people.[36]

Hitler's false ideas about human heredity and his anti-Semitism amplified prejudices that were already widespread in German society, including associations of Jews with uncontrolled sexuality and predatory criminality. (These associations can be seen, for example, in Lang's movie *M*.) Similarly, Hitler's regime fastened on widespread prejudices against "Gypsies" (as it termed the Sinti and Roma peoples) to criminalize this group.[37] In 1935, Dr. Robert Ritter, chief of the Research Institute for Eugenics and Population Biology within the Reich Ministry of Health, announced that the tens of thousands of Gypsies he had been studying through the Bavarian criminal-biological files were "the products of matings with the German criminal asocial subproletariat" and a "people of entirely primitive ethnological origins, whose mental backwardness makes them incapable of real social adaptation."[38] Fusing these ideas about racial hygiene with eugenics, German criminal-biologists produced "an Aryan criminology"[39] that contributed to both projects.

What was the substance of this Aryan criminology? It was based on two fundamental assumptions: that biology determines criminal behavior, with environment having little significant effect; and that the biological factors are genetic and inevitably passed to the next generation. The overriding purpose of Nazi criminal-biology was to confirm these assumptions through research and to identify the men and women who, because they were hereditary criminals, should be prevented from reproducing. Criminal-biologists also studied differential birthrates, showing that criminals were outbreeding good Germans and estimating the impact that sterilization might have in reducing various types of crime. As time went on, the research program expanded to prove that vagrants, homosexuals, communists, prostitutes, and other "asocials" were likewise hereditary deviants. The research program of Nazi criminal-biology was more hereditarian than that of the Weimar period and more explicitly racist in its targeting of Jews and Gypsies.

Criminal-biologists conducted their research through biological examinations of the type pioneered in Bavaria, compiling files on the genetic, intellectual, medical, psychological, and social condition of their subjects. When the Nazis came to power, they nationalized the Bavarian program, opening criminal-biological centers in seventy-three prisons and centralizing the reporting system in the Reich Ministry of Justice.[40] This ambitious research program aimed at producing four practical applications. First, through the criminal-biological examinations Nazi criminologists hoped to be able to genetically classify every prisoner in Germany. Second, they planned to make the results of the examinations useful at sentencing by creating a kind of genetic presentence report upon which judges could base their decisions. Third, the examination results would be useful in identifying those criminals who should be sterilized. And fourth, the head of the program, Robert Ritter, hoped to compile a universal archive of genetic information that would enable him to *predict* who would become criminals so that they could be immobilized before they started committing crimes.[41]

Ritter was a dominant figure in the development of Nazi criminal-biology by virtue of his positions within the Nazi hierarchy. In 1940 he became head of a department that merged the racial hygiene research being done at the Institute for Eugenics and Population Biology, under the Ministry of Health, with the Criminal-Biological Institute collecting genetic data on prisoners for the Ministry of Justice. The following year he became head of a second Criminal-Biological Institute that reported to the Schutz-Staffel, or SS, and compiled genetic databases on wayward youths, vagabonds, and asocial families, using genealogical methods similar to those on which, in the United States, Richard Dugdale and Henry Goddard had based their famous research on the Juke and Kallikak families. However, other criminologists, too, were active in Nazi Germany, including Franz Exner, Hans Gruhle, Siegfried Koller, Heinrich Wilhelm Kranz, and Friedrich Stumpfl, and as Wetzell has shown, many of them did not share Ritter's extreme racism and genetic determinism.[42] "Nazi-era criminology was characterized by a continuing tension between hereditarian biases and an ongoing process of increasing methodological sophistication.... [A] certain amount of 'normal science' continued under the Nazi regime."[43] Even so, criminal-biology lost the eclectic character it had had in the Weimar years, growing ever more uniform. Another factor that sapped whatever vigor was left in German criminology was the diminishment of resources and narrowing of goals that set in when World War II began. Thereafter, criminal-biology had little to do other than to justify exterminating criminals and other asocials.

When Hitler became chancellor of Germany in January 1933, the Nazis moved swiftly to implement their racial hygiene program. In April 1933 they enacted the Law for Restoration of the Professional Civil Service, a ruling that barred Jews and communists from employment in universities and government positions. This order got rid of potential opponents and simultaneously forced those who wanted to keep their jobs into collaboration with the Nazi state. Among the criminologists who were forced to leave Germany in the 1930s were Max Grünhut and Hermann Mannheim; along with the Polish refugee Leon Radzinowicz, they went on to found British criminology.[44] Karl Birnbaum, a key figure in the development of German criminal-biology, emigrated directly to the United States, followed, eventually, by Gustav Aschaffenburg.[45] Hans von Hentig, not a Jew but a close associate of Aschaffenburg and (despite his own hereditarianism) an opponent of the Nazis, also emigrated to the United States, where he taught at various universities and, with his classic *The Criminal and His Victim*, founded the field of victimization studies.[46] Other U.S. emigrants included Georg Rusche and Otto Kirchheimer, whose *Punishment and Penal Structure* laid the foundation for nearly all later theories of penality.[47] Thus through its own racism Germany sent into exile some of its best criminologists, men who might have tempered its criminological biologism with environmentalist perspectives.[48]

## Criminal Justice under the Third Reich

How did criminal-biology affect criminal justice in the Third Reich? To answer that question, we must first look at ways in which the Nazis changed the criminal law and institutions for the administration of justice, for those changes created the circumstances in which they applied criminological theory.

Immediately after coming to power, the Nazis set about turning Germany into a dictatorship. In February 1933, they used a fire in the Reichstag building where the German Parliament met as an excuse for suspending civil liberties. The next month's Enabling Act authorized Hitler to write his own legislation, even if it deviated from the constitution. The new regime centralized the governments of the individual German states; these states, which had enjoyed considerable autonomy in the Weimar Republic, now lost control as responsibility for criminal justice and other matters shifted to the Reich's central administration. In another step, the government in April 1933 created the Geheime Statspolizei, or Gestapo, a secret state police agency that was independent of judicial review. Thus "justice" became a synonym for the needs of the state, and criminal justice institutions became tools for executing Nazi policies. The Nazis carried Lombroso's "social defense" position on criminal justice to an extreme that would have horrified the Italian liberal.

With the opposition silenced by the Law for Restoration for the Professional Civil Service, in July 1933 the Nazis enacted the Law for Prevention of Hereditarily Diseased Offspring, or Sterilization Law, authorizing compulsory sterilization of people said to be afflicted with congenital epilepsy, feeblemindedness, mental diseases such as schizophrenia, alcoholism, and other supposedly heritable afflictions. This law, inspired by American eugenics research and modeled on similar U.S. legislation,[49] took aim more directly at the mentally retarded or "feebleminded" than at criminals. However, it affected the latter group as well. "Feeblemindedness" was vaguely defined in any case, and because it was diagnosed through social as well as intellectual criteria, the term was easily extended to cover those who committed criminal or quasi-deviant acts. "Hereditary alcoholism" was another category that could easily be stretched to include criminals. Hitler himself had wanted to include habitual criminals under the sterilization act, but officials in the Ministry of Justice, in an incident illustrating their commitment to science, resisted the Führer on the grounds that they were not yet sure of the criteria for sorting hereditary from nonhereditary offenders.[50] However, the Sterilization Law was amended in 1935 to provide for "voluntary" castration of those with a "degenerate sex drive,"[51] and in any case those deemed incorrigible criminals were immobilized reproductively by habitual offender legislation passed six months later. This Habitual Offender Law of November 1933 enabled the courts to resentence incorrigibles to indefinite terms. Such terms were, in effect, both life and death sentences, for in the great majority of cases the offenders either died of maltreatment in prison or were eventually shipped to concentration camps to be worked to death.

Historians used to picture the police, courts, and prisons of Germany's traditional criminal justice system as relatively independent of the Third

Reich's police forces and concentration camps. In recent years, however, the older view of a "normal" criminal justice system, parallel to Nazi institutions and often resistant to but helplessly overwhelmed by them, has been rejected. That view in fact was promulgated after World War II by criminal justice officials anxious to cover up their cooperation with the Nazis.[52] Many of these officials had collaborated enthusiastically, and the regular system had actually served to reassure the populace that traditional standards were in place. "The continued operation of the legal bureaucracy," writes Wachsmann, "helped to mask the terrorist nature of the Nazi regime."[53]

Policing in the Third Reich followed a trajectory toward centralization, expansion, takeover of court functions, and obliteration of rights. All policing was organized under the SS, which had expanded from an original small group of bodyguards to become, under Heinrich Himmler, a complex organization with hundreds of thousands of employees. The SS eventually included military units, the Gestapo, a medical corps, the regular police, and concentration camp administrators. Tellingly, even one of Robert Ritter's criminal-biological research units was lodged within the SS bureaucracy— hardly a blueprint for scientific objectivity, but then, objectivity was not what they were after. The regular police, or Kripo, frustrated during the Weimar period by civil rights limitations on their investigative powers, welcomed the opportunity to contribute to "preventative policing" and to improve racial hygiene.[54]

Even though the SS took over functions traditionally lodged with the courts, the regular judicial system nonetheless played a vital role in the effort to cleanse Germany of social misfits. Criminal laws multiplied; for example, it became illegal even to leaflet or make a joke about Hitler. Older laws were rewritten to increase the vagueness with which offenses were defined, making it possible to charge almost anyone with anything. Jurists were advised: "Ask yourself with every decision you take how would the Führer decide in my place?"[55] Many responded vigorously. "Justice is whatever is useful for the German people," declared Judge Hans Frank, head of the Nazi Party's legal office. "The National Socialist state does not negotiate with criminals, it knocks them to the ground."[56]

While some court officials tried to maintain judicial impartiality, many gave in to Nazi pressures, in effect throwing traditional concepts of justice to the winds. Regular courts charged more harshly, allowed fewer appeals, and punished more severely, frequently meting out sentences of death. When prosecutors lacked evidence to convict, they might simply hand defendants over to the SS.[57] To speed up justice and control outcomes in the case of political opponents, the Nazis established special courts, including a people's court that accepted faked charges and determined sentences in advance. Many defendants were simply sent to "protective custody" or "security confinement" to await trial indefinitely; in effect, this meant that they were sent to prison before trial, and because imprisonment often led to slow death, this meant that arrest itself could be a death sentence. Other defendants were eliminated more rapidly. The members of the famous White Rose group of Munich students who leafleted against Hitler, for example, were "tried" in a show of justice and immediately guillotined.[58] "The court and prison systems became key instruments of Nazi repression," Wachsmann explains. "This would have been impossible without the cooperation of the German legal officials."[59]

The jails and prisons of the traditional justice system kept operating under the Third Reich, constituting a carceral network that at times actually held more people than the parallel system of concentration camps.[60] The prisons were kept full by the Habitual Offender Law, which authorized judges to give indefinite "security" sentences to those who, in the court's opinion, had offended due to an underlying "criminal disposition." The same law enabled prison officials to recommend for indefinite sentencing inmates whose terms were about to expire but who had somehow demonstrated incorrigibility. The majority of those sentenced under the eugenic Habitual Offender Law were petty thieves, prostitutes, vagrants, and other minor offenders. In prison they were fed little, worked brutally, and beaten frequently.

Nearly all the Nazi killing programs included criminals, starting with the "euthanasia" operation code-named T4 and initiated in October 1939. T4 aimed at getting rid of the mentally incapacitated, a population that included the criminally insane. Wetzell relates how court officials, when they tried to check up on people they had committed to institutions for the criminally insane, sometimes found that their wards had vanished—disappearances that led some doctors to avoid testifying in diminished responsibility cases for fear that the defendants would be executed before they came to trial.[61] In April 1941, the T4 operation expanded to target people held in concentration camps, including those unable to work, Jews, "asocial psychopaths," and inmates with criminal records—an expansion that coincided with Germany's need to free up resources to fight the war and care for the wounded. Due to public unrest over his "euthanasia" program, Hitler officially terminated it while continuing its operation in secret; now the program gathered "asocials" from workhouses and homes for wayward youth into its murderous embrace. On Hitler's initiative, after 1942 everyone in security confinement was slated for elimination—ostensibly in order to counterbalance the gene pool's loss of good stock through war.[62] Some in security confinement were worked to death in regular prisons; others were shot, hung, or guillotined; yet others were sent to concentration camps for "annihilation through labor."[63] Thus toward the regime's end, the two parallel system, one consisting of traditional penal institutions and the other of concentration camps, began to converge.

Another, more specifically criminological convergence occurred as the various groups of deviants identified as hereditary misfits came to form a vast pool of almost indistinguishable "asocials." These included political opponents of the regime, who were sometimes portrayed in Lombrosian fashion, with deformed heads and twisted features.[64] It further included Jews and Gypsies, groups that research had identified as inherently criminalistic. Sex offenders, prostitutes, homosexuals, Jehovah's Witnesses, juvenile delinquents, "psychopaths," vagrants, the "work-shy," beggars, and alcoholics—these groups, too, were criminologically demonstrated to be hereditary degenerates. The looseness of the identifying criteria encouraged a steady swelling of the "asocials" category. "A good man," wrote the ethologist Konrad Lorenz, "can very easily feel with his deepest instincts whether another is a scoundrel or not. . . . [W]e should rely on the unanalyzed and deeply rooted reactions of our best individuals."[65] Lorenz, a Nazi Party member and future Nobel Prize winner in science, likened asocials to malignant tumors who needed to be eliminated for the health of "the supra-individual organism."[66] The Third Reich, then, was far from hostile to science; rather, at every step of the way it called on science for verification and legitimation—just as science called on it, and for the same reasons.[67] Once the new legal and administrative structures were in place, criminal-biology worked to achieve the Nazi goals of eugenics and racial hygiene.

Illustrating this system's workings, Wachsmann describes the case of a woman committed to prison in June 1936. Magdalena S., thirty-three years old, had a record of sixteen minor convictions for theft and prostitution. She behaved well in prison until guards reprimanded her for not working with sufficient energy, at which point she quit entirely, refusing even to clean her cell and telling officials, "'I cannot bear this life any longer, I cannot say yes to everything and I cannot obey any more.'" The officials sent Magdalena S. to strict detention for five months, feeding her little except bread and water. Deteriorating mentally, she became aggressive toward the guards and her own person. Eventually assigned to an "annihilation through labor" program, Magdalena S. was sent in 1943 to a concentration camp, where she died along with 20,000 other prison inmates.[68]

It is impossible to come up with a total number for the criminals who, like Magdalena S., died as a result of the Nazi belief that by exterminating criminals, they could exterminate crime. Of course, various sorts of figures do exist; we know, for instance, that between 1939 and 1945, German courts meted out 16,000 death sentences and that after August 1942, at least 14,000 habitual offenders were killed in concentration camps.[69] But the figures are often elusive, overlapping, or incommensurable. Do we include in the total number those Poles imported to Germany to work in war industries who were executed by the police for minor infractions?[70] Homosexuals who died in concentration camps? Gypsies at the Birkenau camp who died as a result of exposure, disease, malnutrition, and medical experimentation (13,613), by gassing (6,432), or by being shot in escape attempts (32)?[71] What about Jews who were classified as habitual criminals? And prostitutes identified as Jews? But although it is futile to try to compile a precise tally, that very futility teaches a crucial lesson: in Nazi thought, criminals were not a clearly defined category but rather part of a larger group of degenerates that included Jews, Gypsies, the handicapped, homosexuals, the poor, and other asocials. Race hygiene excluded them all from the Nazi utopia, and for the same fundamental reason of hereditary biological inferiority. Thus Friedlander argues that the term *genocide* must be expanded from its original meaning—the mass murder of a particular ethnic or national group—to include "the mass murder of human beings because they belonged to a biologically defined group."[72] On this argument, criminals too were victims of Nazi genocide. Nazism was an ideology of eugenic purification, a "vision," as Claudia Koonz puts it, "of an exclusive community of 'us' without 'them.'"[73]

## Biocriminology in Fascist Italy: A Comparison

In some respects, the circumstances that led up to the establishment of fascist dictatorships in Italy and Germany were similar. Like the Weimar Republic, Italy in the early 20th century was a liberal state, reformist in thrust but unstable, beset by fundamental economic and political problems against which the government made little progress. Radical political movements on the Left, fed by extremes of poverty in rural areas and industrializing cities, were countered by antiliberal conservatism on the Right. Italy sided with the Allies in World War I, but mainly because it had secretly been promised new territories as a reward; when those rewards failed to materialize on a scale sufficient to satisfy Italy's imperialist hunger, the country reacted with humiliation and frustration, somewhat as Germany reacted to the settlements of the same war. Mussolini founded his Fascist Party in 1919 on assurances that he would stabilize the government, eliminate corruption, and restore the nation to a grandeur it had not known since the days of imperial Rome. He rose to power in part through the violent tactics of his Blackshirts, paramilitary gangs that intimidated the opposition much as Hitler's copycat gangs of Brownshirts were to do in the early 1930s.

These parallels cannot be pushed very far, however. Mussolini established himself as dictator almost a decade before Hitler took over in Germany and in a country long dominated by the Catholic Church, an institution that could effectively oppose the secular government. Moreover, at the time Mussolini rose to power, Italy was not experiencing a hysteria over crime analogous to that of Weimar Germany, although its criminal justice officials were preoccupied on an ongoing basis with "brigandage" in the southern half of the country. However, the nation *was* concerned with problems of governability. ("Brigandage," for example, was sometimes a code word for political resistance by independent southerners to national centralization in Rome.)[74] Riding that wave of concern, in 1922 Mussolini marched into Rome in a grand symbolic gesture, recalling glory days of Italy's past. By 1926 he had established his dictatorship.

Criminologically, too, Italian developments paralleled those of Germany, though again in a rough and imprecise way. Most significantly, criminology in both countries was deeply stamped by Lombroso's criminal anthropology, his commitment to study crime scientifically, and his assumption that any procedures calling themselves science would reveal immutable truths. That Lombroso was a psychiatrist, and that he had begun with the premise that serious criminals must be sick or physically abnormal, meant that in Italy as later in Germany, crime would be interpreted as an individual fault rooted in biological deviation. In addition, Lombroso's "scientific" racism meant that Italy's early 20th-century versions of criminal anthropology, like later German criminal-biology, would be permeated with ideas about racial differences in corrigibility. Lombroso put criminal anthropology on the map in Italy, and there it stayed for decades, perpetuated (with modifications) by second- and third-generation followers such as Enrico Ferri, Raffaele Garofalo, Alfredo Niceforo, Salvatore Ottlenghi, and Scopio

Sighele.[75] Several of these criminal anthropologists joined Mussolini's party, thus yoking criminal anthropology to Fascism.

But even more significant were the differences in the ways Lombrosianism played itself out in Italy and Germany. Apart from his theory of the born criminal as a throwback to a more primitive evolutionary stage, Lombroso was an environmentalist, recognizing a host of social influences on criminal behavior and maintaining that in many cases, biology had little or nothing to do with crime. Because his Italian followers took these distinctions seriously, Italian criminology was better able to incorporate sociological analyses, and these, in turn, buffered it against biological extremism. (In the Weimar years, German sociologists took little interest in criminology, according to Wetzell, thus leaving the field vulnerable to its takeover by biological determinists.)[76] Most significant in setting directions for the criminological future in Italy was the fact that Lombroso, although he was unquestionably biologistic, racist, and crudely deterministic, was also liberal and humanitarian, often sympathetic to criminals and admiring of their subcultures—in sharp contrast to his German followers. These personal characteristics of the towering figure in Italian criminology, along with the fact that he was Jewish, served as a brake, restraining Italians from the Germans' headlong descent into racial hygiene.

Eugenics themes coursed through post-Lombrosian Italian criminal anthropology as they did through German criminal-biology, growing stronger as the 20th century progressed and culminating, in 1927, in Mussolini's public endorsement of eugenics policies. Mussolini's hopes for improving the Italian "race" were built into the Rocco Code of penal reforms enacted in 1930 in the form of enhanced sentences for those who exhibited a "tendency to commit crime"; in the inclusion of a category of "crimes against the integrity and health of the race" (it included having syphilis); and in the criminalization of alcoholism to prevent hereditary diseases and race degeneration.[77] Thus criminal anthropology and fascism came together to produce this mildly eugenical penal code. But in a country in which the major religious institution opposed even birth control, the government took no steps toward sterilization or "euthanasia," and the emphasis fell on positive rather than negative eugenics measures.

This emphasis is obvious, for example, in the article "Eugenics and the Criminal Law" (1914) by law professor Giulio Q. Battaglini of the University of Rome. Speaking enthusiastically about the eugenic potential of the criminal law, Battaglini nonetheless criticizes the sterilization laws recently passed by U.S. states as scientifically unsound and politically intolerable.

Instead, he recommends indeterminate sentencing—not to immobilize offenders reproductively but to improve their moral fiber by offering incentives for "redemption through personal effort."[78] More generally, Battaglini touts the positive eugenic effects of "economic betterment, moral education, and the like"[79]—a program so mild as to be barely recognizable as eugenic in intention.

The racial themes of Fascist biocriminology played out, initially, in the defamation of Africans. Lombroso's facile incorporation of social Darwinist racial hierarchies led him to observe "how closely" criminals' skulls, with their numerous cranial anomalies, "correspond to [the] . . . normal skulls of the colored and inferior races."[80] This sort of association helped undergird Mussolini's imperialist war of 1935–1936 against the Ethiopians, which Fascists justified as a takeover of an inferior people. Racial laws, mass killings, death marches, and internment camps—these measures to subjugate the Ethiopians anticipated later Nazi actions against Jews and Gypsies[81] and were supported by most Italian anthropologists, including criminal anthropologists.[82]

The racial themes of Fascist biocriminology also converged in the criminalization of southern Italians. To criminal anthropologists, the crime problems of southern Italy—the Mafia, the camorra, and brigandage—proved that Sicilians, Sardinians, and other inhabitants of the lower third of the country were racially inferior to the law-abiding citizens of the north. Their darker skins seemed to link them definitively to criminalistic "races" such as Bedouins, Gypsies, and Africans. In his book on homicide, Lombroso's disciple Enrico Ferri used shaded maps to indicate rates for various types of crime; ominously, the maps on parricide, poisoning, assassination, and infanticide were shaded most darkly in their southern regions.[83] Whether we interpret this criminalization of southern Italians as an effort to blame the fallout from northern capitalism on a "subaltern group" (the interpretation put forth by political theorist Antonio Gramsci)[84] or as a step in the forging of the new nation's identity,[85] it was indisputably part and parcel of criminal anthropology under Fascism

The racial equations of Italian criminology shifted in 1938, when Mussolini issued his Racist Scientists' Manifesto, proclaiming that Italians, like Germans, belonged to the Aryan race. The manifesto was followed by a series of racial laws that forbade intermarriage of Arabs, Ethiopians, and Jews with members of "the Italian race" and excluded Jews from public education and state employment. For a moment, Mary Gibson writes, concerns about southern Italians disappeared. "Jews now replaced southerners as the 'inferior' and 'degenerate' race that threatened to weaken Italy."[86] Italy's Jews went underground or were rounded up and sent north to death camps.[87]

But Mussolini, who had earlier helped Jews *escape* from the Nazis, eventually lost interest in these persecutions.[88] Fascist criminology, inoculated against anti-Semitism by Lombroso's own Jewishness and by the relatively low levels of anti-Semitism in Italy, did not become a vehicle for race purification, despite its strong racist themes. Mussolini's racial laws were in fact a sign of the weakening of the Fascist state. Whereas earlier, Hitler had emulated Mussolini, now the Duce, his power ebbing, was trying to emulate the Führer.

Fascist criminologists dreamed of a legal transformation that would bring all aspects of the criminal justice system into line with criminal-anthropological principles.[89] Such dreams were dashed—the hoped-for transformation never came. But criminal anthropology did affect criminal justice practices in nearly all parts of the system. Lombroso's emphasis on crime prevention intensified repressive tendencies already rooted in Italy's authoritarian police agencies.[90] To determine suspects' degree of dangerousness, Fascist police studied criminal anthropology and learned to compile dossiers analogous to (although less hereditarian than) those of the Bavarian criminal-biologists. They also intensified social control of alcoholics, prostitutes, and drug users, groups on whom criminal anthropology cast suspicions of degeneracy and who, collectively, formed a mass of down-and-outers analogous to the Nazis' "asocials." The Fascist hierarchy welcomed such increases in social control, less out of concern to prevent race degeneration than to strengthen their spy networks.[91] But policing under Fascism never became as terroristic as the SS, nor did it attempt to cast political dissent as a biological defect.[92]

In Italy, biological theories evidently had their main impact on the handling of juvenile delinquents, a group Lombroso had identified as highly criminalistic.[93] After 1926, youths showing signs of physical or psychological abnormality could be sent to observation centers for examination by specialists in criminal anthropology, and under the Fascists' Rocco Code of 1930, potentially dangerous youths could be held on three-year indeterminate sentences. As for imprisonment, the Italian practice of *confino*, or internal exile of adults in penal colonies or small southern towns, increased under the Fascists; it, too, was encouraged by criminal anthropologists' concern with crime prevention and the identification of dangerous persons.[94] But the most repressive and brutal aspects of Fascist criminal justice operated independently of criminal anthropology, on orders from Mussolini and his close associates. The Duce might appoint judges, fix trials, and arrange murders, but he did so without appealing to criminologists for scientific justification. Biocriminology was more loosely coupled to Fascism than to Nazism.

How are we to explain this difference between the two fascist dictatorships, in both of which biocriminology served political ends? One factor lay in differences in Lombroso's impact. In Germany, criminal anthropology directly nourished Nazi biocriminology and was in turn amplified by it and carried to its own worst possible conclusions; but in Italy, criminal anthropology's influence was more ambiguous. While it allied itself with Fascism, criminal anthropology also formed a bulwark against Fascism, encouraging a sociological orientation that German interpretations of crime sorely lacked, emphasizing positive rather than negative eugenics measures, and contributing a relatively liberal and less rabidly racist sense of direction. A second factor lay with the Catholic Church, which opposed eugenic measures, and a third with Mussolini's relatively weak control of criminal justice agencies. Then, too, Fascist biocriminologists, despite their dreams of transforming criminal justice, achieved nothing like the transformation of Nazi Germany.

Another explanation for the differences between the impact of biocriminology in Italy and Germany lay with the relative weakness of anti-Semitism in Italy, where Jews were comparatively well integrated into mainstream society. Primo Levi, the Italian Jew who survived imprisonment in the Nazi death camp at Auschwitz, remarked in an interview:

> As a boy and as a young man, being Jewish was not all that important for me. My family was not religious. Jews in Italy speak and spoke only Italian. There was very little difference between me and my friends. . . . This condition ended abruptly with the racial laws promulgated by Mussolini in 1938, which were identical to Hitler's Nuremberg ones. But Italians often disregard laws. This can be a virtue if the laws are bad. . . . It was forbidden to have a Christian maid but everybody had one—when the doorbell rang you told her to go upstairs.[95]

Fascist anti-Semitism, Levi continues, in important ways made "the situation . . . difficult and serious: Jews in jobs or positions dependent upon the government or fascist party were expelled," and of course many, like himself, were sent to Germany for extermination.[96] But "fascism in Italy was not like in Germany, an elite matter of soil and blood. It was accepted cynically. . . . My professor of chemistry, to keep teaching, was obliged to wear a black shirt, but he didn't wear a real one, it was only a triangle in front, when he turned to the left or right you could see the triangle."[97] As a result, biocriminology did not become a deadly weapon against Jews in Italy as in Germany.

## Discovering the Genocide of Criminals

The contours of Nazi criminal-biology are just now becoming clear as historians reassess the nature of Nazi science more generally. In contrast to the earlier view of Nazi science as "bad" science conducted, reluctantly, by researchers who had to toe Hitler's line, the reassessment is discovering that Nazi scientists pursued their research enthusiastically, using what they considered objective methods and hard data. Certainly this is true of the scientists who created Nazi criminal-biology with the aim of exterminating incorrigibles and achieving racial hygiene.

Similarly, the *results* of Nazi criminal-biology are just now becoming clear as historians discover an entirely new class of National Socialism's victims: those designated as criminals. Remarkably, it has taken half a century for historians even to begin documenting the ways in which Nazi police, courts, and prisons worked to exterminate "habitual offenders" and others deemed hereditary misfits. While overlaps with other outcast groups make it impossible to reckon the precise number of criminals exterminated in the name of racial hygiene, this slaughter seems unquestionably to have constituted a form of genocide.

Ultimately, there may be no way to explain what happened in Nazi Germany. "We cannot understand it," Levi writes in his book *The Truce*, "but we can and must understand from where it springs." One of those wellheads was a criminology that, in its biologism, determinism, and calls for social defense, became the tool of a fascist state. As Levi concludes, "We must be on our guard. If understanding is impossible, knowing is imperative, because what happened could happen again."[98]

# 9

# Contemporary Biocriminology

Coming into their own after World War II, sociological explanations of crime dominated theoretical work in the academy for the rest of the century. Biological theories, tainted by associations with Nazi eugenics, fell into disgrace, and the medical model was rejected as a tool of repression. Mainstream sociologists investigated the roles of blocked opportunity and peer associations in the genesis of delinquency, while radical sociologists investigated criminology's own contribution to maintaining the web of power relationships. An iconic sociological text of the 1970s, *The New Criminology*, concluded that "*deviance* is normal."[1]

But then the pendulum started swinging back in the direction of biocriminology. Today it is picking up speed and threatening not to eclipse sociological theories but to break their monopoly. Even though sociological explanations remain dominant in criminology departments, biological theories are developing rapidly elsewhere in the academy, enlisting prestigious sciences such as genetics in their cause and generally showing impressive versatility and vitality.

Two factors in the late 20th-century social context were particularly important in this change of direction: the emergence of a culture pervaded by assumptions about the biological roots of human behavior, on the one hand, and, on the other, a burgeoning interest in the prevention of harms of all types, from cancer to terrorism to criminality. These two factors—a profound cultural involvement with and investment in human biology, including massive funding for genetics research, and an equally profound determination to prevent harms and minimize risks—have persisted into the 21st century and promise to drive the development of biocriminology for decades to come.

We are witnessing a "biologization of human existence," writes sociologist Nikolas Rose. "We live, inescapably, in a biologized culture. Not merely the sicknesses of human beings, but also their personalities, capacities, passions and the forces that mobilize them—their 'identities' themselves—appear at least potentially to be explicable in biological terms, and increasingly in terms of their genetic make-up."[2] American and other Western cultures are now saturated with biological concerns and solutions, in sharp contrast to the environmentalist culture of the mid–20th century, when the sciences that now make newspaper headlines were in their infancy and reformers were more likely to call for "nurture" than "nature" remedies for social problems.

Looking back to the 1950s, 1960s, and 1970s, one can identify the roots of the biological culture that prevails today. Many of them lay in genetics research—on, for instance, sickle cell anemia and the effects of the U.S. atomic bombing of Japan during World War II. The pace of research picked up after Francis Crick and James Watson's identification in 1953 of the three-dimensional structure of the deoxyribonucleic acid (DNA) molecule, a scientific watershed that eventually led to the 1988 initiation of the Human Genome Project, aimed at determining the full sequence of DNA on human chromosomes. With massive increases in funding, historian Daniel Kevles observes, by the 1980s human genetics had "grown from being a quiet hobby, involving merely the collection of pedigrees of rare diseases and deformities, to one of the most complicated and demanding disciplines in the whole of science."[3]

In the criminological arena, one of the first signs of the swing back to biological theorizing was the 1964 publication of *Crime and Personality*, in which British psychologist Hans Eysenck—to the considerable consternation of the then-dominant sociology-of-deviance theorists— revived the medical model by explaining criminality in genetic and neurophysiological terms.[4] Eysenck was the most prominent psychologist in Britain, and although explaining criminality was a digression from his central personality theory, he took *Crime and Personality* through three editions (the second in 1970, the third in 1977). According the Eysenck, the explanation of criminal behavior lies in personality, and the explanation of personality, in turn, lies in the neurobiological equipment one is born with. Criminals and other antisocial types are poor conditioners—that is, they inherit nervous systems that learn moral behavior more slowly than the nervous systems of good (and therefore law-abiding) conditioners. The learning process of most interest to Eysenck was that of classical or Pavlovian conditioning, which involves involuntary behavior and the autonomic (as opposed to the central) nervous system. He portrayed criminals as extraverts, sensation seekers who engage in risky and criminal activities to compensate for the sluggish nervous systems they inherit.

This portrait anticipated that of later neurocriminologists, who depicted offenders as people born with neurological deficits predisposing them to hyperactivity and sensation seeking. In that regard alone, Eysenck's work was remarkably foresighted. But his influence extended far beyond opening up neurological research on criminality. *Crime and Personality* boldly presented the first new biological explanation of crime since William Sheldon had floated bodytype research. At a time when sociological explanations ruled the criminological domain virtually unchallenged, Eysenck's innate-personality theory fired the first shot in the revival of the old struggle between nurture and nature explanations of criminality. Eysenck aggressively invaded the territory of sociological criminologists (he was neither a self-effacing nor a tactful man), taking the initial step in the late 20th-century renewal of biocriminology, a restoration that continues, still accelerating, into the present. In addition, he gave currency to the concept of biosociality—interactions between conditionability and social setting or, more broadly, between biological and environmental factors—that has become central to early 21st-century thinking about the bases of criminal behavior. *Crime and Personality*, then, marked a major turning point, the moment when biological theories regained a toehold in criminological thought.

That toehold was soon expanded by other biological theorizing about the causes of human behavior. In the 1960s researchers claimed that some male offenders have an extra Y chromosome, an XYY configuration that explains their propensity to violence.[5] The XYY theory (discussed in more detail later) proved to be incorrect, but like Eysenck's work, it made sociological criminologists aware that invaders from the biological sciences were starting to circle their walls. Their sense of threat was reinforced by the publication in 1975 of Edward O. Wilson's *Sociobiology*, a work that became famous—in liberal circles, infamous—for arguing that all social behavior, including altruism, is rooted in biology.[6] Several years after it appeared, lawyers for women in England and the United States tried to mount a premenstrual syndrome (PMS) defense to violent crime.[7] Their arguments, while meeting with little success in the courts, again pushed mainstream criminologists to confront the claim that biology—in this case, hormones—might precipitate criminal behavior. More impetus for the biological turn came from disillusionment with environmentalist reforms, especially after President Lyndon Johnson's War on Poverty failed to achieve its goals.

On a very broad scale, the last three decades of the 20th century saw a decline in the social sciences and rise of the natural sciences.[8] The social sciences began to lose explanatory power while the biological sciences gained it. This trend could even be found within disciplines; in psychology, for instance, the study of interpersonal behavior lost ground to evolutionary psychology and neuropsychology. Related to this realignment in the sciences was the trend, identified by sociologist Troy Duster, to look for ever more minuscule causational factors—to "deploy either individual level or even smaller units of analysis (blood, genes, neurotransmitters) to account for scholastic achievement, crime rates, and even racism."[9] The overall result has been, ultimately, a change in the social organization of science itself as funding priorities, the status of various specialities, and the credibility of differing types of explanation shifted in the direction of biology.

Hand in hand with this shift toward biological explanations has come an anxiety about physical security and a new emphasis on risk avoidance in areas as disparate as medicine and airport security. In criminology, risk anxiety shows up in a swing away from the traditional concern with punishing past harms and toward the prevention of future harms. It has contributed as well to criminology's recent tack toward "actuarial justice"— the use of offender statistics to predict dangerousness and introduce postconviction dispositions to incapacitate people deemed high risk.[10] We have arrived at what legal theorists term the *preventive state*[11]—or, rather, *re*-arrived, for the current preoccupation with security echoes anxieties of the early 20th-century eugenics movement, with its emphasis on forestalling crime and immobilizing carriers of bad germ plasm. Today's preventionists, while they show little interest in eugenic measures and rationales per se, further resemble their predecessors by aiming to incapacitate not only serious offenders but also minor repeat criminals.

Precisely this sort of noneugenic prevention scenario can be found in Steven Spielberg's science fiction film *Minority Report* (2002), in which three creatures ("precogs") warn a government official of crimes that are about to occur. The official (played by Tom Cruise) rushes to crime scenes before the offenses are committed, arrests about-to-be criminals in the nick of time, and "halos" them with a device that immobilizes them forever. Knowledge of risk, enabling the official to function as a cop, judge, and jailor simultaneously, thus prevents crime in both the present and the future. But even the precogs cannot accurately predict in all cases who the criminals will be. In Spielberg's analysis, there is an inherent and unresolvable conflict between prediction and justice, science and law. This same tension constitutes a major issue in the trends toward biological explanations and risk prevention: will we adopt new predictive and preventive biocriminological measures that, inevitably, will conflict with our traditional understandings of justice?

This chapter deals with biological explanations of criminality from about 1960 into the early 21st century. Eysenck's *Crime and Personality*, first published in 1964, provides a useful starting point. The period since its appearance has been one of tremendous activity, with biocriminologists cultivating a number of fields at once. It has been characterized not by the dominance of a single theory or even group of related theories but by a multiplicity of contestants—chemical, cognitive, evolutionary, genetic, hormonal, neurological, and psychophysiological explanations—all vying for first place. We find a welter of intersecting and overlapping theoretical initiatives.

My goal in this chapter is twofold. First, I am interested in mapping the big picture: the main lines of development, trends, and promising directions for the future. So far as I know, there is no other recent source for such information.[12] Because the big picture is complicated, and because I trace a number of key trajectories, this chapter is by and large descriptive. Second, I hope to analyze the production of biocriminology over recent decades in ways that will be useful to sociological criminologists. Biological theorizing should be more palatable to sociologists today than it was even a few years ago because the biosocial model has risen to the fore, offering an escape from the endless and unproductive nature-versus-nurture debate. Moreover, biocriminologists themselves now reject out of hand the hard determinism that sociologists (and others) found objectionable in earlier biological theories of crime. In fact, the new work on genetics and crime stresses environment's crucial role in shaping criminal behaviors.[13]

In what follows I categorize developments in late 20th-century and early 21st-century biocriminology by the types of causes they invoke. The chapter is organized around five etiological categories: acquired biological abnormalities, cognitive deficits, evolutionary theories, neuroscientific theories, and genetic explanations of crime. This approach has the drawback of making the categories seem discrete and independent when actually they overlap and intertwine. (For example, cognitive disabilities can be acquired, and many of the causes discussed later in this chapter can be reduced, ultimately, to genetics.) But this approach has the advantage of yielding broad conceptual categories under which more specific explanations (such as those based on hormonal malfunctioning) can be classified. In other words, it keeps the number of explanatory categories manageable and enables us to picture their interrelationships.

Mass murderer Charles Whitman in 1966, age twenty-four. Charles J. Whitman, a twenty-four-year-old student at the University of Texas, killed his wife and mother and then pumped bullets into fifteen people on the university campus from a perch high in the administration building tower. An autopsy discovered a brain tumor. Photograph permission of Associated Press.

## Acquired Biological Abnormalities

William Freeman, the assailant whose case opens this book, provides an early example of a criminal whose behavior was blamed on a biological problem acquired after birth. According to Freeman's supporters, at any rate, a blow on the head by a prison keeper caused his subsequent mental deterioration and eventual murder of the Van Nest family.[14] A similar but more recent example comes from the case of Charles Whitman, the young man who, in 1966, killed his mother and wife and then, having ascended the bell tower of the University of Texas, Austin, fired a rifle at passersby below, killing another fifteen people and wounding thirty-one more before police officers shot him dead. "I wish an autopsy on me to be performed to see if there is any mental disorder," Whitman wrote pathetically on the day he died.[15] The autopsy revealed a brain tumor in the hypothalamus region of this brain, a growth that, some hypothesized, put pressure on his amygdala, an organ associated with emotion and aggression.[16]

To identify influences that promote crime in the general population, scientists today often use not individual cases like those of Freeman and Whitman but longitudinal cohort data that can be mined statistically for correlations between delinquency and biological or social factors. One such study, based on data on almost 1,000 children born at Philadelphia's Pennsylvania Hospital between 1959 and 1962, concluded that lead poisoning—an acquired biological condition—was a top predictor of later criminal activity among boys in this group. When young, some of the children had ingested paint chips and other matter with high levels of lead, a substance that causes neurological damage, which in turn can lead to impulsiveness, cognitive disabilities, and aggression.[17] "A growing body of research shows lead poisoning to be a strong predictor of crime among males," writes Deborah W. Denno, a specialist in this area, "even controlling for other influential biological and social variables."[18] But, Denno continues, these studies really indicate *interactions* among biological and social variables such as family resources. (For example, poor people are most likely to live in homes with flaking leaded paint.) "Social factors," she concludes, "affect the body physiologically."[19] Notably, Denno here not only adopts a biosocial model but gives priority to the impact of social factors.

Other studies focus on groups of people known to suffer from specific problems such as parasomnia, meaning sleep disorders that can lead to dangerous behaviors. Parasomnia mainly affects men, and curiously, during the day these men tend to be good-tempered and gentle. When asleep, however, parasomniacs can become aggressive, committing spouse abuse, sexual assault, other sex crimes, and even homicide.[20] Although somnambulist crime is rare, it and related phenomena are being studied across the United States at sleep disorder centers, where research suggests that they may be caused by stress and depression as well as neurological diseases.[21]

Much more common and severe in its consequences is the environmental factor of childhood trauma, which can lead to brain damage and neuropsychiatric symptoms associated with offending. Bruce Perry and his colleagues at the Baylor College of Medicine point out that each year, millions of young children are exposed to traumas such as incest, beating, witnessing family or community violence, and surviving serious accidents. These traumas, Perry and his team explain, occur at a time when the child's brain is still developing, and the information they impart can affect the child's patterns of neural activation or actually block brain development. Among the results are "malorganization and compromised function in brain-mediated functions such as humor, empathy, attachment, and affect regulation."[22] Some traumatized children learn to use "freezing mechanisms" when they are anxious, reactions that may be diagnosed as oppositional-defiant behavior. Such behavior, as explained later in this chapter, is associated with later criminality. Thus events completely external to the child can become internalized in his or her brain and personality.[23]

Additional acquired problems that have been implicated in crime causation include poor diet (too much coffee or cola, too many refined carbohydrates, too few vitamins), pregnancy complications, and alcoholism.[24] However, none of the acquired biological conditions mentioned in this section has been proven to be, singlehandedly, a cause of crime, and in many instances, social explanations are equally plausible. In Charles Whitman's case, for example, abuse as a child and depression as an adult may have played at least as important a role as his brain tumor in precipitating his homicidal rampage; moreover, his psychological and biological problems may have interacted. Psychologist Adrian Raine, voicing an increasingly common view, explains that "what constitutes a biological variable and what constitutes a social variable is open to question. There is much that is social about biological variables (e.g., head injuries leading to brain dysfunction are caused by the environment) and much that is biological about social variables (e.g., genetic factors, and their biological predispositions, contribute to bad parenting)."[25]

Future studies are likely to discover not a single acquired condition such as brain damage or lead poisoning that, on its own, could cause criminal behavior but rather an interplay among biological and social factors that, if not buffered by other circumstances, could encourage criminality.

## Cognitive Deficits and Crime

Cognitive deficits—problems with either purposeful or unconscious learning and information processing—comprise a second type of cause to which contemporary biological theorists attribute criminal behavior. This sort of explanation has a lengthy genealogy, extending back to degenerationists and criminal anthropologists and eventually reaching its zenith (or nadir), as we have seen, in the feeblemindedness theory of crime. But as the 20th century progressed, such hereditarian explanations became suspect, and theorists shied away from again associating mental weakness with criminality until two publications, one of the 1960s and the other of the 1970s, broke the logjam. The first was Eysenck's *Crime and Personality*, making a case for links between criminality and conditionability, the unconscious learning process dependent on the autonomic nervous system. Eysenck believed that some people condition more easily than others. Extraverts, or sociable, happy-go-lucky types who crave excitement and dislike reading, condition less well than bookish, withdrawn introverts because their autonomic nervous system works less effectively. Extreme extraverts or psychopaths fail entirely to acquire a conscience—which, Eysenck iconoclastically concluded, is in any case nothing more than a conditioned reflex. Moreover, the personality traits of extraversion and introversion are to a large degree inherited. Criminals, in Eysenck's view, are genetically poor at learning moral behavior.[26]

The second harbinger of a return to learning-disability accounts was a 1977 article on intelligence and crime in which criminologists Travis Hirschi and Michael Hindelang argued that delinquents have lower IQs than nondelinquents and therefore do less well in school, with some turning eventually to crime.[27] This analysis, even though it was insistently sociological and made no claim whatsoever about biology, raised eyebrows simply by daring to mention the still verboten variable of intelligence. It, too, helped turn the tide, and it was followed by influential criminological studies that *did* treat learning ability as a biological factor.

One of these was *Crime and Human Nature* (1985), in which James Q. Wilson and Richard J. Herrnstein set forth their theory that in criminal behavior, "constitutional factors" play a major role.[28] Nearly a century had passed since respected scholars had given biology such a prominent place in the etiology of crime, and although neither of these particular scholars was trained in criminology (Wilson taught political science at Harvard, Herrnstein psychology), their work attracted widespread attention. One of their five constitutional factors is intelligence. (The other four are bodytype, sex and hormones, age, and degree of innate psychopathy.) The chapter on intelligence argues that street criminals are on the average eight to ten points lower than noncriminals in their intelligence quotients; that this difference is "somewhat inherited"; and that intelligence correlates with "moral reasoning." "Less intelligent people fail to see what is wrong with their offenses, or merely fail to see quite how wrong their offenses are."[29]

Nearly 300 pages later, in a section headed "History and Culture," Wilson and Herrnstein present a chapter titled "Race and Crime," in which they argue that African Americans have higher crime rates than white Americans due to their average lower intelligence. While this chapter takes note of socioeconomic factors that also may affect African American crime rates, it begins with intelligence—in their view, neither a historical nor a cultural but a "constitutional" factor—thus raising the suspicion that this material is buried away in the "History and Culture" section, far from the earlier material on constitutional factors, to avoid charges of racism. As Wilson and Herrnstein themselves remark, "There is no way to discuss the evidence, such as it is, on constitutional factors underlying the association between race and crime without giving offense."[30] They did indeed give offense: many readers were incensed by their suggestion that black Americans are lower in intelligence than white Americans and innately more inclined to commit crime.

Nine years later, this time in tandem with political scientist Charles Murray, Herrnstein produced his even more inflammatory treatise, *The Bell Curve: Intelligence and Class Structure in American Life*.[31] Whereas *Crime and Human Nature* had taken a multifactorial approach, treating weak intelligence as one cause of crime among many, *The Bell Curve* takes a one-dimensional approach, treating weak intelligence as the single most significant cause of crime and a wide range of other political and social problems. The chapter on crime begins with this summary of its argument:

> Among the most firmly established facts about criminal offenders is that their distribution of IQ scores differs from that of the population at large. Taking the scientific literature as a whole, criminal offenders have average IQs of about 92, eight points below the mean. More serious or chronic offenders generally have lower scores than more casual offenders. The relationship of IQ to criminality is especially pronounced in the small fraction of the population, primarily young men, who constitute the chronic criminals that account for a disproportionate amount of crime.[32]

This passage (and, indeed, the entire *Bell Curve* chapter on crime) studiously avoids mentioning race, but elsewhere the authors make it clear that when they talk about "cognitive disadvantage," they are talking about poor whites, African Americans, and recent immigrants—people whose intellectual deficits, in the Herrnstein and Murray view, incline them to criminal behavior. To cope with this socially problematic underclass, they recommend redesigning society to create "a place for everyone."[33] Inoffensive (and ineffective) as this recommendation may sound, its details, spelled out in *The Bell Curve*, have strong eugenic implications. As noted in chapter 6, the Herrnstein and Murray plan echoes Henry H. Goddard's earlier proposals to assign society's dirty work to "the feebleminded."[34]

*The Bell Curve* generated widespread interest, but it also generated intense criticism from commentators who found it racist, elitist, deliberately misleading, and scientifically wrong.[35] Today most of it is obsolete. Its enduring criminological significance lies in the way it, together with *Crime and Human Nature*, restored IQ to respectability, making cognitive deficits once again a variable that prominent criminologists might discuss without apology. As in the late 19th century, "the" criminal again became a figure with mental disabilities.

*The Bell Curve* was still in press when Adrian Raine, then a University of Southern California psychologist, published *The Psychopathology of Crime*, an argument for viewing criminal behavior as the end result of a wide range of disorders, including cognitive deficits. Raine defines cognitive deficits broadly to include not only IQ (the variable of central concern to Herrnstein and Murray) but also learning ability, academic ability, powers of attention, moral reasoning, and the ability to process social information.[36] This approach enables him to examine a variety of cognitive processes that might affect criminal activity.

One process discussed by Raine is classical conditioning, a type of learned behavior in which an undesirable act such as stealing a cookie, if punished consistently by a parent, will eventually cause the child to feel upset when he or she even *thinks* of stealing a cookie. A moral behavior has been learned and become a conditioned reflex, an automatic response beyond conscious decision-making power. In particular, Raine discusses Eysenck's theory of the criminal as a poor conditioner, someone who learns the lessons of punishment more slowly than lawful people and thus takes longer to feel guilty about that cookie. Raine also describes how he himself extended Eysenck's theory when he and his doctoral supervisor, Peter Venables, discovered an interaction between conditionability and social class. This landmark study found that highly conditionable children (those who, Eysenck had predicted, would grow up to obey the rules) actually became antisocial if they were raised by lower-class (and hence, the authors hypothesized, relatively antisocial) parents, whereas children who conditioned less well but were raised by antisocial parents were *less* likely to become rule breakers.[37]

To explain this "paradox," Raine and Venables drew on an idea that Eysenck himself had tossed out years earlier but not pursued: the notion of an "antisocialization" process in which a highly conditionable child raised in "Fagin's kitchen" or other unsavory circumstances will quickly pick up criminal ways, whereas a child who conditions slowly will not. The Raine and Venables study breathed new life into the idea that learning disabilities in the form of poor conditionability might influence criminal behavior. Moreover, it had impact far beyond its specific findings, for it suggested that biology and social factors interact. No longer could one pit nature against nurture in the etiological sweepstakes, for they seemed to work interactively.[38]

Raine's book also analyzes the possible impact of low intelligence on crime. This discussion, more nuanced than that of Herrnstein and Murray, observes that both IQ and crime could be related to an underlying third factor such as early brain dysfunction, which in turn could be brought on by environmental factors such as head injury, maternal malnutrition, or early experience of child abuse.[39] Raine's conclusion is refreshingly undogmatic in an area long characterized by sweeping claims. "There is little doubt," he writes, "that delinquents and criminals are characterized by cognitive deficits, but there is considerably more doubt as to how such relationships can be best explained."[40] More recent research, maintaining Raine's eclectic and wide-lens approach, also investigates possible links between cognitive deficits and crime on a number of fronts.[41] The *Crime Times* Web site, a comprehensive if unselective source of information on biocriminological research, has more than fifty entries on such disparate factors as drug abuse, excess manganese, and maternal smoking that may affect IQ and criminality.[42]

## Evolutionary Theories of Crime

A third type of cause invoked by contemporary biocriminologists is evolutionary: the idea that human psychology evolved in ways that encourage certain sorts of criminal behavior. Present-day evolutionary criminologists, like many of their 19th-century forerunners, ultimately rest their scientific case on the work of Charles Darwin (especially his *Origin of Species*), but their ideas are otherwise distinct. Cesare Lombroso, Henry Maudsley, J. Bruce Thomson, and other 19th-century Darwinian criminologists pictured lawbreakers as primitive forms of human life, closer to black-skinned savages than to lawful, white Europeans. Today's evolutionary criminologists, in contrast, begin with the claim that criminality is an adaptive trait—or at least was so at one time, even if today it has become so maladaptive as to lead straight to the prison door. Evolutionary criminology has not been well received by mainstream criminologists, but anthropologists and, particularly, psychologists have pursued evolutionary explanations, building up a rich, if controversial, literature. Feeding off this literature, a small band of criminologists continues to pursue the possibility that criminality is (or was) an adaptive trait.

One version of evolutionary criminology calls on natural selection to explain rape. This theory argues that males derive a reproductive advantage from having multiple sex partners and thus that natural selection must have favored "genes promoting brain patterns for 'pushiness' in pursuit of sexual intercourse. . . . [O]ver generations, pushy males will probably be more successful at passing on their genes, including any genes coding for readily learning pushy sexual behavior, than will less pushy males."[43] Two popularizers of this theory, biologist Randy Thornhill and anthropologist Craig Palmer, go so far as to argue that the degree of pain experienced by rape victims depends on the degree to which being sexually assaulted reduces their "reproductive success."

> A rape victim's degree of psychological pain depends on her age (more psychological pain if she is of reproductive age), on her mateship status (more psychological pain if she is married), on the nature of the sex act (more psychological pain if penile-vaginal intercourse occurred), and on whether or not there is evidence that copulation took place without her consent (more psychological pain if there is no physical evidence of resistance).[44]

Thus, Thornhill and Palmer conclude, therapy for rape victims should focus on the victims who have most to lose in terms of reproductive success, with therapists enlightening these women about the evolutionary sources of their pain.[45] Apparently, these researchers could not even imagine social sources of rape victims' pain that could compete in power with evolution.

Evolutionary criminologists agree that what has evolved is not specific forms of criminal behavior such as stickups and tax evasion but rather tendencies to act selfishly and (if we are males) aggressively.[46] Yet they try to account for not only rape but also other specific offenses in Darwinian terms. One is homicide. Psychologists Martin Daly and Margo Wilson, using data that show we are more likely to be killed by a stranger than by a family member, argue that this pattern results from males' evolved tendency to solve problems with violence, unless the potential victim shares the attacker's genes and is thus capable of furthering his overall fitness. (The latter point rests on W. D. Hamilton's famous theory of *inclusive fitness*, according to which collateral relatives as well as descendants are valuable as carriers of similar genes.[47] "Kinship," Daly and Wilson explain, "should be seen to mitigate conflict, all else being equal, and to do so in proportion to its closeness.")[48] Data on stranger killings, Daly and Wilson claim, support the evolutionary argument. For further evidence that natural selection affects homicide patterns, Daly and Wilson break down data on within-family homicides, finding that this kind of killing, when it does occur, predominates among family members who are not genetically related. The most frequent victims, in other words, are again those who cannot maximize the offender's evolutionary fitness by perpetuating some of his or her genes.[49] Child homicide, which occurs far more often at the hands of a stepfather than a biological father, is yet another form of murder that has invited an evolutionary interpretation.[50] Child abuse and neglect, spousal assault, and both violent and property crime by women are other specific offenses that evolutionary criminologists have explained in Darwinian terms.[51]

In addition, evolutionary criminologists offer explanations for two broad patterns that cut across specific offenses: the higher crime rates of males than females, especially for violent crimes, and the higher crime rates of blacks than whites and of whites than Asians. Males (or so the theory goes) evolved to be violent because violence paid off: men who used strong-arm tactics got the most resources, including the most female sex partners, and thus their genes were most likely to be perpetuated. Females, meanwhile, evolved to prefer violent men—those most likely to have high status, obtain resources to feed their young, and thus perpetuate the mother's as well as the father's genes. More generally, women evolved to be less aggressive than men because by avoiding risk taking, they could better ensure the survival of their children and hence their own genes.[52]

To account for racial differences in crime rates, evolutionary criminologists call on the r/K theory of a continuum in reproductive strategies. This theory contrasts the so-called K strategy, in which parents (especially human parents) invest heavily in caring for their young, with the so-called r strategy, in which parents (especially insects and fish, which produce many eggs but have short lives) invest little or nothing in their offspring. People with criminal histories are said to be relatively high on r-type traits when these are translated into human terms (relatively short gestation periods, shorter life expectancy, and so on).[53] As Anthony Walsh, an advocate of the theory, points out, "This is where the controversy and the charges of racism appear. If criminals in general are higher on traits used by biologists to define r-selection species, and if the black-over-white-over-Asian pattern of crime prevalence is consistently found, does it imply a black-versus-white-versus-Asian gradient of r-selection?"[54] Walsh concludes that various studies *do* support the r-selection gradient and that, therefore, the apparently racist explanation is the best account for racial differences in crime rates.

Evolutionary psychology, and with it evolutionary criminology, got an enormous boost from Richard Dawkins's *The Selfish Gene*, a work taking a "gene's eye view" of evolution. Referring to the social cooperation game called Prisoner's Dilemma, Dawkins depicts animal and plant genes "engaged in ceaseless games of Prisoner's Dilemma, played out in evolutionary time."[55] To win at these survival games, Dawkins writes, genes have evolved various strategies, to which he gives picturesque labels such as Cheat, Bully, and Retaliator. Dawkins's overall story is a comforting one: computer simulations show that when these games are played over very long periods, natural selection favors cooperative, forgiving ("tit-for-tat") strategies, whereas cheating and bullying lose out.

While Dawkins's colorful anthropomorphisms popularized population genetics, they created mischief in criminology. Dawkins was talking about nonconscious evolutionary strategies, but what attracted criminologists were words like "selfish," "prisoner," "cheat," and "bully" that sounded as though they had criminological relevance. Some criminologists applied Dawkins's terminology to groups of criminals. "Psychopaths," one author tells us, are "quintessential cheats. . . . [C]heats have evolved mechanisms that serve to hide their true intentions."[56] At best, trying to match up criminal types with Dawkins's genetic strategies proved to be a distraction for criminologists, who ended up with very poor fits between evolutionary concepts and criminological categories. At worst, Dawkins's influence led criminologists to imply that cheats and other groups of criminals could evolve in adaptationist ways, as though they were distinct strains in a reproducing population.

Even though today's evolutionary criminologists are more sophisticated, scientifically, than their social Darwinist predecessors, their work suffers from similar faults. The main one is reductionism: the explanation of complex social phenomena in terms of simple biological causes. When Thornhill and Palmer reduce rape to a single, ultimate evolutionary cause; when they encourage victims to take comfort in the thought that their rapists were acting on an evolutionary imperative; and when they dismiss evidence for social influences on rape, they dig themselves into a monocausal hole that they cannot climb out of. Similarly, it is implausible to reduce differences between biological fathers and stepfathers in child homicide rates to an "ultimate" evolutionary cause when numerous social factors also "ultimately" affect the bonds between children and their primary caretakers. We are all shaped in "ultimate" or fundamental ways by evolution—that goes without saying and is no more than a truism. Offending may eventually be shown to be encouraged by evolved psychology, but it is unproductive to *reduce* it to evolved psychology when additional factors, many of them social, are so obviously in play.

Related is a second major fault with evolutionary criminology: its inability to prove its claims. While evolutionary criminologists do present empirical evidence for their assertions, such as evidence for the r/K theory that the reproductive strategies of some human groups ("races") resemble those of insects and fish, that evidence itself is based on such strained reasoning that it hardly qualifies as scientific. Evolutionary criminologists may eventually amass plausible data to help explain some specific offenses, as Daly and Wilson do for homicide, but they are unlikely to be able to explain offenses such as pedophilia and arson.[57] Moreover, it is unclear how far they will be able to move beyond redundancy ("We are what we evolved to be"). And they are unlikely ever to prove that human evolution is the ultimate or primary cause of a highly social phenomenon such as crime.

Evolutionary criminologists complain that their critics naïvely commit the *naturalistic fallacy* of confusing what *is* with what *ought to be*. That is, they say that their critics simply do not realize that when evolutionary criminologists explain that rape is a product of natural selection, they are not approving of rape but merely reporting on what evolution produced.[58] But, in fact, when Thornhill and Palmer gloss over the social realities of rape with platitudes about evolved male aggression, they themselves are guilty of the naturalistic fallacy. This fault is a direct inheritance from their social Darwinist predecessors, who unabashedly translated their picture of the world as they wanted it to be into "scientific" terms, confusing *ought* with *is*. (Lombroso, for example, thought that criminals should be ugly, and so he found them to be.) Thornhill and Palmer's treatise on rape is really an extended rant about what men and women *ought* to be like—females passive and males aggressive.

More impressive is recent work on the evolution of our ideas about justice, morality, and punishment. Much of it calls on the concept of *mental modules*, or evolved mental faculties analogous to the brain area that enables humans to acquire language.[59] Criminologist Anthony Walsh, among others, has argued that our sense of justice is innate, having originated in natural selection and forming part of evolutionary psychology. "The human sense of justice is a biological adaptation," Walsh writes, "an evolved solution to problems faced by our distant ancestors." The punitive impulse, too, according to Walsh and others, is an evolved set of emotions, another evolutionary strategy that enhances the fitness of punishers.[60] (Walsh's evolved "sense of justice" comes close to the philosophical concept of natural law, according to which all rational beings are endowed with a core set of self-evident truths and rights.) Recognizing that culture contributes heavily to ideas about justice, Walsh holds that both genes and environment influence our ideas of what is fair. However, he keeps the genetic (evolutionary) and environmental contributions separate, picturing genes as first (ultimate or primary) causes and environmental factors as proximate (intermediate or secondary) causes determining a particular culture's ideas about justice. Although Walsh does not picture genes and their environments as interactive factors, he does suggest that the two worked together over evolutionary time to produce humans with an innate sense of justice.

A similar position is taken by Laurence Tancredi in *Hardwired Behavior: What Neuroscience Reveals about Morality* (2005). "Social morality," Tancredi maintains, "begins in the brain."[61]

> The current theory held by most evolutionary biologists is that, through a slow process of mutation over millions of years, the capacity for moral thinking—essential for survival because it provides the bases for human cooperation—became hardwired. . . . The hardwiring of moral ability in our brain, according to [natural] selection, is genetically determined. Throughout our lives we discover, through personal moral challenges, what has already been built into our brains.[62]

Tancredi likens hardwiring to being born with a "template" for morality. "Genes first, then early interaction with cultural experience, etch a pattern that influences thinking and behavior."[63] Tancredi's model is more interactive than Walsh's, with genes (the evolutionary factor) setting the parameters and then interacting with environments (the immediate factor) to determine beliefs about ethical behavior. But in both models, morality is an evolved property of the brain, a kind of mental module.

Neither Walsh nor Tancredi tackles a key problem in any argument that the sense of morality (or justice) has evolved: the conflict between the theory of inclusive fitness, according to which people are unconsciously altruistic toward genetic relatives (but not others), and the broader idea of social justice, according to which we also cooperate in much larger groups including genetic strangers. Nor do Walsh or Tancredi attempt to explain *why* the sense of justice might have evolved (*why* it might have been adaptive). These two issues are addressed in a third work, by the evolutionary theorists Peter Richerson and Robert Boyd: *Not by Genes Alone: How Culture Transformed Human Evolution.*[64]

Richerson and Boyd hypothesize that the answers lie in the *coevolution* of genes and culture, a "coevolutionary dance" in which each partner "influences the evolutionary dynamics of the other."[65] Importantly, Richerson and Boyd really do use the "co-" prefix of "coevolution" to mean that genes and culture are equal partners. Although they recognize, with evolutionary biologist E. O. Wilson, that "genes have culture on a leash," in their view, while "culture is on a leash, all right, . . . the dog on the end is big, smart, and independent. On any given walk, it is hard to tell who is leading who."[66]

The first step in the Richerson and Boyd argument about morality and justice is to point out that because large, coherent, and cooperative groups probably outcompeted small, less coherent, and less cooperative groups, cultural selection probably perpetuated norms of cooperation and systems of rewards and punishment on the group level. Next they argue that "culturally evolved social environments favor an innate psychology that is suited to such environments"; thus, "individual selection will favor psychological predispositions that make individuals more likely to gain social rewards and avoid social sanctions."[67] These predispositions, Richerson and Boyd admit, often conflict with the processes of kin selection and reciprocity involved in inclusive fitness, but they draw on these conflicts to explain why humans so often experience moral tensions between the demands of the family, on the one hand, and those of the larger social group, on the other. The authors conclude that "cultural evolution leads to a social environment in which noncooperators are subject to punishment by others. . . . If generally cooperative behavior is favored in most social environments, selection may favor genetically transmitted social instincts that predispose people to cooperate and identify within larger social groupings. For example, selection might favor feelings such as guilt."[68] Thus do Richerson and Boyd explain how the senses of morality and justice might have evolved. They have acknowledged and accounted for tensions between the evolution of sociality on the group level and on the individual level, where inclusive fitness comes into play. And they have developed a model for considering cultural and genetic evolution simultaneously, one that does not privilege biology over environment but gives each equal weight in the evolutionary process. Future work by evolutionary criminologists, although it might not follow every step of the Richerson and Boyd model, would profit by continuing in the general direction they have pioneered.[69]

## Neuroscientific Explanations of Crime

A fourth type of crime causation investigated by contemporary biocriminologists is neuroscientific. Neuroscience, a rapidly growing field focused on the nervous system, has many branches, including clinical neuroscience, cognitive neuroscience, neurochemistry, neuropharmacology, neurophysiology, neuropsychiatry, and social neuroscience. Although so far only a few neuroscientists have extended these branches into criminology, the points of intersection constitute one of the most heavily medicalized aspects of current biocriminology. These intersections are based on the idea of crime as a psychopathology or clinical disorder. In *The Psychopathology of Crime*, Raine asserts, "*Many* instances of repeated criminal behavior, including theft and burglary, may represent a disorder or psychopathology in much the same way that depression, schizophrenia, or other conditions currently recognized as mental disorders represent psychopathologies."[70] Neuroscientists are less interested in criminal acts or even in criminality as a condition underlying specifically criminal behaviors than in "antisociality," a condition said to underlie a broad range of personal and social pathologies, including depression and schizophrenia as well as lawbreaking. They conceive of criminality as a disease of the brain and central nervous system that may be related to other pathologies as well. In this respect they recall 19th-century degenerationists, who also conceived of criminality as a part of a broader pathology that could manifest itself in any number of individual maladies and social problems.

The neuroscientists' medical model of antisociality meshes well with today's culture of biology, in which many phenomena that previously would have been traced to social or characterological factors are now attributed to biology. In current neuroscientific work, the condition of criminality (or antisociality) is, if not literally a disease, then at least an abnormality or deviation of some sort from biological health and normality. The neuroscientific medical model also fits with today's pervasive concern about risk—the desire to know ahead of time who is likely to cause trouble in order to take preventive measures. Furthermore, neuroscientific explanations exemplify the increasing microization of accounts of human behavior—the trend toward searching for ever more minute causes of phenomena.[71]

In what follows, I first deal with neurochemical explanations of crime, concentrating on hormones and neurotransmitters. Next comes a section on neurophysiological research, including the intriguing results of high-tech brain imaging studies that claim to visually distinguish criminals from noncriminals. I conclude with a section on social neuroscience, an emerging speciality that, as yet, has barely connected with criminology but holds promise for understanding, treating, and perhaps even preventing criminal behavior.

### Neurochemistry and Crime

Hormones—chemical messengers among the cells—perform various tasks in the body, including stimulating or inhibiting growth and regulating the immune system. Criminologically, the most interesting have been the sex hormones, which regulate the reproductive system. This interest was initially stimulated by *The New Criminology: A Consideration of the Chemical Causation of Abnormal Behavior* (1928) and other early works arguing that criminals are more likely than noncriminals to have glandular disorders.[72] Paralleling this argument were experiments by Leo Stanley, chief surgeon at California's San Quentin Prison, who had become convinced that forgers have underdeveloped pituitary glands and murderers overdeveloped thyroid glands. Stanley's first experiment, in 1919, had involved removing the testes of an executed felon and implanting them in a convict with "a decided apathetic attitude."[73] The convict "brightened up," and Dr. Stanley went on to perform other implants, using ram testes "because the amount of human material was limited." He learned to grind up the testicular material "to the consistency of tooth paste" and inject it under his convicts' skin. The injections, he reported, cured "diabetes, acne vulgaris, sexual lassitude, constipation, and asthma."[74] By 1940 he had performed more than 10,000 hormone implantations in prisoners.

Later, attention turned to the criminogenic role of the female sex hormones—or, to be more specific, to the possibility that hormonal changes at the time of menstruation might induce behavioral changes (irritability, depression, irrationality) that could lead to crime. The primary figure in the movement to criminalize menstruation was Katharina Dalton, an English physician and author of numerous works on premenstrual syndrome.[75] Interviews with women incarcerated at Holloway prison led Dalton to conclude that about half had been sentenced for crimes committed during what she termed the paramenstrum period (four days before and four days after the start of menstruation), a finding that led her to suspect a link between offending and menstruation. The link was less apparent to others, however.[76] English courts accepted PMS as a mitigating factor in only four criminal cases decided in the 1980s (in all four, Dalton served as a defense witness). In the few cases in which American courts were asked to accept PMS as a defense to crime, most rejected these arguments.[77] This cold shoulder from the courts, together with the realization that, at best, PMS (or its more severe form, premenstrual dysphoric disorder [PMDD]), would explain only a very small fraction of female offending, led to a decline in studies of menstruation and crime. However, some research continued to examine the possible pathological effects of abnormal interactions of hormonal and neurotransmitter systems in women.[78]

Interest in the possible role of female hormonal dysfunction as a cause of crime revived momentarily with the Andrea Yates case,[79] but the male hormone testosterone has attracted far more research attention. Testosterone has frequently been tied to aggressive criminal behavior and used to explain two key patterns in criminology: the higher crime rates of men than women, and the peaking of crime rates when men are in their teens, a time at which they produce the most sex hormone.[80] Moreover, the higher testosterone levels of black than white males found in some studies have been used to explain racial differences in crime rates, especially violent crime rates for men living in violent subcultures.[81] Some evidence for testosterone-crime links can be found in the results of chemical castration, a procedure that involves injecting male sex offenders with the drug Depo-Provera. This approach, which inhibits the production of testosterone, reduces recidivism in some but not all cases.[82] However, recent research indicates that high-testosterone boys are not necessarily more aggressive than others, and that in any case the relationship between sex hormones and offending is likely to be highly complex, involving social factors as well.[83]

Hormonal explanations of criminal behavior are no longer as popular as they were in the mid–20th century; in fact, today you can read an entire book about neuroscience and morality without finding a word about hormones.[84] In the neurochemical literature on criminal behavior, discussions of hormones are being replaced by research on crime and neurotransmitters.

Neurotransmitters, which are chemicals produced by the brain, have attracted sustained attention due to their apparently key impact on antisociality. Their role in the body is to enable the transmission of electrical impulses in the brain; thus they are crucial to the processing of information.[85] (And thus they also relate to cognitive deficits.) Neurotransmitters act as a kind of bridge between the brain's neurons, but like other bridges, they vary in strength and sometimes collapse entirely. While the levels of neurotransmitters with which we are born seem to be in part determined by genetics, they fluctuate according to environmental factors such as stress and drug intake. Of the neurotransmitters, three—serotonin, dopamine, and norepinephrine—have been implicated in criminal behavior, and of these serotonin has received far and away the most attention.[86]

Neurochemical research shows that antisocial people—schizophrenics and depressives as well as criminals—have low levels of serotonin, deficits that evidently increase impulsivity as well as aggression. Men are more likely than women to inherit these inadequacies.[87] Serotonin inadequacies are treated with drugs such as Prozac that increase the amount of serotonin available in the synapses between brain cells. Dopamine, the second most studied of the three neurotransmitters implicated in criminality, seems to play roles in adult attention disorder, drug addiction, and aggressive behavior, although the nature of those roles is as yet poorly understood.[88] Norepinephrine, the third neurotransmitter in the trio, is implicated in impulsivity, sensation seeking, and aggression. Problems occur not only when the levels of dopamine and norepinephrine become abnormally high or low but also when the balance between them and serotonin is thrown off. According to one authority, for example, such an imbalance can cause sexually deviant behaviors.[89]

Even though today's intense interest in neurotransmitters reflects the broader move toward attributing human behaviors to "hardwired" biological factors, this trend does not signal a return to old-fashioned biological determinism, for researchers who study neurotransmitters and crime emphasize interactions among neurological and environmental factors. For example, prenatal and early life experiences may help fix one's neurotransmitter levels. Thus even discussions of hardwired traits may rest (or at least should rest) on the assumption that such traits are produced through nature-nurture or biosocial interactions.

## Neurophysiology and Crime

Neurophysiologists have produced two types of criminologically relevant research. One calls on psychophysiology, a speciality that investigates relationships between psychological states and physiological conditions. The other involves neuroimaging, a speciality that employs innovative technologies to peer into the brain and study its structures and functioning.

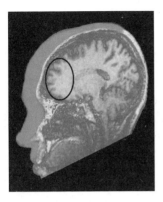

Neuroimaging of a brain. The frontal region of the brain is often implicated in antisocial personality disorder and criminal behavior.

Research in both areas implicates the brain's prefrontal cortex—the area right behind the eyes—in antisocial behavior.

Lombroso and his followers pioneered in psychophysiological research, investigating criminals' reactions to physical and psychological pain in order to demonstrate that they were less sensitive than "normal" men and women. In fact, Lombroso went so far as to invent his own version of the algometer, an electrical device that sent graduated shocks to subjects' hands in order to measure their sensitivity to pain.[90] Since the mid–20th century, when Eysenck and his associates began to suspect that criminals were poor conditioners, psychophysiologists have devised new ways to measure the physiological states associated with antisocial outlooks. One test uses electroencephalograms to determine electrical activity in the brain. (During an EEG, electrodes fastened to the scalp record electrical activity generated by the brain's neurons.) EEG studies tend to conclude either that criminals are more slowly aroused than noncriminals or that violent repeat offenders have abnormal EEG patterns.[91]

Another psychophysiological test measures heart rates; it finds that antisocial people have low resting heart rates, another trait that is then interpreted as an indicator of low arousability.[92] A third psychophysiological measurement is the skin conductance test, which, like the polygraph or lie detector, can detect small changes in the electrical activity of the skin. Weak skin conductance responses, which have been found to be typical of criminals, are taken as further evidence of low arousability or slowness to react physiologically.[93]

Through these tests, neurophysiologists have built up a portrait of psychopaths and other antisocial people as thrill seekers, individuals who ride roller coasters, mug passersby, or carouse to compensate for their chronic understimulation.[94] Because such people were born with underactive central and autonomic nervous systems (the argument continues)—because they are born with a kind of biological drowsiness— they need to drive at top speeds or stalk prey to feel fully alive. For them, according to psychologist David Rowe, "crime is a self-medication for a chronically under aroused [*sic*] brain."[95] Nor are such criminals easily deterred, for due to their biological cushioning against fear, they simply do not take threats as seriously as do law-abiding people. On the other hand, as some neurophysiologists acknowledge,[96] this sort of personality profile can be helpful. If one is trying to escape from a tight spot or make a courageous move, low arousability is just the thing.[97]

Twenty years ago, few would have predicted that neurocriminologists would now be able to look into the human brain to distinguish offenders from nonoffenders. Indeed, such an ambition would have been derided as a holdover from criminal anthropology, according to which born criminals have their own, defective types of brains. Exactly this kind of ambition was lampooned in James Whale's film *Frankenstein* (1931), in which a mad doctor implants an abnormal brain in a cadaver, thereby creating a criminalistic monster. Yet today, neurocriminologists, using brain imaging technologies such as computerized tomography (CT), magnetic resonance imaging (MRI), positron emission tomography (PET), and functional magnetic resonance imaging (fMRI),[98] claim that there are indeed significant differences between the brains of criminals and noncriminals. The leading researcher in this area is psychologist Adrian Raine.

A 1998 study by Raine and his associates provides a good example of this type of research. This was the first brain imaging study to investigate possible differences between two groups of murderers, one consisting of "predators," whose violence was planned, and the other of "affectives," whose violence was impulsive. All twenty-four murderers in the sample (fifteen predators, nine affectives) had either pleaded not guilty by reason of insanity or been found incompetent to stand trial; thus they were preselected for severe mental problems. Using PET scans, the researchers compared the two groups with one another and with a group of forty-one controls, matched for age and sex. The affectives were found to have lower prefrontal functioning than the comparison groups and higher right hemisphere subcortical functioning. In contrast, the predators had normal prefrontal functioning, but they too showed unusually high right subcortical activity. While cautioning that these findings cannot be generalized to other offenders due to the small and highly selected nature

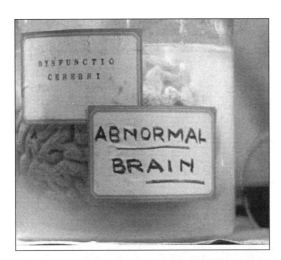

Abnormal brain before implantation by Dr. Frankenstein. In James Whale's movie *Frankenstein*, a demented young physician, hoping to create human life, digs up the body of an executed criminal. By accident, he implants in it an abnormal brain stolen from a laboratory. Photo used by permission of Photofest.

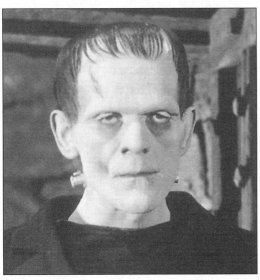

The result: Frankenstein's monster. Due to his abnormal brain, Dr. Frankenstein's creature turns out to be a criminalistic monster. Photo used by permission of Photofest.

of the sample, Raine and his associates conclude that the "emotional, unplanned impulsive murderers are less able to regulate and control aggressive impulses generated from subcortical structures due to deficient prefrontal regulation."[99] The predators, on the other hand, were better able to control their aggressive impulses because they had better prefrontal control over their emotions.

In reaching these conclusions, Raine was building on a body of research on the prefrontal cortex. One function of this area of the brain—particularly important from the criminological viewpoint—is executive: the prefrontal cortex integrates and manages other brain processes.[100] (Hence the book title *The Executive Brain: Frontal Lobes and the Civilized Mind*.)[101] It also seems to be critical in the control of aggression and the formation of moral and social judgments.[102] The prefrontal cortex continues developing after birth, maturing only when people are in their twenties. (Thus it is particularly susceptible to damage from toxic substances ingested in childhood and adolescence. In theory at least, the thrill seekers identified through psychophysiological research are those most likely to abuse alcohol and drugs and thus end up with prefrontal cortex damage.) In addition to its executive functions, the prefrontal cortex may be involved in our ability to form what is called a *theory of mind*, meaning an idea of what is going on in the minds of others.[103] "The prefrontal cortex," Rowe explains, "may create our knowledge of mind—that other people are themselves thinking about us—and allow us to adjust our behavior to the needs and concerns of others."[104] Those who are unable to understand other people's mental states are less able to sympathize with others and predict their reactions.

To date, the central finding of brain imaging technologies is that the prefrontal cortex functions less well in criminals than in noncriminals.[105] These studies are redefining the meaning of "criminality," which neuroscientists increasingly interpret as a function of prefrontal cortex impairment. Their research is still in its infancy, and it leaves a lot to be desired. It uses very small, highly selected samples; its procedures are not standardized; and its findings are inconsistent.[106] As yet, we do not know what a "normal" brain looks like, although we do know that the brain differs among people and even in a single individual over time.[107] We still know very little about how the various parts of a single brain system such as the limbic system (which includes the amygdala, hippocampus, hypothalamus, and pituitary gland) interrelate and how its parts might compensate for one another if damaged. (A student of mine who had lost an amygdala in surgery liked to point out that she was not a serial killer, perhaps because her second amygdala had taken over the functions of the other.) Moreover, the latest research suggests that *many* parts of the brain are involved in social perception and interaction, with the prefrontal cortex functioning more like a symphony conductor than a soloist in the processing of social information.[108] Furthermore, we do not know if there are behavioral differences between those in whom dysfunctionality begins in childhood, perhaps as a result of physical or psychological trauma, and those who acquire it later as a result of tumors, operations, or head blows.

These caveats notwithstanding, brain imaging research remains the most powerful method to emerge in biocriminology in recent years. It does not signal a simple return to criminal anthropology because now we can actually see into the brain and watch it working. Moreover, unlike Lombroso and the mad Dr. Frankenstein, today's neuroimagers do not claim that there is a simple dichotomous distinction between the criminal and the noncriminal brain. Rather, they picture a continuum of abnormality that at some point (yet to be defined) passes over a threshold from normality and into criminality.

### Social Neuroscience and Crime

One of the most innovative branches of neuroscience is social neuroscience, the study of the neural processes that underlie social behavior. An emerging field, social neuroscience builds on the core disciplines of neurology and social psychology but also draws on evolutionary biology, genetics, and psychiatry to study what happens, neurologically, during social exchanges. Its criminological relevance has not yet been articulated, but social neuroscience (or social cognitive neuroscience, as it is sometimes called) has enormous potential for deepening our understandings of what goes on in people's minds while committing a crime, experiencing victimization, and reacting to punishment. Over the next few decades, as social neuroscientists learn more about the neurobiological underpinnings of human interaction and social-information processing, social neuroscience is likely to transform ways in which criminologists think about their field.

In an introduction to social cognitive neuroscience, Ralph Adolphs, a neurologist at the University of Iowa, identifies the types of processes studied by the field, nearly all of which have strong implications for criminology. They include research on the neurobiology of self-regulation; on motivational and emotional factors in the ways we interpret social situations; and on the "moral emotions" (guilt, shame, embarrassment, jealousy). Social neuroscientists also examine the brain processes involved in assessments of danger and trustworthiness.[109]

Extrapolating from Adolphs's overview, we can predict ways in which social neuroscience will be applied to criminology. Crime is an inherently social event, a kind of social exchange, albeit a negative one. It frequently involves close contact and, on the part of both perpetrator and victim, a close reading of the other's mind. It further involves what Adolphs calls "the construction of an internal model of the social environment" and assessments of the "value of one's actions in the context of a social group."[110] Crime is often triggered by jealousy or other of the so-called moral emotions, including pride and shame, that "require an extended representation of oneself as situated within a society."[111] Violent crime in particular involves a breakdown of self-regulation, a phenomenon that social neuroscientists are already examining neurologically. At all these levels—personal, interpersonal, group, and societal—social neuroscience holds promise for vastly improving understandings of the biological dynamics of criminal events.

Social neuroscience could help us devise more effective aids to victim recovery, since it has the potential to sort out which responses by criminal justice officials and counselors are helpful. These responses occur not only in the brain but throughout the body, for brain reactions set off responses in other areas, such as the hormonal and vascular systems. (The evidence so far suggest that the brain responds biologically to sympathetic counselors and to efforts to overcome emotional isolation, with these responses then cascading through the body to improve overall physiological well-being. Conversely, a lack of a sympathetic counselor and emotional isolation lead to opposite physiological responses.)[112] In the area of punishment, we may soon be able to specify what goes on neurologically during the social transactions that lead (or that punishers hope will lead) to guilt and shame. Eventually, using social neuroscience, criminal justice officials may be able to make punishment more effective and perhaps less physically and socially punitive. Moreover, social neuroscience, with its interest in brain plasticity and development, and its studies of ways in which environmental factors can affect brain processes in both childhood and adulthood, may be able to suggest ways to forestall the development of neurological processes that encourage crime and to strengthen other neurological processes that buffer against it.[113]

Some social neurological research focuses on theory of mind, the capacity to form an idea of what others are thinking. Social neuroscientists have identified "mirror neurons," cells that enable us to follow the emotional states of people we encounter, interpret their intentions, and then actually replicate their presumed states in our own brains by activating the same areas active in the other person.[114] Science writer Daniel Goleman uses the phrase "wired to connect" to speak of this capacity of our brains to respond, physiologically, to what we think is going on in someone else's mind. Goleman is harnessing this extraordinary capacity by developing empathy programs that teach young people to control impulses, resist peer pressure, and refrain from violence and substance abuse.[115] In time, criminologists may be able to integrate this new work on theory of mind with some of the older work on symbolic interactionism and labeling, which also focused on interpersonal interactions, though not at the neurological level.[116]

## Genetic Explanations

The fifth strand in contemporary biocriminology consists of genetic explanations. These are far from new, for mid-19th-century degenerationsts argued that criminality is heritable through devolving germ plasm, and late 19th-century criminal anthropologists developed more deterministic hereditarian explanations for lawbreaking. But these precursors knew nothing about the mechanisms of heredity, which were not discovered until the early 20th century; and in any case, their pregenetic approaches were submerged by the development of sociological criminology. Little work on genetics and crime was undertaken until Eysenck broke the ice in 1964 by asserting, "beyond any question, that heredity plays an important, and possibly a vital part, in predisposing a given individual to crime."[117]

An early sign of the revival of genetic approaches to crime, as noted earlier, was the furor in the 1960s over the identification of the XYY chromosomal configuration in some men who had been seriously aggressive. In contrast to other men, with their XY chromosomes, XYY males were reported to be taller, to have lower IQs, and to suffer from acne and personality disorders as well as a tendency to commit violent crime.[118] Subsequent research failed to confirm these claims, however (aside from that pertaining to height). Moreover, because the original studies had been conducted on highly selected, incarcerated populations, and because XYY men were too rare ever to contribute much to understandings of violence, this line of research eventually petered out.[119] That it drew so much attention in the first place perhaps signified a yearning for "harder" scientific explanations of crime based on biology.

If the XYY research anticipated the coming resurgence of genetic theories of crime, the finding that a small core of chronic delinquents in a birth cohort committed most of the cohort's crime stimulated new genetic research.[120] This finding, by criminologist Marvin Wolfgang, was later reinforced by a study in which psychologist Terrie Moffitt distinguished two types of delinquents: a large group of "adolescence-limited" offenders who got into trouble when they were teenagers but then simply grew out of crime, and a small group of early-onset "life-course persistent" offenders who, like Wolfgang's chronic offenders, did not.[121] Wolfgang's and Moffitt's research prompted questions about what made the serious offenders different from other delinquents—questions that, some thought, might be answerable by the new field of behavioral genetics.[122]

But mainstream criminologists resisted the biological turn, so vigorously that they and their allies managed to shut down a 1992 conference on genetics and crime. The National Institutes of Health (NIH) initially funded the conference, to be held at the University of Maryland, but withdrew its support in the face of well-publicized fears that the establishment of links between genes and crime could lead to racist results and even the sedation of inner-city black youths.[123] Mainstream criminologists were already up in arms over Wilson and Herrnstein's *Crime and Human Nature*, with its emphasis on "constitutional" factors in crime. The proposed NIH conference merely hardened their resistance. Psychologists David Rowe and D. Wayne Osgood tried to clear the air by writing for sociologists, urging more collaboration and explaining that the new genetic studies of crime did not entail the old biological determinism. "There are social explanations consistent with large genetic components," Rowe and Osgood pointed out, "and biological explanations consistent with large environmental components."[124] But their peacemaking efforts had little impact on sociological criminologists, some of whom even today simply dismiss genetic explanations out of hand or condemn them as a new form of biological determinism.

### Classic Genetic Research: The Nature or Nurture Question

Until recently, behavioral geneticists interested in crime posed their research questions in terms of the relative contributions of genes and the environment to criminal behavior. They conducted what might be called *relationship studies*, using research on families, twins, and adoptees to parse out the proportional influence of nature and nurture, considered separately. The family seemed the ideal unit for investigating the relative contributions of nature and nurture to behavior, particularly if one member had a criminal record and others did not. Better yet would be families with twins, especially monozygotic (MZ) twins, who have identical genes and thus (at least in theory) hold the "nurture" variable constant. Also valuable, it seemed, would be studies of the relative rates of criminality among fraternal, or dizygotic (DZ), twins and other siblings who were genetically related.

The family study method goes back to Richard Dugdale and the eugenicists who, following his lead, charted the genealogy of criminality in bad families.[125] Uniformly, the family studies found a strong genetic effect: crime runs in families and is passed down through the generations. But these researchers used no control groups, and their work was a methodological nightmare. Moreover, because none of them (aside from Dugdale) had the slightest interest in environmental influences, the original bad-family studies made no effort to sort out the relative effects of genetics and environment.[126]

More rewarding were the twin studies pioneered by Francis Galton and the German criminologist Johannes Lange.[127] The twin study that Lange reported in *Crime as Destiny* (1930) found a higher concordance for criminal behavior among identical twins (77 percent) than fraternal twins (12 percent)[128]—a result that seemingly proved that heredity plays the major role in crime causation, thus delighting Nazi criminal-biologists. However, Lange's approach still left unanswered the question of the relative impact of environment on criminal behavior—a drawback that he acknowledged but the Nazis conveniently ignored.

Numerous twin studies followed, some comparing MZ with DZ twins in terms of criminal behavior, some examining the effects of environment on criminality when MZ and DZ twins were reared apart. Nearly all these studies reached the same conclusion: nature in the form of genes affects criminal behavior, but so does nurture in the form of family circumstances.[129] But the twin studies tended to suffer from multiple methodological problems, including biases in sample selection, inaccurate determinations of monozygosity, and use of inappropriate statistical procedures.[130] Thus criminological researchers turned to adoption studies, which avoid the problems of twin studies by instead examining rates of criminality in children who were adopted away from their birth families.

The best known of the adoption studies is that in which Sarnoff Mednick and his colleagues compared the court convictions of nearly 15,000 adoptees with those of their biological and adoptive parents.[131] Published in 1984, Mednick's research utilized records from Denmark, a country with a relatively homogeneous population that kept detailed records on its citizens. All the children had been adopted by nonfamily members. If either the mother or the father (biological or adoptive) had a court conviction, those parents were coded as criminal. Mednick's basic question was: if the biological parent had a criminal record, did that increase the probability that a child adopted-away would also have a criminal record? Looking only at the data on male adoptees, he found the following:

- If neither the biological nor the adoptive parents had been convicted, 13.5 percent of the sons were convicted.
- If the adoptive parents had a conviction but the biological parents did not, the results were about the same—just under 15 percent of the sons were convicted.
- If the adoptive parents had no convictions but the biological parents did, 20 percent of the sons were convicted.
- If both the adoptive and the biological parents had a conviction, then about 25 percent of the sons were convicted.

These figures, Mednick concluded, support the claim that there is a genetic element in the etiology of criminal behavior. (Of course, they also indicate that there is an even larger environmental influence.)

Like Wolfgang (and anticipating Moffitt), Mednick also found a core group of recidivists—4 percent of the male adoptees. These men had three or more convictions and were responsible for 69 percent of all the male adoptees' convictions—"a high concentration of crime," as Mednick put it, "in a small fraction of the cohort."[132] This finding, too, suggested that genetic influences might be at work.

While Mednick's study remains a milestone in genetic research on family relationships, it, too, has been criticized. It did not consider the possible impact of biological but nongenetic factors such as perinatal complications.[133] It did not control for the families' social class.[134] It assumed that one's genetic constitution is fixed at birth, whereas genetic influences, like environmental influences, appear to change throughout life, and the effects of heritability may vary by age.[135] Most important, its design assumed that environmental and genetic influences are mutually exclusive, whereas the evidence today points to interactivity. In other words, Mednick and others who conducted relationship studies framed the question in terms of a nature-nurture dichotomy, but later evidence in behavioral genetics showed that this was not the most effective way to pose the question.[136]

Recent Genetic Research: The Nature-Nurture Question

Recasting the question, subsequent research on genetics and crime has asked how nature and nurture *interact* to increase someone's vulnerability or resistance to crime. While the relationship studies looked at global factors—the relative influence of genes and environment in populations— the newer research has focused more specifically, even minutely, on biosocial interactions at the genetic and molecular level.[137] These studies have not looked for a gene "for" a trait but rather for variants of a single gene that can put individuals at risk. Some have been less interested in genes per se than in adjacent regulatory "promoter" regions that keep genes company and affect their expression. The newer studies, because they are concerned with risk factors that might make one person more likely than the next to commit crime, conceive of criminality not as an either-or condition but as a continuum. Some people, in this view, are more predisposed than others to commit crime, but no one is destined to become a criminal.[138]

What traits, then, have the newer studies examined? One is impulsivity, a characteristic that, as we saw earlier, has been associated with low levels of serotonin and norepinephrine, a low resting heart rate, weakness on skin conductance tests, and functional weaknesses in the prefrontal cortex. Impulsive people have been shown to lack capacity for long-term planning, weighing consequences, and thinking of trade-offs between immediate gratification and later rewards—in other words, the executive function of their prefrontal cortex seem to be impaired. All these characteristics have been shown to have genetic bases.[139] Other research has examined the childhood conditions known as attention deficit with hyperactivity disorder (ADHD), conduct disorder (CD), and oppositional defiant disorder (ODD).[140] All three of these childhood conditions have been associated with later criminality and found to be partially genetic in origin. Related research has focused on the specific genes associated with these disorders and with neurotransmitter deficiencies.

In 1993, the Dutch geneticist Hans Brunner attracted a storm of attention with a report on a criminalistic Dutch family that, over a hundred-year period, had produced a large number of men notable for two traits: low intelligence and a tendency to violence.[141] Brunner's report, combining the older family study method with the newer technique of gene mapping, traced the family's problem to a gene that codes for the enzyme monoamine oxidase A (MAOA). MAOA's job in the body is to break down (or "mop up," as the behavioral genetics literature often puts it) the neurotransmitter serotonin after it has done its work in the brain. The violent men suffered from defective MAOA. Brunner's report inspired sensational headlines such as "A Violence in the Blood,"[142] implying that he had discovered a gene for aggression. This media hype notwithstanding, critics realized that Brunner had not controlled for the violent men's shared environment. Moreover, like the XYY men of the 1960s, the Dutch family constituted but a rare instance in which a genetic abnormality (in this case, a hereditary abnormality) may have contributed to violent behavior.[143] Most men do not inherit a defective MAOA gene.

Despite the misinterpretations and critiques of Brunner's study, interest in the connection between MAOA and crime persisted as study after study implicated the MAOA gene in problems with neurotransmitters, particularly serotonin, a neurotransmitter repeatedly linked to violence. But the ways in which MAOA works are not well understood, and according to some research, men with the MAOA gene are aggressive only if they were maltreated as children[144]—a finding that reminds us that to understand the operations of genes, we need to look at the circumstances, past and present, in which they operate. Studies that take environment into account indicate that the same gene can produce different behavior in different people, depending on context. MAOA may be a susceptibility gene or risk factor, but it is not a unitary or inevitable cause of crime.[145]

Evidence of a strong genetic effect on some types of offending comes from the Minnesota Twin Family Study, ongoing research on social problems among male, reared-together twins and their parents. Specifically, the researchers have found that early-onset (or "life-course persistent") delinquency is more affected by genetic factors than late-onset (or "adolescence-limited") delinquency.[146] Among the late starters, for whom offending is more of a passing phenomenon, a major influence seems to be antisocial activity among peers. But for the early starters, for whom "offending is more akin to a disorder,"[147] genetically linked factors such as impulsivity, poor self-control, low scores on tests of mental ability, ADHD, and ODD evidently play a major role. Moreover, the early starters have more immediate relatives with records of antisocial behavior; and while they resemble the late starters in having antisocial peers, their friends are even more antisocial.[148]

Behavioral genetics is redesigning the picture of biocriminology's enduring poster boy: the psychopath (poster *boy* because psychopaths are rarely described as female, although the literature does identify female cases). This figure, as we have seen, was initially described as *morally insane*—lacking in conscience, though normal in other respects. Lombroso and Maudsley described him as a *born criminal*, lacking not only conscience but also most other civilized traits. Today, psychologists and psychiatrists continue to put forth descriptions of the psychopath.[149] Although these accounts differ, their basic points are the same: psychopaths are unable to empathize with others; they lack remorse and foresight; they have poor impulse control and low tolerance of frustration; they are risk takers and fail to understand risks; and the syndrome, starting in childhood, is unresponsive to treatment. The American Psychiatric Association currently defines psychopathy as an antisocial personality disorder characterized by disregard for the rights of others, failure to conform to social rules and expectations, lawbreaking, deceitfulness, impulsiveness, failure to consider the consequences of actions, and aggressiveness.[150]

Among the hundreds of descriptions of psychopaths, however, until recently there have been few that attempted to identify the source of the condition. Even Robert D. Hare, in his well-known book *Without Conscience: The Disturbing World of the Psychopaths among Us*, says only that "psychopaths have little aptitude for experiencing the emotional responses—fear and anxiety—that are the mainsprings of conscience" and that they are oriented toward the present, not the future.[151] But Hare himself, in his more scholarly work, has done neurophysiological research on psychopathy, and he helped open the door through which behavioral and psychiatric geneticists are moving to flesh out the picture of the psychopath's inner conditions. Essentially, they draw on many of the findings already mentioned in this section—those pertaining to the childhood syndromes of ADHD, CD, and ODD, and to the adult conditions of impulsivity, aggressiveness, risk taking, and lack of foresight—and then apply these findings to the concept of antisocial personality disorder.[152] All these problems, as we have seen, have been shown to have a genetic aspect.[153] "Predominantly," reports a summary of the research, "significant genetic factors do appear to be influencing antisocial-behavior-related psychiatric disorders such as conduct disorder and antisocial personality disorder."[154]

Most interesting is research that examines gene-environment interactions; this includes two well-known studies by Avshalom Caspi, Terrie Moffitt, and others, one on the criminal effects of child abuse (2002), the second on a factor less directly related to criminology—depression (2006). The first study examined a representative general population sample of males to determine why some who were maltreated as children grew up to develop antisocial behavior but others did not. Notably, the study began with an environmental factor: child abuse. The researchers found that different versions of the MAOA gene affected the results of maltreatment. Maltreatment effects were weaker on males whose version conferred *high*

MAOA activity, which evidently constituted a kind of protection, whereas males with the version conferring *low* MAOA activity were more likely to develop childhood conduct disorders and to be convicted of a violent crime in adulthood. Caspi and his colleagues concluded, "These findings may partly explain why not all victims of maltreatment grow up to victimize others, and they provide epidemiological evidence that genotypes can moderate children's sensitivity to environmental insults."[155] Some children were genetically more susceptible than others to the destructive effects of abuse.

The second study by Caspi and Moffitt examined differences in the serotonin transporter gene, asking whether they affected levels of depression induced by stressful life events.[156] As it turned out, individuals with one or two "short" versions of the gene exhibited more clinical depression during stressful life events than those with two copies of the "long" version. Again, a problem was explained not by genes or environment in isolation but rather by an interaction between the two. Genetic variations apparently help explain differences in people's reactions to stressful life events. As Moffitt put it in an interview, "Nature works via nurture."[157]

Other work, too, pursues this possibility, although not always with Caspi and Moffitt's apparent success in documenting interactions at the genetic level.[158] A 2002 review analyzes thirty-nine studies of biosocial interaction effects for antisocial behavior from such disparate areas of research as brain imaging, environmental toxins, genetics, hormones, neurology, neuropsychology, neurotransmitters, obstetrics, and psychophysiology.[159] A subsequently published study asks about the effects of gene-environment interactions not on offending but on victimization. In it, Kevin Beaver and his colleagues, using data on adolescents, found that different variants of the dopamine D2 receptor gene (DRD2) were related to victimization in the case of white males. Future work along the same lines, as Caspi and Moffitt predict, should "move beyond single genetic polymorphisms . . . to identify gene systems and study sets of genetic polymorphisms that are active in the pathophysiology of a disorder."[160] That is, future research on genetics and crime is likely to move beyond the study of variants for single genes to investigate how genes and their variants interact with one another and their environments to increase one's risk of antisocial behavior.[161]

## *The Current State of Biocriminological Research*

There is, then, a tremendous amount of activity in current biocriminological research.[162] This research includes work on acquired biological abnormalities such as those caused by lead poisoning, brain tumors, and child abuse that may create predispositions to criminal activity by damaging the prefrontal cortex or other parts of the brain. It also includes research on learning deficits, especially low IQ but also other cognitive impairments and even autonomic nervous system weaknesses that seem to be associated with criminality. Third and more speculatively, it includes evolutionary theories proposing that proclivities to specific types of crime, or to crime more generally, result from the trajectories of human evolution. This type of evolutionary theorizing is now being supplemented by work on the evolution of the concepts of justice, morality, and punishment; some of this new work analyzes the *co*evolution of genes and culture to produce universal ideas about right and wrong.

Neuroscientific explanations of criminality, a fourth type of research in the current biocriminological deck, are developing rapidly and in many directions: into research on neurochemistry and crime, including the effects of hormonal imbalances and neurotransmitter deficits; and into neurophysiology, with investigations of physiological correlates of crime such as low resting heart rate levels and prefrontal cortex problems that may impair the brain's executive functions and its ability to form a theory of mind. The newest branch of neuroscience, social neuroscience, has only just begun to connect with criminology but holds promise for improving understandings of the neurobiology of criminal behavior, experiences of victimization, and reactions to punishment.

The same is true of current research on genetics and crime, the fifth type of work in today's biocriminology, which has moved beyond its original relationship studies (family, twin, and adoption studies), with their nature-versus-nurture questions, to newer work on nature-nurture interactions. One of the strongest messages to emerge from current behavioral genetics research is that, while criminality seems to have a strong genetic component, no one is destined to commit crime. Today's behavioral geneticists picture criminality as a continuum along which some people are more genetically predisposed to offend than others; but in their view, even those most at risk may be protected by genetic and environmental factors.

Never in the history of biocriminology has there been anything like this explosion of interest, this diversity of perspective and approach, or this intensity of research activity. Never before have governments funded biological research at current levels or scholars produced so many publications on biology and crime. It is almost as if, during the post–World War II decades when biological analyses were shunned and scorned, pressure built up until finally the sociological lid blew off, enabling biological ideas to shoot off in all directions.

But it is also true that the current proliferation of biocriminology has been well nurtured by its social context. It has occurred in a culture suffused with biological ideas about the causes of human behavior. It has further coincided with a widespread preoccupation, even obsession, with risk and the prevention of harms. This social context has helped to make the current explosion of theory and research in biocriminology possible. Biocriminology, in turn, feeds back into this social context, reinforcing assumptions about the priority and efficacy of biological explanations and intensifying the old suspicion that some people are biologically dangerous.

# PART III

# Biological Theories in the 21st Century

# 10

# A Criminology for the 21st Century

No one has ever been able to answer the questions about criminals' brains raised by William Freeman's massacre of the Van Nest family. Might Freeman's head injury have caused him to kill the Van Nests? Or was he a calculating, cold-blooded killer who for some unfathomable reason decided to wipe out a family he hardly knew? How can we distinguish between mental disorder and evil intent—and should we even try? What is the best relation of medicine and related sciences to law? (In Freeman's day, those specialities were phrenology and psychiatry; today, they include psychiatry, neurology, and genetics.) Similar questions arose again in the Andrea Yates case, in which the first jury found her guilty of deliberately drowning her children in a bathtub, but the second (convened not because of doubts about Yates's condition but because of false testimony by a prosecution witness) found her not guilty due to a biological condition—postpartum psychosis. Do we need to rethink traditional dualisms (mind versus body, free will versus determinism) in light of the new biosocial reasoning and the current view that it is impossible to clearly distinguish between mind and body? The debates over such issues are really controversies about how we as a social group or "thought community"[1] want to think about the relationship of bodies to behavior, biology to crime.

Today as in William Freeman's time, debates over specific cases involving criminal biology are inflamed by strains in the broader society, in our case, agitation about human cloning and stem-cell research; worries about the wisdom of transgenic foods and so-called test-tube babies; and alarm about proposals to create "posthumans"—genetically engineered men and women, and people who are part machine. Once again, there is widespread uneasiness about the implications of new sciences, together with broad-based uncertainty about how much weight to give scientific opinion in legal matters. Reflecting this lack of social consensus about the meanings of scientific discoveries is the plethora of attempts in recent years to raise new biological legal defenses: sleepwalking defenses; premenstrual tension defenses and those based on postpartum psychosis; mental retardation defenses; defendants arguing that they came from a family with a history of violence, as in the Hans Brunner study;[2] and, increasingly, defenses based on genetic abnormalities and MAOA deficiencies.[3] Our culture of biology, with its daily avalanche of news on scientific discoveries, generates an uneasiness about the causes of crime not unlike that which erupted in the mid-19th century when the Van Nest killings became a lightning rod for tensions between older and newer ways of thinking about crime and biology.

In the years ahead, biological explanations are likely to play an increasingly prominent role in efforts to understand criminal behavior. Just as, according to predictions, the 21st century will be "the century of biology," so too, on a more specific scale, is it likely to be the century of biocriminology. On the basis of what this book has found about earlier biological theories, this chapter speculates about the development of biocriminology in the years ahead and ways it will come to relate to sociological explanations of crime. It asks whether there have been patterns or trends in the evolution of biological theories over time and whether today's biological explanations differ fundamentally from those of the past or are basically more of the same. It also asks whether today's explanations have the same potential for misuse as those of past and, if so, how we can guard against such tragedies.

In what follows, I first trace trends in the development of biological theories of crime over time and then compare the theories of the past to those of the present. I go on to argue that today the danger for misuse lies not with the scientists who are investigating biological causes of crime but rather with simplistic or politically manipulative understandings of their work. To avoid the misappropriation of biocriminology for political ends, as happened during the period of eugenic criminology in the United States and Hitler's reign in Germany, we need to learn how to question science intelligently and acknowledge our own ignorance.

## Trends in Biocriminology

Over time, biological theories of crime have evolved over six broad trajectories. First, they have developed in terms of their *theoretical scope*. Moral insanity theory addressed just one form of offending—that which was repeat, remorseless, and uncontrollable; today's theories, in contrast, attempt to explain many or even all forms of offending. Second, biological theories have expanded in *theoretical focus*. Phrenologists dealt with crime almost incidentally, in the course of attempting to explain all human behavior. While today's sciences of the criminal brain are also part of broader endeavors (genetics, neuroscience), ever since Lombroso conceived of a science of criminal behavior, most biocriminologists have concentrated exclusively on explaining crime.

Third, biological theories have changed in *personnel*—the types of scientist involved in their development. Whereas the earliest theories were articulated almost entirely by medical men, especially those involved in the study of mental diseases, today's biocriminologists come from diverse fields, especially genetics, neurology, and psychology but, increasingly, also from sociological criminology. Herein lies the historical significance of Lombroso's conception of criminology as a field that could accommodate not only psychiatrists like himself but also specialists from other areas such as anthropology. Some of his successors tried to close the field's boundaries, but today Lombroso's vision of a multidisciplinary criminology is being realized.

Fourth, biocriminology has evolved in *scientific sophistication*. Its first endeavors mixed science with religion and focused on just a few deviant cases. Benjamin Rush thought of criminological investigation as a "moral science" and did not hesitate to draw examples from the Bible. Lombroso, in contrast, explicitly rejected the intrusion of religious reasoning into criminology, and while even his contemporaries ridiculed his scientific efforts, he at least tried to use objective and experimental methods. Today's biocriminologists are scientifically respectable, although their work, like all scientific endeavors, is open to critique.

Fifth, biocriminology has evolved in its focus *from the mind to the brain*. Early criminologists did not dare equate the mind with the brain because to do so would imply that, like the brain, the mind could die— seemingly a denial of the immortality of the soul. But phrenologists boldly elided mind with brain, and their assumption of equivalence passed on to Lombroso, other evolutionary criminologists, and early 20th-century feeblemindedness theorists, who also did not distinguish between mind and brain. The somatotypers took a step backward by assuming that mind was somehow related to body shape; but today's biocriminologists focus almost exclusively on the brain. Sixth and finally, *the unit of study* has changed over time, from macro-factors such as brain size and shape to micro-factors such as genes. Herein lies the significance of Galton, the first scientist to conclude that if criminal tendencies were heritable, they must involve some difficult-to-detect, genelike factor.

Similar trajectories characterize the evolution of other fields, too, over the same time period. Criminology is just a little fish in the scientific pond. It is also inextricably and unavoidably part of the social contexts in which it develops, drawing fundamental preconceptions from the world in which it grows and matures. This was true in the late 19<sup>th</sup> century, when evolutionism hit criminology like a meteor, blasting old assumptions and forcing a major change in course. It is equally true today as the culture of biology forces criminology to undergo a radical change in direction.

## Comparing Biological Theories of Crime, Past and Present

Past and current biological theories of crime can be compared along five key dimensions: (1) their degree of reliance on the medical model of crime; (2) the degree to which they engage in reductionism and biological determinism; (3) the extent to which their content is racist or sexist; (4) the extent to which they emphasize human differences; and (5) their compatibility with sociological explanations of crime. The comparisons indicate that, even though today's biocriminologies perpetuate some of the dubious assumptions of their past, significant change has nonetheless taken place, so much so that one can now enlist them in crime-control programs aimed at improving social conditions.

1. *The medical model of crime.* Like their predecessors, today's biocriminologists focus on the criminal, not the crime or social factors that encourage crime, and that is no doubt inevitable, given the questions (such as, how do offenders differ from nonoffenders?) that interest them. Less inevitable is a traditional concomitant of focusing on criminals: biocriminology's reliance on the medical model of the criminal as ill or somehow abnormal, a reliance made manifest, for instance, by the title of Adrian Raine's book *The Psychopathology of Crime: Criminal Behavior as a Clinical Disorder* (1993).

There are better frameworks than the medical model for the sciences of deviance, be they biological or social.[4] The long-standing but faulty assumptions behind comparisons of criminals with the physically or mentally ill need to be unraveled and scrutinized. Many groups of deviants are not deemed ill—the blind, for example, and punk rockers, and right-wing survivalists. Some have physical disorders, and others do not, but even the former are not automatically considered sick. Moreover, deviations are not always negative, a point made by the autism rights movement, with its demands for tolerance for neurodiversity, and by the gay rights movement, with its decades-long struggle to demedicalize homosexuality. While criminals are deviants in a legal sense, they are not necessarily ill in a medical sense.

The idea of criminality as an illness took root because most 19th-century scientists of the criminal were physicians. It meshed perfectly with the powerful, persistent, and ubiquitous concept of degeneration, and it was a professional boon, for it legitimized physicians' efforts to gain jurisdiction over criminals.[5] But the medical model never was accurate, literally or metaphorically, and it proved lethal during the eugenics movement, in the United States as well as Germany. Even if someone has an unusually small brain or a variant MAOA gene, that does not make him or her ill in the same sense as would having typhoid or schizophrenia . Some criminals— one thinks of William Freeman and Andrea Yates—obviously *are* physically or mentally ill, but most differ little from the rest of us, and it is not useful to stigmatize them as "psychopathological" and "clinically disordered." Genes may put one at risk, but how those genes are expressed depends on social factors. The old-fashioned medical model does not fit well with today's biosocial explanations of human behavior.

Biocriminologists continue to latch on to the medical model because—working in their labs on neurological problems, or running psychophysiological tests on offenders—they have little occasion to learn about the medical model's past criminological abuses. To judge from their writings, few of them are familiar with the history of biological theories of crime, and few have much awareness of the social dimensions of science. Thus they repeat past mistakes, including the almost instinctive adoption of the medical model.

2. *Reductionism and biological determinism.* A second dimension along which past and present biological theories can be compared is the degree to which they engage in reductionism and determinism. At times, biocriminology continues to be as reductionist as criminal anthropology and the feeblemindedness theory of crime, boiling the complexities of criminal behavior down to a single biological factor (or very few). In 2005, for instance, the Canadian psychologist Peter Hurd announced that "measuring a man's index finger length relative to his ring finger length predicts his predisposition to being physically aggressive." Men with shorter index fingers, relative to their ring fingers, have more prenatal testosterone, according to Hurd, and are thus more likely to be physically aggressive in adulthood.[6] Another example appears in the recommendation of criminologist James

A. Fox to the Massachusetts Parole Board that a convicted killer be released because his brain had physically changed since he was committed to prison as a teenager.[7] A third example turns up in responses to an announcement by Adrian Raine that in a highly selected sample, men prone to rage and violence had less prefrontal gray matter (by about 11 percent) than other men. Although Raine stressed that he was talking about a *predisposition* to antisocial behavior,[8] not an inevitability, that message was not conveyed by popular media gleefully reporting that criminals have smaller brains than the rest of us.

But even though biocriminologists can still be as reductionist as Lombroso (or made to sound that way), it is nonetheless true that their work is less reductionist than it was in the past. Responsible researchers no longer claim that biology alone causes behavioral problems, for they recognize that behavior results from interactions between nature and nurture, biology and environment. This is a major difference from the past. Similarly, responsible biocriminologists today reject biological determinism. This, too, is a significant change from the past, when biological theorists hurried to claim that people with anomalies of one sort or another were bound to commit crime. Maudsley, Lombroso, and other prophets of doom are gone, replaced (for the most part) by scientists who avoid determinist conclusions about criminals' brains (and index fingers).

3. *Racism and sexism.* Biological theories today also fare better in the third comparison, along the dimension of racism and sexism. Biological theories of crime, as we have seen, have a long history of racism and sexism. Rooted in 19th-century "scientific" racism and social Darwinism, early biological explanations reinforced a hierarchical view of human worthiness in which white males topped the pyramid. Lombroso's pronouncements about female inferiority and African innate savagery; Hooton's use of racial and ethnic stereotypes to illustrate differences in crime rates; *Crime and Human Nature*'s arguably racist analyses—these constitute a heritage of which biocriminologists need be aware. But the new biocriminologies, unlike many of their predecessors, do not begin from racist or sexist premises.

The exception here is evolutionary criminology, which assumes that evolution produced marked gender differences, and which sometimes implies (or can be made to imply) that people of color must be evolutionarily predisposed to crime. But evolutionary psychology is not necessarily sexist, as the feminist work of psychologist Anne Campbell demonstrates.[9] Moreover, other recent biological explanations can be actively antiracist in their applications. For example, geneticists who emphasize the negative developmental effects of poverty are addressing an important cause of racial difference in crime rates.

4. *Emphasis on human differences.* Past and present biological theories can further be compared according to the extent that they stress human differences. Traditionally, the emphasis of biological theories of crime fell on what distinguishes "us" from "them." Today, although biocriminologists search for ever more minute factors—genes and neurons—to account for those differences, the emphasis remains the same. This stress on difference, though perhaps inevitable, obscures the larger picture in which we are all basically alike. "Humans are a remarkably homogeneous species," writes geneticist Eric S. Lander, "with any two people, regardless of racial or ethnic group, being 99.9 percent identical at the genetic level."[10] When biological theorists look for differences, they are looking at that tiny bit of leeway. With respect to genetic differences in particular, sociologists Dorothy Nelkin and M. Susan Lindee argue that:

> The emphasis on . . . differences reflects cultural priorities rather than the specific details of molecular biology, for one of the fundamental insights of contemporary genomics is that all human beings—indeed, all species—share a great deal of DNA. Genetic differences—diseases, talents, and presumably even personality traits—exist, but humans have so much DNA in common that the social message of molecular genetics could be that we are all fundamentally the same. While the science of genetics focuses on biological differences between individuals (because such differences provide insight into the processes of heredity), it has also revealed striking similarities both within and between species.[11]

Perhaps the preceding paragraph should be a required preface to all books on biology and crime for the next few decades. In any case, biocriminologists need to begin by emphasizing that most criminals are basically like the rest of us. If some offenders differ biologically, those differences alone cannot tell the full story. For example, Andrea Yates suffered from postpartum psychosis, but she also had to raise her children in a school bus and live with a man who repeatedly impregnated her despite their doctor's warnings. A de-emphasis on difference could lead to greater tolerance, healing of social wounds, and a draining away of prejudice.

5. Compatibility with sociological explanations of crime. Fifth and finally, we can compare past and present biological theories in terms of their

compatibility with sociological theories of crime. Traditionally, biological theorists belittled the possibility that social factors might affect criminal behavior. This was not true of Lombroso, who studied a range of social factors that he thought were associated with crime, but even he emphasized the biological over the social. No significant change occurred until Eysenck published *Crime and Personality,* with its interactive, biosocial model. Although Eysenck himself ignored this model's implications until very late in life, others picked up on it, and today it dominates biocriminology. "Genes cannot be expressed in any way without an environment," writes Anthony Walsh. "Without the environment, one's genome would create 'nothing more than a damp spot on the carpet.'"[12] This view almost totally reverses the biological determinism of the past, a reversal with major implications for research, treatment, public policy, and relationships among researchers. For the first time, there is a genuine possibility for collaborations between social scientists and cognitive, genetic, and neurological scientists working on crime. But sociological theorists must do their part and acknowledge that biological factors affect crime.

Today's biocriminologies, then, are *not* more of the same. While they continue to rely on the medical model and to be preoccupied with human differences, they can no longer automatically be charged with reductionism or biological determinism, and (aside from some versions of evolutionary criminology) they are no longer overtly sexist or racist. They are compatible with sociological theories of crime and could be yoked to progressive programs addressing crime through amelioration of social conditions. There are endless points where intervention might begin—removing environmental sources of lead, improving children's diets, reducing inner-city unemployment rates and, with them, substance abuse, providing treatment for neurodevelopmental problems, training children to process social information, and educating parents about the need for consistent discipline. A biosocial model can be used to address biosocial problems.

## The Potential for Misuse

Today as in the past, biological explanations of criminal behavior carry considerable potential for misuse. Most gravely, they could feed into new eugenics programs designed to eliminate supposedly criminalistic genes. While coercive eugenics died out at the end of World War II, it has been replaced by a "new" or "liberal" eugenics in which elimination of "bad" genes (or enhancement of "good" genes) occurs by choice:[13] aborting fetuses that test positive for mental retardation or other unwanted characteristics; choosing the sex of babies (in China, a whole nation can play); modifying germ lines—eggs, sperm, or embryos—in ways that can be reproduced in the next generation; and creating banks of sperm from "geniuses" so that women can select presumably high-quality donors. Now that memories of Nazi eugenics have faded, people openly write books touting "new" eugenic solutions (*Redesigning Humans*, for example, and *Future Human Evolution: Eugenics in the Twenty-first Century*),[14] although some still avoid the term *eugenics*.

Next time around, if there is one, the misusers are unlikely to be biocriminologists themselves. No new Henry Goddard will campaign for eugenic criminology, nor will born-again criminal-biologists design a futuristic version of Nazism. A new wave of eugenic criminology would be led not by biocriminologists, who (after all) have themselves developed the biosocial model, but rather by manipulative politicians and ignorant citizens.

Futuristic movies like *Robocop* and *Minority Report* get it right: political danger lies less with mad scientists than with messianic or cynical political leaders who understand that a quick way to gain control is to encourage people to cede authority over the criminal justice system to experts offering easy, if drastic, solutions. These could easily include programs based on genetic profiling and selective breeding. While some of the mass media warn against such simplistic responses, others encourage them, such as a recent television special on sex offenders during which a forensic investigator whipped out a chart showing that a specific criminal had two deviant genes. His explanation of the criminal's behavior was simple and dramatic, and it fit nicely into the time-honored narrative mold in which a heroic scientist points the way to salvation.

People will grasp at what seem to be easy genetic solutions if they are not informed that crime is a biosocial, not a biological, phenomenon. Negative environments lead to gene expression that is sometimes suboptimal, from the viewpoint of crime control, but because the problem is social, it is foolish to propose genetic solutions. Responsibility for misunderstandings about genes lies in part with the behavior geneticists and neurologists who endorse a biosocial model of human development and yet downplay or ignore the model's "social" part when they do research and speak to the public. Science historian Garland Allen observes, "Although most who claim that there is a genetic basis for criminal or violent behavior pay lip service to the environment . . . , in reality both researchers and popularizers focus the vast majority of their attention only on the gene."[15]

But the ultimate responsibility is much wider, and it lies with our culture of biology, which continues to promulgate the nature-nurture dichotomy and to suggest that the solutions to life's problems are primarily biological. If eugenics returns, warns Simon Cole, a specialist in the pitfalls of criminal identification, it is most likely to be ushered in not by genetic testing or profiling but by simplistic understandings of genes. Cole warns that "the media and a few misguided or unscrupulous researchers are laying the groundwork for the gene to become the latest biological marker to be enlisted in the eugenic program, despite the protests of most geneticists. . . . The pernicious aspect of eugenics is the stubborn belief that complex phenomena like race, health, behavior, and ability can be explained by looking at biological markers."[16]

While ignorance can result from bias and unfamiliarity with the subject matter, it can also follow from the subject matter itself. New "hard" scientific findings, when they first arrive, seem persuasive, unarguable. Media reports seldom mention that the experiment has yet to be replicated or that professional interests may have influenced the results. We can be sure that time will eventually reveal the constructed and contingent nature of recent findings that today seem authoritative and convincing. They, too, will "soften." (What "hard" science may mean, experientially, is that we are socialized to accept that particular finding without much question.) This does not imply that there is no objective world "out there" for science to grasp. Rather, it means that all science has an interpretive element, difficult as it may be, at first, to recognize.

What can we do about the "hardness" problem? How can we become more sophisticated in our responses to scientific claims about genes, neurons, and other biological factors implicated in crime? One way is to read more in the history and sociology of science, and an exemplary place to begin is with Nelkin and Lindee's book *The DNA Mystique: The Gene as a Cultural Icon*, which problematizes today's popular acceptance of genetic explanations. DNA, these authors show, has become "an object to think with," a "malleable idea or cognitive framework which different interpretive communities use to express diverse, even contradictory, concerns." The authors continue,

> Genetic metaphors are used to buttress class differences (the result of "good breeding") and to reinforce social stereotypes ("differences lie in the genes"). They serve to explain human exceptionalism on the basis of different DNA ("the genes of genius"), but also to claim the rights of animals on

the basis of shared DNA . . . . Genetics can justify social harmony (based on common ancestry) or social divisions (based on race).

"Clearly," Nelkin and Lindee conclude, "the gene is . . . a symbol, a metaphor," as well as a segment of DNA,[17] and it is difficult to separate its various meanings when we hear the word. But with the help of sociological historians such as these, we can become more aware of the symbolic freightage of the word "gene"—and more sophisticated about the construction of meaning in science generally.[18]

If we acknowledge that genetic research is still in its early stages, we will be less ready to jump to hasty conclusions about the meanings of genetic variants. Western culture idealizes "normality" and looks suspiciously on variations and deviations. But when we speak of genes, it is crucial to remember that we do not actually know that most variations are negative. After all, many of them could be neutral, or positive—or perhaps "creative" responses to hostile environments. Eric Lander drives this point home in his article on the meanings of the human genome project, asking,

> To what extent will we seek to pigeonhole people based on their genes? . . .
> Will we speak of genetic defects or genetic variants? Clearly, some DNA
> changes are unquestionably negative mutations, destroying the function
> of a crucial protein. But many of the common ones are likely to confer
> mixed blessings—perhaps an increased risk of infection by one pathogen,
> but greater resistance to another. It's easy to slip into speaking of devia-
> tions from an "ideal" genotype.[19]

Similarly, we might question another ingrained but untested assumption: the premise that so-called risk factors are always bad. Sociological criminologists are just as invested as their biological counterparts in this assumption, embracing risk reduction as part of their professional identity. No one who has been a crime victim or watched the 9/11 planes slice through the World Trade Center towers will object to risk reduction, and yet we need to beware of "dangerization" processes that breed fears unnecessarily.[20] We need to remember that in constructing difference, we construct ourselves. Do we want a criminology (or social policies) devoted to identifying difference when science itself indicates that key differences are not innate, and when we could devote attention and funds to, for instance, improving public schools so as to further erase differences and reduce crime? Neuroscience and behavior genetics themselves point to crime solutions *outside* the body.

Biosociality is likely to become the leading model in 21st-century criminology, but its path is full of potholes. We are *used* to sciences that, insisting on determinism, reinforce hierarchies and throw the blame for social problems onto those who suffer most from them. We wake up in the morning to a newspaper that reports (for example) that in the Baby M custody dispute, "it will not make much difference which family brings up the child since her personality is already determined by her genes."[21] At the office around the water cooler we argue with colleagues over whether women really do lack scientific aptitude, as asserted by Harvard's ex-president Lawrence Summers. On the way home, we drop by the hospital to visit a friend with cystic fibrosis, a degenerative disease caused by a genetic mutation (but also, in fact, affected by environmental factors, although those are seldom recognized).[22] The day closes with a eugenics-themed episode of *Star Trek*. Thus bombarded with false or incomplete scientific information about genetics, perhaps our best bet at the end of such a day is to sign off with a prayer that we may listen critically to scientific messages and avoid the temptation of quick fixes. Perhaps we can recognize our own ignorance.

## A Criminology for the Future

The field of criminology has burst its traditional boundaries. Until recently, it was what David Garland and Richard Sparks call a "modernist" project, characterized by instrumental reasoning, faith in a technocratic state, and commitment to social progress.[23] Remnants of the modernist project remain, but for the most part criminology has been reharnessed (or so Garland and Sparks argue) to suit the ends of the new regulatory state in which government's role, increasingly, is to manage risk and regulate private security providers.[24] Be that as it may (and we can certainly argue about criminology's future direction), this analysis is useful for what it says about changes in criminology itself. "Given the centrality, the emotiveness and the political salience of crime issues today, academic criminology can no longer aspire to monopolize 'criminological' discourse or hope to claim exclusive rights over the representation and disposition of crime."[25]

Having broken free of the discursive fetters that constrained it in the 20th century, criminology can now more easily incorporate other discourses. History is one (slowly, the discipline is realizing that it needs to know something about its own origins and development); popular culture is another (currently, the discipline is incorporating "cultural criminology"); and biology is a third (a subject originally embraced by criminology but then rejected along with Lombrosianism and eugenics). In the decades ahead, biological theories are likely to constitute a significant discourse within mainstream criminology. Should biological theories cling to the medical model, they might drag criminology back into the pathologization of individual offenders that used to characterize their research on crime. But they could also help turn the field toward becoming a truly *biosocial* criminology, one that investigates, much more precisely than in the past, the impact of negative environments on gene expression and behavior.

For decades, scholars on the Left dismissed biological explanations of crime as a way of pinning blame for social problems on bad individuals and hence avoiding social solutions. At the same time, scholars on the Right argued that the solutions lay in downplaying environmental improvements and doing something about the bad people. Today, new understandings of the complexity, flexibility, and indeterminacy of genetic and neuroscientific development open the way to formulating new positions outside of the old nature-nurture debate. We no longer have to pit nature against nurture; now we can picture the two as working together to achieve gene expression and produce the individual. We can now see that biocriminology itself indicates that ameliorating social environments is the most effective of all anticrime measures.

Thus I envision a new or third way in which we harness biocriminological explanations to programs of social improvement that would lead to crime reduction. I am interested not in a compromise between the former positions of the Left and Right but rather in moving beyond those disputes to splice biocriminology to sociology in order to reduce crime *and* social inequality. I want to enlist modern genetics in progressive social change.

# Notes

CHAPTER 1

1. Arpey, 2003: 8.

2. Dunn and Jones, 1955: par. 11.

3. Arpey, 2003: 65.

4. Arpey, 2003: 15 ("depravity"), 36 ("catastrophe"), 80.

5. Seward as quoted by Arpey, 2003: 60.

6. Dunn and Jones, 1955: par. 30, quoting Brigham's postmortem report.

7. As quoted in Arpey, 2003: 32.

8. Seward as quoted in Arpey, 2003: 71.

9. Arpey, 2003.

10. Rose, 2000.

11. The term *biocriminology* was coined in Rose, 2000.

12. Michael Woroniecki, as quoted at http://crime.about.com/od/current/p/andreayates.htm.

13. For these and other details on the case, I have relied on Denno, 2003, and West and Lichtenstein, 2006.

14. Charen, 2006.

15. http://digg.com/world_news/BREAKING_Andrea_Yates_found_NOT_GUILTY_of_drowning_her_5_children.

16. See also Degler, 1991.

17. Barbassa, 2005.

18. Kaiser Daily Women's Health Policy, 2003.

19. Raine, 1993; Walsh, 2002.

20. E.g., *Biology and Crime* (Rowe, 2002) confuses phrenology with criminal anthropology.

21. Proctor, 1991: 159.

22. E.g., Foucault 1977, 1988.

23. Fink, 1938.

24. Werlinder, 1978. The same year saw publication of a partly historical review of criminology, *The Search for Criminal Man* (Rennie, 1978).

25. See, e.g., Becker and Wetzell, 2006; Beirne, 1993, 1994; Cole, 2002; Davie, 2005; Garland, 1985, 1988, 2002; Gibson, 2002; Hood, 2004; Horn, 2003; Laub, 1984; Laub and Sampson, 1991; Regener, 2003; Wetzell, 2000.

26. Rafter, 1992b.

27. Rock, 1994: xiii

28. Smith, 1988, 1997; see also Richards, 1987.

29. On ways in which socio-intellectual climate can influence the content of criminology, see Rafter, 1997, and Savelsberg, 2004; on the effects of competition among criminologists, see Laub and Sampson, 1991; and on the impact of government funding policies on criminology, see Savelsberg, King, and Cleveland, 2002, and Savelsberg, Cleveland, and King, 2004.

30. See also Duster, 2006; Rafter, 1990b.

31. See, esp., Douglas, 1966.

CHAPTER 2

1. Beccaria, 1764; Bentham, 1789.

2. Here and throughout this book, I do not attempt to impose today's criteria for "scientific" on the past but instead investigate how earlier researchers who regarded their work as scientific established and implemented their criteria for scientificalness. That is, I use "science" descriptively, not judgmentally.

3. King, 1991.

4. Rush, 1786: 181.

5. Rush, 1786: 183.

6. Rush terms these conditions *anomia* and *micronomia*, respectively (Rush, 1786/1947: 192). While the distinction remained criminologically important, Rush himself eventually abandoned the awkward terminology.

7. Rush, 1786: 187–188.

8. Rush, 1786: 184–185, citing the *Memoirs* of the Duke of Sully, v. 3: 216–217.

9. Rush, 1786: 193.

10. Rush, 1786: 201.

11. Rush, 1786: 209.

12. Rush, 1812: 10.

13. Rush, 1812: 12.

14. Rush, 1812: 358.

15. Werlinder, 1978: 24, n. 25. See also Carlson and Simpson, 1965.

16. Tony Robert-Fleury, *Pinel Déliverant les aliénés*.

17. Bynum, 1981. Meanings of the term *moral* fluctuated considerably in early psychiatric texts. Benjamin Rush used the term to mean "ethical"; for him, *moral insanity* was a derangement of what we might call the ethical capacity. Other writers used *moral* to mean "psychological" or "affective." As the next section shows, J. C. Prichard distinguished between intellectual and moral insanity, the first

affecting the mind and resulting in (for example) hallucinations, and the second affecting feelings, temper, and habits and resulting in (for example) kleptomania. In addition, Pinel and other early 19th-century psychiatrists on both sides of the Atlantic endorsed "moral treatment," which involved creating a benign, therapeutic environment to help the mentally ill recover (see, e.g., Digby, 1985).

18. Pinel, *Traité*, 1806: 46, as quoted by Werlinder, 1978: 18.

19. Pinel, 1806: 1, 2, 3.

20. Dain, 1964: 64–67.

21. Pinel, 1806: 150.

22. Pinel, 1806: 152–153.

23. Pinel, 1806: 151–152.

24. Werlinder 1978: 30.

25. Prichard, 1835: 5. The earlier, anthropological, book is Prichard, 1813.

26. Prichard, 1835: 4.

27. Prichard, 1835: 14.

28. Prichard, 1835: 112.

29. Prichard, 1835: 479.

30. Prichard, 1835: 386.

31. Prichard, 1835: 393.

32. Tuke, 1891.

33. Dain, 1964: 74–75; Werlinder, 1978: 40.

34. Arpey, 2003.

35. Augstein, 1996; Carlson and Dain, 1962; Bynum, 1981.

36. Augstein, 1996: 311.

37. Tuke, 1885b; see also Hughes, 1882.

38. Carlson and Dain, 1962.

39. Franz Joseph Gall, the founder of phrenology, actually discusses moral insanity in one of his later works (Gall, 1825, v. 1: 434–444), endorsing the distinction between general and partial mental alienation. However, Gall's ideas on this head are based on Pinel's work and do not constitute a significant contribution to the identification and definition of moral insanity.

40. See, e.g., Eigen, 1995; Mohr, 1993; Moran, 2000; Robinson, 1998; Rosenberg, 1968; Smith, 1981.

41. Hughes, 1882; Dain and Carlson, 1962.

42. This is an odd genealogy, given that Ray was thoroughly familiar with the even earlier work of his compatriot Benjamin Rush. Ray may have been trying to align himself with the more scientific Pinel and to thereby give moral insanity a more respectable ancestry. In Ray's day, Rush would still have been remembered for not only his bloodlettings but also his horrific therapeutic tools, which included a "tranquillizing chair" into which he locked mentally ill patients.

43. Ray, 1838: 138.

44. Moreover, although Ray later became an asylum superintendent, at the time he produced the first edition of his *Treatise on the Medical Jurisprudence of Insanity* he was still a general practitioner in Maine, under thirty years old and lacking much personal experience with the insane. For background, see Overholser, 1962, 1972.

45. Actually, Ray contradicts himself on this last point by reporting (1838: 191) that in some cases a morally insane offender will turn himself in to the police, overwhelmed with guilt.

46. Ray, 1838: 196.

47. See, e.g., Spitzka, 1878.

48. Rosenberg, 1968; Waldinger, 1979.

49. Gray as quoted in Bynum, 1981: 39–40.

50. See also *American Journal of Insanity*, 1863.

51. Dain and Carlson, 1962.

52. Pick, 1989. Degeneration theory is discussed in detail later, in chapters 4 and 5.

53. Cf. Dain and Carlson, 1962.

54. Rafter, 1997; see also chapter 6.

55. The superintendent of Broadmoor, as quoted in Tuke, 1891: 58.

56. Kitching, 1857:335.

57. Tuke, 1885a; the photographs appear on p. 360.

58. Tuke, 1885a, repr. in Tuke, 1891: 361–363.

59. See also Digby, 1985.

60. From Rush onward, psychiatrists had noted that mental disease tended to run in families. But early 19th-century mad-doctors did not claim that bad heredity is the central cause of madness, as late 19th-century psychiatrists did.

61. Savage, 1881: 152.

62. For more detail on the influence of Spencer, Darwin, and Maudsley on the development of biological theories of crime, see chapters 4 and 5.

63. Gasquet, 1882; Manley, 1883; Manning, 1882–1883; Needham, 1882; Smith, 1885; Tuke, 1885a, 1885b.

64. Tuke, 1885b, repr. in Tuke, 1891: 85.

65. Tuke, 1885b, repr. in Tuke, 1891: 89.

66. J. Wiglesworth, in Tuke, 1891: 99.

67. Tuke, 1885a, repr. in Tuke, 1891: 110.

68. Lombroso, 2006 (orig. 1876).

69. See note 16.

70. Bloor, 1991: 62–68.

71. Spurzheim, 1815: 8.

72. Spurzheim, 1815: 10.

73. Ray, 1838: 108.

74. Dain, 1964: 43.

75. Luman Sherwood as quoted by Arpey, 2003: 87.

76. Tyndall, 1878: 116.

77. Rothman, 1971.

CHAPTER 3

1. Spurzheim, 1815: 308.

2. The system's founder, Franz Joseph Gall, identified twenty-seven organs; his closest follower, Johann Gaspar Spurzheim, identified thirty-three.

3. As the next section explains, it was not Gall himself but Spurzheim who introduced the hopeful idea that the faculties might be modified by exercise and other forms of treatment.

4. *Phrenological Journal and Miscellany*, 1834–1836: title page.

5. Foucault, 1977; McLaren, 1981.

6. Rush, 1786.

7. Lavater, n.d.: 27.

8. Woodrow, 2001–2002.

9. Lavater, n.d.: 50.

10. Lavater, n.d.

11. Cooter, 1984: 5; see also Gray, 2004.

12. Spurzheim, 1815: 257. Gall's own (and almost identical) account of the genesis of his doctrine appears in Gall, 1825, v. 1.

13. Spurzheim, 1815: 258.

14. Spurzheim, 1815: 263.

15. Gall, 1825.

16. Gall, 1835.

17. Gall, 1825, v. 1: iv.

18. Van Wyhe, 2002.

19. Gall, 1825, v. 1: esp. 150–51.

20. Spurzheim, 1828: 187.

21. Spurzheim, 1828: 187; see also Spurzheim 1825: 182.

22. Walsh, 1972. It took me years to locate Spurzheim's tomb, although once you know the location, it is easy to find. Gall was one of the first people to be buried in the newly opened Mount Auburn Cemetery in Cambridge, Massachusetts, the country's first large landscaped burial ground and one filled with historical notables. Spurzheim's grave is near the main entrance, lot 181 on Central Avenue. There is some debate over whether his body actually lies under the stone sarcophagus (the Boston Phrenological Society laid claim to his skull, heart, and brain, and no record testifies to the internment), but according to Mount Auburn officials, the body, at least, is probably there.

23. Cantor 1975; Cooter, 1984; Shapin, 1979.

24. Cantor, 1975; Carlson, 1958; Cooter, 1981, 1984; Dain, 1964; McLaren, 1981; Shapin, 1979, 1982.

25. Spurzheim, 1828: 280.

26. Cooter, 1984.

27. For an example of these implicit tendencies, see Spurzheim, 1828, especially the chapter "On the Law of Hereditary Descent." In this chapter (p. 44), he remarks: "Children born of healthy parents, and belonging to a strong stock, always bring into the world a system formed by nature to resist the causes of disease; while children of delicate, sickly parents, are overpowered by the least favorable circumstance." From such passages it was but a small step to the degenerationist thought of the second half of the 19th century.

28. Galton, 1869, 1883.

29. Spurzheim, 1815: 6.

30. Spurzheim, 1815: 10.

31. Spurzheim, 1815: 250.

32. Abernathy, 1821: 5.

33. Guerry, 1833; Quetelet, 1835; Poisson, 1837. On the history of crime statistics, see Beirne, 1993, and Stigler, 1986. A. M. Guerry, in his *Essai sur la statistique morale de la France* (1833), tried to correlate arrests with literacy rates and also examined recidivism. Quetelet's *Treatise on Man and the Development of His Faculties* (1835) observed that crime rates, like suicide rates and birth ratios, remain stable in large numbers over time, thus calling individual free will into question; he also developed the criminologically important concept of the average or typical man. Poisson's main book (1837) dealt with probability theory but also examined conviction rates and made comparisons of crimes against persons with crime against property.

34. Spurzheim, 1815: 305 ("kill birds"), 306 ("desire to kill"), 310 (mental organization), 312–315 (Pinel).

35. Gall, 1825, v. 4: 64.

36. Spurzheim, 1815: 317–318.

37. Spurzheim, 1815: 320–321.

38. Phrenologists sometimes spoke of the "will," but they recognized no faculty of the will, and the concept of volition tended to get lost in their discussions of the faculties' influence on behavior. See Gall, 1825, v. 1: 220–246, and v. 6: 427, and Spurzheim, 1825, esp. 32–35.

39. Sampson, 1843: 9.

40. Sampson, 1843. This extreme version of the medical model was satirized in Samuel Butler's novel *Erewhon* (1872), which portrays a country where the sick are punished and the criminals treated solicitously until they recover. Although the novel does not speak directly of phrenology, it can be read as a satire on phrenology and related deterministic ideas about human nature and social improvement.

41. Combe, 1841, v. 1: 204–207.

42. Combe, 1841, v. 2: 9–10, 16.

43. Simpson, 1834: 281–282, emphasis in original.

44. Lombroso, 2006 (orig. 1876); Rafter, 1992b. Lombroso's work is discussed in chapter 4.

45. As quoted in Barker, 1995: 678. The source of the report was probably John M. Harlow, the physician who first treated Phineas Gage.

46. See, esp., Simpson, 1834: 12–13, arguing for improvements in the living conditions of the poor in order to replenish the laboring population and make it healthier.

47. Simpson, 1834: 289.

48. Combe, 1854: 29.

49. Sampson, 1843: 6, 10.

50. Spurzheim, 1828: 278.

51. Combe 1854: 35, emphasis in original.

52. Mittermaier in Combe and Mittermaier 1843: 5 (both quotations). Mittermaier could not possibly have known this at the time, but his small grandson, Richard von Krafft-Ebing (1840–1902), would grow up to be a pioneer sexologist and authority in medical jurisprudence. The grandson's interest in legal issues was probably stimulated by his grandfather's interests along the same lines; see Oosterhuis, 2000.

53. Foucault, 1988.

54. Arpey, 2003: 76–77.

55. Ray, 1838: 139–140.

56. Kitching, 1857: 38.

57. E.g., Combe and Mittermaier, 1843: 4.

58. Many phrenologists who advocated replacing execution with life sentences for first-degree murderers also advocated eventual release should the convict reform.

59. Sampson as quoted by Wharton, 1841: 26, emphasis in original.

60. Wharton, 1841: 32.

61. Cooter, 1981: 90.

62. Gall, 1825: v. 1, 339, emphasis in original.

63. The proceedings of the Cincinnati meeting are collected in Wines, 1871.

64. Davies, 1955.

65. Brockway, 1871: 39, 38, 40.

66. Combe in Combe and Mittermaier, 1843: 9.

67. Combe, 1841: 19.

68. Mittermaier in Combe and Mittermaier, 1843: 6.

69. Farnham, 1846. Farnham's additions to the 1846 edition of Marmaduke Sampson's *Rationale of Crime* were illustrated by the soon-to-be-famous Civil War photographer Mathew Brady. Farnham asked Brady to photograph prisoners so she could illustrate her text with actual examples of phrenological doctrine. The

photographs were turned into lithographs for reproduction. They illustrate head shapes considered telling by Farnham and are accompanied by her textual analyses.

70. Rafter, 1990a.

71. Livingston, 1827, 1833.

72. E.g., Simpson, 1834: Appendix I.

73. Wines, 1871.

74. Maconochie, 1847; Wines, 1871: 66–74.

75. de Guistino, 1975; but see Clay, 2001.

76. Combe, 1841.

77. Combe in Combe and Mittermaier, 1843: 13.

78. Combe in Combe and Mittermaier, 1843: 16; see also Combe, 1841, and Combe, 1854.

79. E.g., Livingston, 1827: 58.

80. E.g., Combe, 1841, v. 2: 207.

81. Combe, 1854: 3.

82. de Guistino, 1975, puts Maconochie in this category.

83. Abernethy, 1821: 66–67, 8.

84. McLaren, 1981: 19–20; Carlson, 1958: 536.

85. Cantor, 1975: 211–218.

86. See also Young, 1990.

87. Pick, 1989.

88. Wilson, 1975.

89. See also Gander, 2003.

90. For a critical overview, see Uttal, 2003.

91. With thanks to Lynn Chancer for helping me clarify this final point.

CHAPTER 4

1. Lombroso, 1871: 10.

2. Dickie, 1999; Gibson, 1998; Melossi, 2000.

3. Wolfgang's 1972 biography remains a useful guide to Lombroso's life, while more recent works such as Frigessi, 2003, Gibson, 2002, and Villa, 1985, have added depth and new analyses to his life story.

4. Lacassagne, 1909: 894.

5. Lombroso, 1911: xxiv–xxv.

6. Lombroso shaped this myth over time, adding the dramatic details. An earlier version appears in Lombroso, 1871; see also Horn, 2003.

7. Mayhew and Binny, 1862: 89.

8. Thomson, 1870b.

9. Maudsley, 1874: 24.

10. Lombroso, 1876, 1878, 1884, 1889, 1896–1897. The editions grew in length, with the last one comprising four volumes. The new translation (Lombroso, 2006)

includes the significant parts of all five editions, showing Lombroso's development over time.

11. Lombroso, 2006: 45, 48.

12. Lombroso, 2006: 48.

13. Lombroso, 2006: 51.

14. Lombroso, 2006: 72.

15. Lombroso, 2006: 69.

16. Lombroso, 2006: 163.

17. Lombroso, 2006: 224. This is the figure he used in the third edition; by the fifth, the proportion had fallen to 35 percent (Lombroso, 2006: 338), and it varied at other times as well.

18. Lombroso, 2006: 67.

19. Lombroso and Ferrero, 1893, originally translated as *The Female Offender* (1895), recently retranslated as *Criminal Woman, the Prostitute, and the Normal Woman* (Lombroso and Ferrero, 2004). The introduction to the new edition traces the book's influence on subsequent thinking about female criminality.

20. Lombroso and Ferrero, 2004: 64.

21. Lombroso and Ferrero, 2004: 99.

22. Lombroso, 1871.

23. It is instructive to reflect on why Lombroso, whose background lay in medicine and psychiatry, decided to cast himself as a specialist in anthropology. Villa (1985: 135) contends that "neither in Italy nor abroad was Lombroso considered an 'anthropologist.'" His qualifications, in Villa's view, lay in anthropometry—"Lombroso was essentially a measurer." But *L'uomo bianco e l'uomo di colore* must have given him a sense of expertise in anthropology, even though his research for it was strictly armchair anthropology.

24. d'Agostino, 2002.

25. Lombroso, 1871: 170. Darwin himself did not say this in *The Origin of Species*.

26. Lombroso (1871) mentions these sources on pp. 13, 121–122, 161 (referring to recapitulation theory without naming Haeckel) and 214 (same). He also frequently cites Paolo Marzolo, "the leader of Italian anthropologists" (p. 7) and one of his scientific heroes. For background materials on Lombroso and Darwinism, see Pancaldi, 1991.

27. Lombroso, 1871:10.

28. Lombroso, 1871: 44, 221, 171, 151.

29. Lombroso, 2006: 91.

30. Lombroso, 2006: 196.

31. Lombroso, 2006: 81.

32. Lombroso, 2006: 222.

33. Lombroso, 2006: 247. On Lombroso and epilepsy, see Chio et al., 2004. At the time Lombroso was relating epilepsy to crime, other European theorists, too,

were discussing the affliction (including "latent" or "hidden" epilepsy) and diagnosing it in new populations; see Hacking, 1996.

34. On Lombroso and degeneration theory, see Pick, 1989.

35. Lombroso, 2006: 92, 43.

36. Bentham, 1789; Beccaria, 1764.

37. Cf. Beirne, 1991.

38. Lombroso, 2006: 235–236, 100; Dugdale, 1877.

39. Lombroso, 2006: 53. Because this translation condenses Lombroso's writings, these two statements did not necessarily appear on the same page in the original.

40. Nye, 1976: 391.

41. Nye, 1976: 342, n. 23.

42. Villa, 1985.

43. As quoted in Dolza, 1990: 34.

44. Dolza, 1990: 34.

45. As of this writing, the city of Turin is planning to reopen the Lombroso museum.

46. Lombroso, 2006: 99.

47. Lombroso, 2006: 331, 135.

48. Sekula, 1986.

49. Lombroso, 2006: 146. This eugenical passage is from the second (1878) version of *Criminal Man.*

50. Lombroso, 2006: 348.

51. Lombroso, 2006: 92. The roots of Lombroso's social defense philosophy lay in phrenology; see chapter 3.

52. Garland, 1988.

53. Wolfgang, 1972: 239, writes of the many opportunities Lombroso "had as prison physician at Turin to examine clinically thousands of prisoners, for Lombroso was fortunate that the head of the Italian prison administration was an interested scholar and diligent historian. Beltrani-Scalia put at Lombroso's disposal the entire body of official criminal and penal material and opened all Italian prisons to him and his pupils."

54. Thanks to Jonathan Simon for his contribution to this analysis.

55. Wolfgang, 1972: 235.

56. Guarnieri, 1993.

57. Duggan, 1994: 130.

58. Pick, 1986: 63; see also Pick, 1989.

59. Pick, 1986: 61. More generally, see Foucault, 1977.

60. Kuhn, 1962.

61. Horn, 2003: 11.

62. See Dolza, 1990: 29–30: "Belonging to the generation of Jews who came of age after the 1848 law of emancipation," Lombroso did not consider the Jewish world "the sole source of his cultural and intellectual identity. Through his

precocity and his hunger for . . . knowledge, he soon encountered contradictions presented by the rigid religious education imparted to him by his family . . . . Lombroso rather early rejected the religious and ritual components of Judaism that, from youth, seemed to him to conflict with his rationalist tendencies, and, later, his scientific materialist convictions." In the movement for Italian unification he found "the promise of integration in a new society, more free and just, to whose formation he would be about to contribute." See also D'Antonio, 2001.

63. Garland, 2002: 8–9.

64. On France, see Mucchielli, 2006; on Italy, Gibson, 2002; on Germany, Wetzell, 2000; on Portugal, Saldaña, 1933; on Spain, de Quiros, 1912; on the United States, Rafter, 1992b, 1997, and the following chapters in the present book; on Britain, Davie, 2005.

65. Moffitt, 1993.

CHAPTER 5

1. But see Pick, 1989.

2. Strahan, 1892: 1.

3. Wiebe, 1967.

4. Wiener, 1990: 11.

5. "Most men at the beginning of the nineteenth century thought the world had been created only some six thousand years before," writes J. W. Burrow (1968: 20), "though perhaps few would have cared to be so specific as the famous pronouncement of a seventeenth-century vice-chancellor of Cambridge University according to whom 'man was created by the Trinity on October 23 4004 B.C. at nine o'clock in the morning.'"

6. Lamarck, 1809, v. 1: 221–222.

7. Jordanova, 1984; Packard, 1901.

8. Lamarck, 1809, v. 1: 235.

9. Darwin, 1871: 199.

10. Darwin, 1871: 96.

11. Darwin, 1871: 97–98.

12. Darwin, 1871: ch. 3.

13. Spencer, 1876a: part I.

14. Spencer, 1876b: 530.

15. Spencer, 1864–1867/1898: 553.

16. Haeckel presented these images in his book *Natürliche Schöpfungs-Geschichte (Natural History of Creation)* (1898; originally 1868). According to Weisstein, n.d., some of Haeckel's illustrations were immediately challenged as deceptive, and Haeckel admitted touching up the woodblock images of fetuses to make his point. However, Weisstein continues, because the charges against Haeckel were made in German, few people outside of Germany learned about them.

17. Gould, 1981: 114.

18. Geoffroy Saint-Hilaire, 1822.

19. Geoffroy Saint-Hilaire, 1832.

20. Darwin, 1859: 101. Darwin attributed "monstrosities" such as cleft palates and microcephalous brains to arrested development (Darwin, 1871: 121).

21. Boies, 1893: 266.

22. Darwin, 1871: 173.

23. Spencer, 1864–1867/1898: 233.

24. E.g., J. Wiglesworth, in Tuke, 1891: 99.

25. Some criminologists also discussed crime as a result of *arrested development*. However, few distinguished clearly among arrested development, atavism, and reversion or degeneration; rather, they tended to use all three concepts interchangeably to explain criminality as backward evolution, a downward deviation from the norm of civilized behavior.

26. Maudsley, 1874: 29–30.

27. Noyes, 1887: 31. Noyes had read the then-new French translation of *Criminal Man.*

28. McKim, 1900: 282–283.

29. Strahan, 1892: 10.

30. Darwin, 1859: 76.

31. Strahan, 1892: 8.

32. Early in his *Traité*, Morel (1857) defines degeneration in a relatively neutral way, in terms of departures from or elaborations of an original human type, an idea analogous to deviations from a statistical mean. (This usage followed the lead of the German anthropologist J. F. Blumenbach and other monogenists, according to whom humanity began as a single family, with racial variations spinning off from the original template as a result of climate or other environmental factors. The monogenist position opposed itself to the polygenist thesis, according to which God made the races in separate acts of creation.) When Morel uses degeneration in this neutral sense, he is thinking merely of deviations from a "primitive" type caused by natural selection ("une lutte incessante contre tant d'éléments accumulés de destruction" [Morel, 1857: 7–8]). Later, however, he uses degeneration to refer to maladaptations or morbid deviations from normality, caused by (as well as producing) degenerative conditions.

33. Morel, 1857: 6, 33.

34. Morel, 1857: 72. Morel sometimes suggests ways to combat degenerative tendencies, but most of the time he views degeneration as an incurable, hopeless condition.

35. Morel, 1857: vii–ix. By "precocity," Morel meant that youth crimes were occurring at ever-younger ages.

36. Morel, 1857: 660.

37. Pick, 1989; Rafter, 1997.

38. McKim, 1900: 23.

39. Boies, 1893: 268.

40. Strahan, 1892: 289.

41. McKim, 1900: 64.

42. Dugdale influenced Lombroso, but not vice versa; thus I cover Dugdale first, even though his book was not first chronologically.

43. Maudsley, 1874: 29.

44. Collie, 1988; Scull, MacKenzie, and Hervey, 1996. Later in life, Maudsley became less dogmatic; see, for instance, Maudsley, 1888.

45. Maudsley, 1874: 22, 25, 28, 33, emphasis in original.

46. Maudsley, 1874: 29, 32. Even more emphatically, in *Body and Mind*, Maudsley describes degeneracy as "the *unkinding*, so to say, of the human kind" (1873: 53, emphasis in original), a phrase that cuts criminals off almost entirely from the human species.

47. Maudsley, 1874: 60–62. The year before publication of *Responsibility in Mental Disease*, in a new edition of *Body and Mind* (1873), Maudsley had drawn on Haeckel's biogenetic law to account for moral reversion. Explaining that every human brain develops through "the same stages as the brains of other vertebrate animals," Maudsley reasoned that "arrested development" can lead to "a display of criminal instincts." He concluded that "there is truly a brute brain within the man's; and when the latter stops short of its characteristic development as *human*—when it remains arrested at or below the level of an orang's brain, it may be presumed that it will manifest its most primitive functions, and no higher functions" (1873: 52, emphasis in original). But Maudsley did not return to this Haeckelian explanation of criminality in *Responsibility in Mental Disease*, instead adopting a more degenerationist account.

48. Thomson, 1870a: 488.

49. Thomson, 1870b: 321.

50. Thomson, 1870b: 327, 331.

51. Collie, 1988: 17.

52. Maudsley, 1874: 22.

53. Maudsley, 1874: 23.

54. Earlier, Galton devised a similar method of pedigree analysis for his book *Hereditary Genius* (1869). My guess is that the prison association official for whom Dugdale worked, Dr. Elisha Harris—a better-read and more sophisticated man— had read *Hereditary Genius* or one of J. B. Thomson's inflammatory tracts on criminal heredity (or both) and then, with them in mind, commissioned Dugdale to nose around in county jail records to see if he could identify any bad families. Apparently Dugdale himself had not read Galton's book.

55. In the conclusion to *"The Jukes"* ("Tentative Generalizations on Heredity and Environment"), Dugdale holds that the effects of bad heredity are nearly always "capable of marked modification for better or worse by the character of the

environment" (1877: 65). Earlier in the text, however, he makes more emphatically hereditarian observations (e.g., "it would seem that chastity and profligacy are hereditary characteristics" [p. 20]).

56. Rafter, 1997.

57. A brief contemporary memorial (Shepard, 1884) suggests that Dugdale did not attend college and that he was by and large self-taught.

58. Dugdale, 1877: 7.

59. Dugdale, 1877: 8, emphasis in original.

60. Those who cited *"The Jukes,"* reprinted it, and did follow-up studies ignored the quotation marks that Dugdale had carefully placed around the family name in his title. But while Dugdale had the integrity to use quotation marks, he undeniably fostered the impression of interrelatedness by creating a vast family tree headed by a single sire.

61. Dugdale, 1877: 70.

62. In a sign of his lack of familiarity with the social theory of his day, including degeneration theory, Dugdale uses not "degeneration" but "heredity." However, Elisha Harris, in his introduction, speaks of "degenerate stock."

63. Rafter, 1988.

64. Lombroso, 2006: 123. The section runs pp. 123–126.

65. Lombroso, 2006: 118–119.

66. Lombroso, 2006: 146.

67. In the new translation of *Criminal Man*, Lombroso (2006) cites Morel only twice, and in neither case is the subject the inheritance of degeneration.

68. Darwin, 1871: 9.

69. Darwin, 1871: 39.

70. Darwin's influence is even more marked in *Criminal Woman* (Lombroso and Ferrero, 2004) than in *Criminal Man*, probably because Darwin wrote extensively about sex differentiation, a key theme in *Criminal Woman*.

71. Frigessi, 2003: 127; see also chapter 4 of the present book.

72. Villa, 1985: 139–140.

73. Frigessi, 2003: 138; see also Pancaldi, 1991.

74. Oosterhuis, 2000.

75. Oosterhuis, 2000.

76. Krafft-Ebing, 1899: 2.

77. Krafft-Ebing, 1899: 6.

78. Krafft-Ebing, 1899: 326–328.

79. Krafft-Ebing, 1899: 79–80, n. 3.

80. Oosterhuis, 2000: 54–55.

81. Krafft-Ebing, 1899: 75–76.

82. To track changes in Krafft-Ebing's ideas over time, the ideal method would be to compare various editions of *Psychopathia Sexualis*. However, even in Oxford's Bodlean Library I had access only to an English edition of 1899, and so I

supplemented it with Krafft-Ebing's work on criminal responsibility (1875) and with secondary sources on Krafft-Ebing's work and its development, of which Oosterhuis, 2000, is particularly useful.

83. Krafft-Ebing, 1899: 332–339, 392. Krafft-Ebing was encouraged in this interpretation by the work of Karl Heinrich Ulrichs, the original gay rights advocate, who as early as 1864 had drawn on embryological concepts to demonstrate that homosexuality is an organic trait (Kennedy, 2001; Krafft-Ebing, 1899).

84. Krafft-Ebing, 1899: 111–112.

85. Galton, 1875; Gillham, 2001: 5 and ch. 14.

86. Galton, 1883: 3.

87. Galton, 1883: 42–43.

88. Galton, 1883: 199–200.

89. Cowan, 1972: 389. See also Bulmer, 2003, and Sweeney, 2001.

90. Cowan, 1972: 412; see also Bulmer, 2003: ch. 4; Sweeney, 2001, esp. pp. 50–51. Galton's "law of ancestral inheritance," Bowler explains (2003: 257), "bears no resemblance to the laws of Mendelian genetics, but it does encapsulate the basic idea of hard heredity, because Galton insisted that the environment could not influence how the package of ancestral inheritance could be expressed. Thus Galton's followers were able to use it as the basis for an analysis of the effect of selection on a population."

91. Galton, 1883: 1.

92. On the latter, see Rafter, 2001.

93. Moffitt et al., 2001; Wright et al., 2001. See also chapter 9 of the present book.

94. Ellis and Walsh, 1997; Thornhill and Palmer, 2000.

95. E.g., Raine et al., 2000.

96. Rose, 2000.

CHAPTER 6

1. *Buck v. Bell, Superintendent,* 274 U.S. 200 (1927).

2. *Buck v. Bell, Superintendent,* 274 U.S. 200, 205–207.

3. Lombardo, 1985: esp. p. 55.

4. Theodore Roosevelt as quoted in Bruinius, 2006: 6.

5. On the eugenics movement generally, see Haller, 1963, and Kevles, 1985.

6. You can see their photographs, respectively, in Rafter, 1997: opposite p. 149, and in Bruinius, 2006: opposite p. 237. For related photographs, see Paul, 1995.

7. See, esp., Bruinius, 2006.

8. Barnicle, 1990; Vega, 2003.

9. Thomson, 1870b: 333, emphasis in original.

10. Lombroso, 2006: 72.

11. Benedikt, 1881: 157, viii.

12. Ellis, 1890: 133–134, 135.

13. See also Rafter, 1997, esp. p. 88.

14. Goring, 1913: 370.

15. Lombroso-Ferrero, 1914: 209. "Goring becomes more Lombrosian than Lombroso," Lombroso-Ferrero continued (1914: 210). "He not only admits one but several criminal types."

16. Note in the *Journal of the American Institute of Criminal Law and Criminology* prefacing Lombroso-Ferrero, 1914: 207.

17. Beirne, 1988.

18. Or so I would hold, but there is dispute on this matter in the secondary literature. Cf. Garland, 1988: 141, arguing that Goring conceived "of criminality as normal, rather than morbid or pathological," with Davie, 2005: 242, arguing that Goring's conclusions were very similar to those of Lombroso. See also Leps, 1992: 37, who holds the same position as Davie and I do.

19. Goring, 1913: 372, emphasis in original.

20. Goring, 1913: 258 (typical offenses), 372 (rates of reproduction).

21. Goddard's work has been analyzed extensively; see, e.g., Gould, 1981; Haller, 1963; Rafter, 1997; Zenderland, 1998.

22. Gelb, 1995.

23. These family studies and the Kite study mentioned later in this paragraph are reprinted in Rafter, 1988.

24. Goddard, 1912: esp. 29–30 (quotes).

25. Goddard, 1912: 53.

26. Goddard himself, working with Charles B. Davenport, seems to have invented this iconography, which was then used extensively in other bad-family studies. See Rafter, 2001.

27. Kite, n.d.: 24.

28. Kite, n.d.: 9.

29. Goddard, 1910: 27.

30. Goddard, 1910: 28.

31. Goddard, 1910: 29–30.

32. Rafter, 1992a.

33. Goddard, 1915. This book—*The Criminal Imbecile*—is discussed in Rafter, 1997, and Zenderland, 1998, among other works.

34. Goddard, 1914.

35. Goddard, 1914: 8.

36. Barr, 1895: 529–530. Barr's umbrella term for these high-grade types was *moral imbeciles*; Goddard had not yet coined the terms *morons* or *criminal imbeciles*.

37. Earlier, J. Bruce Thomson (1870b: 333) had anticipated this usage when he observed that juvenile delinquents of imbecile mind "reminded me strongly of the children of the mining population in some Scottish districts, who never could keep pace with the teaching and training of the factory operatives, the miners

being decidedly the lowest in caste of any of the industrial operatives." For Barr, too, to be poor and troublesome was a sign of mental deficiency.

38. Hahn, 1980; Rafter, 1997; see also Allen, 1975.

39. New York State Prison Survey Committee, 1920.

40. See also Rafter, 1997, and Walkowitz, 1999. For related analyses pertaining to Britain, see Davie, 2005; Freeden, 1979; and Ray, 1983.

41. See also Burnham, 1960.

42. Ray, 1983: 214.

43. Barr, 1904: 190.

44. Goddard, 1920: 37.

45. Goddard, 1920: 63.

46. Goddard, 1920: 120.

47. Goddard, 1920: 116.

48. Bruinius, 2006: 8.

49. Ross, 1994: 1.

50. On the difficulties of definition, see, esp., Ross 1994; on modernist science, see Pauly, 1994.

51. Harrington, 1996; Harwood, 1993; Herf, 1984; Lears, 1981.

52. Harrington, 1996: xvi.

53. Herf, 1984.

54. Rafter, 1997.

55. Cravens, 1987.

56. Healy, 1915.

57. Burt, 1925.

58. Currell and Cogdell, 2006, among others, argue that in the United States, eugenics remained strong through the 1930s, culturally though not scientifically. As the next chapter shows, it in fact even retained some scientific vitality into the 1950s.

59. Fernald, 1909–1910: 33 (orig. 1908); Fernald, 1918–1919: 98; see also Goddard, 1928.

60. Sutherland, 1931: 313.

61. Hoag and Williams, 1923: 5–6.

62. Glueck and Glueck, 1934: 69, 303.

63. Barnes and Teeters, 1944.

64. Herrnstein and Murray, 1994: 23.

65. Herrnstein and Murray, 1994: 54, 515.

66. Herrnstein and Murray, 1994: 532. A quotation from Burke prefaces *The Bell Curve*.

67. Herrnstein and Murray, 1994: 354.

68. Donohue and Levitt, 2001.

69. A review of this discussion appears on the Internet encyclopedia wikipedia.org under "legalized abortion and crime."

70. Lombardo, 1985.
71. Lombardo, 1985.
72. Bruinius, 2006: 17; Kevles, 1985: 347, n. 21.
73. *Buck v. Bell, Superintendent*, 274 U.S. 200, at 202.

CHAPTER 7

1. See, for instance, Sheldon's book *The Varieties of Human Physique* (1940), which is subtitled *An Introduction to Constitutional Psychology*.
2. Hooton, 1938.
3. Cortes and Gatti, 1972; Garrett and Kellogg, 1928; Gibson, 2002; Sheldon, 1940; Wertheimer and Hesketh, 1926.
4. Cantor, 1936. For a fuller description of the rise of Nazi criminology, see chapter 8.
5. Garrett and Kellogg, 1928. For related research, see Patterson, 1930; Wertheimer and Hesketh, 1926.
6. Hooton, 1939a, 1939b.
7. Hooton, 1948a.
8. Hooton, 1945a. W. W. Howells, a former Hooton student who became a colleague, makes the important observation that Hooton "was a self-made anthropologist. His mentors at Oxford and elsewhere were anatomists . . . . So there was not much to guide him outside of the French and German formalized methods of measurement" (1992: 6). The thinness of Hooton's background in anthropological techniques and analysis helps explain the methodological weakness of his later criminals study.
9. Hooton, 1925, 1930. These two early works sorted series of skulls into types—basically the same procedure that Hooton used in his later criminal study with living subjects. Howells (1992: 6–7) points to a problem with the early efforts: Hooton used "statistics to validate what were nonrandom samples to begin with." The same statistical naïveté would bedevil the later criminals study.
10. Hooton, 1931, 1937, 1939c.
11. Hooton, 1940b, 1942, 1945b, 1947.
12. Hooton, 1939b: 181.
13. For example, Morris Edward Opler (1939), a professor of anthropology at the Claremont Colleges in California, wrote Hooton a tactful but anguished five-page letter in which he all but called Hooton an embarrassment to the field. Opler begged Hooton to pay less attention to racial differences, since such attention was bound to be misunderstood by "the popular imagination." He explained, "You are representing in the popular eye scores of anthropologists who are younger, less important, and less articulate. With all respect to your obligations to your public and your right to vigorously and colorfully present your own ideas, there remains the question of whether the American public is not being led [by Hooton's

speeches and writings], concerning certain [race] problems, to draw a picture of the position of Anthropology which the vast majority of anthropologists could not support."

14. In addition to his participation in war efforts, Hooton spoke regularly before school and professional groups about topics he considered of pressing civic interest. See Rafter, 2004, 2006a.

15. Hooton, 1939c; Rafter, 2006a.

16. Hooton, 1939c: opposite p. 48.

17. E.g., Hooton, 1940a.

18. Hooton 1939a: 31.

19. Hooton, n.d.-a.

20. Hooton, 1939a: 18.

21. Hooton himself jinxed the original plan by insisting on publication of all the tables generated in his statistical laboratory. He was probably trying to emulate the table-filled text of Goring's *The English Convict* (1913), but potential publishers were intimidated by the printing costs.

22. Hooton, 1939a: 299.

23. Hooton, 1939b:177.

24. Hooton, 1939b: 59.

25. Hooton, 1939b: 139.

26. Hooton, 1939a: vii–viii.

27. Hooton, 1939a: 309.

28. Hooton, 1939b: 388, 391, 392, 397.

29. Hooton, 1954: 1.

30. Glueck and Glueck, 1934: vii; Glueck and Glueck, 1950: x, xii.

31. Glueck and Glueck, 1956: v.

32. Sheldon, 1938.

33. Hooton, 1948b.

34. Hooton, 1950. Still later, with F. L. Stagg, Hooton did a bodytype study of 2,631 Harvard men, classes of 1880 through 1912, relating bodytype to career.

35. Hooton, 1938.

36. Hooton, 1939d.

37. Hooton, 1938.

38. Hooton n.d.-b: 5–6. Hooton's notes to himself in this document include this remark: "In my opinion, 'anthrotyping' alone [is] not sufficient" and "I suggest the term 'Somatype' instead of 'Anthrotype.'"

39. Hooton, 1939d.

40. Carter and Heath, 1990; Garrett and Kellogg, 1928. Naccarati died in a car crash in Italy just as Sheldon finished his dissertation work.

41. Sheldon, 1936.

42. Sheldon, 1936. In Greek mythology, Prometheus was a demigod who created a man of clay, stole fire from the gods, and gave mankind both fire and the

arts. To punish his audacity, Zeus chained Prometheus to a rock, where every day a vulture plucked out his liver. To Sheldon, Prometheus was a Christ figure who martyred himself for the good of mankind.

43. Sheldon, 1949b: 55–56.

44. Sheldon, 1949b: 50.

45. Huxley, 1944: 520.

46. Rafter, 2007.

47. E.g., Sykes, 1950.

48. The story of this rupture, which involved Sheldon doing something to greatly upset Leonard Elmhirst's younger brother, whom Sheldon was supposed to be mentoring in Chicago, is told in somewhat more detail in Rafter, 2007, although the particulars remain cloudy.

49. Sheldon, 1940.

50. Sheldon, 1949b: 13–16, writes that he identified the temperaments by closely observing thirty-three associates, but it seems clear that he found what he was looking for and that this preliminary study was merely social-scientific window dressing.

51. Sheldon, 1942: 437.

52. Sheldon, 1949b: xvi.

53. Sheldon, 1949b: table 11, pp. 721–25.

54. Sheldon, 1949b: 762.

55. Sheldon, 1949b: 752 ("essential inadequacy"), 759 ("spoor of insufficiency"), 822 (third quotation; emphasis in original).

56. Sheldon, 1949b: 826 ("biological catastrophe"), 837–838 ("irresponsible reproduction"), 877 ("biological humanics").

57. Sheldon, 1954: xiii.

58. Rosenbaum, 1995.

59. Datson and Galison, 1992.

60. Banks, 2001: 45.

61. Sheldon, 1936: 62–63, emphasis in original.

62. Sheldon, 1936: 239 ("man of character"), 78 ("new light").

63. From 1936 to 1939, Sheldon received a total of about $12,000 in grants from the Elmhirsts and the Whitney Foundation. See Rafter, 2007: 817, n. 13.

64. Sheldon, 1935a.

65. Sheldon, 1935a, capitalization as in the original.

66. Sheldon, 1935b.

67. Sheldon, 1949a: xi.

68. Sheldon, 1949a: 3.

69. American Numismatic Society, 1999.

70. Sheldon, 1949b: 18, 810, n. 12; see also Gatlin, 1999.

71. E.g., Sutherland, 1951.

72. E.g., Cortes and Gatti, 1972; Humphreys, 1957.

73. Eysenck, 1953, 1964; Humphreys, 1957; Jensen, 1950. Contemporary social science reviewers were mainly concerned with age, but race and ethnicity, too, might have complicated the picture. Sheldon was actually aware of this, for in *Varieties of Delinquent Youth* (1949b: p. 791), to explain the strong predominance of mesomorphs among 1,000 male bathers whom he had informally surveyed at Coney Island, he noted a heavy representation of Jews and Italians in that population. Social class as well as race/ethnicity could help explain the somatotype differences in the samples, especially because at the time the admissions policies of U.S. colleges tended to favor Anglo-Saxons. However, Sheldon did not acknowledge any of these possible influences on his formal bodytype findings.

74. A former assistant charged that he had asked her to fudge the data (Carter and Heath, 1990). Other critics argued that Sheldon ignored factors that might complicate his assumption that one inherits a somatotype that then, with no modification by environmental factors, determines personality or behavior (e.g., Glueck and Glueck, 1956). Age was one potentially confounding factor: mesomorphs may mature earlier than ectomorphs (McCandless, Persons, and Roberts, 1972); and the college men with whom Sheldon compared his "delinquents" were probably older (Montemayor, 1985).

75. See the studies by Gibbens, 1963; Cortes and Gatti, 1972; McCandless, Persons, and Roberts, 1972; and Hartl, Monnelly, and Elderkin, 1982. For details and citations to additional studies, see Raine, 1993; Sampson and Laub, 1997; and Wilson and Herrnstein, 1985.

76. Glueck and Glueck, 1950.

77. Glueck and Glueck, 1950: 187.

78. Glueck and Glueck, 1950: 192.

79. Glueck and Glueck, 1950: 273.

80. Glueck and Glueck, 1950: 348.

81. Glueck and Glueck, 1956: 226.

82. Glueck and Glueck, 1956: 226.

83. Glueck and Glueck, 1956: 269.

84. Glueck and Glueck, 1956: 270.

85. Sampson and Laub, 1997: 181.

86. Sampson and Laub, 1997: 183.

87. Sampson and Laub, 1997: 184.

88. Glueck and Glueck, 1934.

89. Laub and Sampson, 1991: 1406.

90. Wilson and Herrnstein, 1985: 23.

91. Wilson and Herrnstein, 1985: 70.

92. Wilson and Herrnstein, 1985: 71–77. On the methodological madness of Hooton's criminological work, see Rafter, 2004. Hooton was not careless, but he was methodologically unsophisticated and at times self-deluded.

93. Wilson and Herrnstein, 1985: 90.

94. Wilson and Herrnstein, 1985: 528.

95. Eysenck, 1964: 138. For an analysis of Eysenck's *Crime and Personality* and his place in the development of biocriminology, see Rafter, 2006.

96. Eysenck and Gudjonsson, 1989: 41.

97. Raine, 1993: 203, emphasis in original, 204.

98. Datson and Galison, 1992.

CHAPTER 8

1. The phrase comes from a book by Alfred Hoche and Rudolf Binding, *Release and Destruction of Lives Not Worth Living* (Leipzig, 1920), as discussed and cited by Proctor, 1988: 178, 333.

2. Wachsmann, 2001.

3. Wetzell, 2000; Wachsmann, 2004.

4. Müller-Hill, 1988; Proctor, 1988.

5. Proctor, 1988, 1991; Szöllösi-Janze, 2001a, 2001b; Weiss, 2006; Wetzell, 2000.

6. See, esp., Proctor, 1991.

7. Wachsmann, 2001, 2004; Wetzell, 2000, 2006.

8. Day and Vandiver, 2000; Yacoubian, 2000.

9. For Italy, the key new source is Gibson, 2002.

10. Passmore, 2002.

11. Benito Mussolini as quoted by Smith, 1993: 100.

12. Wachsmann, 2004.

13. Lees, 2006.

14. Ayass, 1988.

15. Gellately and Stoltzfus, 2001: 3.

16. Tatar, 1997; Evans, 1996.

17. Aschaffenburg, 1913; Bondio, 2006.

18. Lange, 1930: 173–174.

19. E.g., Aschaffenburg, 1913.

20. Bondio, 2006: 205.

21. Kraepelin, 1904; Aschaffenburg, 1913; Kurella, 1910; see also Evans, 1999.

22. Wetzell, 2006: 417–418.

23. Kretschmer, 1925.

24. Kretschmer, 1925: 39.

25. Lange, 1930: 41.

26. Cantor, 1936; Liang, 2006.

27. Liang, 2006.

28. Wetzell, 2006; see also Cantor, 1936.

29. Wachsmann, 2001: 169.

30. Max Planck as quoted in Müller-Hill, 1988: 25.

31. Eugen Fischer as quoted in Müller-Hill, 1988: 18.

32. Wetzell, 2000: 186–187; see also Kevles, 1985, esp. pp. 117–118.

33. Wetzell, 2000: 187.

34. Hitler, 1939: 243, 240.

35. Hitler, 1939: 239–240.

36. Hitler, 1939: 275.

37. Milton, 2001.

38. Robert Ritter as quoted in Müller-Hill, 1988: 57.

39. Cantor, 1936: 418.

40. Wetzell, 2000: 183–184.

41. Liang, 2006; Wetzell, 2000, 2006.

42. Wetzell, 2000.

43. Wetzell, 2006: 415.

44. Hood, 2004.

45. Wetzell, 2000.

46. Hentig, 1948. For biographical information on Hentig, see Evans, 1999, *Journal of Criminal Law, Criminology and Police Science*, 1967, and Hentig, 1947.

47. Rusche and Kirchheimer, 1939.

48. Aschaffenburg, for example, was an environmental degenerationist and opponent of the belief in born criminals.

49. Bruinius, 2006; Kevles, 1985; Proctor, 1988.

50. Evans, 2005: 511; Wachsmann, 2004: 152–153.

51. Wachsmann, 2004: 146–147.

52. Black, 2006; Wachsmann, 2004.

53. Wachsmann, 2004: 373; see also Black, 2006.

54. Black, 2006.

55. Wachsmann, 2004: 388.

56. Wachsmann, 2004: 74.

57. Evans, 2005.

58. Several films have been made about the White Rose group, including *The White Rose* (1982) and *Sophie Scholl: The Final Days* (2005).

59. Wachsmann, 2004: 71.

60. Wachsmann, 2004: 211.

61. Friedlander, 1995: 117–118; Wetzell, 2000: 286.

62. Wachsmann, 2004: 285.

63. Wachsmann, 2004.

64. Gellately and Stoltzfus, 2001: 5.

65. Konrad Lorenz as quoted in Müller-Hill, 1988: 56.

66. Konrad Lorenz as quoted in Müller-Hill, 1988: 14.

67. Szöllösi-Janze 2001a.

68. Wachsmann, 2004: 137. Magdalena S.'s mug shots appear in Wachsmann, 2004, opposite p. 143.

69. Wachsmann, 2004.

70. Gellately, 2001.

71. Milton, 2001.

72. Friedlander, 1995: xii.

73. Koonz, 2003: 274.

74. Gibson, 1998; Lombroso, 2006; Pick, 1989.

75. Gibson, 1998, 2002, 2006.

76. Wetzell, 2000: 107–108.

77. Gibson, 2002.

78. Battaglini, 1914: 14.

79. Battaglini, 1914: 15.

80. Lombroso, 2006: 48.

81. Axelrod, 2002.

82. Gibson, 2002. Bosworth (2002) suggests that the Ethiopian campaign was motivated by imperialism more than racism—belatedly, Italy had decided to join other European powers in their African landgrab.

83. See Lombroso, 2006: 116, where Ferri's maps are reproduced.

84. Gramsci, 1992.

85. Dickie, 1999.

86. Gibson, 2002: 119.

87. The deportation of Italian Jews is dramatically depicted in Vittorio De Sica's famous film *The Garden of the Finzi-Contini* (1970).

88. Bosworth, 2002: 334, 344.

89. Gibson, 2002, suggests that Ferri and Salvatore Ottolenghi, another prominent criminal anthropologist, may have joined the Fascist Party at least in part to encourage enactment of their programs.

90. Gibson, 2002; Dunnage, 1997.

91. Dunnage, 1997.

92. Dunnage, 2003.

93. Gibson, 2002.

94. *Confino* is depicted in the Italian film *Christ Stopped at Eboli*. The title is ironic: neither the train nor Christian compassion goes farther than the station at Eboli, from which the lead character is taken to the remote village where he will be confined.

95. Levi, 2001: 24.

96. Levi, 2001: 24.

97. Levi, 2001: 30 (punctuation as in original).

98. Levi, 1987: 396.

CHAPTER 9

1. Taylor, Walton, and Young, 1973: 282, emphasis in original.

2. Rose, 2000: 6.

3. Kevles, 1985: 250.

4. Eysenck, 1964. On the consternation among sociologists and Eysenck's significance to criminology more generally, see Rafter, 2006b.

5. Jacobs et al., 1965; Daly, 1969; see also Rennie, 1978.

6. Wilson, 1975.

7. Dalton, 1980; Grose, 1998; Horney, 1978.

8. Duster, 2006. Cf. Wilson, 1999, arguing for a convergence of the various fields and disciplines.

9. Duster, 2006: 2.

10. Feeley and Simon, 1994; Rose, 2006.

11. See, e.g., Zedner, 2007.

12. Raine, 1993, is comprehensive but somewhat dated.

13. E.g., Tibbetts, 2003, in press.

14. Arpey, 2003.

15. N.a., n.d., http://en.wikipedia.org/wiki/Charles_Whitman (accessed 13 September 2006).

16. N.a., n.d., http://en.wikipedia.org/wiki/Charles_Whitman (accessed 13 September 2006).

17. Denno, 2005.

18. Denno, 2005: 177.

19. Denno, 2005: 177–178.

20. Browne, 2003; Cartwright, 2004.

21. Goode, 2003.

22. Perry et al., 1995: 276.

23. Perry et al., 1995; see also Anda et al., 2006.

24. Elliott and Mirsky, 2002. Information on these and related factors is available at www.crime-times.org. See also Raine, 2002, for an especially thorough review of the literature on the effects of pregnancy and birth complications.

25. Raine, 2002: 312.

26. Eysenck, 1970 (orig. 1964).

27. Hirschi and Hindelang, 1977.

28. Wilson and Herrnstein, 1985.

29. Wilson and Herrnstein, 1985: 149, 169, 172.

30. Wilson and Herrnstein, 1985: 468.

31. Herrnstein and Murray, 1994.

32. Herrnstein and Murray, 1994: 235.

33. Herrnstein and Murray, 1994: ch. 22, esp. pp. 543–544.

34. Goddard, 1920.

35. This literature is large; see, e.g., Fraser, 1995, and Gould, 1994.

36. Raine, 1993: 215.

37. Raine, 1993: 220–221. The original Raine and Venables study was published in 1981.

38. Raine, 1993: 220–221.

39. Raine, 1993: 234–235.

40. Raine, 1993: 241.

41. See, e.g., Elliott and Mirsky, 2002.

42. See www.crime-times.org.

43. Ellis and Walsh, 1997: 235.

44. Thornhill and Palmer, 2000: 103.

45. Thornhill and Palmer, 2000: 188.

46. Rowe, 2002: ch. 3; Walsh, 2002: 59.

47. Hamilton, 1964.

48. Daly and Wilson, 1988: 10.

49. Daly and Wilson, 1988: 23.

50. Daly and Wilson, 1988: esp. 83–93; Raine, 1993: 43–44.

51. Ellis and Walsh, 1997; Campbell, 1999; Campbell, Muncer, and Bibel, 2001.

52. Campbell 1999; Walsh, 1995: ch. 7.

53. Walsh, 2002: 72.

54. Walsh, 2002: 72.

55. Dawkins, 1989: 203.

56. Walsh, 2002: 63, 65.

57. Raine, 1993: 45.

58. Walsh, 2002: 58; Thornhill and Palmer, 2000: 107–110.

59. The idea of mental modularity—that specific areas of the brain are responsible for specific tasks—goes back to phrenology but was revived in the 1950s by linguist Noam Chomsky's work on a universal, innate grammatical structure in the human brain. Building on Chomsky's work, Jerry Fodor reintroduced the concept of mental modularity in his book *Modularity of Mind* (1983). Thereafter, Leda Cosmides and John Tooby integrated the concept of mental modularity with evolutionary psychology, arguing that mental structures evolved in response to natural selection (see Barkow, Cosmides, and Tooby, 1995). The concept of mental modularity has been attacked by William Uttal in *The New Phrenology* (2003). The idea that humans' moral capacity has evolved seems to be supported by recent research on conciliation and empathy in chimpanzees; see de Waal, 1996, and Wade, 2007.

60. Walsh, 2000: 841, 854.

61. Tancredi, 2005: ix.

62. Tancredi, 2005: 81.

63. Tancredi, 2005: 29.

64. Richerson and Boyd, 2005.

65. Richerson and Boyd, 2005: 190.

66. Richerson and Boyd, 2005: 194.

67. Richerson and Boyd, 2005: 196.

68. Richerson and Boyd, 2005: 215.

69. On the evolution of morality, see also de Waal, 1996.

70. Raine, 1993: 2, emphasis in original.

71. Duster, 2006; Rose, 2007.

72. Schlapp and Smith, 1928.

73. Stanley, 1940: 110. I am grateful to Professor Clay Mosher for introducing me to this source.

74. Stanley, 1940: 110, 113.

75. Dalton, 1977, 1980; see also Fishbein, 1992.

76. Horney, 1978.

77. For a detailed review of both the British and American cases, see Grose, 1998; see also Brown, 1991.

78. Fishbein, 1992.

79. Denno, 2005; West and Lichtenstein, 2006.

80. Zuckerman, 2002.

81. Walsh, 2002: 193. Note that it is also possible that living in a violent subculture could raise testosterone levels.

82. Testosterone studies are reviewed in Raine, 1993, and Rowe, 2002.

83. Sylvers et al., in press.

84. See, e.g., Tancredi, 2005.

85. Fishbein, 2001: 35–36; Raine, 1993: 83; Walsh, 1995: 48–50.

86. Ishikawa and Raine, 2002a.

87. Walsh, 2002: 208.

88. Fishbein, 2001: 37.

89. Tancredi, 2005: 110.

90. Lombroso and Ferrero, 2004; Lombroso, 2006; Horn, 2003.

91. Ishikawa and Raine, 2002b; Raine, 1993: 174–178; Walsh, 2002: 115–116.

92. Ishikawa and Raine, 2002b; Raine, 1993: 165–174.

93. Ishikawa and Raine, 2002b; Rowe, 2002; Raine, 1993.

94. Ebstein and Belmaker, 2002; Ishikawa and Raine, 2002b; Zuckerman, 2002.

95. Rowe, 2002: 80; see also Raine, 2002: 315.

96. Ebstein and Belmaker, 2002; Rowe, 2002: 81.

97. For a review of the recent research on psychophysiology and crime and its theoretical implications, see Sylvers et al., in press.

98. For details on the technologies, see Raine, 1993; Rowe, 2002. Functional MRIs scan brains while people are functioning—performing tasks or perceiving specified things.

99. Raine et al., 1998: 319.

100. Goldberg, 2001; Walsh, 2002.

101. Goldberg, 2001.

102. Goldberg, 2001; Raine et al., 1998; Walsh, 2002.

103. Goldberg, 2001; Tancredi, 2005.

104. Rowe, 2002: 86.

105. Raine et al., 1998; Rowe, 2002; Tancredi, 2005; see also Goldberg, 2001.

106. Carey, 2005. Some of the inconsistencies could be due to the possibility (an emerging hypothesis) that the prefrontal abnormalities differ by the sex of the offender and by the type of crime (e.g., affective vs. predatory violence). Raine, 1993, reports that frontal lobe dysfunction seems to underlie violent criminal behavior, whereas temporal lobe dysfunction seems to lie behind sex offending.

107. Doidge, 2007.

108. Goldberg, 2001.

109. Adolphs, 2003.

110. Adolphs, 2003: 166.

111. Adolphs, 2003: 166.

112. Perry et al., 1995.

113. See, esp., Perry et al., 1995.

114. Goleman, 2006; see also Gazzaniga, 2005.

115. Goleman, 2006.

116. This older work includes Goffman, 1982; Lemert, 1972; and Mead, 1967.

117. Eysenck, 1970: 68–69; see also Rafter, 2006b. Exceptions include Johannes Lange, 1930, and other twins researchers who did genetics research in this interim period without trying to directly study genes. The exceptions also include the eugenical family studies; see Rafter, 1988.

118. Jacobs et al., 1965; Daly, 1969; see also Perlin, 1999; Walters and White, 1989.

119. Blackburn, 1993.

120. Wolfgang, Figlio, and Sellin, 1972.

121. Moffitt, 1993.

122. Also important in raising and pursuing answers to such questions was the work of David P. Farrington; for a later review, see Farrington, 1998.

123. Duster, 2006.

124. Rowe and Osgood, 1984: 527–28.

125. Dugdale, 1877; Goddard, 1912; Rafter, 1988.

126. For more detailed reviews of the family studies, see Walters and White, 1989.

127. Galton's twin research is discussed in chapter 14 of Gillham, 2001.

128. Lange, 1930.

129. Blackburn, 1993; Ishikawa and Raine, 2002a; Walters and White, 1989. For an example of a twin study using questionnaires and self-reports of delinquent activities, see Rowe and Osgood, 1984.

130. Walters and White, 1989; Blackburn, 1993; see also Rhee and Waldman, 2002.

131. Mednick, Gabrielli, and Hutchings, 1984.

132. Mednick, Gabrielli, and Hutchings, 1984: 224.

133. Blackburn, 1993: 141.

134. Walters and White, 1989: 477.

135. Baker, Bezdjian, and Raine, 2006: 17.

136. Raine, 2002.

137. I have taken the global-genetic distinction from Baker, Bezdjian, and Raine, 2006.

138. Raine, 1993; Ishikawa and Raine, 2002a.

139. Baker, Bezdjian, and Raine, 2006.

140. Baker, Bezdjian, and Raine, 2006; Elliott and Mirsky, 2002.

141. Brunner et al., 1993; Mestel, 1993.

142. Richardson, 1993.

143. In addition, other researchers have not been able to replicate aspects of the Brunner study; see Stamps et al., 2001.

144. Caspi et al., 2002.

145. See, esp., Baker, Bezdjian, and Raine, 2006: 37–39.

146. The terms in quotation marks are those used by Moffitt, 1993.

147. Taylor, Iacono, and McGue, 2000: 634.

148. Taylor, Iacono, and McGue, 2000.

149. E.g., Hare, 1993; Millon et al., 2002; Zuckerman, 2002.

150. American Psychiatric Association, 2000.

151. Hare, 1993: 76–78.

152. Baker, Bezdjian, and Raine, 2006; Ishikawa and Raine, 2002b; Zuckerman, 2002.

153. Baker, Bezdjian, and Raine, 2006: esp. 20; Ebstein and Belmaker, 2002; Raine, 1993; Rowe, 2002; Zuckerman, 2002.

154. Baker, Bezdjian, and Raine, 2006: 23; see also Blair, Mitchell, and Blair, 2005, and Sylvers et al., in press. Raine (1993) reviews the evidence on psychopathy and concludes (p. 79) that there is no good evidence for it as a heritable trait.

155. Caspi et al., 2002: 851.

156. Caspi and Moffitt, 2006.

157. Moffitt as quoted in N.a., 2003.

158. "Apparent" because the first study, at least, has not fared well in attempted replications. See Morris et al., 2007.

159. Raine, 2002; see also Ishikawa and Raine, 2002b.

160. Beaver et al., 2006; Caspi and Moffitt, 2006: 588.

161. See also Lykken, 2006.

162. A useful theoretical summary of much of this research can be found in Tibbetts, 2003. Less theoretical but also thorough and useful is Sylvers et al., in press.

CHAPTER 10

1. Zerubavel, 1997: 9.

2. Brunner et al., 1993.

3. Denno, 2006; Farahany and Bernet, 2006; Farahany and Coleman, 2006.

4. One alternative would be a statistical model of deviance.

5. Rafter, 1997.

6. *Health Day News*, 2005.

7. Ellement, 2007.

8. Raine et al., 2000: 126; see also Yang et al., 2005.

9. Campbell, 2006.

10. Lander, 2000, p. 3 of 5. Thanks to Simon Cole for calling this article to my attention.

11. Nelkin and Lindee, 1995b: 388.

12. Walsh, 2002: 30, quoting David Lykken (textual citation omitted).

13. Agar, 1999; Allen, 2001; Duster, 1990; Haller, 1963; Kevles, 1985; Kristof, 2003.

14. Stock, 2002; Glad, 2006.

15. Allen, 2004: 294.

16. Cole, 2004: 77.

17. Nelkin and Lindee, 1995a: 16.

18. Also helpful in this regard is *GeneWatch*, a magazine published by the Council for Responsible Genetics.

19. Lander, 2000: p. 3 of 5.

20. Lianos and Douglas, 2000.

21. Nelkin and Lindee, 1995a: 1, citing John S. Long, "How Genes Shape Personality," *U.S. News and World Report*, 12 April 1987, 60–66.

22. Allen, 2004: 301–302.

23. Garland and Sparks, 2000: 8.

24. See also Braithwaite, 2000.

25. Garland and Sparks, 2000: 3.

# References

Abernethy, John. 1821. *Reflections on Gall and Spurzheim's System of Physiognomy and Phrenology*. London: Longman, Hurst, Rees, Orme, and Brown.

Adolphs, Ralph. 2003. Cognitive neuroscience and human social behavior. *Nature Reviews/Neuroscience* 4:165–178.

Agar, Nicholas. 1999. Liberal eugenics. In *Bioethics: An Anthology*, ed. Helga Kuhse and Peter Singer, 171–181. Oxford: Blackwell.

Allen, Garland E. 1975. Genetics, eugenics and class struggle. *Genetics* 79 (June, Supplement): 29–45.

———. 2001. Is a new eugenics afoot? *Science* 294:59–61.

———. 2004. DNA and human-behavior genetics: Implications for the criminal justice system. In *DNA and the Criminal Justice System*, ed. David Lazer, 287–314. Cambridge, MA: MIT Press.

*American Journal of Insanity*. 1863. On moral insanity (discussion of paper by Dr. McFarland). 20:63–106.

American Numismatic Society. 1999. An update report on early U.S. cents previously stolen from the ANS. www.numismatics.org/newsletter/wtr99/research.htm.

American Psychiatric Association. 2000. *Diagnostic and Statistical Manual of Mental Disorders*. 4th ed . Washington, DC: American Psychiatric Association.

Anda, Robert F., V. J. Feletti, J. D. Bremner, J. D. Walker, C. Whitfield, B. D. Perry, S. R. Dube, and W. H. Giles. 2006. The enduring effects of abuse and related adverse experiences in childhood. *European Archives of Psychiatry and Clinical Neuroscience* 256:174–186.

Arpey, Andrew W. 2003. *The William Freeman Murder Trial: Insanity, Politics, and Race*. Syracuse, NY: Syracuse University Press.

Aschaffenburg, Gustav. 1913 (orig. 1903). *Crime and Its Repression*. Repr., Montclair, NJ: Patterson Smith, 1968.

Augstein, Hannah F. 1996. J. C. Prichard's concept of moral insanity: A medical theory of the corruption of human nature. *Medical History* 40:311–343.

Axelrod, Alan. 2002. *The Life and Work of Benito Mussolini*. Indianapolis: Alpha/Pearson.

Ayass, Wolfgang. 1988. Vagrants and beggars in Hitler's Reich. In *The German Underworld: Deviants and Outcasts in German History*, ed. Richard J. Evans, 210–237. London: Routledge.

Baker, Laura A., Serena Bezdjian, and Adrian Raine. 2006. Behavioral genetics: The science of antisocial behavior. *Law and Contemporary Problems* 69 (7): 7–46.

Banks, Marcus. 2001. *Visual Methods in Social Research*. London: Sage.

Barbassa, Juliana. 2005. Politics: Bennett under fire for remarks on blacks, crime. http://www.cnn.com/2005/POLITICS/09/30/bennett.comments/ (accessed 27 October 2005).

Barker, F. G., 2d. 1995. Phineas among the phrenologists: The American crowbar case and 19th-century theories of cerebral localization. *Journal of Neurosurgery* 82:672–682.

Barkow, Jerome H., Leda Cosmides, and John Tooby, eds. 1995. *The Adapted Mind: Evolutionary Psychology and the Generation of Culture*. New York: Oxford University Press.

Barnes, Harry Elmer, and Negley K. Teeters. 1944. *New Horizons in Criminology*. New York: Prentice-Hall.

Barnicle, Mike. 1990. A life ruined, or one misspent. *Boston Globe*, 9 January 1990, 17.

Barr, Martin. 1895. Moral paranoia. In Association of Medical Officers of American Institutions for Idiotic and Feeble-Minded Persons, *Proceedings for 1895*: 522–531.

———. 1904. *Mental Defectives: Their History, Treatment and Training*. Repr., New York: Arno, 1973.

Battaglini, G. 1914. Eugenics and the criminal law. *Journal of Criminal Law and Criminology* 5:12–15.

Beaver, Kevin M., John Paul Wright, Matt DeLisi, Leah E. Daigle, Marc L. Swatt, and Chris L. Gibson. 2006. Evidence of a gene X environment interaction in the creation of victimization: Results from a longitudinal sample of adolescents. *International Journal of Offender Therapy and Comparative Criminology* 7:1–26.

Beccaria, Cesare. 1764. *On Crimes and Punishments*. Repr., trans. Henry Paolucci. Indianapolis: Bobbs-Merrill, 1963.

Becker, Peter, and Richard F. Wetzell, eds. 2006. *Criminals and Their Scientists: The History of Criminology in International Perspective*. New York: Cambridge University Press.

Beirne, Piers. 1988. Heredity versus environment: A reconsideration of Charles Goring's *The English Convict* (1913). *British Journal of Criminology* 28:315–339.

———. 1991. Inventing criminology: The "science of man" in Cesare Beccaria's *Dei delitti e delle penne* (1764). *Criminology* 29:777–820.

———. 1993. *Inventing Criminology: Essays on the Rise of Homo Criminalis*. Albany: State University of New York Press.

———, ed. 1994. *The Origins and Growth of Criminology: Essays on Intellectual History, 1760–1945*. Aldershot: Dartmouth.

Benedikt, Moriz. 1881. *Anatomical Studies upon Brains of Criminals.* New York: William Wood. Repr., New York: Da Capo Press, 1981.

Bentham, Jeremy. 1789. *The Principles of Morals and Legislation.* Repr., New York: Hafner, 1948.

Black, Peter. 2006. Review of *Hitler's Kriminalisten* by Patrick Wagner (Munich, 2002). *Holocaust and Genocide Studies* 20:129–131.

Blackburn, Ronald. 1993. *The Psychology of Criminal Conduct: Theory, Research and Practice.* New York: Wiley.

Blair, James, Derek Mitchell, and Karina Blair. 2005. *The Psychopath: Emotion and the Brain.* Malden, MA: Blackwell.

Bloor, David. 1991. *Knowledge and Social Imagery.* 2nd ed. Chicago: University of Chicago Press.

Boies, Henry. 1893. *Prisoners and Paupers.* New York: G. P. Putnam's Sons.

Bondio, Mariacarla Gadebusch. 2006. From the "atavistic" to the "inferior" criminal type: The impact of the Lombrosian theory of the born criminal on German psychiatry. In *Criminals and Their Scientists: The History of Criminology in International Perspective*, ed. Peter Becker and Richard Wetzell, 183–206. New York: Cambridge University Press.

Bosworth, R. J. B. 2002. *Mussolini.* New York: Oxford University Press.

Bowler, Peter J. 2003. *Evolution: The History of An Idea.* 3rd ed. Berkeley: University of California Press..

Braithwaite, John. 2000. The new regulatory state and the transformation of criminology. In *Criminology and Social Theory*, ed. David Garland and Richard Sparks, 47–70. New York: Oxford University Press.

Brockway, Zebulon R. 1871. The ideal of a true prison system for a state. In *Transactions of the National Congress on Penitentiary and Reformatory Discipline, 1870*, ed. E. C. Wines, 38–65. Albany, NY: Weed, Parsons.

———. 1912. *Fifty Years of Prison Service: An Autobiography.* Repr., Montclair, NJ: Patterson Smith, 1969.

Brown, DeNeen L. 1991. PMS defense successful in Va. drunken driving case. *Washington Post*, 7 June, 1.

Browne, Chip. 2003. The man who mistook his wife for a deer and other tales from the new sciences of extreme sleep. *New York Times Magazine*, 2 February, 34–41, 63, 72, 79.

Bruinius, Harry. 2006. *Better for All the World: The Secret History of Forced Sterilization and America's Quest for Racial Purity.* New York: Vintage.

Brunner, H. G., M. Nelen, X. O. Breakefield, H. H. Ropers, and B. A. van Oost. 1993. Abnormal behavior associated with a point mutation in the structural gene for monoamine oxidase A. *Science* 262:578–580.

Bulmer, Michael. 2003. *Frances Galton: Pioneer of Heredity and Biometry.* Baltimore: Johns Hopkins University Press.

Burnham, John Chynoweth. 1960. Psychiatry, psychology and the Progressive movement. *American Quarterly* 12:457–465.

Burrow, John W. 1968. Editor's introduction to Charles Darwin, *The Origin of Species*. London: Penguin.

Burt, Cyril. 1925. *The Young Delinquent*. London: University of London Press.

Butler, Samuel. 1872. *Erewhon*. Repr., New York: Airmont, 1967.

Bynum, William F., Jr. 1981. Rationales for therapy in British psychiatry, 1780–1835. In *Madhouses, Mad-doctors, and Madmen*, ed. Andrew Scull, 35–57. London: Athlone Press.

Campbell, Anne. 1999. Staying alive: Evolution, culture, and women's intrasexual aggression. *Behavioral and Brain Sciences* 22:203–252.

———. 2006. Feminism and evolutionary psychology. In *Missing the Revolution: Darwinism for Social Scientists*, ed. J. Barkow, 63–100. Oxford: Oxford University Press.

Campbell, Anne, Steven Muncer, and Daniel Bibel. 2001. Women and crime: An evolutionary approach. *Aggression and Violent Behavior* 6:481–497.

Cantor, G. N. 1975. The Edinburgh phrenology debate: 1803–1828. *Annals of Science* 32:195–218.

Cantor, Nathaniel. 1936. Recent tendencies in criminological research in Germany. *American Sociological Review* 1:407–418.

Carey, Benedict. 2005. Can brain scans see depression? *New York Times Science Times*, 18 October, D1, D6.

Carlson, Eric T. 1958. The influence of phrenology in early American psychiatric thought. *American Journal of Psychiatry* 115:535–538.

Carlson, Eric T., and Norman Dain. 1962. The meaning of moral insanity. *Bulletin of the History of Medicine* 36:130–140.

Carlson, Eric T., and Meribeth M. Simpson. 1965. Benjamin Rush's medical use of the moral faculty. *Bulletin of the History of Medicine* 39:22–33.

Carter, J. E. Lindsay, and Barbara Honeyman Heath. 1990. *Somatotyping: Development and Applications*. Cambridge: Cambridge University Press.

Cartwright, Rosaline. 2004. Sleepwalking violence. *American Journal of Psychiatry* 161:1149–1158.

Caspi, Avshalom, Joseph McClay, Terrie E. Moffitt, Jonathan Mill, Judy Martin, Ian W. Craig, Alan Taylor, and Richie Poulton. 2002. Role of genotype in the cycle of violence in maltreated children. *Science* 297 (5582): 851–854.

Caspi, Avshalom, and Terrie E. Moffitt. 2006. Gene-environment interactions in psychiatry: Joining forces with neuroscience. *Nature Reviews/Neuroscience* 7:583–590.

Charen, Mona. 2006. Andrea Yates, insanity and guilt. 28 July. http//:www.southernillinoisian.com/articles/2006/07/30/opinions/columnists/charen (accessed 30 July 2006).

Chio, A., R. Spreafico, G. Avanzini, P. Ghiglione, M. Vercellino, and R. Mutani. 2004. Cesare Lombroso, cortical dysplasia, and epilepsy: Keen findings and odd theories. *Neurology* 63 (1): 194.

Clay, John. 2001. *Maconochie's Experiment*. London: John Murray.

Cole, Simon A. 2002. *Suspect Identities: A History of Finger Printing and Criminal Identification*. Cambridge MA: Harvard University Press.

———. 2004. Fingerprint identification and the criminal justice system: Historical lessons for the DNA debate. In *DNA and the Criminal Justice System*, ed. David Lazer, 63–90. Cambridge, MA: MIT Press.

Collie, Michael. 1988. *Henry Maudsley: Victorian Psychiatrist. A Bibliographical Study*. Winchester, England: St. Paul's Bibliographies.

Combe, George. 1841. *Notes on the United States of North America during a Phrenological Visit in 1838-9-40*. 3 vols. Edinburgh: Maclachlan, Steward.

———. 1854. *Remarks on the Principles of Criminal Legislation and the Practice of Prison Discipline*. London: Simpkin, Marshall.

Combe, George, and C. J. A. Mittermaier. 1843. On the application of phrenology to criminal legislation and prison discipline. *Phrenological Journal* 21, n.s.: 1–19.

Cooter, Roger. 1981. Phrenology and British alienists, ca. 1825–1845. In *Madhouses, Mad-doctors, and Madmen*, ed. Andrew Scull, 58–104. London: Athlone Press.

———. 1984. *The Cultural Meaning of Popular Science: Phrenology and the Organization of Consent in Nineteenth-Century Britain*. Cambridge: Cambridge University Press.

Cortes, Juan B., and Florence M. Gatti. 1972. *Delinquency and Crime: A Biopsychosocial Approach*. New York: Seminar Press.

Cowan, Ruth Schwartz. 1972. Francis Galton's contribution to genetics. *Journal of the History of Biology* 5:389–412.

Cravens, Hamilton. 1987. Applied science and public policy: The Ohio Bureau of Juvenile Research and the problem of juvenile delinquency, 1915–1930. In *Psychological Testing and American Society 1890-1930*, ed. Michael M. Sokal, 158–194. New Brunswick, NJ: Rutgers University Press.

Currell, Susan, and Christina Cogdell, eds. 2006. *Popular Eugenics: National Efficiency and American Mass Culture in the 1930s*. Athens: Ohio University Press.

d'Agostino, Peter. 2002. Craniums, criminals, and the "cursed race": Italian anthropology in American racial thought, 1861–1924. *Comparative Studies in Society and History* 44:310–343.

D'Antonio, Emanuele di. 2001. Aspetti della rigenerazione ebraica e del sioismo in Cesare Lombroso. *Società e Storia* 92:281–309.

Dain, Norman. 1964. *Concepts of Insanity in the United States, 1789-1865*. New Brunswick, NJ: Rutgers University Press.

Dain, Norman, and Eric T. Carlson. 1962. Moral insanity in the United States 1835–1866. *American Journal of Psychiatry* 118:795–800.

Dalton, Katharina. 1977. *The Premenstrual Syndrome and Progesterone Therapy.* London: William Heinemann Medical Books.

———. 1980. Cyclical criminal acts in premenstrual syndrome. *Lancet* 2:1070–1071.

Daly, Martin, and Margo Wilson. 1988. *Homicide.* New York: Aldine de Gruyter.

Daly, Richard F. 1969. Neurological abnormalities in XYY males. *Nature* 221:472–473.

Darwin, Charles. 1859. *The Origin of Species.* Repr., London: Penguin, 1968.

———. 1871. *The Descent of Man, and Selection in Relation to Sex.* Repr., Princeton, NJ: Princeton University Press, 1981.

———. 1872. *The Expression of the Emotions in Man and Animals.* Repr., ed. Paul Ekman, London: HarperCollins/FontanaPress, 1999.

Datson, Lorraine, and Peter Galison. 1992. The image of objectivity. *Representations* 40 (Autumn): 81–128.

Davie, Neil. 2005. *Tracing the Criminal: The Rise of Scientific Criminology in Britain, 1860–1918.* Oxford: Bardwell Press.

Davies, John. 1955. *Phrenology: Fad or Science, A 19th-Century Crusade.* New Haven, CT: Yale University Press.

Dawkins, Richard. 1989 (orig. 1976) *The Selfish Gene.* New York: Oxford University Press.

Day, L. Edward, and Margaret Vandiver. 2000. Criminology and genocide studies: Notes on what might have been and what still could be. *Crime, Law and Social Change* 34:43–59.

de Guistino, David. 1975. *The Conquest of Mind: Phrenology and Victorian Social Thought.* London: Croom Helm.

de Quiros, Bernaldo. 1912. *Modern Theories of Criminality.* Boston: Little, Brown.

Degler, Carl N. 1991. *In Search of Human Nature: The Decline and Revival of Darwinism in American Social Thought.* New York: Oxford University Press.

Denno, Deborah W. 2003. Who is Andrea Yates? A short story about insanity. *Duke Journal of Gender, Law and Policy* 10:141–148.

———. 2005. Commentary. , In *Understanding Crime: A Multidisciplinary Approach*, ed. Susan Guarino-Ghezzi and A. Javier Trevino, 175–180. N.p.: Anderson Publishing.

———. 2006. Revisiting the legal link between genetics and crime. *Law and Contemporary Problems* 69:209–257.

Dickie, J. 1999. *Darkest Italy: The Nation and Stereotypes of the Mezzogiorno, 1860–1900.* London: Macmillan.

Digby, Anne. 1985. *Madness, Morality and Medicine: A Study of the York Retreat, 1786–1914.* Cambridge: Cambridge University Press.

Doidge, Norman. 2007. *The Brain That Changes Itself.* New York: Viking.

Dolza, Delfina. 1990. *Essere figlie di Lombroso: Due donne intellecttuali tra '800 e '900.* Milan: Franco Angeli.

Donohue, John J., III, and Steven D. Levitt. 2001. The impact of legalized abortion on crime. *Quarterly Journal of Economics* 116:379–420.

Douglas, Mary. 1966. *Purity and Danger: An Analysis of Concepts of Pollution and Taboo.* New York: Routledge and Kegan Paul.

Dugdale, Richard. 1877. *"The Jukes": A Study in Crime, Pauperism, Disease and Heredity; also Further Studies of Criminals.* New York: G. P. Putnam's Sons.

Duggan, Christopher. 1994. *A Concise History of Italy.* Cambridge: Cambridge University Press.

Dunn, James Taylor, and Louis C. Jones. 1955. Crazy Bill had a down look. *American Heritage* 6 (5). http://www.americanheritage.com/articles/magazine/ah/1955 (accessed 12 January 2006).

Dunnage, Jonathan. 1997. Continuity in policing politics in Italy, 1920–1960. In *The Policing of Politics in the Twentieth Century*, ed. Mark Mazower, 57–90. Oxford: Berghahn Books.

———. 2003. The policing of an Italian province during the Fascist period: Siena, 1926–1943. In *Conflict and Legality: Policing Mid-Twentieth Century Europe*, ed. Gerard Oram, 23–41. London: Francis Boutle.

Duster, Troy. 1990. *Backdoor to Eugenics.* New York: Routledge.

———. 2006. Comparative perspectives and competing explanations: Taking on the newly configured reductionist challenge to sociology. *American Sociological Review* 71:1–15.

Ebstein, Richard P., and Robert H. Belmaker. 2002. Genetics of sensation or novelty seeking and criminal behavior. In *The Neurobiology of Criminal Behavior*, ed. Joseph Glicksohn, 51–80. Boston: Kluwer Academic Publishers.

Eigen, Joel Peter. 1995. *Witnessing Insanity: Madness and Mad-Doctors in the English Court.* New Haven, CT: Yale University Press.

Ellement, John. 2007. Parole board rejects Rod Matthews [*sic*] bid for freedom. *Boston Globe*, 29 June. http://www.boston.com/news/globe/city-region/breaking-news/2007/06/parole-board (downloaded 8 May 2007).

Elliott, Adrienne K., and Allan F. Mirsky. 2002. Cognitive antecedents of violence and aggression. In *The Neurobiology of Criminal Behavior*, ed. Joseph Glicksohn, 111–136. Boston: Kluwer Academic Publishers.

Ellis, Havelock. 1890. *The Criminal.* London: Walter Scott.

Ellis, Lee, and Anthony Walsh. 1997. Gene-based evolutionary theories in criminology. *Criminology* 35:229–276.

Evans, Richard J. 1996. *Rituals of Retribution: Capital Punishment in Germany, 1600–1987.* London: Penguin.

———. 1999. Hans von Hentig and the politics of German criminology. In *Grenzgange: Deutsche Geschichte des 20*, ed. Angelika Ebbinghaus and Karl Heinz Roth, 238–264. Luneberg, Germany: Rechtssprechung und Historischer Forschung.

———. 2005. *The Third Reich in Power, 1933–1939*. London: Allen Lane/Penguin.

Eysenck, Hans J. 1953. *The Structure of Human Personality*. London: Metheun.

———. 1964. *Crime and Personality*. St. Albans: Paladin.

———. 1970. *Crime and Personality*. 2nd ed., rev. London: Paladin.

Eysenck, Hans J., and G. H. Gudjonsson. 1989. *The Causes and Cures of Criminality*. New York: Plenum.

Farahany, Nita A., and William Bernet. 2006. Behavioural genetics in criminal cases: Past, present, and future. *Genomics, Society and Policy* 2 (1): 72–79.

Farahany, Nita A., and James E. Coleman, Jr. 2006. Genetics and responsibility: To know the criminal from the crime. *Law and Contemporary Problems* 69:115–164.

Farnham, Eliza B. 1846. Introductory preface. In M. B. Sampson, *Rationale of Crime*, xiii–xxi. New York: D. Appleton.

Farrington, David P. 1998. Predictors, causes, and correlates of male youth violence. *Crime and Justice* 24:421–475.

Feeley, Malcolm, and Jonathan Simon. 1994. Actuarial justice: The emerging new criminal law. In *The Futures of Criminology*, ed. David Nelken, 173–201. London: Sage.

Fernald, Walter E. 1909–1910 (orig. 1908) The imbecile with criminal instincts. *Journal of Psycho-Asthenics* 14:16–36.

———. 1918–1919. Remarks. *Journal of Psycho-Asthenics* 23:98–99.

Fink, Arthur E. 1938. *Causes of Crime: Biological Theories in the United States, 1800–1915*. Repr., New York: A. S. Barnes, 1962.

Fishbein, Diana H. 1992. The psychobiology of female aggression. *Criminal Justice and Behavior* 19:99–126.

———. 2001. *Biobehavioral Perspectives on Criminology*. Belmont, CA: Wadsworth.

Fodor, Jerry A. 1983. *The Modularity of Mind*. Cambridge, MA: MIT Press.

Foucault, Michel. 1977. *Discipline and Punish: The Birth of the Prison*. New York: Pantheon.

———. 1988. The dangerous individual. In *Michel Foucault: Politics, Philosophy, Culture*, ed. Lawrence D. Kritzman, 125–151. New York: Routledge.

Fraser, Steven, ed. 1995. *The Bell Curve Wars: Race, Intelligence, and the Future of America*. New York: Basic Books.

Freeden, Michael. 1979. Eugenics and progressive thought: A study in ideological affinity. *Historical Journal* 22:645–671.

Friedlander, Henry. 1995. *The Origins of the Nazi Genocide: From Euthanasia to the Final Solution*. Chapel Hill: University of North Carolina Press.

Frigessi, Delia. 2003. *Cesare Lombroso*. Turin: Einaudi Editore.

Gall, Frans Josef. 1825. Sur les functions du cerveau et sur celles de chacune des parties. Paris: J. B. Ballière.

Gall, Franz Joseph. 1835. *On the Functions of the Brain and of Each of Its Parts*. 6 vols. Trans. Winslow Lewis, Jr., M.D. Boston: Marsh, Capen, and Lynn.

Galton, Francis. 1869. *Hereditary Genius*. London: Watts.

———. 1875. *English Men of Science: Their Nature and Nurture*. New York: Appleton, 1875.

———. 1883. *Inquiries into Human Faculty and Its Development*. 2nd ed., 1907. London: J. M. Dent.

Gander, Eric M. 2003. *On Our Minds: How Evolutionary Psychology Is Reshaping the Nature-versus-Nurture Debate*. Baltimore: Johns Hopkins University Press.

Garland, David. 1985. The criminal and his science. *British Journal of Criminology* 25 (2): 109–137.

———. 1988. British criminology before 1935. *British Journal of Criminology* 28 (2): 1–17.

———. 2002. Of crimes and criminals: The development of criminology in Britain. In *The Oxford Handbook of Criminology*, 3rd ed., ed. Mike Maguire, Rod Morgan, and Robert Reiner, 7–50. New York: Oxford University Press.

Garland, David, and Richard Sparks. 2000. Criminology, social theory and the challenge of our times. In *Criminology and Social Theory*, ed. David Garland and Richard Sparks, 1–22. New York: Oxford University Press.

Garrett, H. E., and W. N. Kellogg. 1928. The relation of physical constitution to general intelligence, social intelligence, and emotional stability. *Journal of Experimental Psychology* 11:113–129.

Gasquet, J. R. 1882. On moral insanity. *Journal of Mental Science* 28:1–6.

Gatlin, Stephen H. 1999. William H. Sheldon and the culture of the somatotype. Ph.D. diss., Virginia Polytechnic Institute and State University, 1997.

Gazzaniga, Michael S. 2005. *The Ethical Brain*. New York: Harper Perennial.

Gelb, Steven A. 1995. The beast in man: Degenerationism and mental retardation, 1900–1920. *Mental Retardation* 33 (1): 1–9.

Gellately, Robert. 2001. Police justice, popular justice, and social outsiders in Nazi Germany. In *Social Outsiders in Nazi Germany*, ed. Robert Gellately and Nathan Stoltzfus, 256–272. Princeton, NJ: Princeton University Press.

Gellately, Robert, and Nathan Stoltzfus. 2001. Social outsiders and the construction of the community of the people. Ch. 1 (pp. 3–19). In *Social Outsiders in Nazi Germany*, ed. Robert Gellately and Nathan Stoltzfus, 3–19. Princeton, NJ: Princeton University Press.

Geoffroy Saint-Hilaire, Etienne. 1822. *Philosophie anatomique. Des monstruosités humaines*. Paris: Chez l'auteur.

Geoffroy Saint-Hilaire, Isidore. 1832 (vol. 1), 1836 (vol. 2). *Histoire générale et particulière des anomalies de l'organisation, des monstruosités, ou traité de tératologie*. 3 vols., with Atlas. J-B Ballière.

Gibbens, T. C. N. 1963. *Psychiatric Studies of Borstal Lads*. London: Oxford University Press.

Gibson, Mary. 1998. Biology or environment? Race and southern "deviancy" in the writings of Italian criminologists. In *Italy's "Southern Question": Orientalism in One Country*, ed. Jane Schneider, 99–115. New York: Berg.

———. 2002. *Born to Crime: Cesare Lombroso and the Origins of Biological Criminology*. Westport, CT: Praeger.

———. 2006. Cesare Lombroso and Italian criminology: Theory and politics. In *Criminals and Their Scientists: The History of Criminology in International Perspective*, ed. Peter Becker and Richard Wetzell, 137–158. New York: Cambridge University Press.

Gillham, Nicholas Wright. 2001. *A Life of Sir Francis Galton*. Oxford: Oxford University Press.

Glad, John. 2006. *Future Human Evolution: Eugenics in the Twenty-first Century*. Schuylkill, PA: Hermitage.

Glueck, Sheldon, and Eleanor T. Glueck. 1934. *Five Hundred Delinquent Women*. New York: Knopf.

———. 1950. *Unraveling Juvenile Delinquency*. New York: Commonwealth Fund.

———. 1956. *Physique and Delinquency*. New York: Harper and Brothers.

Goddard, Henry Herbert. 1910. Four hundred feeble-minded children classified by the Binet method. *Journal of Psycho-Asthenics* 15:17–30.

———. 1912. *The Kallikak Family: A Study in the Heredity of Feeble-Mindedness*. New York: Macmillan.

———. 1914. *Feeble-mindedness: Its Causes and Consequences*. New York: Macmillan.

———. 1915. *The Criminal Imbecile: An Analysis of Three Remarkable Murder Cases*. New York: Macmillan.

———. 1920. *Human Efficiency and Levels of Intelligence*. Princeton, NJ: Princeton University Press.

———. 1928. Feeblemindedness: A question of definition. *Journal of Psycho-Asthenics* 33:219–227.

Goffman, Erving. 1982. *Interaction Ritual: Essays on Face-to-Face Behavior*. New York: Pantheon.

Goldberg, Elkhonon. 2001. *The Executive Brain*. New York: Oxford University Press.

Goleman, Daniel. 2006. Friends for life: An emerging biology of emotional healing. *New York Times*, 10 October, D5.

Goode, Erica. 2003. When the brain disrupts the night. *New York Times*, 2 January, D1, D7.

Goring, Charles. 1913. *The English Convict: A Statistical Study*. London: His Majesty's Stationery Office. Repr., Montclair, NJ: Patterson Smith, 1972.

Gould, Stephen Jay. 1981. *The Mismeasure of Man*. New York: Norton.

———. 1994. Curveball. *New Yorker*, 28 November, 139–149.

Gramsci, Antonio. 1992. *Prison Notebooks*. Vol. 1. New York: Columbia University Press.

Gray, Richard T. 2004. *About Face: German Physiognomic Thought from Lavater to Auschwitz*. Detroit, MI: Wayne State University Press.

Grose, Nicole R. 1998. Note: Premenstrual dysphoric disorder as a mitigating factor in sentencing: Following the lead of English criminal courts. *Valparaiso University Law Review* 33:201–229.

Guarnieri, Patrizia. 1993. *A Case of Child Murder*. Cambridge: Polity Press.

Guerry, A. M. 1833. *Essai sur la statistique morale de la France*. Paris: Crochard.

Hacking, Ian. 1996. Automatisme ambulatoire: Fugue, hysteria, and gender at the turn of the century. *Modernism/Modernity* 3 (2): 31–43.

Haeckel, Ernst 1898 (orig. 1868). *Natürliche Schöpfungs-Geschichte*. 2 vols. Berlin: Durck und Verlag von Georg Reiner.

Hahn, Nicolas F. [Nicole F. Rafter]. 1980. Too dumb to know better: Cacogenic family studies and the criminology of women. *Criminology* 18:3–25.

Haller, Mark H. 1963. *Eugenics: Hereditarian Attitudes in American Thought*. New Brunswick, NJ: Rutgers University Press.

Hamilton, W. D. 1964. The genetical evolution of social behaviour, I and II. *Journal of Theoretical Biology* 7:1–16 and 17–52.

Hare, Robert D. 1993. *Without Conscience: The Disturbing World of the Psychopaths among Us*. New York: Guilford Press.

Harrington, Anne. 1996. *Reenchanted Science: Holism and German Culture from Wilhelm to Hitler*. Princeton, NJ: Princeton University Press.

Hartl, Emil M., Edward P. Monnelly, and Roland D. Elderkin. 1982. *Physique and Delinquent Behavior: A Thirty-Year Follow-Up to W. H. Sheldon's Varieties of Delinquent Youth*. New York: Academic Press.

Harwood, Jonathan. 1993. *Styles of Scientific Thought: The German Genetics Community, 1900–1933*. Chicago: University of Chicago Press.

*Health Day News*. 2005. Fingers point to male aggression. www.ajc.com/health/content/shared-auto/healthnews/psyc/524409.html.http://story.news.yahoo.com/news?tmpl (accessed 25 March 2006).

Healy, William. 1915. *The Individual Delinquent*. Boston: Little, Brown.

Hentig, Hans von. 1947. *Crime: Causes and Conditions*. New York: McGraw-Hill.

———. 1948. *The Criminal and His Victim*. New Haven: Yale University Press.

Herf, Jeffrey. 1984. *Reactionary Modernism: Technology, Culture, and Politics in Weimar and the Third Reich*. Cambridge: Cambridge University Press.

Herrnstein, Richard J., and Charles Murray. 1994. *The Bell Curve: Intelligence and Class Structure in American Life*. New York: Free Press.

Hirschi, Travis, and Michael J. Hindelang. 1977. Intelligence and delinquency: A revisionist review. *American Sociological Review* 42:571–587.

Hitler, Adolf. 1939. *Mein Kampf*. 2 vols. in 1. London: Hurst and Blackett.

Hoag, Ernest Bryant, and Edward Huntington Williams. 1923. *Crime, Abnormal Minds and the Law*. Indianapolis: Bobbs-Merrill.

Hood, Roger. 2004. Hermann Mannheim and Max Grünhut: Criminological Pioneers in London and Oxford. *British Journal of Criminology* 44:469–495.

Hooton, Earnest A. 1925. *The Ancient Inhabitants of the Canary Islands*. Harvard African Studies, vol. 7 .Cambridge, MA: Peabody Museum of Harvard University.

———. 1930. *The Indians of Pecos Pueblo*. With Habib Yusuf Rihan and Edward Reynolds. New Haven, CT: Published for the Department of Archaeology, Phillips Academy, by the Yale University Press.

———. 1931. *Up from the Ape*. New York: Macmillan.

———. 1937. *Apes, Men and Morons*. New York: G. P. Putnam's Sons.

———. 1938. Letter to E. C. Lindeman, Chair, Advisory Comm. of the William C. Whitney Foundation, 2 June. Earnest A. Hooton Records, Accession Number 995-1, Archives of the Peabody Museum, Harvard University. Correspondence files, Box 24: Sheldon.

———. 1939a. *The American Criminal*. Cambridge, MA: Harvard University Press.

———. 1939b. *Crime and the Man*. Cambridge, MA: Harvard University Press.

———. 1939c. *Twilight of Man*. New York: G. P. Putnam's Sons.

———. 1939d. Letter to Anna Bogue of the Whitney Foundation, 11 December. Earnest A. Hooton Records, Accession Number 995-1, Archives of the Peabody Museum, Harvard University. Hooton Correspondence files, Box 24.

———. 1940a. Future Quality of the American People. Lecture delivered at the Littauer Center, Harvard University, 25 July. Earnest A. Hooton Records, Accession Number 995-1, Archives of the Peabody Museum, Harvard University. Manuscripts and Data files, Box 1.

———. 1940b. *Why Men Behave Like Apes and Vice Versa, or Body and Behavior*. Princeton, NJ: Princeton University Press.

———. 1942. *Man's Poor Relations*. Garden City, NY: Doubleday, Doran.

———. 1945a. Letter to Edgar C. Taylor, 28 February. Earnest A. Hooton Records, Accession Number 995-1, Archives of the Peabody Museum, Harvard University. Correspondence files, Box 25.

———. 1945b. *"Young Man, You Are Normal": Findings from a Study of Students*. New York: G. P. Putnam's Sons.

———. 1947. *Up from the Ape*. Rev. ed. New York: Macmillan.

———. 1948a. Letter to Associated Press, Obituary Department, 13 March. Earnest A. Hooton Records, Accession Number 995-1, Archives of the Peabody Museum, Harvard University. Correspondence files, Box 1.2.

———. 1948b. Letter to William H. Sheldon, 14 October. Earnest A. Hooton Records, Accession Number 995-1, Archives of the Peabody Museum, Harvard University. Correspondence files, Box 24.

———. 1950. Letter to Robert M. Yerkes, 19 February. Earnest A. Hooton Records, Accession Number 995-1, Archives of the Peabody Museum, Harvard University. Hooton Correspondence files, Box 27, "XYZ."

———. 1954. The Physiques of Juvenile Delinquents. Sample column submitted to *New York Herald Tribune*. Earnest A. Hooton Records, Accession Number

995-1, Archives of the Peabody Museum, Harvard University. Correspondence, Box 17: "M" General Correspondence.

———. N.d.-a. Lecture Notes. Earnest A. Hooton Records, Accession Number 995-1, Archives of the Peabody Museum, Harvard University. Manuscript and Data files, Box 18–20.

———. N.d.-b. Notes on Sheldon's "Anthrotyping" Method. Earnest A. Hooton Records, Accession Number 995-1, Archives of the Peabody Museum, Harvard University. Earnest A. Hooton Papers, Correspondence files, Box 6.1, s.v. Constitution Project (Commonwealth Fund).

Horn, David. 2003. *The Criminal Body: Lombroso and the Anatomy of Deviance.* New York: Routledge.

Horney, Julie. 1978. Menstrual cycles and criminal responsibility. *Law and Human Behavior* 2 (1): 25–36.

Howells, W. W. 1992. Yesterday, today and tomorrow. *Annual Review of Anthropology* 21:1–17.

Hughes, C. H. 1882. Moral (affective) insanity. *Journal of Psychological Medicine* 8:64–74.

Humphreys, Lloyd G. 1957. Characteristics of type concepts with special reference to Sheldon's typology. *Psychology Bulletin* 54:218–228.

Huxley, Aldous. 1944. Who are you? *Harper's*, November, 512–522.

Ishikawa, Sharon S., and Adrian Raine. 2002a. Behavioral genetics and crime. In *The Neurobiology of Criminal Behavior*, ed. Joseph Glicksohn, 81–110. Boston: Kluwer Academic Publishers.

———. 2002b. Psychophysiological correlates of antisocial behavior: A central control thesis. In *The Neurobiology of Criminal Behavior*, ed. Joseph Glicksohn, 187–230. Boston: Kluwer Academic Publishers.

Jacobs, Patricia A., Muriel Brunton, Marie M. Melville, R. P. Britain, and W. F. McClemont. 1965. Aggressive behaviour, mental sub-normality and the XYY male. *Nature* 208:1351–1352.

Jensen, H. E. 1950. Review of William H. Sheldon's *Varieties of Delinquent Youth*. *Social Forces* 29 (October):105.

Jordanova, L. J. 1984. *Lamarck*. New York: Oxford University Press.

*Journal of Criminal Law, Criminology, and Police Science*. 1967. Hans von Hentig, eighty years old. 58:427.

Kaiser Daily Women's Health Policy. 2003. Program that offers money to drug users, 23 July. http://www.kaisernetwork.org/daily_reports/ (accessed 3 August 2006).

Kennedy, Hubert. 2001. Research and commentaries on Richard von Krafft-Ebing and Karl Heinrich Ulrichs. *Journal of Homosexuality* 42:165–178.

Kevles, Daniel J. 1985. *In the Name of Eugenics: Genetics and the Uses of Human Heredity*. New York: Knopf.

King, Lester S. 1991. *Transformations in American Medicine: From Benjamin Rush to William Osler*. Baltimore: Johns Hopkins University Press.

Kitching, John. 1857. Lecture on moral insanity. *British Medical Journal*: April 25: 334–336; May 9: 389–391; May 30: 453–456.

Kite, Elizabeth S. N.d. *The Binet-Simon Measuring Scale for Intelligence: What It Is; What It Does; How It Does It; With a Brief Biography of Its Authors, Alfred Binet and Dr. Thomas [sic] Simon*. Philadelphia: The Committee on Provision for the Feeble-Minded.

Koonz, Claudia. 2003. *The Nazi Conscience*. Cambridge, MA: Belknap Press of Harvard University Press.

Kraepelin, Emil. 1904. *Lectures on Clinical Psychiatry*. Revised and edited by Thomas Johnstone. London: Ballière, Tindall, and Cox.

Krafft-Ebing, le Dr. de. 1875. *La Responsabilité Criminelle et la Capacité Civile*. Translated from the German (n.d.) by le Dr. Chatelain. Paris: G. Masson.

Krafft-Ebing, Richard von. 1899. *Psychopathia Sexualis*. Translation of the 10th German ed. London: Aberdeen University Press and Rebman, Limited. (1st ed. 1886.).

Kretschmer, Ernst. 1925. *Physique and Character*. New York: Harcourt Brace.

Kristof, Nicholas D. 2003. The new eugenics. CNN.com, 4 July. (accessed 26 January 2007).

Kuhn, Thomas. 1962. *The Structure of Scientific Revolutions*. Chicago: University of Chicago Press.

Kurella, Hans. 1910. *Cesare Lombroso: A Man of Science*. New York: Rebman.

Lacassagne, Alexandre. 1909. Cesare Lombroso (1836–1909). *Archives d'Anthropologie Criminelle* 24:881–894.

Lamarck, Jean-Baptiste Pierre. 1809. *Philosophie zoologique: Ou, exposition des considérations relative à l'histoire naturelle des animaux*. Paris: Dentu et l'Auteur.

Lander, Eric. 2000. In wake of genetic revolution, questions about its meaning. *New York Times*, 12 September. http://geneticsandsociety.org/article.php?id=174&&printsafe=1..

Lange, Johannes. 1930. *Crime as Destiny*. London: George Allen and Unwin.

Laub, John. 1984. *Criminology in the Making: An Oral History*. Boston: Northeastern University Press.

Laub, John H., and Robert J. Sampson. 1991. The Sutherland-Glueck debate: On the sociology of criminological knowledge. *American Journal of Sociology* 96:1402–1440.

Lavater, J. C. N.d. *Essays on Physiognomy*. Abridged from Mr. Holcroft's translation. London: Printed for G. G. J. & J. Robinson.

Lears, T. J. Jackson. 1981. *No Place of Grace: Antimodernism and the Transformation of American Culture, 1880–1920*. New York: Pantheon Books.

Lees, Andrew. 2006. Moral discourse and reform in urban Germany, 1880s–1914. In *Criminals and Their Scientists*, ed. Peter Becker and Richard F. Wetzell, 85–104. Cambridge: Cambridge University Press.

Lemert, Edwin. 1972. *Human Deviance, Social Problems and Social Control*. 2nd ed. rev. Englewood Cliffs, NJ: Prentice-Hall.

Leps, Marie-Christine. 1992. *Apprehending the Criminal: The Production of Deviance in Nineteenth-Century Discourse*. Durham, NC: Duke University Press.

Levi, Primo. 1987. *The Truce*. In *If This Is a Man* and *The Truce*. Translated by Stuart Woolf. London: Abacus/ Sphere Books.

———. 2001. *The Voice of Memory: Interviews 1961–87*. Ed. Marco Belpoliti and Robert Gordon. Cambridge: Polity Press.

Liang, Oliver. 2006. The biology of morality: Criminal biology in Bavaria, 1924–1933. In *Criminals and Their Scientists: The History of Criminology in International Perspective*, ed. Peter Becker and Richard Wetzell, 425–446. New York: Cambridge University Press.

Lianos, Michalis, with Mary Douglas. 2000. Dangerization and the end of deviance: The institutional environment. In *Criminology and Social Theory*, ed. David Garland and Richard Sparks, 103–126. New York: Oxford University Press.

Livingston, Edward. 1827. *Introductory Report to the Code of Prison Discipline: Explanatory of the Principles on which the Code is Founded. Being Part of the System of Penal Law prepared for the State of Louisiana*. Philadelphia: Carey, Lea and Carey.

———. 1833. *A System of Penal Law, for the State of Louisiana*. Philadelphia: James Kay, Jun. & Co.

Lombardo, Paul A. 1985. Three generations, no imbeciles: New light on *Buck v. Bell*. *New York University Law Review* 60:30–62.

Lombroso, Cesare. 1871. *L'uomo bianco et l'uomo di colore*. Padua: Sacchetto.

———. 1876. *L'uomo delinquente studiato in rapporto all' antropologia, alla medicina legale ed alla discipline carcerarie*. Milan: Hoepli.

———. 1878. *L'uomo delinquente in rapporto all'antropologia, giurisprudenza e alle discipline carcerarie*. 2nd ed. Turin: Bocca.

———. 1884. *L'uomo delinquente in rapporto all'antropologia, giurisprudenza ed alle discipline carcerarie*. 3rd ed. Turin: Bocca.

———. 1889. *L'uomo delinquente in rapporto all'antropologia, alla giurispridenza ed alle discipline carcerarie*. 2 vols. 4th ed. Turin: Bocca.

———. 1896–1897. *L'uomo delinquente in rapporto all' antropologia, alla giurisprudenza ed alla psichiatria*. 3 vols. and *Atlante*. 5th ed. Turin: Bocca.

———. 1911. Introduction. In Gina Lombroso-Ferrero, *Criminal Man According to the Classification of Cesare Lombroso*, xxi–xxx. Repr., Montclair, NJ: Patterson Smith, 1972.

———. 2006. *Criminal Man*. A new translation with introduction and notes by Mary Gibson and Nicole Hahn Rafter. Durham, NC: Duke University Press.

Lombroso, Cesare, and Guglielmo Ferrero. 1893. *La donna delinquente, la prostituta e la donna normale*. Torino: Roux.

———. 1895. *The Female Offender*. New York: D. Appleton.

———. 2004. *Criminal Woman, the Prostitute, and the Normal Woman*. Newly translated and edited by Nicole Hahn Rafter and Mary Gibson. Durham, NC: Duke University Press.

Lombroso-Ferrero, Gina. 1914. The results of an official investigation made in England by Dr. Goring to test the Lombroso theory. *Journal of the American Institute of Criminal Law and Criminology* 5:207–223.

Lykken, D. T. 2006. Commentary: The mechanism of emergenesis. *Genes, Brain and Behavior* 5:306–310.

Maconochie, Captain [Alexander]. 1847. *Norfolk Island*. London: J. Harchard and Son.

Manley, John. 1883. Commentary on some cases of moral insanity. *Journal of Mental Science* 28:531–532.

Manning, H. 1882–1883. Moral insanity: Case of homicidal mania. *Journal of Mental Science* 28:369–375.

Maudsley, Henry. 1873. *Body and Mind*. Enlarged and revised edition. London: Macmillan.

———. 1874. *Responsibility in Mental Disease*. London: Henry S. King.

———. 1888. Remarks on crime and criminals. *Journal of Mental Science* 34:159–167.

Mayhew, Henry, and John Binny. 1862. *The Criminal Prisons of London*. www.victorianlondon.org/publications5/prisons.htm

McCandless, Boyd R., W. Scott Persons III, and Albert Roberts. 1972. Perceived opportunity, delinquency, race, and body build among delinquent youth. *Journal of Consulting and Clinical Psychology* 38:281–287.

McKim, W. Duncan. 1900. *Heredity and Human Progress*. New York: G. P Putnam's Sons.

McLaren, Angus. 1981. A prehistory of the social sciences: Phrenology in France. *Comparative Studies in Society and History* 23:3–22.

Mead, Georg Herbert. 1967. *Mind, Self, and Society*. Chicago: University of Chicago Press.

Mednick, Sarnoff A., William F. Gabrielli, and Barry Hutchings. 1984. Genetic influences in criminal convictions: Evidence from an adoption cohort. *Science*, n.s., 224:891–894.

Melossi, Dario. 2000. Changing representations of the criminal. In *Criminology and Social Theory*, ed. David Garland and Richard Sparks, 149–182. Oxford: Oxford University Press.

Mestel, Rosie. 1993. Does the "aggressive gene" lurk in a Dutch family? (Genetic disorders). *New Scientist* 140 (1897): 6.

Millon, Theodore, E. Simonsen, M. Birket-Smith, and R. D. Davis, eds. 2002. *Psychopathy: Antisocial, Criminal, and Violent Behavior*. New York: Guilford Press.

Milton, Sybil H. 2001. "Gypsies" as social outsiders in Nazi Germany. In *Social Outsiders in Nazi Germany*, ed. Robert Gellately and Nathan Stoltzfus, 212–232. Princeton, NJ: Princeton University Press.

Moffitt, Terrie E. 1993. "Adolescence-limited" and "life-course persistent" antisocial behaviour: A development taxonomy. *Psychological Review* 100:674–701.

Moffitt, Terrie E., Avshalom Caspi, Michael Rutter, and Phil A. Silva. 2001. *Sex Differences in Antisocial Behavior*. Cambridge: Cambridge University Press.

Mohr, James C. 1993. *Doctors and the Law: Medical Jurisprudence in Nineteenth-Century America*. Baltimore: Johns Hopkins University Press.

Montemayor, Raymond. 1985. Men and their bodies: The relationship between body types and behavior. In *Biology, Crime and Ethics*, ed. Frank H. Marsh and Janet Katz, 176–186. Cincinnati, OH: Anderson.

Moran, Richard. 2000. *Knowing Right from Wrong: The Insanity Defense of Daniel McNaughtan*. New York: Free Press.

Morel, B. A. [Bénédict Auguste]. 1857. *Traité des dégénérescences physiques, intellectuelles et morales de l'espèce humaine*. Paris: J. B. Baillière.

Morris, Corey, Aimee Shen, Khadija Pierce, and Jon Beckwith. 2007. Deconstructing violence: MAOA variants and behavior genetics. *GeneWatch* 20 (2): 3–10.

Mucchielli, Laurent. 2006. Criminology, hygienism, and eugenics in France, 1870–1914: The medical debates on the elimination of "incorrigible" criminals." In *Criminals and Their Scientists: The History of Criminology in International Perspective*, ed. Peter Becker and Richard Wetzell, 207–230. New York: Cambridge University Press.

Müller-Hill, Benno. 1988. *Murderous Science: Elimination by Scientific Selection of Jews, Gypsies, and Others, Germany, 1933–1945*. Trans. George R. Fraser. Oxford: Oxford University Press.

N.a. 2003. Depressed? Your genetic "safety catch" isn't on. . . . *Straits Times*, 22 October. http://straitstimes.asia1.com.sg/health/story (accessed 21 October 2003).

N.a., n.d. Charles Whitman. Wikipedia: http://en.wikipedia.org/wiki/Charles_Whitman._

Needham, Frederick. 1882. Moral or emotional insanity. *Journal of Mental Science* 27:554–555.

Nelkin, Dorothy, and M. Susan Lindee. 1995a. *The DNA Mystique: The Gene as a Cultural Icon*. New York: Freeman.

———. 1995b. The media-ted gene: Stories of gender and race. eds., In *Deviant Bodies*, ed. Jennifer Terry and Jacqueline Urla, 387–402. Bloomington: Indiana University Press.

New York State Prison Survey Committee. 1920. *Report of the Prison Survey Committee*. Albany, NY: J. B. Lyon.

Noyes, William. 1887. The criminal type. *American Journal of Social Science* 24:31–42.

Nye, Robert A. 1976. Heredity or milieu: The foundations of modern European criminological theory. *Isis* 47:335–355.

Oosterhuis, Harry. 2000. *Stepchildren of Nature: Krafft-Ebing, Psychiatry, and the Making of Sexual Identity*. Chicago: University of Chicago Press.

Opler, Morris Edward. 1939. Letter to Earnest A. Hooton, 16 November. Earnest A. Hooton Records, Accession Number 995-1, Archives of the Peabody Museum, Harvard University. Correspondence files, Box 25.

Overholser, Winfred. 1962. Introduction to Isaac Ray, *A Treatise on the Medical Jurisprudence of Insanity*. Repr., Cambridge, MA: Belknap Press of Harvard University Press.

———. 1972. Isaac Ray (1807–1881). In *Pioneers in Criminology*, ed. Hermann Mannheim. 2nd ed., enlarged. Montclair, NJ: Patterson Smith.

Packard, Alpheus S. 1901. *Lamarck, the Founder of Evolution: His Life and Work*. With translations of his writings on organic evolution. New York: Longmans, Green.

Pancaldi, Giuliano. 1991. *Darwin in Italy: Science across Cultural Frontiers*. Bloomington: Indiana University Press.

Passmore, Kevin. 2002. *Fascism: A Very Short Introduction*. Oxford: Oxford University Press.

Patterson, Donald G. 1930. *Physique and Intellect*. New York: Century.

Paul, Diane. 1995. *Controlling Human Heredity*. Atlantic Highlands, NJ: Humanities Press.

Pauly, Philip. 1994. Modernist practice in American biology. In *Modernist Impulses in the Human Sciences, 1870–1930*, ed. Dorothy Ross, 272–289. Baltimore: John Hopkins University Press.

Perlin, Michael L. 1999. "Big ideas, images and distorted facts": The insanity defense, genetics, and the "political world." In *Genetics and Criminality*, ed. Jeffrey R. Botkin, William M. McMahon, and Leslie Pickering Francis, 37–66. Washington, DC: American Psychological Association.

Perry, Bruce D., R. A. Pollard, T. L. Blakley, W. L. Baker, and D. Vigilante. 1995. Childhood trauma, the neurobiology of adaptation, and "use-dependent" development of the brain: How "states" become "traits." *Infant Mental Health Journal* 16:271–291.

Pick, Daniel. 1986. The faces of anarchy: Lombroso and the politics of criminal science in post-unification Italy. *History Workshop Journal* 21:60–86.

———. 1989. *Faces of Degeneration: A European Disorder, c. 1848–c. 1919*. Cambridge: Cambridge University Press.

Pinel, Philippe. 1806 (orig. 1801). *A Treatise on Insanity*. Translated from the French by D. D. Davis, M.D. Sheffield, England: Printed by W. Todd for Messrs. Cadell and Davies, London.

Poisson, Siméon-Denis. 1837. *Recherches sur la probabilité des jugements en matière criminelle*. Paris: Bachelier.

Prichard, James Cowles. 1813. *Researches into the Physical History of Man*. London: John and Arthur Arch and B. and H. Barry.

———. 1835. *A Treatise on Insanity*. London: Sherwood, Gilbert, and Piper.

Proctor, Robert. 1988. *Racial Hygiene: Medicine under the Nazis*. Cambridge, MA: Harvard University Press.

——. 1991. *Value-Free Science? Purity and Power in Modern Knowledge*. Cambridge, MA: Harvard University Press.

Quetelet, Adolphe. 1835. *Treatise on Man and the Development of His Faculties*. Paris: Bachelier.

Rafter, Nicole H. 1988. *White Trash: The Eugenic Family Studies, 1877–1919*. Boston: Northeastern University Press.

——. 1990a. *Partial Justice: Women, Prisons, and Social Control*. New Brunswick, NJ: Transaction Press.

——. 1990b. The social construction of crime and crime control. *Journal of Research in Crime and Delinquency* 27:376–389.

——. 1992a. Claims-making and socio-cultural context in the first U.S. eugenics campaign. *Social Problems* 39:17–34.

——. 1992b. Criminal anthropology in the United States. *Criminology* 30:525–545.

——. 1997. *Creating Born Criminals*. Urbana: University of Illinois Press.

——. 2001. Seeing and believing: Images of heredity in biological theories of crime. *Brooklyn Law Review* 67 (1): 71–99.

——. 2004. Earnest A. Hooton and the biological tradition in American criminology. *Criminology* 42:735–773.

——. 2006a. Apes, men and teeth: Earnest A. Hooton and eugenic decay. In *Popular Eugenics, National Efficiency, and American Mass Culture in the 1930s*, ed. Susan Currell and Christina Cogdell, 249–268. Athens: Ohio University Press.

——. 2006b. H. J. Eysenck in Fagin's kitchen: The return to biological theory in 20th-century criminology. *History of the Human Sciences* 19 (4): 37–56.

——. 2007. Somatotyping, antimodernism, and the production of criminological knowledge. *Criminology* 45:101–129.

Raine, Adrian. 1993. *The Psychopathology of Crime: Criminal Behavior as a Clinical Disorder*. San Diego: Academic Press.

——. 2002. Biosocial studies of antisocial and violent behavior in children and adults: A review. *Journal of Abnormal Child Psychology* 30:311–326.

Raine, Adrian, Todd Lencz, Susan Bihrle, Lori LaCasse, and Patrick Colletti. 2000. Reduced prefrontal gray matter volume and reduced autonomic activity in antisocial personality disorder. *Archives of General Psychiatry* 57:119–127.

Raine, Adrian, J. Reid Meloy, Susan Bihrle, Jackie Stoddard, Lori LaCasse, and Monte S. Buchsbaum. 1998. Reduced prefrontal and increased subcortical brain functioning assessed using positron emission tomography in predatory and affective murderers. *Behavioral Sciences and the Law* 16:319–332.

Ray, Isaac. 1838. *A Treatise on the Medical Jurisprudence of Insanity*. Repr., Cambridge, MA: Belknap Press of Harvard University Press, 1962.

Ray, L. J. 1983. Eugenics, mental deficiency and Fabian socialism between the wars. *Oxford Review of Education* 9:213–222.

Regener, Susanne. 2003. Criminological museums and the visualization of evil. *Crime, History, and Societies* 7 (1): 43–56.

Rennie, Ysabel. 1978. *The Search for Criminal Man*. Lexington, MA: Lexington Books.

Rhee, Soo Hyun, and Irwin D. Waldman. 2002. Genetic and environmental influences on antisocial behavior: A meta-analysis of twin and adoption studies. *Psychological Bulletin* 128:490–529.

Richards, Graham. 1987. Of what is history of psychology a history? *British Journal of History of Science* 20:201–211.

Richardson, Sarah. 1993. A violence in the blood. *Discover* 14 (10). http://www.discover.com/issues/oct-93 (accessed 18 December 2006).

Richerson, Peter J., and Robert Boyd. 2005. *Not by Genes Alone: How Culture Transformed Human Evolution*. Chicago: University of Chicago Press.

Robison, Daniel. 1998. *Wild Beasts and Idle Humors: The Insanity Defense from Antiquity to the Present*. Cambridge, MA: Harvard University Press.

Rock, Paul, ed. 1994. *History of Criminology*. Aldershot, England: Dartmouth.

Rose, David. 2006. Lives of crime. *Prospect Magazine* 125. http://www.prospect-magazine.co.uk (accessed 16 August 2006).

Rose, Nikolas. 2000. The biology of culpability: Pathological identities in a biological culture. *Theoretical Criminology* 4 (1): 5–34.

———. 2007. *The Politics of Life Itself: Biomedicine, Power, and Subjectivity in the Twenty-first Century*. Princeton, NJ: Princeton University Press.

Rosenbaum, Ron. 1995. The great Ivy League nude posture photo scandal. *New York Times Magazine*, 15 January, 26–31, 40, 46, 55–56.

Rosenberg, Charles E. 1968. *The Trial of the Assassin Guiteau: Psychiatry and the Law in the Gilded Age*. Chicago: University of Chicago Press.

Ross, Dorothy. 1994. Modernism reconsidered. Introduction to *Modernist Impulses in the Human Sciences, 1870–1930*, ed. Dorothy Ross, 1–25. Baltimore: John Hopkins University Press.

Rothman, David. 1971. *The Discovery of the Asylum*. Boston: Little, Brown.

Rowe, David C. 2002. *Biology and Crime*. Los Angeles: Roxbury.

Rowe, David C., and D. Wayne Osgood. 1984. Heredity and sociological theories of delinquency: A reconsideration. *American Sociological Review* 49:426–540.

Rusche, Georg, and Otto Kirchheimer. 1939. *Punishment and Social Structure*. New York Columbia University Press.

Rush, Benjamin. 1786. The influence of physical causes upon the moral faculty. Repr. in Dagobert Runes, ed., *The Selected Writings of Benjamin Rush*. New York: Philosophical Library, 1947.

———. 1812. *Medical Inquiries and Observations upon the Diseases of the Mind*. Philadelphia: Kimber and Richardson.

Saldaña, Quintiliano. 1933. The new criminal anthropology. *Journal of Criminal Law and Criminology* 24 (1): 333–350.

Sampson, Marmaduke B. 1843. *The Phrenological Theory of the Treatment of Criminals Defended.* London: Samuel Highley.

Sampson, Robert J., and John H. Laub. 1997. Unraveling the social context of physique and delinquency. In *Biosocial Bases of Violence*, ed. Adrian Raine, P. A. Brennan, David P. Farrington, and Sarnoff A. Mednick, 175–188. New York: Plenum Press.

Savage, George H. 1881. Moral insanity. *Journal of Mental Science* 27:147–155.

Savelsberg, Joachim J. 2004. Criminological knowledge: Period and cohort effects in scholarship, with Sarah M. Flood. *Criminology* 42:1009–1041.

Savelsberg, Joachim J., Ryan D. King, and Lara L. Cleveland. 2002. Politicized scholarship? Science on crime and the state. *Social Problems* 49:327–348.

Savelsberg, Joachim J., with Lara Cleveland and Ryan King. 2004. Institutional environments and scholarly work: American criminology, 1951–1993. *Social Forces* 82:1275–1302.

Schlapp, Max, and Edward A. Smith. 1928. *The New Criminology: A Consideration of the Chemical Causation of Abnormal Behavior.* New York: Boni and Liveright.

Scull, Andrew, Charlotte MacKenzie, and Nicholas Hervey. 1996. Degeneration and despair: Henry Maudsley (1835–1918). In *Masters of Bedlam: The Transformation of the Mad-Doctoring Trade*, ed. Andrew Scull, Charlotte MacKenzie, and Nicholas Hervey, 226–267. Princeton, NJ: Princeton University Press.

Sekula, Allan. 1986. The body and the archive. *October* 39: 3–64.

Shapin, Steven. 1979. Homo phrenologicus: Anthropological perspectives on an historical problem. In *Natural Order: Historical Studies of Scientific Culture*, ed. B. Barnes and S. Shapin, 41–71. Beverly Hills: Sage.

———. 1982. History of science and its sociological reconstruction. *History of Science* 20:157–211.

Sheldon, William H. 1935a. Letter to Leonard and Dorothy Whitney Elmhirst, 1 February. Dartington Hall Trust Archive, Totnes, England, folder DWE G9.

———. 1935b. Letter to Leonard Elmhirst, 8 February. Dartington Hall Trust Archive, Totnes, England, folder LKE UA 6.

———. 1936. *Psychology and the Promethean Will.* New York: Harper and Brothers.

———. 1938. Letter to Earnest A. Hooton, 8 May. Earnest A. Hooton Records, Accession Number 995-1, Archives of the Peabody Museum, Harvard University. Correspondence files, Box 24.4.

———. 1940. *The Varieties of Human Physique: An Introduction to Constitutional Psychology.* With the collaboration of S. S. Stevens, and W. B. Tucker. New York: Harper and Brothers.

———. 1942. *The Varieties of Temperament: A Psychology of Constitutional Differences.* With the collaboration of S. S. Stevens. New York: Harper and Brothers.

———. 1949a. *Early American Cents, 1793–1814: An Exercise in Descriptive Classification*. With the collaboration of H. K. Downing and M. H. Sheldon. New York: Harper and Brothers.

———. 1949b. *Varieties of Delinquent Youth: An Introduction to Constitutional Psychiatry*. With the collaboration of Emil M. Hartl, and Eugene McDermott. New York: Harper and Brothers.

———. 1954. *Atlas of Men: A Guide for Somatotyping the Adult Male at All Ages*. With the collaboration of C. Wesley Dupertuis and Eugene McDermott. New York: Harper and Brothers.

Shepard, Edward Morse. 1884. *The work of a social teacher. Being a memorial of Richard L. Dugdale*. Economic Tracts XII: 1–14.New York: Society for Political Education.

Simpson, James. 1834. *Necessity of Popular Education as a National Object; with Hints on the Treatment of Criminals, and Observations on Homicidal Insanity*. Edinburgh: Adam and Charles Black, and London: Longman Rees.

Smith, Denis Mack. 1993. *Mussolini*. London: Weidenfeld.

Smith, Percy. 1885. Two cases of moral insanity. *Journal of Mental Science* 31:366–370.

Smith, Roger. 1981. *Trial by Medicine: The Insanity Defense in Victorian England*. Edinburgh: Edinburgh University Press.

———. 1988. Does the history of psychology have a subject? *History of the Human Sciences* 1:147–177.

———. 1997. *The Human Sciences*. New York: Norton.

Spencer, Herbert. 1864–1867/1898. *The Principles of Biology*. Vol. 1. Revised and enlarged. London: Williams and Norgate.

———. 1876a. *Principles of Sociology*. Abridged ed., 1969, ed. Stanislav Andreski. London: Macmillan

———. 1876b. *The Principles of Sociology*. Vol. 1. London: Williams and Norgate.

Spitzka, Edward C. 1878. Reform in the scientific study of psychiatry. *Journal of Nervous and Mental Disease* 5:201–229.

Spurzheim, J. G. 1815. *The Physiognomical System of Drs. Gall and Spurzheim*. 2nd ed. London: Printed for Baldwin, Cradock, and Joy.

———. 1825. *A View of the Philosophical Principles of Phrenology*. Repr. in vol. 1 of Roger Cooter, ed., *Phrenology in Europe and America*. London: Thoemmes Press, 2001.

———. 1828. *A View of the Elementary Principles of Education: Founded on the Study of the Nature of Man*. 2nd ed. London: Treuttel, Würtz, and Richter.

Stamps, V. R., N. G. Abeling, A. H. van Gennip, A. G. van Cruchten, and H. Gurling. 2001. Mild learning difficulties and offending behaviour: Is there a link with monoamine oxidase A deficiency? *Psychiatric Genetics* 11:173–176.

Stanley, Leo L. 1940. *Men at their Worst*. New York: D. Appleton-Century.

Stevenson, Robert Louis. 1886. *Dr. Jekyll & Mr. Hyde*. Repr., London: Folio Society, 1948.

Stigler, Stephen M. 1986. *The History of Statistics: The Measurement of Uncertainty before 1900.* Cambridge, MA: Belknap Press of Harvard University Press.

Stock, Gregory. 2002. *Redesigning Humans: Our Inevitable Genetic Future.* Boston: Houghton Mifflin.

Strahan, S[amuel] A. K. 1892. *Marriage and Disease: A Study of Heredity and the More Important Family Degenerations.* New York: D. Appleton.

Sutherland, Edwin H. 1931. Mental deficiency and crime. Repr. 1956, in *The Sutherland Papers,* ed. Albert Cohen, Alfred Lindesmith, and Karl Schuessler, 308–326. Bloomington: Indiana University Press, 1956.

———. 1951. Critique of Sheldon's *Varieties of Delinquent Youth. American Sociological Review* 16:10–13.

Sweeney, Gerald. 2001. *Fighting for the Good Cause: Reflections on Francis Galton's Legacy to American Hereditarian Psychology.* Philadelphia: American Philosophical Society.

Sykes, Gerald. 1950. Review of William H. Sheldon's *Varieties of Delinquent Youth. Nation* 171:318.

Sylvers, Patrick, Stacy R. Ryan, S. Amanda Alden, and Patricia A. Brennan. In press. Biological factors and the development of persistent criminality. In *The Development of Persistent Criminality,* ed. Joanne Savage. New York: Oxford University Press.

Szöllösi-Janze, Margit. 2001a. National Socialism and the sciences: Reflections, conclusions and historical perspectives. In *Science in the Third Reich,* ed. Margit Szöllösi-Janze, 1–36. Oxford: Berg.

———, ed. 2001b. *Science in the Third Reich.* Oxford: Berg.

Tancredi, Laurence. 2005. *Hardwired Behavior: What Neuroscience Reveals about Morality.* New York: Cambridge University Press.

Tatar, Maria M. 1997. *Lustmord.* Princeton, NJ: Princeton University Press.

Taylor, Ian, Paul Walton, and Jock Young. 1973. *The New Criminology.* New York: Harper and Row.

Taylor, Jeanette, William G. Iacono, and Matt McGue. 2000. Evidence for a genetic etiology of early-onset delinquency. *Journal of Abnormal Psychology* 109:634–643.

Thomson, J. Bruce. 1870a. The hereditary nature of crime. *Journal of Mental Science* 15:487–498.

———. 1870b. The psychology of criminals. *Journal of Mental Science* 16:321–350.

Thornhill, Randy, and Craig T. Palmer. 2000. *A Natural History of Rape: Biological Bases of Sexual Coercion.* Cambridge, MA: MIT Press.

Tibbetts, Stephen G. 2003. Selfishness, social control, and emotions: An integrated perspective on criminality. In *Biosocial Criminology,* ed. Anthony Walsh and Lee Ellis, 81–101. Hauppauge, NY: Nova Science Publishers.

———. In press. Perinatal and developmental determinants of early onset offending. In *Persisting Offending,* ed. Joanne Savage. New York: Oxford University Press.

Tuke, D. Hack. 1885a. Case of congenital moral defect, with commentary. Paper presented at the annual meeting of the Medico-Psychological Association, August; orig. in *Journal of Mental Science* 31:360–366. Repr. in D. Hack Tuke, *Prichard and Symonds, in Especial Relation to Mental Science, with Chapters on Moral Insanity*. London: J. and A. Churchill, 1891.

———. 1885b. Moral or emotional insanity. Paper written for presentation at the July 1884 meeting of the British Medical Association and orig. published in *Journal of Mental Sciences* 31 (1885–1886):174–190. Repr. in D. Hack Tuke, *Prichard and Symonds, in Especial Relation to Mental Science, with Chapters on Moral Insanity*, 65–100. London: J. and A. Churchill, 1891.

———. 1891. *Prichard and Symonds, in Especial Relation to Mental Science, with Chapters on Moral Insanity*. London: J. & A. Churchill.

Tyndall, Prof. 1878. Prof. Tyndall on consciousness and organization, free will, heredity, responsibility, &c. *Journal of Mental Science* 24:107–116.

Uttal, William R. 2003. *The New Phrenology: The Limits of Localizing Cognitive Processes in the Brain*. Cambridge, , MA: MIT Press.

Van Wyhe, John. 2002. The history of phrenology on the Web. http://pages. britishlibrary.net/phrenology/ (accessed 20 April 2004).

Vega, Cecilia M. 2003. Cash-for-sterilization plan starts slowly in New York. *New York Times*, 6 January, A19.

Villa, Renzo. 1985. *Il deviante e i suoi segni: Lombroso e la nascita dell'antropologia criminale*. Milan: Franco Angeli.

Waal, Frans de. 1996. *Good Natured: The Origins of Right and Wrong in Humans and Other Animals*. Cambridge, MA: Harvard University Press.

Wachsmann, Nikolaus. 2001. From indefinite confinement to extermination: "Habitual criminals" in the Third Reich. In *Social Outsiders in Nazi Germany*, ed. Robert Gellately and Nathan Stoltzfus, 165–191. Princeton, NJ: Princeton University Press.

———. 2004. *Hitler's Prisons*. New Haven, CT: Yale University Press.

Wade, Nicholas. 2007. Scientist finds the beginnings of morality in primate behavior. *New York Times*, 20 March, D3.

Waldinger, Robert J. 1979. Sleep of reason: John P. Gray and the challenge of moral insanity. *Journal of the History of Medicine and Allied Sciences* 34:163–179.

Walkowitz, Daniel J. 1999. *Working with Class: Social Workers and the Politics of Middle-Class Identity*. Chapel Hill: University of North Carolina Press.

Walsh, Anthony. 1972. The American tour of Dr. Spurzheim. *Journal of History of Medicine and Allied Sciences* 27:187–205. http://inside.salve.edu/walsh/spurzheimsamericantour.pdf.

Walsh, Anthony. 1995. *Biosociology: An Emerging Paradigm*. Westport, CT: Praeger.

———. 2000. Evolutionary psychology and the origins of justice. *Justice Quarterly* 17:841–864.

————. 2002. *Biosocial Criminology*. Cincinnati, OH: Anderson.

Walters, Glenn D., and Thomas W. White. 1989. Heredity and crime: Bad genes or bad research? *Criminology* 27:455–485.

Weiss, Sheila Faith. 2006. Human genetics and politics as mutually beneficial resources: The case of the Kaiser Wilhelm Institute for Anthropology, Human Heredity and Eugenics during the Third Reich. *Journal of the History of Biology* 39:41–88.

Weisstein, Eric W. N.d. Haekel [*sic*], Ernst (1834–1919). http://scienceworld. wolfram.com/biography/Haekel.html (accessed 9 June 2004).

Werlinder, Henry. 1978. *Psychopathy: A History of the Concepts*. Uppsala: Uppsala University, Ph.D. diss. Distributed by Stockholm: Almqvist and Wiksell International.

Wertheimer, F. I., and Florence E. Hesketh. 1926. The significance of the physical constitution in mental disease. *Medicine* 5:375–463.

West, Desirée, and Bronwen Lichtenstein. 2006. Andrea Yates and the criminalization of the filicidal maternal body. *Feminist Criminology* 1:173–187.

Wetzell, Richard F. 2000. *Inventing the Criminal: A History of German Criminology, 1880–1945*. Chapel Hill: University of North Carolina Press.

————. 2006. Criminology in Weimar and Nazi Germany. In *Criminals and Their Scientists: The History of Criminology in International Perspective*, ed. Peter Becker and Richard Wetzell, 401–424. New York: Cambridge University Press.

Wharton, J. J. S. 1841. *Criminal Jurisprudence Considered in Relation to Man's Responsibility: Repudiating Mr. M. B. Sampson's Phrenological Theory, and His Philosophy of Insanity*. London: A. Maxwell.

Wiebe, Robert H. 1967. *The Search for Order, 1877–1920*. New York: Hill and Wang.

Wiener, Martin. 1990. *Reconstructing the Criminal: Culture, Law, and Policy in England, 1830–1914*. Cambridge: Cambridge University Press.

Wilson, Edward O. 1975. *Sociobiology*. Abridged edition. Cambridge, MA: Belknap Press of Harvard University Press.

————. 1999. *Consilience*. New York: Vintage.

Wilson, James Q., and Richard J. Herrnstein. 1985. *Crime and Human Nature*. New York: Simon and Schuster.

Wines, E. C., ed. 1871. *Transactions of the National Congress on Penitentiary and Reformatory Discipline, 1970*. Albany, NY: Weed, Parsons.

Wines, Frederick Howard. 1888. *Report on the Defective, Dependent, and Delinquent Classes of the Population of the United States as returned at the Tenth Census* (June 1, 1880). Washington, DC: Government Printing Office.

Wolfgang, Marvin. 1972. Cesare Lombroso, 1835–1909. In *Pioneers in Criminology*. ed. Hermann Mannheim, 232–291. 2d ed. Montclair, NJ: Patterson Smith.

Wolfgang, Marvin E., Robert M. Figlio, and Thorsten Sellin. 1972. *Delinquency in a Birth Cohort*. Chicago: University of Chicago Press.

Woodrow, Ross. 2001–2002. Digital Lavater: Essays on Physiognomy. Introduction. Index. www.newcastle.edu.au/department/fad/fi/lavater (accessed 10 April 2004).

Wright, Bradley R. Enter, Avshalom Caspi, Terrie E. Moffitt, and Phil A. Silva. 2001. The effects of social ties on crime vary by criminal propensity: A life-course model of interdependence. *Criminology* 39:321–348.

Yacoubian, George S., Jr. 2000. The (in)significance of genocidal behavior to the discipline of criminology. *Crime, Law and Social Change* 34:7–19.

Yang, Yaling, Adrian Raine, Todd Lencz, Susan Bihrle, Lori LaCasse, and Patrick Colletti. 2005. Volume reduction in prefrontal gray matter in unsuccessful psychopaths. *Biological Psychiatry* 57:1103–1108.

Young, R. M. 1990. *Mind, Brain and Adaptation in the Nineteenth Century.* Oxford: Clarendon.

Zedner, Lucia. 2007. Seeking security by eroding rights: The side-stepping of due process. In *Security and Human Rights*, ed. Benjamin Goold and Liora Lazarus, 257–276. Oxford: Hart.

Zenderland, Leila. 1998. *Measuring Minds: Henry Herbert Goddard and the Origins of American Intelligence Testing.* Cambridge: Cambridge University Press.

Zerubavel, Eviatar. 1997. *Social Mindscapes: An Invitation to Cognitive Sociology.* Cambridge, MA: Harvard University Press.

Zuckerman, Marvin. 2002. Personality and psychopathy: Shared behavioral and biological traits. In *The Neurobiology of Criminal Behavior*, ed. Joseph Glicksohn, 27–50. Boston: Kluwer Academic Publishers.

# Index

# About the Author

NICOLE RAFTER is Senior Research Fellow in the College of Criminal Justice at Northeastern University and Fellow of the American Society of Criminology. She is the author of numerous books, most recently *Shots in the Mirror: Crime Films and Society*. She has translated (with Mary Gibson) the foundational texts of criminology, Cesare Lombroso's *Criminal Man* and *Criminal Woman*.